T0320268

AMERICA
IN
DECLINE

AMERICA
IN
DECLINE

Mike Sharpe

Routledge
Taylor & Francis Group

LONDON AND NEW YORK

First published 2012 by M.E. Sharpe

Published 2015 by Routledge
2 Park Square, Milton Park, Abingdon, Oxon OX14 4RN
711 Third Avenue, New York, NY 10017, USA

Routledge is an imprint of the Taylor & Francis Group, an informa business

Copyright © 2012 Taylor & Francis. All rights reserved.

No part of this book may be reprinted or reproduced or utilised in any form or by
any electronic, mechanical, or other means, now known or hereafter invented,
including photocopying and recording, or in any information storage or retrieval
system, without permission in writing from the publishers.

Notices
No responsibility is assumed by the publisher for any injury and/or damage to
persons or property as a matter of products liability, negligence or otherwise,
or from any use of operation of any methods, products, instructions or ideas
contained in the material herein.

Practitioners and researchers must always rely on their own experience and
knowledge in evaluating and using any information, methods, compounds, or
experiments described herein. In using such information or methods they should
be mindful of their own safety and the safety of others, including parties for
whom they have a professional responsibility.

Product or corporate names may be trademarks or registered trademarks, and
are used only for identification and explanation without intent to infringe.

Library of Congress Cataloging-in-Publication Data

Sharpe, M.E., 1928–
America in decline / by M.E. Sharpe.
    p. cm.

        "This collection gathers ninety-one essays that appeared in the pages of
        Challenge from 1973 through 2011."

Includes bibliographical references and index.
ISBN 978-0-7656-3391-0 (pbk. : alk. paper)
    1. United States—Economic conditions—20th century. 2. United States—Economic conditions—21st
century. 3. United States—Economic policy—20th century. 4. United States—Economic policy—21st
century. 5. United States—Politics and government—20th century. 6. United States—Politics and
government—21st century. 7. United States—Foreign relations. I. Title.

HC106.7.S36497 2012
330.973—dc23   2011044837

ISBN 13: 9780765633910 (pbk)

Again

For my wife Carole

and my children

Susanna, Matthew, Elisabeth, Hana

Table of Contents

Preface   xi
Acknowledgments   xvii
A Note on Dates, Comments, and Presidents   xviii
Advice on Reading This Book   xix

Planning Versus Stagflation, 1973–1979

To the Lilies of the Field Who Toil Not   3
Economics for Sybarites   5
Why Economists Disagree   9
The Galbraithian Revolution   12
Of Sticky Prices and Stinking Fish: The Wage-Price Spiral   17
Gunnar Myrdal's Challenge   21
Portrait in Oil   24
2074   28
As You Like It   33
The Praise of Folly   40
Inflation and Defunct Ideas: President Ford's
   Economic Summit   43
The Economic Consequences of Friedrich A. von Hayek   46
The Fear of Planning   48
The Planning Bill   51
Reply to a Critic of Planning   59
Recovery Without Recovery   63
The Continued Existence of New York City Is
   Not Essential to National Security   66
Ten Rules for Full Employment Without Inflation   70
The Lost Papers of Jack Tanner   75
Do Economists Discover Economic Laws or Are
   They Passed by Congress?   78
How to Plan the Economy   80
Apologia Pro Vita Mea   84
The Last Chronicle of Barset   86
Advising Carter and Congress   90
The Backward Art of Giving Advice   94

JKG Versus the Angel   97
What Is an Incomes Policy All About?   102
Little Red Riding Hood   106
Searching for *Homo sapiens*   109
Why a Tax-Based Incomes Policy Won't Work   115
Anniversaries   118
Once More, Capitalism, Socialism, Democracy   122
Is Inflation Inevitable in Post-Keynesian Capitalism?   127
When Britain Ran Out of Wood   129

Back to Laissez Faire, 1988–1999

Thirty Years of *Challenge*   135
The Speaker Speaks   138
The Rise and Fall of the New Deal   142
Ownership and Control   147
Labor's Future   151
What's Wrong with Economists?   158
The Good Society and Its Enemies   163
Adam Smith: Right and Wrong   167
Short Takes: Pleasant and Unpleasant Reviews   172
The Labor Movement and Black Ghettos: Two Reviews   177
The Short Twentieth Century   181
The Theft of Russia   188
Forty-Thousand Years of History   195
The Past and Future of Socialism: *The Communist
    Manifesto* at 150   202
The Truman Show   207
World Development for the Few   211
Remembering Wassily Leontief, 1905–1999   214
Social Health and Social Illth   217

Further Down the Downward Spiral, 2005–2011

Robert Heilbroner, 1919–2005   221
The Biography of John Kenneth Galbraith   222
The Way Out of Iraq   227
One President, Five Disasters   228

New Orleans: A Modest Proposal 230
The Country Left the Man 232
Garbage 234
John Kenneth Galbraith, 1908–2006 237
The Heavy Burden of Wealth 239
He's Got the Whole World in His Hands 243
Iraqonomics 246
How to Become a Friend of the Next President 249
America's Suicide Pact with George W. Bush 251
Poor People 254
The New New Deal 257
A Sick Society 260
Hard Times 265
Racism and Polite Conversation 267
Super-Bubble 268
The Case for Government 270
Barack Obama and the Revolution of November 4, 2008 272
What Keynes Knew 275
Postscript on the G20 Summit: What Members Can
    Learn from the WPA 281
Recovery? 283
Camp Runamuck 288
Dissatisfaction Guaranteed: An Account of Two Bubbles 291
Obama's Failures 294
The Freefall That Isn't Free 297
Tea Party Politics 303
The Futility of Force 306
The Crisis of Capitalism 309
The Failure of Capitalism 326
Big Money 333
Violent Nation 337
    Postscript: The Egyptian Revolution, February 11, 2011 342
The Poorest Rich Country in the World: Address to the
    Graduating Class of 2011 344
Ice-T and the Pathology of Poverty 346
China and the Future of the World 350

The First Blossoms and Thorns of the Arab Spring   355

Index   357
About the Author   372

Preface

I started writing these essays in 1973 when I became publisher of *Challenge*. The title of the first section, "Planning Versus Stagflation, 1973–1979," indicates my preoccupation with stagflation and how to get out of it with a coordinated set of economic policies. Demand management as conceived by John Maynard Keynes, input-output analysis as conceived by Wassily Leontief, and planning for the public sector as conceived by John Kenneth Galbraith are explicitly or implicitly behind my writings in this period. The period came to an end just as I thought it should not have: by battering the economy to near death with high interest rates.

I resumed writing for *Challenge* in 1988. My preoccupation then is reflected in the section title "Back to Laissez Faire, 1988–1999." The revival of laissez-faire economics began much earlier, in the mid-1970s. Keynesian economics was eclipsed by a revival of market fundamentalism and a move to deregulation: Markets are best left alone free of government meddling. This view became dominant with the election of Ronald Reagan in 1980. I will try to make amends for my omission of the Reagan ascendency later in this preface.

My final section is called "Further Down the Downward Spiral, 2005–2011." I write "further down" because the downward spiral began in the 1970s, accelerated in the 1980s and 1990s, and continued further down in the 2000s.

I have to admit that I became fully aware of the downward spiral only in retrospect. I thought that the spiral could be bent back upward from the moment that I started writing for *Challenge* and I still think that it can. But the fact is that we have lived through more than a third of a century in a downward spiral and nothing on the horizon suggests that we will reverse it.

What Is Declining?

Indicators of well-being are declining. We compare unfavorably with the rest of the affluent world in almost all of them: health, longevity, infant mortality, education, medical care, poverty, and incarceration, particularly among the historically ghettoized minorities. The concentration of wealth and income has increased among the very richest, who have all the means of persuasion that money can buy to increase the disparities in their favor. At the same time, organizations that speak for the majority have been reduced to a pathetic semblance of their former selves, particularly unions. Cultivated ignorance of the public interest prevails, ending in the hapless thrashing around of the Tea Party. In a word, the plutocracy has the power to have its way, even more so through the mishandled Great Recession, as it is called. It is no different from a Great Depression for its victims. The bankers who were in the saddle during the boom remain in the saddle during the bust. As workers became more productive, their condition became more precarious. The present mantra is "cut benefits." We are a rich country but act like a poor country. To make a bad situation worse, we are engaged in war without end with nothing to show for it but death, destruction, and enmity.

Deindustrialization

I see nothing wrong with deindustrialization if it is not at the expense of employment and well-being. We have gone through deagriculturalization because the rise of productivity in agriculture enables well under 2 percent of the workforce to supply all the agricultural needs of the entire population, allowing for what we import and export. The rise in industrial productivity enables just under 22 percent of the workforce to supply all our industrial needs, again save for what we import and export. There's the problem. When we import things made by sweatshop labor under miserable conditions at a fraction of the compensation of American workers, most of us lose and the disparity in income and wealth here and abroad increases. A service society is appealing, provided that enough of the public has the means to buy the services as well as the products of industry and agriculture without going hopelessly into debt. If labor income rose at the same rate as productivity, everyone would be able to buy the same things as before while working fewer hours. The opposite is happening. Labor income is falling as employed labor works longer hours. The benefits of increased productivity are going to the top few percent, who have the means to buy more of everything, with enough funds left over to control almost everything, economic and political. Nor do the benefits of scientific research, as some fallaciously argue, have to be the by-product of military spending. Scientific research can be conducted both privately and publicly, not for military purposes, but for purposes directly intended to raise the standard of living.

Deindustrialization cannot be blamed for the loss of the necessities and the luxuries of life that is the inevitable result of unemployment. Nor can it be blamed for the inevitable loss that is the result of undereducation. Nor for the loss from self-serving practices of private businesses that put a burden on the public by polluting rivers and air, moving away from viable cities and towns and letting them rot instead of helping to find alternative occupations for the people who live there. All these practices make us fall short of the standard of living that we could achieve if common sense prevailed. Nothing prevents us from devising policies to prevent such losses except the indifference of the miniscule minority that benefits from them.

War Without End

The big wars in Korea, Vietnam, Afghanistan, and Iraq all ended or are ending with nothing accomplished except public disillusionment, a massive waste of resources, and the unspeakable loss of lives. The concept of endless war against "terrorism," against a few hundred or a few thousand terrorists, has seized the policymakers' imagination and has accomplished the opposite of what was intended. We don't defeat the enemy, we don't build nations, we don't win friends; we do the opposite. Only a nation in decline is led by men and a few women who have no capacity to learn from history.

"Never Again"

Never were words spoken that have meant so little. A fraction of the hardware and humanware of war could be used to save lives instead of destroying them. After the last gasp of the Ottoman Empire in the mass murder of Armenians and the last gasp of the Third Reich in the mass murder of Jews, the Great Powers committed themselves to preventing genocide from taking place ever again. Then followed genocide in Rwanda, Darfur, Kosovo, Bosnia, Cambodia, Sudan, Congo. Whom have I forgotten? What happened to the solemn promise of "never again"?

The United States, the dominant power after World War II, with quite adequate assets to wage an endless series of wars, could not muster enough assets to *prevent* genocide, the endless slaughter of innocents who belonged to another nation, tribe, religion, ethic group, political organization, or were just in the way of the perpetrators.

Leaving aside the bottomless depravity of genocide, which should move any decent person in any civilized nation to action, the practical result of nonintervention has been the instability of vast regions in which state and military marauders pillage with impunity, giving the go-ahead to more pillaging with impunity. Whenever the self-designated civilized nations intervene with the timid injunction, "Now, now, don't be bad," the madmen turn their madness against *us*.

The excuses for doing nothing escalate. The leadership in Washington didn't know. But they did know. The public wouldn't accept intervention. But the public knew too little until they read about genocide in the morning paper. Our leaders in Washington hid behind the lame excuse that we shouldn't get stuck in regional conflicts. But by omission we were stuck. We didn't have to be stuck. Before military action is even contemplated, warnings are a deterrent. World condemnation *before* genocide is a deterrent. Cutting off the supply of arms is a deterrent. Jamming communications systems is a deterrent. Cutting off funds is a deterrent. The threat of military action is a deterrent. Never has the United States resorted to any of these diplomatic maneuvers *before* the beginning of genocide.

The cost has been the loss of hundreds of thousands of lives that could have been saved had we chosen to intervene short of war. We, the so-called civilized world, could have avoided the cost of supporting hundreds of thousands of refugees and the rampant spread of disease. The excruciating details of genocide after genocide can be found in the long *cri de coeur* by the deeply informed Samantha Power, *"A Problem from Hell."*

Ronald Reagan Triumphant

Ronald Reagan was president from 1981 to 1989. He was Mr. Congeniality, which allowed him to charm the public, at least that part that votes, and get elected and reelected on a platform of supply-side economics, a wonderful concoction of ideas for taking wealth from the general population and transferring it upward. If the wealthy have more money to invest, the idea goes, the act of investing will create more jobs. The proponents of trickle-down economics, as it was called, overlooked the fact that investment takes place when people have jobs that provide them with the money to buy the products of investment. Without demand for products, investors save their money. A cover for Reaganomics, another term of art, was provided by the Laffer Curve, drawn on the back of an envelope by Arthur Laffer, showing that a reduction of taxes on the wealthy would encourage investment, which in turn would increase economic activity, which in turn would generate more revenue to make up for the reduction in taxes. The fact that no such thing ever happened in history went unnoticed. During the Reagan era, wealth did not trickle down but was siphoned up.

Another supporting view was provided by George Gilder in his book *Wealth and Poverty*, in which he points out that a few farsighted men get richer by producing the wealth that the less-than-farsighted masses then consume. We have no poverty problem, but a moral problem. The "so-called poor," as he called them, compared with the poor of the world, are not poor, they are lazy. Moreover, family values would be enhanced by sending women back to the kitchen where they belong. At the same time Charles A. Murray, in *Losing Ground: American Social Policy, 1950–1980,* affirmed that wealth and poverty simply reflected levels of intelligence. He wrote, "In order to succeed, the poor need most of all the spur of their poverty." John Kenneth Galbraith summarized Murray's views succinctly when he wrote: "As the rich needed the incentive of more money, so the poor needed the incentive of less" (in *A Journey Through Economic Time*). The government could do nothing about such issues, except reduce taxes. Reagan covered this ground in his statement that government was not the solution to the problem, government was the problem.

At the outset of his presidency, Reagan acted on his free-market credo by firing the striking members of the air traffic controllers' union, which gave a signal to business that it's all right, even desirable, to bust unions. The move of corporations to the nonunion South and Southwest and parts abroad accelerated, effecting an accelerating decline of unions.

While reducing taxes and breaking unions, Reagan expanded military spending to unprecedented levels, practicing military Keynesianism while simultaneously increasing the national debt to unprecedented levels in apprehension of the Soviet menace. Yet when Mikhail Gorbachev came to power, Reagan was able to reach a rapprochement as the Soviet Union lay on its deathbed, suffering from a backward and completely unworkable system. The administration left the matter of paying off the national debt to some unspecified future, the long run, but meanwhile stimulated a sustained rate of economic growth that benefited the well-to-do and excluded everyone else. To be fair to Reagan, after reducing taxes, he later increased them by a lesser amount under severe budgetary pressure. On his own terms, Reagan was a success.

What Hope?

Each president since Ronald Reagan has followed in his footsteps, each with slightly different coloration and emphasis. George H.W. Bush, Bill Clinton, George W. Bush, and Barack Obama have continued along the lines of deregulating business, keeping business taxes low, expanding military spending except for a short decline after the Soviet Union disintegrated, increasing the deficit of payments with foreign countries, and increasing the national debt except for a short period of surplus under Clinton. All the while wealth has been transferred from the masses to the classes. Domestic and foreign policy is bipartisan, notwithstanding slightly different rhetoric. A current exception to the rule must be made for the Tea Party, whose principal contribution to public discourse is their menacing tone: Government stay out of this or that—or else.

The condition for a good society remains public understanding of its own interests. The means to serve its own interests manifestly must be the fair use of both the public and private sectors for all, not just a small minority. We look around and see a neglect of public works. When I drive down a street in an affluent suburb, I see manicured lawns, but the strips along the street outside the private lawns are wild with weeds. Our entire public sector is wild with weeds. Public works have become anathema and we cannot afford them. What is the purpose of the world's richest economy if we don't use it?

What hope? The public sometimes reacts to disaster by learning what its own interests really are and by organizing. We know when this happens in retrospect. We rarely know when this will happen beforehand. We just know that it must happen if humans are to realize their humanity. Hope lies in the expectation that it will happen sometime in the future—give or take a few hundred years.

October 2011

Acknowledgments

Thanks, Carole Brafman Sharpe and Susanna Sharpe, for insisting that I not stray too far from what passes as standard English. Thanks again, Susanna, for fearlessly copyediting all ninety-one articles. Thanks, Irina Burns, for making everything go without a hitch in the production of this book. Thanks, Jeff Madrick, editor of *Challenge*, and thanks, the entire staff of M.E. Sharpe, for immeasurable moral support. Thanks, Carole, Susanna, Matthew, Elisabeth, and Hana Sharpe for tolerating and sustaining me. Any errors are the fault of the abovementioned people.

A Note on Dates, Comments, and Presidents

Challenge is published six times a year. The date after each article indicates the month and year of publication.

I have written postscripts to those articles for which I wanted to present a context to current readers; to clarify issues in light of subsequent events; or to remark on issues about which I later changed my mind. I have also made several minor changes in the text in the interest of clarity.

The following presidents were in office during the period covered in *America in Decline*. The purpose of this list is to assist readers in identifying the president responsible for each particular disaster.

Richard Nixon, January 20, 1969–August 9, 1974
Gerald Ford, August 9, 1974–January 20, 1977
Jimmy Carter, January 20, 1977–January 20, 1981
Ronald Reagan, January 20, 1981–January 20, 1989
George H.W. Bush, January 20, 1989–January 20, 1993
Bill Clinton, January 20, 1993–January 20, 2001
George W. Bush, January 20, 2001–January 20, 2009
Barack Obama, January 20, 2009–

Advice on Reading This Book

You could regard this book as a collection of jellybeans. You will find jellybeans of many different colors. If you don't like the red ones, go on to the green. If you don't like the green ones, go on to the blue. As in all jellybean packages, you will find quite a few of the same color. If you don't want two, three, or four of the same color, try a different color. If you don't like jellybeans of any color, put down this package and try something else.

To be blunt, I have repeated myself in articles written over a period of thirty-eight years. Repetition goes with the territory of periodical writing— as well as refreshing novelty.

The Author

Planning Versus Stagflation, 1973–1979

To the Lilies of the Field Who Toil Not

The Bible says that a person must be born again if he is to enter the kingdom of heaven. It doesn't say whether this applies to magazines. Nor does it say whether magazines are even permitted to circulate in heaven. An editor can only assume the affirmative on both counts. Certainly *Challenge* deserves St. Peter's sympathetic consideration, for with Volume 16, Number 1, it is born again. In its previous incarnation, *Challenge* was published for fifteen years and expired quietly in its sleep in 1967. The cause, I believe, was financial anemia. As a faithful reader of *Challenge*, I was sorry to see it go. At that time I was a publisher by day and an economist by night. It was practically inevitable that the idea of reviving *Challenge* should occur to me one evening at twilight.

Challenge used to be Everybody's Economic What's What. Everybody's because it was written for both economists and laymen. And also because it represented a wide band of opinion, and wasn't afraid of stirring up an argument. Economic because it was written by economists on every conceivable subject that can come under the heading economics. What's What because it dealt with issues and policies and made the vital connection between economics and the rest of life.

We are going to continue in that tradition. No other magazine did the job that *Challenge* did. *Challenge* was needed as a source of readable, up-to-date economic thinking; it still is. Even economists occasionally like to read articles that they can understand. *Challenge* defied classification as highbrow, lowbrow, or middlebrow. It simply disregarded brow level and discussed issues important to all of us.

We are honored to have a star-studded editorial advisory board. The editor will seek its counsel and try to keep *Challenge* on the paths of righteousness. But if we err, the board is to be held blameless. Members of the board have graciously consented to give advice from time to time, but they are in no way accountable for anything in *Challenge* which may distress the reader. At the same time, it is only proper that they should be praised for anything that the reader likes.

Even the editor cannot be blamed for everything. Our pages are open to all reasonable points of view, and to some unreasonable ones too, provided that they are reasonably stated. Hence the authors themselves are

3

responsible for what they say. The editor will take the liberty of stating his own opinions on the editorial page, and will see to it that his ideas are expressed in a way which evokes universal assent.

Economists constitute that curiously rare profession which looks forward to the day when its importance is greatly diminished. The eminent economist Frank H. Knight wrote (with the deep modesty so characteristic of the entire tribe): "It ought to be the first aim of economic policy to reduce the importance of economic policy in life as a whole." He went on to explain: "So it ought to be the highest objective in the study of economics to hasten the day when the study and the practice of economy will recede into the background of men's thoughts, when food and shelter, and all provision for physical needs, can be taken for granted without serious thought, when 'production' and 'consumption' and 'distribution' shall cease from troubling and pass below the threshold of consciousness and the effort and planning of the mass of mankind may be mainly devoted to problems of beauty, truth, right human relations, and cultural growth."

Wordsworth put it a little differently, but was thinking along the same lines:

> The world is too much with us; late and soon,
> Getting and spending, we lay waste our powers:
> Little we see in Nature that is ours . . .

Translated into the language of economics textbooks, that means: don't hassle me with your demand and supply curves.

To that bright future, when economics falls into its properly subordinate place, *Challenge: The Magazine of Economic Affairs* is dedicated.

March 1973

Economics for Sybarites

Heaven forbid that I pick a fight with a member of the editorial advisory board of *Challenge*. But a recent comment by Robert M. Solow cannot pass uncontested. In a *New York Times* review he flatly announced that "nobody but a professional would read economics for pleasure or for mere understanding." No statistics, sample surveys, or theoretical underpinnings were offered in support of this assertion. Accordingly I shall also omit all references to theory and research, and proceed with the discussion.

Let's begin with Professor Solow himself. In our last issue a sprightly piece appeared under his name entitled "Is the End of the World at Hand?" I have personally encountered several noneconomists who actually claimed to have obtained pleasure from reading it. They also claimed to have understood it.

Professor Solow might with justice reply that a mere handful of testimonials is not enough to overthrow a general law, especially if the testimonials were obtained from acquaintances moved by the desire to compliment the editor. In order to prove that nonprofessionals can read economics for pleasure we must offer cases that are above suspicion.

Very well. We need go no further than Chapter One of *The Wealth of Nations,* that prodigious font of modern economics. It is a dull dog indeed who cannot enjoy Adam Smith's account of pinmaking and learn something about the division of labor in the bargain. Enter Adam Smith as Exhibit A.

Talk about reading economics for pleasure! We have only to turn to George Bernard Shaw. Never mind that he had no degree in economics. Neither did Adam Smith. And never mind that you don't agree with everything that Shaw wrote. You don't agree with everything that Smith wrote either. I have always wanted an excuse to quote the opening paragraph of Shaw's first entry in *Fabian Essays.* Here we learn something about the capriciousness of step-mother Earth. It's a quaint blend of Henry George and Karl Marx, to be sure. Just enjoy it. Enter GBS as Exhibit B.

Let me now call on another well-known economist. What could be more timely than his teachings about gold in *Timon of Athens?*

> *What is here?*
> *Gold? yellow, glittering, precious gold? . . .*
> *Thus much of this will make black white, foul fair,*
> *Wrong right, base noble, old young, coward valiant.*
> *Ha, you gods! why this? what this, you gods?*

Why, this
Will lug your priests and servants from your sides,
Pluck stout men's pillows from below their heads:
This yellow slave
Will knit and break religions; bless the accursed;
Make the hoar leprosy adored; place thieves,
And give them title, knee and approbation
With senators on the bench: this is it
That makes the wappen'd widow wed again;
She, whom the spital-house and ulcerous sores
Would cast the gorge at, this embalms and spices
To the April day again. Come, damned earth,
Thou common whore of mankind, that put'st odds
Among the rout of nations, I will make thee
Do thy right nature.

I have offered three exhibits which prove beyond the shadow of a doubt that things economic can be and are read for pleasure by anyone who takes the trouble to read them. The real question is, which economists take the trouble to write them?

This brings me to Solow's Fourth Law: "baloney outsells meat and potatoes." Why should this be the case? Nobody is stopping those who sell meat and potatoes from exercising as much cunning as those who sell baloney. It is not intuitively obvious that baloney-sellers have a corner on talent. The meat of the matter, if I may so express it, is that it takes a certain amount of literacy to recognize that baloney is inferior to filet mignon.

Here's where *Challenge* comes into the picture. If economics can't be made interesting, we might as well fold up our tent and steal away. But beyond that, the economic chefs who serve up filet mignon have a vested interest in educating the palates of their nonprofessional brothers and sisters. No one expects that all economics be written for pleasure any more than all physics or chemistry be written for pleasure. But the findings of economists can be popularized just as the findings of physicists and chemists can.

But isn't one man's filet mignon another man's baloney? Not really. Of course there are differences of opinion among professionals about the nature of the economic world in which we live; about the means to attain ends; and about what ends we ought to attain. But to clarify and define what these differences are is essential for clear thinking about economics and economic policy. And an increase in clear thinking is naturally followed by a decrease in the consumption of baloney.

To all economists who write with irresistible charm and scintillating clarity: kindly come forward and identify yourselves to the editor of *Challenge.*

Adam Smith on Pins

One man draws out the wire, another straights it, a third cuts it, a fourth points it, a fifth grinds it at the top for receiving the head; to make the head requires two or three distinct operations; to put it on, is a peculiar business, to whiten the pins is another; it is even a trade by itself to put them into the paper; and the important business of making a pin is, in this manner, divided into about eighteen distinct operations, which, in some manufactories, are all performed by distinct hands, though in others the same man will sometimes perform two or three of them. I have seen a small manufactory of this kind where ten men only were employed, and where some of them consequently performed two or three distinct operations. But though they were very poor, and therefore but indifferently accommodated with the necessary machinery, they could, when they exerted themselves, make among them about twelve pounds of pins in a day. There are in a pound upwards of four thousand pins of a middling size. Those ten persons, therefore, could make among them upwards of forty-eight thousand pins in a day. Each person, therefore, making a tenth part of forty-eight thousand pins, might be considered as making four thousand eight hundred pins in a day. But if they had all wrought separately and independently, and without any of them having been educated to this peculiar business, they certainly could not each of them have made twenty, perhaps not one pin a day; that is, certainly, not the two hundred and fortieth, perhaps not the four thousand eight hundredth part of what they are at present capable of performing, in consequence of a proper division and combination of their different operations.

George Bernard Shaw on Step-Mother Earth

All economic analyses begin with the cultivation of the earth. To the mind's eye of the astronomer the earth is a ball spinning in space without ulterior motives. To the bodily eye of the primitive cultivator it is a vast green plain, from which, by sticking a spade into it, wheat and other edible matters can be made to spring. To the eye of the sophisticated city man this vast green plain appears rather as a great gaming table, your chances in the game depending chiefly on the place where you deposit your stakes. To the economist, again, the green plain is a sort of burial place of hidden treasure, where all the forethought and industry of man are set at naught by the caprice of the power which hid the treasure. The wise and patient workman strikes his spade in here, and with heavy toil can discover nothing but a poor quality of barley, some potatoes, and plentiful nettles, with a few dock leaves to cure his stings. The foolish spendthrift on the other side of the hedge, gazing idly at the sand glittering in the sun, suddenly realizes that the earth is offering him gold—is dancing it before his listless eyes lest it should escape him. Another man, searching for some more of this tempting gold, comes upon a great hoard of coal, or taps a jet of petroleum. Thus is Man mocked by Earth his step-mother, and never knows as he tugs at her closed hand whether it contains diamonds or flints, good red wheat or a few clayey and blighted cabbages. Thus too he becomes a gambler, and scoffs at the theorists who prate of industry and honesty and equality. Yet against this fate he eternally rebels. For since in gambling the many must lose in order that the few may win; since dishonesty and since inequality is bitter to all except the highest, and miserably lonely for him, men come greatly to desire that these capricious gifts of Nature might be intercepted by some agency having the power and goodwill to distribute them justly according to the labor done by each in the collective search for them.

May 1973

Why Economists Disagree

Economics is like a Bruegel painting. All sorts of odd people are doing all sorts of odd things. Some are sawing wood and some are baking bread; some are hawking fish and some are just staring out windows; some are busy carousing while others are lying in the shade of a tree asleep; some are flying kites and others are washing dirty laundry in a brook. It's a disorderly, noisy scene. What can you expect from such a motley bunch? When they get together of an evening at the inn, you can hardly count on them to agree on much.

Let me explain at once that jostling, shoving, and arguing are commonplace among economists, who engage in them with gusto. They are part of an honorable tradition that dates back to the beginnings of the science. This manner of behavior is quite in order. But at times the din reaches the proportions of Babel and the uninformed person may feel a slight sense of apprehension. We have arrived at one of those times. Each disputant loudly proclaims his own opinion about inflation and unemployment; wage and price controls; the deficit in the balance of payments; antitrust and unions; growth and the environment; even about which social system is best. Is it not a strange science that has a hundred answers for every question? No, no. Quite normal. There are reasonable explanations for all these disagreements.

To begin with, the world is difficult to understand. Other sciences have their little problems too, but the public is less aware of them. Astrophysicists, for example, have been debating whether the universe will go on expanding indefinitely or will collapse into one big black hole in forty billion years. A 5 percent error in measuring the rate at which quasars are receding could spell the difference. This dispute has not captured the headlines. The point is, as J.B.S. Haldane put it, the universe is inexhaustibly queer, and that makes it hard to know what it is up to and why. Since the earth is one of the rather more queer places in an already queer universe, the problems astrophysicists face are nothing compared to those of economists. Just imagine, as Kenneth Boulding suggests, a world in which g is not constant; then you have some idea of what social scientists are up against.

This brings us to the second reason for disagreement. The world which economists study is one of conflicting interests—class, national, and ideological—and it is a world that is always in transition from one state to another: mercantile, industrial, and managed economies in all their varieties; and we know not what next. G, or social gravity, is in a constant state of flux, pulling Malthus this way and Ricardo that; Marx one way and Jevons another; Pigou hither and Keynes yon. We are a bit like a flock of positively and negatively charged particles. It's all very confusing for an economist caught in this social cyclotron. It ought to be his business to know which way he is charged; but it isn't easy.

Another reason for disagreement is the Big-End, Little-End problem. You may recall that a long, bloody war raged in Lilliput between the Big-Endians and the Little-Endians. One faction obstinately maintained that an egg should be cracked at the big end and the other maintained with equal obstinacy that it should be cracked at the small end. This describes the normal state of affairs in a science between crises. In such periods scholars engage in learned disputes about minute but apparently vital distinctions. Some think it best to follow Senior and explain that capitalists' profits are a reward for abstinence from consumption. Others think it best to follow Marshall and explain that profits are a reward for waiting rather than abstinence. Some prefer the sunspot theory of business cycles; others deny that business cycles are possible. The process described here is known as "the internal development of science" and it consists of solving problems raised by the major assumptions of the science that prevail at any given time. In economics the solution of such problems usually has done very little harm.

The next source of disagreements is the split between practitioners of The Higher Economics and practitioners of The Lower Economics. The trouble starts with the fact that these subspecies speak different languages: one mathematics; the other English. The first is concerned with elegance, truth, and beauty; the latter is bogged down with messy things like sociology, politics, and anthropology. Communicants of The Higher Economics customarily study the celestial mechanics of a nonexistent universe (I am indebted to Professor Boulding for this insight); those of The Lower Economics study the grubby, disorderly, intractable business of daily economic life; they have terrible trouble generalizing.

These are some of the perfectly ordinary, normal reasons for disaccord among economists. None is a cause for undue alarm or dismay. We have done nothing but describe the regular path of progress. But as I said at the outset, the squabble is unusually raucous at the moment and so we must go beyond all the regular explanations to find out why.

From time to time the underlying assumptions of economics cease giving satisfaction. This last happened in the thirties. Economists had assured themselves that general gluts were impossible. Such a position was unusually awkward during the Great Depression. Keynes saved the profession from this recondite nonsense. At a single stroke he reunited economics, statecraft, and common sense, and provided a rallying point for a new generation of economists who refused to put up with unemployment.

Three decades later economics is floundering again and threatens to come unstuck from statecraft and common sense. Keynes's legacy is a good first approximation for economic management; but major new challenges threaten to knock the underlying assumptions to pieces. The unemployment-inflation dilemma; the imbalance between private affluence and public squalor; the spectacle of poverty amidst riches; the disruption of the environment; the disarray of the international economy: the fumbling efforts at solutions point to scientific arteriosclerosis.

Aside from those who practice business-as-usual, two main camps have formed, each advocating a diametrically opposite line of march from the other. One camp warns: you who have sinned, go back to the competitive model; break up large corporations and unions before it is too late; dismantle the government bureaucracy; let the invisible hand do its work, or be scourged. The other camp replies: it's too late to go back; big institutions are the facts of modern life; and even if you wanted to break them up, it would take a revolution to do it. We have bitten the apple of knowledge of large organizations and can't disgorge it; we had better finish the apple and learn how to control the organizations we live in. The separation of economics from politics and power is a delusion. Go onward or be scourged.

You might wonder, after all this, whether economists actually have anything in common. Rest assured that they do. George Stigler, a distinguished member of our board, once wrote an essay to prove that all economists are united in their conservatism. He was successful beyond all measure—principally by defining economists as conservative and those not conservative as not economists. If we update the definition to include all members of the profession who favor preserving this little planet, we could at small expense gain universality: we are all conservative, even those in search of radical changes.

July 1973

The Galbraithian Revolution

Bernard Shaw once wrote: "The reasonable man adapts himself to the world: the unreasonable one persists in trying to adapt the world to himself. Therefore all progress depends on the unreasonable man." Most economists will agree that John Kenneth Galbraith is an unreasonable man. They may, however, shrink from Shaw's conclusion that the unreasonable man is the cause of progress. In the present instance the issue will eventually be resolved by the place accorded *Economics and the Public Purpose.* It is the complete Galbraith. All his previous books are prelude. This one invites comparison with Keynes's *General Theory,* for it is Galbraith's general theory; and it is very general indeed. Previous economics is thrown unceremoniously on the rubbish pile. A new social order is sketched out in all necessary detail and the required methods of reform comprehensively presented. It has been a long time since so celebrated an author has undertaken so much in a single book. If there is to be a Galbraithian revolution, it will be bigger than Keynes's by several orders of magnitude.

I hasten to add that there is nothing new or original in this book. It has all been said before in one way or another by James Madison, John Stuart Mill, Elizabeth Cady Stanton, Karl Marx, John Ruskin, Thorstein Veblen, Sidney and Beatrice Webb, Finley Peter Dunne, Joseph Schumpeter, Antonio Gramsci, C. Wright Mills, and countless others, any or all of whom Professor Galbraith may justly choose to disavow. No one carries all the genes of all his intellectual progenitors nor even knows who they all are. In fact I doubt that Galbraith came to his views through any particular intellectual tradition. Unlike many other critics of society's ills, he stands outside radical schools and movements. Ideologically he is a self-made man. He diagnosed the disease in his own way, mixed the medicine according to his own prescription, and offered it to the patient in his own good time. And that is about all the originality that any economist can hope for.

In the textbook world, the consumer and the citizen possess power; the corporation and the state do their bidding. In the Galbraithian world, the bureaucracies of the corporation and the state possess power; the consumer and the citizen are managed, manipulated, cajoled, and persuaded. In the textbook world, the consumer maximizes his pleasures by choosing the shirts and soaps and soups and saloons that he likes best. In the Galbraithian world, the larger strategy of consumption is decided on high: the consumer will have cars and highways instead of trains and tracks because public and private authorities have invested the funds accordingly. In the textbook world, various branches of the economy develop in proportion to consumer need. In the Galbraithian world, they develop unevenly, in proportion to the power the producer commands. The consumer-citizen will enjoy the services of all the missiles he possibly can use because a strong munitions industry has a strong symbiotic relationship with a strong government bureaucracy—the Pentagon. He will go begging for housing because powerful housing corporations don't exist—nor do they have any powerful counterpart in the federal executive. All these contrasts can be easily summarized. In textbook economics, things have a tendency to work out for the best for everyone. But as Galbraith puts it, "Left to themselves, economic forces do not work out for the best except perhaps for the powerful."

"But," interjects an irate reader, "you have to be pretty stupid to take textbook economics at face value. Anyone in his right mind knows that all those propositions have to be qualified before they can be applied to reality." I'm sure Galbraith would agree. His point is that they have to be qualified so much that they are qualified out of existence. It is better to throw out the original assumptions and start with new ones that take the economy as it is.

If you wanted to compress Galbraith's message into three words, they would be power and uneven development. The economy is divided into two parts: the planning system and the market system. The first has about one thousand firms; the second twelve million. The thousand produce more of the gross national product than the twelve million combined. The four largest corporations in the planning system have total sales that exceed those of the three million farmers in the market system. These are the bare facts of power. Power resides in the planning system: the power to plan prices and outputs; to deploy modern technology and to grow; to sway consumers and the state. And the power to extract extremely favorable terms of trade from the market system. The two systems develop unevenly: the planning system from strength; the market system from weakness. The strong go to the state and get the services they need; the weak do without. Hence the highly uneven development of public services.

Galbraith, by the way, has at last integrated the housewife into modern economics. She is the administrator of consumption. Through a neat division of labor in the household, the husband seeks the ever-increasing utility of ever-increasing consumption because he does not suffer the ever-increasing disutility of managing more possessions. Housewives, converted into a crypto-servant class, become the unwitting allies of the planning system and its inexorable drive to cover the earth with more artifacts. When the odious connection between wifely virtue and corporate convenience dawns on American wives, the death knell of corporate power will have sounded.

The first two-thirds of *Economics and the Public Purpose* is devoted to how things are, the last third to how they ought to be. Much of the first two-thirds is plagiarized from *The New Industrial State*—Galbraith's own book, I hasten to add for the information of those who don't know—but Galbraith had to recapitulate so the stage could be set for his reforms. And the recapitulation smooths over many of the irritating spots of his last big book and offers enough qualifications of all propositions so that he can fall back to previously prepared positions, whatever and wherever the attack.

Most of the reforms can be classed as the five socialisms. But before coming to them, we must emphasize what Galbraith emphasizes: reforms depend on belief, not machinery. You can't get important reform by setting up a commission, putting a public representative on the board of directors, or making a list of regulations. "Law cannot anticipate understanding." The emancipation of belief comes first, which is to say that public opinion must change. Galbraith's quintessential conviction is that public opinion—belief—is now in the service of the planning system rather than in the service of the public itself. People are convinced that they need what the planning system can deliver—more commodities of the kind that the planning system is good at producing. This myth is perpetuated by economic pedagogy, which teaches that the economy is best when intervention is least. But uneven development, inequality of income, the paucity of services, environmental disruption, inflation, the imbalance of payments, and all the other economic horrors cause pain. "Pain," says Galbraith, "or even modest discomfort is better for persuasion than more abstract argument." The emancipation of belief is taking place because circumstance will have it so; Galbraith will just help it along.

The first job of those who attain public cognizance—Galbraithian shorthand for the state of mind of those who can distinguish the needs of the public from those of the planning system—is to pry the state loose from the grip of the planning system and place it at the disposal of the public. Emancipation of the state must be the central issue of the electoral process. Half a party already exists that is more or less ready to serve that purpose—the reform wing of the Democrats. More or less, because they grasp the situation only imperfectly—through political instinct—and need further exposure to the beneficial influence of rational economic thought. A sprinkling of Republicans are in the same class.

Now to the five socialisms. Galbraith's aims are to equalize power, competence, and income; to safeguard the environment; to expand the use of public resources to serve public rather than private interests; and to stop the stop-and-go dilemma of inflation and deflation.

Socialism one—the new socialist imperative: run the weak parts of the market system by public authority, especially housing, urban transportation, and medical care. Don't be pusillanimous about it. Face the fact that it must be done and do it well.

Socialism two—guild socialism: encourage small and weak firms to merge, form trade associations, fix output and prices, aid them with R&D and generally equalize their terms of trade with the planning system.

Socialism three—the elimination of bureaucratic symbiosis: nationalize the military contractors. They're public in everything but name anyway. The weapons bureaucrats work with Pentagon bureaucrats and together they hit Congress and the public from two sides for ever more money. One bureaucracy is better than two and will take off some of the pressure for support of a bloated military establishment.

Socialism four—the euthanasia of the stockholder: stockholders of large corporations have lost their social function. The rich who own most of the equity get richer on capital gains. Exchange their stock for fixed-interest-bearing public bonds and let the capital gains accrue to the public treasury. The corporations will go on being managed just as before, they will simply be public—like Renault in France or IRI in Italy—and more susceptible to the pressures of the public cognizance. Meanwhile the rich will dissipate their funds through estate taxes, divisions among heirs, and high living, and we shall end up with greater equality of income and less concentration of illegitimate private power.

Socialism five—planning: the planning system needs to be planned. The automobile industry doesn't know what the petroleum industry is doing and the electric appliance industry doesn't know what the electric power industry is failing to do. Coordination is needed. Furthermore, wage and price increases can't be allowed to exceed average productivity increases, or we shall have a perpetual source of inflation. Wages and prices are privately administered in the planning system, and but a single step is required to administer them publicly in the public interest.

The five socialisms do not exhaust Galbraith's reforms. A minimum wage, a guaranteed income, abandonment of full employment, legal limits for the use and abuse of the environment, revenue-sharing, much less resort to monetary policy, and others complete the battery of Galbraith's reforms.

Must I comment? Perhaps my job is done if I have managed to send you to *Economics and the Public Purpose* to read for yourself. This book will exert an enormous influence. There is planning in our future. Galbraith is quite blunt about it, much less urbane than usual. His work belongs to the genus mixed economy, in which, I need hardly add, planning bulks much larger than most American economists have dared contemplate. If there is a Galbraithian revolution, it will be bigger than Keynes's because Keynes let the market alone and was content to manage the level at which it operated. Galbraith would manage the market itself, and replace much of it with planning. Keynes also let most of the core of economic doctrine alone. Galbraith slashes away at its vitals—consumer sovereignty and the market—and damns it as flummery.

Those who shudder at the implications of such vast projects must remember that Galbraith is an optimist and a pragmatist. Never mind the dangers; we have to experiment. It is more dangerous to stand still. Never mind the risks of democratic public power; can't be worse than private. Never mind the dangers of centralized planning; if we abolish the extremes of wealth and poverty and have an aware public watching the planners, it will all come out right.

I leave the reader, Professor Galbraith, and myself with Bertrand Russell's cautionary maxim: "It matters little what you believe, so long as you don't altogether believe it."

September 1973

I attributed the phrase "the five socialisms" to Galbraith. But when I looked for the phrase subsequently, I couldn't find it. Possibly I made it up myself. But Galbraith did advocate the five socialisms as listed.

I did not discuss Galbraith's concept of the "technostructure," the corporate technicians who are experts in the field in which the corporation operates. Granted that the power of technical discovery and application is in the hands of experts in the technostructure and that they might take a long view of their responsibilities. But the top corporate management reacts to immediate exigencies and the main chance for short-run profits. They do not know what is around the corner. Galbraith acknowledged this view in later writings. I should add that Galbraith is usually considered a member of the institutional school of economics.

Of Sticky Prices and Stinking Fish: The Wage-Price Spiral

Several readers have confessed that they do not know the difference between demand-pull and cost-push inflation. A knowledge of this distinction is the ticket of admission to the great debate on stabilization policy. It is impossible to understand the exquisite mental torture suffered by leading members of the Nixon administration without an insight into the thoroughly depressing choices available to them. A short explanation is in order.

Demand-pull inflation occurs when demand goes up faster than supply. The increased demand bids prices up until they reach a level where supply and demand are equal. As long as demand goes up faster than supply, prices will continue to rise. An infallible way to produce inflation is to expand the quantity of money in circulation without a corresponding increase in supply. This invariably happens in wartime. The government needs money to buy munitions. It rarely if ever relies entirely on taxes but manufactures money which it then spends. The new money is spent in turn by those who receive it, and after the economy starts to work at full capacity there is no place for the money to go but into higher prices.

Cost-push inflation is quite different. It occurs when businesses and unions have the power to raise their prices and wages without an increase in demand for their products. This is typically the case in industries dominated by a handful of very large corporations and unions. Let us say that steel manufacturers decide to raise their prices. A price rise in steel means that buyers of steel will have higher production costs and will raise their prices if they can. These higher prices become higher costs to others who then will want to raise their prices. Soon the increase becomes general. The United Steel Workers, to stay with our illustration, now has an incentive to seek higher wages. Since the steel manufacturers can pass on a wage increase by raising prices, they have little reason to resist. The result is the well-known wage-price spiral. Readers who do not like the fact that the illustration starts with an increase in prices can use another in which the process starts with an increase in wages. The results will be the same.

In either case there is a kind of tripartite arrangement among business, labor, and government to sponsor inflation. The roles of business and labor have already been described. The government enters the picture because it must validate the price and wage increases by expanding the quantity of money. If it does not, unemployment will result because there will not be sufficient demand to clear the market at the higher prices. Since the government is committed to full employment, it has no choice but to comply. All the parties are quite innocent of any desire to bring about inflation, but they bring it about nevertheless. The motive of the government is to maintain full employment. The motive of business and labor is to get larger profits or wages or simply not to fall behind in an ongoing inflation.

Once inflation gets started, it is kept going by inflationary expectations. If prices are increasing at the rate of 5 percent a year, employees will have to get a 5 percent increase just to stand still. Businesses will have to raise prices 5 percent. Banks will be obliged to charge 5 percent more than they hope to make on loans. Owners of savings accounts will require 5 percent over and above anticipated earnings. The merry-go-round doesn't go anywhere, but if anybody gets off or can't get on he falls behind everybody else. No one enjoys being on the merry-go-round and it is a nonsensical place for grown-ups. So the question is how to stop it.

The first of several ways is to have a resounding recession. There is nothing like a resounding recession to put an end to inflationary expectations. This cure, like the following ones, can't be undertaken halfheartedly. You have to go all the way or not bother. You have to stage enough of a recession to break the unions and businesses that engage in the game of wage-price leapfrog. You can't faint at the sight of 7, 8, 9 or 10 percent unemployment but must grit your teeth long enough for all the inflationary fires to burn themselves out. After that, everything will be all right. The only drawback to the shattering rate of unemployment incident to the therapy is that it creates an ugly mood. A certain obtuseness to the fine points of economic theory among the general public has discouraged the present administration from seeing this course of treatment through to its logical conclusion. Economics cannot be blamed for that.

Devotees of the second type of cure would do something about wages and prices that are sticky downward. As we have seen, all wages and prices that go up do not come down because the people who set them do not want them to come down and have the power to prevent it. The simple thing to do is to take that power away. Break up the big businesses and unions. Then, if there is excess demand and inflation, the authorities can engineer a slack through the customary monetary and fiscal devices and the force of competition will bring wages and prices down. Nor will there be much unemployment to speak of because wages will go down until they are low enough for everybody to be hired again at the lower level of demand. The chief difficulty with this remedy for inflation is that half the economy—the oligopolistic half—has to be disestablished before it can work. An intrepid band of crusaders has been working at it since the Sherman Antitrust Act was passed eighty-three years ago. May success crown their efforts.

The next cure for inflation isn't strictly a cure at all but a resolve to learn to live with it. If we all step on an escalator and go up at the same rate, inflation can be made just as comfortable as noninflation. After all, inflation is just a rise in prices (including wages) and prices are only numbers. If all the numbers go up by 10 percent during the course of the year, nothing real has changed; everybody is in the same place as he was before. If a person is poor at $50 a week, he is still poor at $55 a week. If he is rich at $2,000 a week, he will be no richer at $2,200. The trick is to get all the numbers to go up at the same rate. Difficult, but not impossible. But what happens if plumbers decide to go up by 15 percent when the prevailing rate of escalation is 10 percent? They may want to do so if there is a bad harvest and grocery prices go up by 15 percent. Then the electricians will want to hike their wages by the same rate. And the policemen, the firemen, the teachers, the auto workers, and so on. Soon everybody will be hell-bent on trying to race faster than the universal escalator. Those who can will.

Those who can't won't. We will be right back where we started from before we installed the escalator and will have gone to a great deal of trouble with nothing to show for it.

We are left with the last cure, which is nothing but a mishmash of eclecticism. It relies on monetary and fiscal policy to balance aggregate supply and demand, public service employment to mop up the remaining unemployment among the unskilled, and controls to intercept the wage-price spiral. Proponents of eclecticism can't get it through their heads that their regimen has failed: failed in the United States; failed in Europe; failed everywhere. They keep wanting to try again. In the case of Mr. Nixon, they claim that his timing was off, his heart wasn't in it, or he was thinking about one thing while doing another. Some people are never satisfied.

Despite this apparently poor record, eclecticism is all we've got, and we had better reconsider it. It is manifestly impossible to get full employment by monetary and fiscal means alone because the labor market is divided into two boxes, and full employment is reached in the skilled box before it is reached in the unskilled. By raising aggregate demand when the larger part of the labor market is already tight you get inflation. There is no sense in disrupting the whole economy with the turmoil of inflation when a straightforward expedient is available. Full employment in the unskilled box is the job of an adequate public service program; and plenty of public services need to be performed.

Equally impossible is the effort to arrest cost-push inflation by monetary and fiscal restraint without creating more unemployment than people are willing to put up with. Controls have the virtue of being specific. They publicly administer prices and wages that are already privately administered in a thousand large firms, but they do it so that prices and wages rise on the average at the same rate as productivity. Controls can be equitable if they embody the principle of leveling up and they can be efficient if they allow for price variations corresponding to surpluses and shortages. Controls do not require agreement among business, labor, and government on every decision any more than an election does. But controls do require agreement on the rules. Controls do require a public understanding that there is no alternative but inflation or recession. That is an educational job for economists, and one might as well work at something that can work. When it becomes known that inflation is a futile game in which the efforts of the players to outdo each other must cancel out; that it is impossible for us collectively to get more than 100 percent of the national income by raising wages and prices; that controls will be applied equitably; that they are as permanent as the businesses and unions that necessitate them and should be taken seriously: then controls will work.

Until that time we will undoubtedly continue with the malpractice of economics and stagger from recession to inflation and back again, enjoying the worst of both. The way this is done is explained in the parable of the stinking fish, told by Abba P. Lerner in his excellent little book on inflation.

The prisoner of a Russian autocrat is forced to choose among three punishments. He must eat a stinking fish, receive a hundred lashes, or pay a fine of a thousand rubles. He decides to eat the stinking fish, but before finishing it he becomes violently ill and can't go on. He then submits to the hundred lashes, but before they are completed, he fears that he is near death and so he pays the thousand-ruble fine.

Well, pass your plate.

November 1973

Gunnar Myrdal's Challenge

Gunnar Myrdal has already performed four lifetimes of work. Forty-five years ago he wrote *The Political Element in the Development of Economic Theory*, which so thoroughly demolished the credibility of value theory that it would have ceased being taught had anyone read the book. After that he became an institutional economist and exercised his penchant for writing encyclopedias by producing *An American Dilemma* and *Asian Drama*. In the meantime came contributions on the welfare state, of which, as a Swedish senator and then minister of trade and commerce, he is a Founding Father. Now Gunnar Myrdal has returned to the land that attracts and exasperates him and has brought along an account of his one-man crusade against preciousness in economics called *Against the Stream*.

The stream referred to is mainstream economics. Myrdal is confident that it will reverse direction in the next ten or fifteen years and flow his way. His way is, of course, institutional economics. Some may wonder exactly what that is.

One clue is Myrdal's comment that all economists are planners, even those who plan nonintervention. "Put an economist in the capital of an underdeveloped country and give him a few assistants, and he will in no time produce a plan. No political scientist, statistician, sociologist, psychologist, or what have you, would ever think of behaving in this way." Economists are not afraid to plan for a country or even the whole world, he says. No noninstitutionalist would make a remark like that.

Another clue is the assertion that you can't really understand a social problem if you make an arbitrary demarcation between economic and noneconomic factors. The only tenable distinction is between more relevant and less relevant ones. You cannot, for example, study a poor country in terms of capital/output ratios and let it go at that. You must also think of the literacy, health, and habits of the people who are expected to work with the capital. This kind of preoccupation has earned Myrdal that hideous label sociologist. No thanks, says he. I'm an economist and expect great things of economics.

Where do the clues lead? Certainly not to the conclusion that some economists are institutional and others are analytical. All economists are institutional economists because they ultimately deal with social relations that take place in institutions. Even Robinson Crusoe had a mother and a father. All economists are also analytical, which is to say that they try to adhere to rules for finding out what is relevant to their particular subject. Differ as they may on the nature of the institutions and the fitness of the rules, all economists, be they mainstream or institutional, will become incensed at the very thought that their work is not both analytical and in touch with institutional reality.

As you read Myrdal, the clues gradually fit together: institutionalism is really a code word, and that code word signifies discontent with market economics.

If you swim against the stream you swim against market economics. You say that the market no longer exists apart from other social influences, if it ever did; that it cannot be understood in isolation; that it is no longer primarily self-regulating; and that social control of economic life has to replace automatic control. The big corporation, the big union, the big state, and market failure have changed the rules. What proof? Well, put the case that economists cannot deal with stagflation by means of simplified aggregate models but need to inform the public that more exacting demands on business and labor are in order. Or put the case that economists must call for long-range planning *before* an event like the oil shortage occurs.

Looking for new rules, you cannot limit your investigation to the confines of the market system but have to reexamine everything. Thus, "the central idea in the institutional approach is that history and politics, theories and ideologies, economic structures and levels, social stratification, agriculture and industry, population developments, health and education and so on, must be studied not in isolation but in their mutual relationship" *(Asian Drama)*.

Is Myrdal's criticism useful? In science, scrupulous criticism is always useful, especially when the record leaves something to be desired. "To be 'behind its time' is the regular methodological weakness of establishment economics." Myrdal makes this remark in the course of discussing stagflation. Robert Heilbroner has been saying the same thing: conventional economics has failed to anticipate the main shifts in the past several decades—the Depression; the postwar prosperity; the problems of development; recessionary inflation; the raw materials crisis. It is no accident Myrdal calls the weakness methodological. The methodology has been excessively static, excessively abstract, and excessively committed to the proposition that things work out best if let alone.

What would happen to the world if mainstream economics suddenly disappeared? It won't. But I suspect that unless the batting average improves, economists will eventually suffer the equivalent of disappearance: they will be ignored. There is no fate worse than being ignored. Good reason to suppose that Gunnar Myrdal's challenge will not go unnoticed and that his words will be pondered: "Economists have a duty to be ahead of their time and not only to adjust."

January 1974

Portrait in Oil

I have borrowed the above title from the autobiography of Nabur Gulbenkian, who was one of the richest oil men in the world. He steadfastly followed the credo "I believe in comfort. I enjoy myself. I enjoy life. I enjoy everything I do." According to his obituary in the *New York Times*—certainly the most jocular obituary the *Times* ever published—Mr. Gulbenkian was once asked whether he preferred old brandy or young women, horses or Rolls Royces, city life or country life. After stroking his beard a moment, he replied: "I prefer everything."

That of course is the American credo too. If there is a shortage of oil, we will find a way to get around it. If we must invent substitutes, we will do it by 1980 and damn those who say we can't. That is the only sensible way of looking at it. After all, old brandy, young women, horses, Rolls Royces, and city and country life cannot be enjoyed without energy. Yes, we will find a way to get what we want. But everything about us will be revealed in the course of it.

The first step is to find out who is to blame. An article in the January issue of *Fortune* says: "Despite clear and insistent warning from his own officials beginning as long ago as 1970, President Nixon failed to take adequate action to cope with energy problems until it was far too late." True, and oil experts knew even earlier. But before we pin this on Mr. Nixon, let us consider that the same facts were available to Mr. Heath, M. Pompidou, Herr Brandt, Mr. Tanaka, and Mrs. Gandhi. They all enjoy the services of bigger planning agencies than we do. It is too much of a strain to believe that all the presidents and prime ministers in the world made the same mistake at the same time. The inaction must be explained as an inherent difficulty governments have in reckoning with turning points, in this case a turning point in the world oil situation. People who say "we can't go on like this" have no status in government. All the status belongs to yea-sayers who assume that tomorrow will be very much like today. Since this is rarely the case, we should take some of that status and give it to a planning board whose job is to assume that, indeed, we really cannot go on like this.

Then surely the Arabs are to blame. They cut supplies and raised prices. They acted in their own selfish interest and didn't consider the rest of the world. That sounds very wicked until you realize that they are just playing a game whose rules were made by Europeans and North Americans. For many years the prices of raw materials exported by poor countries fell while the prices of industrial products exported by rich countries rose. Was there a hue and cry at the suffering this caused in the poor countries? Of course not. For many years we restricted agricultural acreage as a means of keeping farm prices up, even though much of the world went hungry. Diabolical? Not at all. Just good business practice. Now the Oil Producing and Exporting Countries, a club which includes Venezuela, Iran, Nigeria, and Indonesia in addition to the Arabs, have awakened to the knowledge that oil is a wasting asset and will all be gone by 2010, give or take a few years. Any self-respecting cartel in possession of that information will try to get the most from what it has by raising its price to a level that approaches the cost of substitutes and by restricting its output to a level that stretches out the benefits as long as possible. Suddenly every non-Arab has become a follower of Henry George and is wondering out loud what the members of OPEC have ever done to deserve all that oil. This is a line of reasoning we must resist until we are ready to apply the same standards to ourselves.

In fairness we must also clear the oil companies of any blame in this affair. On the international scene, the producing and consuming countries are more and more coming to make their arrangements on a state-to-state basis, with oil and aid as the bargaining counters. The once proud companies are reduced to the menial job of drawing oil from beneath the sands and dispensing it according to the dictates of others. An oil concession is accompanied by a noose and the wearer must act the part of a "tax collecting agency," to use the anguished expression of the chairman of BP. Of late a new and even more lucrative arrangement called "participation" has been devised by Sheikh Yamani, oil minister of Saudi Arabia. The exporting countries come to own a share in the oil companies; the companies do all the work, including marketing the oil everywhere a motor runs or a wheel turns. The oil countries then collect a share of the revenues in addition to the tax.

Domestically the oil companies have not begun construction of any refineries amid all this hubbub, nor will any be completed this year (it takes three years to build one) even though they knew that demand was rising. This is a reaction to adversity: several lean years of too much oil; a price war; a reduced depletion allowance; frozen prices; and environmentalist alarm over Alaskan pipelines and offshore rigs. By not building refineries the majors have been able to deal with these difficulties and end up with terrific profits. Using a refreshingly direct metaphor for an oil executive, the president of Shell said that he and his colleagues had to "claw our way back." If several of those claws have gotten lodged in painful places, that comes under the heading of external diseconomies of scale, by common consent not the concern of business.

We have shown that all the parties are blameless. The point is: Don't blame people for doing things that flow naturally from the positions they occupy in life. The next question is: Don't blame them for what? The Arabs, about to raise prices for reasons already mentioned, did so with a flourish in the winter of 1973–74. They combined a healthy price rise with an embargo imposed for the purpose of promoting a better understanding of their views on Israel. This unfortunately coincided with a shortage of refining capacity in the United States. The Arabs, being in a recalcitrant mood, could hardly be expected to permit the multinationals to ship refined oil from the Middle East to make up our shortfall. Those who argued that there was no world shortage of oil were right; but that was hardly the point.

What happens next is that very much higher oil prices make it feasible to perfect the techniques needed to use other sources of energy: nuclear fission, liquefied coal, and shale in the next few years; the sun, the wind, the tides, nuclear fusion, and the internal heat of the earth in the next fifty. Higher prices also guarantee that we will have more oil, possibly much more oil, from Alaska, offshore, and places yet undreamed of.

Everybody who has put pen to paper about oil has been proved wrong on one point or another and it may be that the coming boom in prospecting will again prove everybody wrong: the oil age may not come to an end in forty years after all. It is not too far-fetched to suppose that we may again be up to our necks in oil with prices coming down. But after the traumatic price rise this winter we are not likely to return to our old ways. The big car appears finished and mass transit has a chance: the reversal of the auto economy alone will change the character of the country. The waste of energy in the way we heat, cool, and insulate buildings is coming under scrutiny. Manufacturers of energy-intensive products like aluminum have suddenly discovered ways to save 30 or 40 percent of their electric bill. Opportunities to be rational are upon us.

The prerequisite is reliable statistics. The daily fumble with figures and the wildly divergent opinions of the highest authorities about what is going on in the oil industry make mandatory reporting of accurate information by the industry a proposition that everybody can agree on.

Then comes planning. Here is another instance where we have backed into planning because there was no choice. The most doctrinaire antiplanner is not going to defend the helter-skelter arrangement we had in which the Treasury, the Department of State, the Office of Emergency Preparedness, the Texas Railroad Commission, the Bureau of Mines, the American Petroleum Institute, and the companies themselves all had a hand in the mismanagement of the industry. Nor is there much to be said in favor of leaving it to the companies. They cut down on research at the precise moment that research was most needed. They stopped building refineries when they were most needed. They were favored with enormous incentives through the depletion allowance and even more enormous ones through the tax write-off allowed for royalties paid to the producing countries. Apparently the 5 percent in federal taxes the companies must pay is too burdensome and must be replaced with a subsidy if they are to continue as viable private institutions.

We have found to our discomfort that energy is too important to leave to the energy men. The research will now be done by the government. The information will be collected by the government. The planning will be done by the government. But under the present setup the public will not be the prime beneficiary. The eighteen majors will be the prime beneficiary because, whether our efforts are directed to oil, coal, shale, or gas, they have the largest proprietary interest. They will also be the first in line when public lands and shores are auctioned off for exploration. And they will in due course collect the money as gas rises to a dollar a gallon. The public will pay the bill. The public will swim in the oil slicks and live in the strip-mined counties. The energy companies—that is the euphemism for vertically integrated oligopolies that go in for horizontal integration—will remain the strongest interest group in the field and have things their way. So it will go unless we dare to put the public interest first and nationalize the majors, or at least place them under public regulation. No doubt public bureaucracy presents problems of its own, no worse, I imagine, than those recently imposed by private bureaucracy. Had a nationalized oil industry possessed the temerity to execute the maneuvers of the last few years we would now be at the barricades.

That leaves the Arabs and their oil-rich confrères. Whether we like it or lump it, they are in a strong position. With fifty billion dollars a year flowing in (or is it one hundred billion?) they have practically imposed economic development on themselves. They need Europe and Japan for that just as Europe and Japan need them for oil. Mutual forbearance is the best attitude under the circumstances. The industrialized nations built their postwar economies on cheap oil. Now they face the most colossal redistribution in modern times. Let us accept poetic justice with good grace.

March 1974

2074

Here it is 2074, and at the age of 145 I am now the oldest editor in the country, not to mention the world. Having written 607 editorials for *Challenge,* it is a little difficult for me to find a fresh topic. Several days ago, looking over the shelves of my library in search of something to write about, my eyes fastened on a musty old book. I lifted it up, sneezing and coughing from the dust that swirled into the air. It was *An Inquiry into the Human Prospect* by Robert Heilbroner. Recollections of the remote past began to wander back to mind. I opened the cover, turned the yellowed pages and came upon a date: 1974. "Why," I exclaimed, "this volume was published exactly a century ago!" This celebrated antiutopia, read by every student along with *Brave New World* and *1984,* saw the light of day in that dark time of Watergate, shortages, and inflation. The world seemed quite mad then, in a mood of self-destruction. Heilbroner captured the mood perfectly. With agitation I reread the momentous question on the opening page: "Is there hope for man?" Then I reread the terrifying answer at the end: "No." No hope? How could that be? I could not swallow it. When I first read the book in 1974, I wanted to protest, argue, remonstrate. But I hesitated. How could I bring myself to write on so large a subject as the next hundred years, about which I knew nothing? The prevailing attitude of pessimism restrained me further. So I maintained silence. Sitting in my study the other day, book in hand, I mused: a hundred years have passed. The time has come for me to speak out.

Admittedly, it is not entirely fair to criticize a book after such a long lapse of time and with full knowledge of what has actually happened. So I shall try to be as dispassionate as possible. I begin, as best I can, by reproducing Robert Heilbroner's narrative. While the populations of the developed countries are stabilizing (as it appeared in 1974), those in the underdeveloped countries are doubling every twenty-five years or so. At that rate the poor lands of the world will have to support some forty billion people by 2074, a manifestly impossible task. If the trend is not arrested, mass famine and disease will intervene. The chances of any democratic government's rousing itself and imposing population control measures are nil. Parliamentary states are too indecisive. The only hope of forestalling an uncontrollable population explosion is through the imposition of authoritarian regimes which have the will and the power to take the harsh steps necessary to get the job done. Such governments will not stop at birth control, but will lead their uncomprehending peoples in a forced march along the route of agrarian reform and economic development.

The leaders of these iron governments, viewing the wealth of rich nations with envy, will be tempted to embark on wars of redistribution. Armed with nuclear weapons, which will soon be within the reach of almost any nation, they will be capable of playing a deadly game of nuclear blackmail. Should any rich nation refuse to ransom one of its cities by making a massive transfer of wealth to the blackmailer, the city might be reduced to ashes. A world atomic war could follow; or with better fortune, the first earnest steps toward world disarmament. In either case, the continuance of nation-states as the main form of social organization virtually guarantees the eruption of limited wars with grim regularity.

The poor countries, bent on following a course of industrialization, will be frustrated by the coming exhaustion of natural resources. All their efforts to reach the current levels of the advanced countries will be in vain. The latter, too, will reach a point where further growth is impossible. Both the developed capitalist and socialist countries will be forced to adapt to no growth through the imposition of stringent planning. An unprecedented goods hunger will arise and lead to such a severe struggle over the distribution of income that all prospects for democratic government will be destroyed.

In an amazing *tour de force*, Heilbroner reasoned that these disasters would come to plague his contemporaries not because they were inherently unavoidable, but because they were the payoff of human nature. Back in 1974, the wellsprings of human action were not as well understood as they are now. Heilbroner turned to Sigmund Freud as his guide and boldly sketched a psychological theory of political behavior. A tragic predicament existed because mankind's growing command over nature far outreached his feeble mechanisms of social control. Behind the political inflexibility was the child in the adult. Children learn to identify with their mothers and fathers and accept their authority. When they grow up they transfer their need for identification to the nation and their need for authority to national leaders. Since the crucial problems are now worldwide, this propensity is fatal. Grown-up children can adjust to ordinary conditions but are unfortunately far too set in their ways to adjust to extraordinary ones. They cannot choose to change; calamity will force them to change. Unhappy ending.

Readers, from our vantage point of 2074, we are well aware of the contrast between this hypothetical sequence and the actual course of events. I will not burden you by reciting the details. But it might be well to refresh our memories with a narrative of the broad outlines.

Heilbroner's assumptions, of course, were wrong. During the last quarter of the twentieth century, a growing number of leaders in the then less developed countries (as they were called) became alarmed at the impending doubling of the population and went to China to find out how to launch effective birth-control programs. In the same period a simple contraceptive method was invented which worked by being poured into the water supply. Consequently, populations in the formerly less developed countries became stabilized at ten billion by 2025. You may recall that as of 1974, birth-control policies had been discussed seriously for only a decade and international awareness of the danger of overpopulation required another decade to sink in. Meanwhile, the green revolution had just begun and the world's ever-normal granary was in the offing, providing civilization with a margin of time within which to organize population control.

By the year 2000, a good many of the formerly poor countries had acquired strong governments which embarked on social reform. Since elections and revolutions occurred every few months in the underdeveloped world, it was just a matter of time before enough effective regimes came to power. This process was aided by a searching discussion of development that took place in the 1970s, at the end of which the mistakes of the previous thirty years were known to every literate person throughout the world. Since both North and South Korea had pioneered in effective development policies, left-wing governments sent representatives to the North to see how it was done and right-wing governments sent representatives to the South. Both put heavy emphasis on agrarian reform, education, health, and employment, avoiding the capital-intensive growth characteristic of the then advanced countries. The requisite finances for development were obtained through the formation of raw materials cartels patterned after the successful oil exporters' cartel of that period. Thus the menace of redistributive wars never arose. In fact, the nuclear threat receded after the cold war ended in the early 1970s, a feature of the time strangely overlooked by Heilbroner. Although the balance of terror was maintained for many years, the recognition of mutual self-interest among the great powers gave them a vested interest in world order. Through combined influence they enforced peaceful settlements of local conflicts, those in Indochina and the Middle East being among the last.

Looking backward, it is hard to understand Heilbroner's despair over the advent of strong states in the poor countries. Some were parliamentary; some were not. The primary issue for the impoverished masses was social discipline, not the form of government. All those that promoted equitable development had a modicum of popular support. We detested Draconian rule just as Heilbroner did, but recognized that sometimes the inescapable sequence was full bellies first, popular elections later.

The industrialized societies did not fare as badly as Heilbroner expected either. The growth of industrial production did slow down, but only over a protracted time. Substitutes became available to replace scarce materials and the steady state is not yet in sight. An intractable struggle over income distribution was allayed by the continued expansion of services. In the United States, the Democrats, elected in 1976 and now in office for their twenty-fifth consecutive term, have almost plugged all the tax loopholes as promised, and are finishing plans for an attractive public service employment program. A national planning board has been established as suggested by Herbert Stein, a leading authority of the time on wage-price controls, and in gratitude for the wonderful results achieved, the Democratic Party has erected a statue in his honor in front of the old Executive Office Building. In the Soviet Union, Chairman Brezhnev turned to light industry and services and declared the competition with capitalism won. Happy ending.

With the advantage of a hundred years of history behind us, let us consider this question: What if Robert Heilbroner, back in the year 1974, had predicted the exact path that events have followed? Would we have to regard him as more perspicacious than he was? No, for the simple reason that nobody can possibly know the trajectory of the future. The future is only partly determined in the present; the rest of it is determined in the future itself. People will make choices in the future and we don't know what choices they will make. People will have more knowledge in the future and we don't know what knowledge they will have. The bare possibility of novel reactions to novel problems opens the door to a wide variety of possible futures. The absence of this conception in *An Inquiry* casts it with the deterministic systems of the past of Smith, Malthus, Ricardo, and Marx, all of which foundered on the rocks of real events.

The premise of *An Inquiry* is that the future can, in general outline, be foreseen because political man and woman are conditioned to walk a predictable path before they leave the nursery. But the adult's sense of identification and acceptance of authority are not received in finished form in the nursery and are not infallible indicators of which ideals, movements, and leaders he or she will follow; they are mediated by all that a man or woman learns or comes to value throughout life. Since general psychological principles do not predestine people to act in any particular way in any particular historical situation, they are useless as guides to the future. Equipped with the most advanced principles of identification and authority, we still do not know whether Rome fell because the Romans identified with their mothers and fathers or because the barbarians identified with theirs. In what circumstances will people succeed and in what will they fail? Many examples, from the Survival of the Ice Age to the Battle of Britain, warn us not to assume that the greater the challenge, the greater the chance of failure.

Thus we can regard *An Inquiry into the Human Prospect* as prophecy; as allegory; as social science fiction; but not as social science. For no single narrative line about the future can be anything but fiction. Because of its plausibility, Heilbroner's was great fiction, sorely needed by his contemporaries as a warning of what could happen if they did not mend their ways. This is a biblical function that must be performed in each generation, and Heilbroner performed it.

But as social science speculation, the economics, politics, and psychology of *An Inquiry* tightened a ring around his contemporaries from which there was apparently no escape. Yet much of this ring was evanescent. It was distilled from forebodings in the air. "Is there hope for man?" Heilbroner sensed this question in people's minds. But his book tells us more about 1974 than about 2074. We read in Winston Churchill's *History of the English-Speaking Peoples* that the period of Roman Britain was a good time to live in: "there was law; there was order; there was peace; there was warmth; there was food, and a long-established custom of life." No one knew that the decline of Rome lay in the future. If we read Huizinga's *The Waning of the Middle Ages* we discover that "a sombre melancholy weighs on people's souls" and that a preoccupation with death pervades the air. Yet the Renaissance was in the making.

Robert Heilbroner ends his book by invoking the myth of Atlas, who bears the heavens on his shoulders with endless fortitude. We will go through terrible times, but if we do not falter, we will survive. There is another myth, that of Hercules. Hercules was forced to perform twelve great labors. With his indomitable strength and will he accomplished them and was made to dwell among the stars as a god by Jupiter. Myths, as Heilbroner writes, "are immense projections of our own hopes and capabilities." Let us invoke Hercules, whose noble spirit dared to overcome all difficulties.

May 1974

I regret writing this article. Bob Heilbroner was a good friend and I should not have mocked his thesis concerning the human prospect. On every other issue we were in close agreement and I admired him greatly. Nevertheless, I still believe what I wrote to be true.

As You Like It

S cene: the Oval Office of the White House, Washington, D.C.
Time: January 21, 1977. Dramatis personae: the newly elected president; his chief economic adviser; ballerina; waiter.

The president is sitting at his desk lost in thought. Music is playing. The chief economic adviser enters from the left.

PRESIDENT. Come in and enjoy the music.

ADVISER. Are my senses intact? I never thought I would live to hear the Ciaconna from Bach's Second Partita for Solo Violin in the Oval Office of the White House at two o'clock in the afternoon.

PRESIDENT. I hope your knowledge of economics is as impressive as your knowledge of music.

ADVISER. It is.

PRESIDENT. Good. Because you will be out on Pennsylvania Avenue if it isn't.

ADVISER. I'll try harder for a president who loves Bach.

PRESIDENT. It's my duty to raise the tone of this place. Bach is above suspicion.

ADVISER. Who's fiddling?

PRESIDENT. Nathan Milstein. He's also above suspicion and is now in the Green Room practicing for a concert this evening. I have a little device in my desk, installed by Gerald Ford's predecessor, which allows me to hear what's going on in the Green Room or any other room.

ADVISER. The bugging of Bach: Another first.

PRESIDENT. *Chacun à son goût.* [The music ends.] Now tell me what I must do to fulfill my campaign promises of full employment, a stable price level, and no shortages.

ADVISER. Say that it will require a second term. In the first term, set up an economic planning board.

PRESIDENT. That sounds un-American. In fact, it sounds European. Tell me: Why have we been able to get along until now without planning?

ADVISER. We haven't. We've had a hundred different plans instead of one. We've had a patchwork of departments and agencies, each doing its own planning. We've had plenty of problems that intelligent planning could have dealt with but have been diverted from it because another theory has

33

prevailed. In the last quarter-century, Keynesianism was at center stage. Whenever we had a problem, the Keynesians thought they had the answer. If the prescription didn't work, a rationalization was always at hand. But now the Keynesian intellectual capital has been spent. The age of Keynes is over and, for good or ill, the age of planning has begun.

In the last few years, we've seen one failure after another, inevitable in an economy of administered prices and wages because fiscal and monetary policy has a poor chance of producing a match between overall supply and demand if specific supplies and demands are mismatched. There is a long string of mismatches beginning with the supply and demand for different kinds of labor and going on through housing, medical facilities, transportation, energy, and even farm produce. We have a jigsaw puzzle in which the pieces don't fit together right. Planning starts with the act of seeing the problem as a whole; seeing where the pieces go; seeing the relation of each part to all the others.

PRESIDENT. What would a planning board do?

ADVISER. A planning board would assemble all the required information in a central place. It would gather together not just aggregate information but details about the supply and demand for particular goods and services, for different types of labor and for investments.

Then it would prepare a number of different plans for a period of, say, five years, based on different goals. It would look ahead to see what steps would be necessary to realize those goals. If it anticipated a shortage of refining capacity, it would recommend that additional capacity be built. If it anticipated a 20 percent expansion of automobile production, it would indicate that a corresponding increase of steel and other materials would be needed.

In the course of drawing up prospective plans, the planning board would have to consult business, labor, and local government as well as specialists in technology, education, health, urban development, and a long list of others to determine the needs and impacts in their respective fields.

Thus the planning board would be concerned not only with aggregate figures like gross national product, national income, investment, and employment but also with their composition. The proportions of the economy would have to be right. Among other things, economics is the science of proportions. We cannot take it for granted that the market will ensure that these proportions are always coherent. They often aren't. Then, too, there is the matter of priorities. We cannot assume that if we want adequate mass transit in ten years, the market will see to it that we have it. There is no way for the public to vote for mass transit through the market under existing conditions. Or even for adequate supplies of paper and plastics, as we have learned to our dismay. The only way it can vote to secure its priorities is through the political process.

PRESIDENT. The planning board may set forth several plans, each of which is self-consistent and realizable in theory. But who decides which plan to adopt?

ADVISER. The planning board cannot decide this. The plans have to be submitted to the president and Congress and it is up to them to pick one. The administration, Congress, and ultimately the electorate determine who benefits and how. Economists as technicians can provide no clue as to which projects ought to have a high priority and which ought to have a low priority. The planning board can only say that if we want to increase housing twofold in a decade, we must have the labor and materials necessary for the job and we cannot use the same labor and materials for something else.

PRESIDENT. Does a planning board do anything further?

ADVISER. In theory it can have responsibility to oversee the fulfillment of the plan. It can act as a coordinator and general manager. Or this job can be done by various executive departments of the federal government. Also, in collecting statistics, the planning board evaluates past performance: Was the plan fulfilled successfully or not?

PRESIDENT. How big a planning board do we need?

ADVISER. The French Commissariat au Plan is composed of 40 members and has the support of 3,000 people divided into 30 committees. That might be a good working figure.

PRESIDENT. Can't the planning board get snowed under by a mountain of out-of-date statistics?

ADVISER. That situation has not been unknown, but with the use of computers and a good reporting system, the chances of success improve. If the planning board concentrates on strategic points and does not try to replace the market, its chances of success are that much better.

PRESIDENT. What is the relation between planning and the market?

ADVISER. The plan does not replace the market. The planning board does not make decisions for people. It recommends the use of indirect means, such as taxes, subsidies, and regulations as incentives and penalties in order to induce people to engage in economic activities (or cease to engage in them) that fulfill the plan. If a paper shortage is anticipated because of insufficient pulp-processing capacity, inducements to invest would be in order.

In those cases where the government itself is a producer, for example the Tennessee Valley Authority (TVA), it can issue guidelines to management but it cannot make the decisions of management. In other industries it can set up yardstick corporations like TVA and run them according to its guidelines, offering competition to private industry. It can run the public sector according to consistent policies and it can use the public sector to help reach the goals of the plan.

PRESIDENT. Does planning cut down freedom?

ADVISER. Yes and no. Yes, in the sense that there may be different rules, regulations, and taxes which induce people to do or refrain from doing certain things. No, in the sense that we avoid the consequences of a failure to look ahead.

PRESIDENT. Does planning intrinsically serve any particular interest group in society?
ADVISER. No. It can be made to serve the interest of capital, labor, the general public, some particular section of any of these, or a compromise of the interests of all.

PRESIDENT. Does planning imply nationalization of industry?
ADVISER. No. This is a separate question. A planning agency can work with private corporations as well as public ones.

PRESIDENT. Doesn't planning undermine antitrust?
ADVISER. Yes, in the sense that it tries to get different components of the economy to concert their efforts. No, in the sense that it doesn't promote mergers. Planning does not eliminate individual firms, their profit motive, or their desire to get more customers.

PRESIDENT. What is to guarantee the objectivity of a planning board?
ADVISER. Nothing, except the traditions of a good, highly educated, intelligent civil service. In short, professional ethics. Also the institutional arrangement. It should be established at the outset that the planning board, except for the directors, is nonpartisan.

PRESIDENT. What about red tape and bureaucracy?
ADVISER. Less, in doing things right to begin with than in having to undo them if they are done wrong. Less, in having a centralized agency doing consistent planning instead of a hundred separate agencies each planning in its own bailiwick and each at odds with all the others.

PRESIDENT. How do you recommend that a planning board be organized?
ADVISER. Right at the center of power if it's not going to be an innocuous body. I recommend that you establish a cabinet post called the Secretary of the Economy to head a Department of the Economy.

This department would have the responsibility of coordinating all the economic activities of the federal government, including the collation of economic information. A planning board should be established within this department, the executive committee of which would consist of all the cabinet members. If you run down the list—Treasury, Labor, Commerce, Interior, Housing, Transportation, Health, Education and Welfare—you will see that they all have economic responsibilities that need to be concerted.

The committee would be chaired by the Secretary of the Economy and the working leadership would consist of that office and the secretary of the Treasury, together with the director of the Bureau of Management and Budget, who should sit *ex officio*. The planning board needs four councils: one for research; one for short-term planning of one year; one for long-range planning; and one for monitoring implementation.

PRESIDENT. What about the Federal Reserve Board and the Council of Economic Advisers?

ADVISER. The Council of Economic Advisers would be redundant and should be phased out. In effect, it would become the council of the planning board responsible for short-run planning. Since the planning board ought not have a rival, the Federal Reserve Board should be placed under the Treasury.

PRESIDENT. How do we avoid rivalry among the various executive departments and independent agencies?

ADVISER. We don't. But since the heads of departments will comprise the executive committee of the planning board, their participation in the process of planning is ensured and a forum is provided to air differences in an attempt to reach a consensus. As for the independent agencies, legislation is required instructing them to act in a manner consistent with the economic plan adopted by Congress.

PRESIDENT. How long should the planning period be?

ADVISER. At least five years is needed to change or develop anything. Even longer-term plans are needed for scientific research, technology, resource development, and the development of new industries.

PRESIDENT. What kinds of things must we include in the plan?

ADVISER. An assessment of current economic and social conditions. A review of results under the previous plan. A statement of objectives. A set of targets and the measures to reach them. Special plans for special areas: science and technology; housing; transportation; social services; energy; agriculture; environment; arms. The plan especially has to provide for anticipated shifts in resources, for example, the closing down of a military installation. The reemployment of personnel and the economic impact on the region have to be dealt with rather than left to chance.

PRESIDENT. What is the difference between indicative and imperative planning?

ADVISER. Indicative planning is the projection of a plan without compulsory measures to realize it. Imperative planning is a plan that entails mandatory compliance. An indicative plan is said to have an announcement effect, that is, the very announcement of the plan is said to inspire confidence that it will be realized and induces private firms to try to live up to it.

PRESIDENT. Which do you prefer?

ADVISER. In practice there is no such thing as a purely indicative plan or a purely imperative plan. A government that issues an indicative plan also adopts some inducements to go along with it. A government that issues an imperative plan cannot control every decision that is made in the economy. I prefer an indicative plan with clout. That is, a plan that is voluntary in the private sector but contains potent economic inducements to comply; in the public sector it sets down general mandatory guidelines.

PRESIDENT. Why can't the CEA do the job?

ADVISER. The CEA deals with aggregates relating to full employment under the Employment Act of 1946. It has a small staff and lacks the information to do the job.

PRESIDENT. What is necessary in order for a plan to succeed?

ADVISER. The plan has to make economic sense. It must have the support of the president, the chief members of the executive branch, of Congress, and the public. Leading decision-makers in the economy must take part in making the plan. They must control the crucial decisions in implementation. Consultation must take place around a table and through a network of planning committees throughout the country. The annual plans must be consistent with the long-range plan.

PRESIDENT. What is the relationship between the federal budget and an economic plan?

ADVISER. The federal budget deals with the economic activities of the federal government, which constitutes about 20 percent of the entire economy. Taxing, spending, and various other levers are used to influence the other 80 percent. In a sense, a plan is a budget for the whole economy, not just for the federal government. But it is more than the sum of accounting items. It is also a matrix of interindustry flows and balances.

PRESIDENT. What is the role of priorities in planning?

ADVISER. Since we don't have enough resources to have everything we want, we have to choose some things over others. That means allocating enough resources for the things we want most. The assumption behind planning is that this will not happen automatically.

PRESIDENT. One last question. Will I succeed if I take your advice?

ADVISER. Your question reminds me of a story by Oscar Wilde. A young man invented a theater box or stall that ingeniously economized space. A friend of his invited twenty millionaires to dinner so that they might be interested in the invention. The young man completely convinced them of the saving to be made in a theater holding six hundred people and they were ready to advance the necessary funds. Unfortunately he then proceeded to calculate the profits to be made in all the theaters in the world; all the churches in the world; all the legislatures in the world; and then went on to discuss the moral and religious effects of his invention. By the end of an hour he had estimated a profit of several billion, at which time the millionaires quietly went away, convinced that the unfortunate inventor was *non compos mentis.*

Being fairly warned, I will promise little in the hope of being pleasantly surprised. But I think planning will be helpful.

PRESIDENT. One good story deserves another. When Jack was President, he had trouble remembering the difference between monetary and fiscal policy. Since William McChesney Martin was then head of the Federal Reserve Board, and both Martin and monetary began with an "M," that helped him remember that the Fed had to do with money. One great virtue of having an economic planning board is that it is perfectly clear what it is supposed to do. So I presume we will have to have one. Now I should like to ask for your proposals in writing.
ADVISER. I thought they were all on tape.

PRESIDENT. Sorry. Tapes are *streng verboten.*
ADVISER. Had I only known. [A ballerina enters dancing.] What now?

PRESIDENT. I've been doing some planning too. I made a deal with Brezhnev. He sends ballerinas; we send bulldozers. Each side specializes in what it does best.
ADVISER. Comparative advantage.

PRESIDENT. And I couldn't resist conspiring with one of them to dance through here as a signal that it's time for my nap. Meet Maya Plisetskaya.

PLISETSKAYA. *Ochen rada s Vami poznakomitsia.*
ADVISER. Likewise. [Enter waiter with champagne.]

PRESIDENT. Drink up, everybody. A nap goes better preceded by champagne. By the way, did I ever tell you you're one of the tallest economists I've ever met?

July 1974

Wassily Leontief's concept of input-output relations among industries comes shining through in this dialogue. In retrospect, I unduly denigrated Keynesian monetary and fiscal policy. I did not mean to do so.

I cannot remember who I had in mind as president. The context suggests Senator Edward Kennedy. Those who read this in the twenty-second century and beyond will need to know that the tall economist is John Kenneth Galbraith.

The Praise of Folly

When an economist says, "We don't really know what to do about inflation," his statement, like many in the Bible, is subject to interpretation. One interpretation is that we do know what to do. The proof is that we knew what to do in World War II. We imposed price and wage controls and instituted rationing. President Ford and his advisers have forgotten.

Although there were shortages of commodities and superfluities of money, although demand pulled and costs pushed, controls stood the test with admirable resilience. The reasons are quite simple.

Controls are designed to stabilize and temporarily sustain a disparity between demand and supply. Under normal circumstances, meaning in an uncontrolled market, price is the allocator and rationer, always moving to bring quantities demanded and supplied into balance. Let demand rise; prices will rise. Let supply fall; prices will rise again. In wartime, when supply cannot readily catch up, this can spell disastrous inflation. The same in peacetime. Controls enable us to live with such a disequilibrium of demand and supply, limiting demand and rationing supply by means other than price.

The subject of controls is divisible into several parts. First there is price control and resource allocation in concentrated industries. Galbraith has remarked that "it is relatively easy to fix prices that are already fixed." The prices charged by large corporations are administered. It is but one further step to provide the administrators with authoritative counsel. The managements of the thousand largest corporations are accustomed to dealing in controlled prices. They are also accustomed to allocating supplies to customers or dealers. It is not difficult for the supplier to engage in rationing because it is simply an extension of the process of allocation that he engages in during the course of the day's business.

The problem is different in competitive markets. There it is necessary to supplement price control with a rationing apparatus. Rationing limits demand. A customer not only needs dollars; she needs coupons. Presumably the number of coupons issued will be limited so that demand will be artificially reduced to equate with supply at the going price.

The chief consideration in the control of wages is equitability. Wages can only be controlled if people think they are being treated fairly. Fairness must reign between recipients of wages and profits and among different groups of wage earners themselves. Controls do not mean that wages and prices can never change in the interest of efficiency and equity or that they must tend toward uniformity, even though there may be pressure in that direction. As Galbraith reported in his remarkably timely book, *A Theory of Price Control* (1952), he was advised in the days of Office of Price Administration (OPA) to fix one price, five dollars, for everything. Taking into account the subsequent depredations of inflation, the appropriate price now appears to be fourteen dollars and ninety-seven cents.

A control system buys time in which to maneuver. Credit and materials can be used to alleviate shortages. Marginal producers can be subsidized until better processes are developed or more efficient plants are built. Expensive imports can be subsidized until domestic production expands or conservation measures become effective. Anyone with a fertile imagination can extend the list of means available to bring demand and supply back into alignment. Meanwhile we can live with disequilibrium for quite a long time provided people are willing to go along with it. If they think it reasonable, why shouldn't they?

The experience of World War II shows that inflation can be contained effectively and that it can be contained for a matter of years. Skeptics will immediately reply that controls are an exercise in suppressing inflation and that sooner or later the piper has to be paid. They will remind us that there was a rapid increase in prices when controls were removed after the war. Precisely. Controls were lifted precipitately and not very wisely. Had decontrol been lengthened out enough for civilian production to get a running start, supply would have caught up with demand at a considerably lower price level. As is often the case, the most disruptive course was advocated by conservatives, who consider themselves the most intrepid foes of disruption.

No doubt much of the current inflation could have been contained had we used the instruments available. Someone will protest that we had phases I, II, III, III1/2, and IV and they were a dismal failure. But as a well-known economist remarked, putting this administration in charge of a program of controls was like putting a minister in charge of a whorehouse. Possibly it was more like putting a whore in charge of a ministry. In any event, when strict controls were the order of the day, as they were during phase II, the rate of inflation did indeed decline. Those heady days were followed by heart-rending efforts to restrain agricultural prices without rationing and to moderate petroleum prices by a strict regime of silent meditation and prayer.

We have learned in recent months that the stuff of which panics are made still exists. If the managers of multinationals wake up one morning and decide to sell their CDs, there is precious little to stop them. Much to our discomfort, we are apprised that banks can run out of money. So can countries. In spite of all the admirable developments since the 1930s, we have acquired a new and astonishing piece of information. Our economies are not depression-proof after all.

Where is the new Keynes? asked the editors of *BusinessWeek,* with a wary eye cocked on the bumblings of the finance ministers of the Western World and Japan, so hypnotized by their minimal versions of the old Keynes that they cannot think of anything to do except to repeat the same formulas that led us to the edge of disaster in the first place. Yet salvation does not lie in waiting for some new oracle who will reveal hitherto unknown truths, but rather in taking hold of the truths that are already known. The usual sequence, of course, is disaster first, imagination later. Then the new Keynes or Keyneses, if there are several, will be lionized and saluted with awestruck amazement over his (her, their) dazzling originality.

Meanwhile the government characteristically blames the public. But the public has a retort, as suggested by a colloquy between G.K. Chesterton, who was very fat, and George Bernard Shaw, who was very thin. Encountering Shaw at a banquet, Chesterton remarked: "Looking at you, one would think there was a famine." To which Shaw replied: "Looking at you, one would think you were the cause of it."

September 1974

Inflation and Defunct Ideas: President Ford's Economic Summit

A mass meeting of sages at the summit is an impressive spectacle, but no one in his right mind expects that economic truths will be revealed by majority vote. If a group of cartographers were assembled and solemnly proclaimed the earth to be cylindrical, that would not be helpful, especially if the administration persisted in believing it to be cubical. Only one Columbus is required to announce the truth. A hotelful is neither necessary nor obtainable. But it is a wise sovereign who knows his Columbus. Alan Greenspan, unflinching opponent of newfangled ideas like the progressive income tax and protective consumer legislation, does not possess that certain innovative turn of mind necessary to qualify. He is obviously a flat earth man. When the sovereign keeps counsel with a flat earth man, the rest of us can reasonably expect that policy will be guided by the fear of falling off edges that don't exist.

Yet there are plenty of economists who understand that the earth is round, James Tobin for one. Amid rivers of swill, his recent article in the *New York Times* is high ground on which one can take refuge. He states simply and clearly that there are three kinds of inflation and that we have two. We do not have excess demand inflation. Unemployment has been rising and production has been falling; these are sure signs of slack in overall demand. We do have inflation induced by commodity shortages and we have a wage-price spiral. The shortages in farm products and petroleum are well known. Those in steel, nonferrous metals, paper, and other products are less well known. In each case, the shortage results in higher costs for the user, and if this is a manufacturer, the increase is passed on to the consumer. Consumers in their capacity as workers demand higher wages to recoup their losses. Employers then raise prices to recoup theirs and, not implausibly, to come out ahead. The process is self-perpetuating. To top it off, the depreciation of the dollar gave the inflationary wheel another spin by making imports more expensive and exports cheaper. Foreign demand, particularly for basic agricultural and industrial products, increased, compounding the shortages and price increases.

Under the circumstances, tight money and budget cutting, appropriate when inflation is induced by a general excess of demand, can only make matters worse. They contribute nothing to the alleviation of shortages and they do nothing to arrest the wage-price spiral. In fact, measures that cause a contraction of investment only deepen the malady. And investment is sure to contract as demand contracts, perpetuating the downslide of the economy that is already under way while leaving prices free to rise.

Advocates of tight money and budget cutting argue that by steadfastly restricting demand, prices will eventually come down regardless of the immediate causes of the inflation. This may well be true, depending on how long "eventually" is, but it means holding the entire economy hostage until the treatment takes effect. Accept 6 or more percent unemployment, accept a decline in output, give up essential social programs, give up economic growth, and maybe the thing will work. But the public will rebel long before that hoped-for hour, and will demand a shifting of gears into an expansionary phase. This phase will last until inflation again becomes intolerable, and then the gears will be shifted back once more. This upward-and-downward movement is what the Polish economist Michal Kalecki called the political business cycle. It is the result of a failure of diagnosis and a refusal to use the appropriate economic tools. As long as we restrict ourselves to the use of monetary and fiscal instruments, pretending that they are suitable for the treatment of all three types of inflation, we are limited to the primitive tactics of stop-and-go.

But there is another way, and that is to deal directly with the problems we have. Wage-price controls are relevant to both the wage-price spiral and inflation-inducing commodity shortages. But before controls can even be discussed rationally, we must get over the childish taboo against them that originated in the muddle of exhortation, optimistic prediction, reluctant tinkering, and quick changes of costume called "controls" by the late administration of Richard Nixon. Controls do not have to be a muddle, as the freeze of August 15, 1971, and the subsequent phase II demonstrated. Administered by people who believe in what they are doing, as was the case in World War II, controls play a role for which there is no substitute. They can halt the leapfrog of wages and prices. And where there are shortages, they can hold the price line or even effect a rollback while industries have a chance to increase capacity. Then there is rationing. That, I suppose, should not even be mentioned. But if we could calm our nerves sufficiently, we might recognize that in some cases rationing is a useful supplement to controls for the purpose of holding down demand until supply catches up. The price we have to pay for a high rate of inflation in terms of misallocated resources, upset priorities, and income maldistribution should make these proposals positively alluring.

But this is not the end of the story. We not only need a change of heart and mind with respect to wage-price controls as normal, natural, beneficial economic tools; we need the same change with respect to economic planning. An economic planning board can anticipate shortages before they occur. Shortages are imbalances between one section of the economy and another. The market as it is presently arranged does not do anything to prevent shortages but only records them after they have occurred. A planning board must be in a position to recommend steps that will guide the market in the desired direction. But the anticipation of shortages is only the most elementary function of a planning board, one that is merely preventive. Its positive function is to produce a plan in which all aspects of the economy are in balance, in conformity with national economic objectives as predetermined by the administration and Congress after due consultation with the public. The recent establishment of a National Commission on Supplies and Shortages is a first tentative step in the right direction. But as long as fiscal policy is made by one body, manpower policy by another, monetary policy by yet a third, the federal budget by a fourth, and now supply policy by still a fifth, planning will come to nothing. In a fit of typical American extravagance, we will have five planning boards, each working its own beat, and in the end we will conclude that planning is a sham after all and wonder what to try next. But if we are really serious about supplementing monetary and fiscal techniques, which can only speed up or slow down economic activity indiscriminately, with a technique that is expressly designed to secure coherence, balance, and proportionality among the various parts of the economy (at the microlevel, as economists are fond of calling it), then we must not play with planning boards but do the job right.

As the mist from the summit clears, it becomes apparent that Mr. Ford likes to appear to be listening for new ideas; but possibly he is dozing. There is an apocryphal story about Joseph Haydn which claims that he placed a resounding chord in the slow movement of the Surprise Symphony because his London audiences had the habit of falling asleep. Upon hearing the chord, they awakened with a start. Apparently the most that could be mustered at the summit were a few restrained *mezzo fortes* through which the president comfortably slept.

November 1974

The Economic Consequences of Friedrich A. von Hayek

The ways of the Nobel committee are exceedingly strange. Before the economics prizes were awarded in October 1974, nobody on this earth ever thought of Gunnar Myrdal and Friedrich A. von Hayek at the same time, on the same day, or even in the same week. Now they are joined in eternal confraternity by virtue of being co-recipients of last year's award. The catholicity of taste of the Nobel committee staggers the imagination and is certainly unsurpassed in the annals of prize-giving.

I assume that the prize is proffered in recognition of notable advances in economic science. But since Myrdal and Hayek have been advancing in opposite directions for the past fifty years, this leaves the committee with some explaining to do. In physics, chemistry, and medicine, I don't doubt that, aside from petty professional jealousies, general agreement prevails in the respective fields that Nobel laureates have made some laudable contribution to the storehouse of human knowledge. No one could assert that about both Myrdal and Hayek and be adjudged sane by an impartial panel of specialists. Myrdal has spent his life blasting the free market as a snare and a delusion, while Hayek has spent his blasting all attempts to manage the free market as the work of the devil. The conclusion ineluctably follows that the Nobel committee is collectively insane.

Or is there another explanation? The most generous view conceivable is that the committee cannot tell the difference between "forward" and "backward" in economics as it can in, say, physics, chemistry, and medicine. The following conversation probably took place:

Chairman: Ladies and gentlemen of the committee. Having discussed the economics prize for six weeks and being still deadlocked between Myrdal and Hayek, let us play it safe and award two prizes: one for the most advanced economist and one for the most backward. Since we are unable ourselves to decide which is which, we will simply leave it up to the public.

Committee member: How will the public know that we have made this distinction if we don't say so openly?

Another member: My dear Bruno, the public is not stupid. By a process of deductive logic, someone is bound to figure out that Myrdal and Hayek cannot both be the most advanced economists of 1974, that one of the two must be the least advanced; and this will spare us the embarrassment of having to say so ourselves.

Assorted members: Hear, hear!

Chairman: I take it, then, that, as they say in America, we shall get ourselves off the hook by making a joint award. Let the minutes so record.

I eschew any impulse to become embroiled in a controversy of this nature. Suffice it to say that I read in the *New York Times* of last November 15 Friedrich A. von Hayek's tremendous blast against all novel economic ideas that have been inflicted on us since 1935 by Lord Keynes and the disreputable crowd that surrounded him. It is quite true that "the seductive doctrine" of government deficits would have been denounced by "every reputable economist" before Keynes. They, it goes without saying, preferred balanced budgets à la Herbert Hoover.

"What we are experiencing," says Hayek, "are simply the economic consequences of Lord Keynes." This sets one to wondering, in a most amiable sort of way, whether Keynes would have endorsed the economic policies of Johnson, Nixon, and Ford. Alas, we shall never know.

Now here is a further puzzlement. Hayek says, in his disarmingly simple manner, but with all the authority of a Nobel laureate: either we go back to the pre-Keynesian—I almost said glorious pre-Keynesian—"recurring cycles of booms and depressions" where the booms were more modest than our protracted postwar boom and the busts much more modest than the one that is coming as a consequence of said current protracted postwar boom; or we go forward—well, not forward, of course—we go toward a "command economy in which everyone is assigned his job."

This is a terrible, dismal set of choices. Since economics is known as the dismal science, it does, however, lend credence to the view that Hayek is the true, secret winner of the 1974 Nobel prize. But before making a final decision, I believe it only fair to ask Gunnar Myrdal if he thinks there are any other possibilities.

January 1975

The Fear of Planning

"Frankly," said I to my barber, "I am afraid of economic planning."
My barber is the most literate person I know. No matter how early I arrive for a haircut, he has already read every word of the *New York Times*.

"But Monsieur," he replied, since he is French, "you are a businessman. It is not becoming to a businessman to be afraid of planning." He picked up the *Management Review* and leafed through its pages.

"Read this ad," he said, jabbing a finger at a headline. "'Any organization that doesn't plan for its future isn't likely to have one.' That is what a corporate planning service has to say. Businessmen will agree. Family heads will agree. The Joint Chiefs of Staff will agree. The Mafia will agree. But suggest that the president and the Congress of the United States plan, and you are in trouble."

He fastened the apron around my neck. "Everyone knows that businesses have to be run by people; but the economy, *mon Dieu!* the economy runs itself."

I muttered something about the invisible hand as the scissors clicked around my head.

"The will to believe in miracles: what a wonder! Long ago nature was generous; workers were obliging; and the economy was small and simple. Those days are gone, Monsieur, gone. We must plan. But first we must cast out fear."

"Fear, yes, fear," I said as I sank into the chair. "I fear that planning means the end of something we all cherish: the free market system."

"You say this to a Frenchman? To me, the only French barber in America? We French have been planning for thirty years. Do we not still have a free market system? Our planning tries to make the market work well. You Americans are very practical. Maybe you will do better than the French.

"Let us try to be sensible," he continued, applying lather to my neck. "Suppose the Congress and the president, perhaps Mr. Ford's successor, decided in a general way how to spend our national income between now and the year 2000. So much for consumption; so much for investment; so much for housing, mass transit, health care, energy, and research. Then suppose the economists told them what kinds of incentives and controls would be necessary, not to destroy the market, but to guide it. Is this a terrible thing?"

"But Pierre," I interjected, "the economy is an intricate web. A vague idea of how all the strands tie together will not do."

"True," he replied, stropping his razor. "Planning will require a much more intimate knowledge of the economy than we now have. Summary figures of gross national product, employment, and price levels will not do. Detailed information about the transactions between one industry and another will be required. It will take a big staff to get the information and it will take a lot of money.

"But what is the alternative? We have no means at present, none at all, neither automatic nor deliberate, to see to it that the structure of the economy will be as we wish it in ten or twenty years. How many cars, trains, trucks, ships, and planes will we have by the year 2000? How much energy will we have to run them? Do not tell me that the commuter and the shipper will decide such matters. Am I to believe that the auto industry grew; roads were built; railroads declined; blacks moved from the rural South to the urban North; the middle class fled to the suburbs; Lake Erie was polluted; energy-using metal containers replaced returnable bottles; indestructible synthetic fibers replaced biodegradable cottons and woolens; and multinational corporations exported jobs to Hong Kong and Korea because the public wanted it that way? *Sacre bleu*! You Americans will believe anything."

This remark was accompanied by a savage slash at my right sideburn. I began to perspire. It seemed best to concede a point. "Let us admit that planning might help the market satisfy our needs a little better than it does now. Still I do not want to go down a road that will destroy private enterprise and end in socialism and dictatorship," said I as firmly as circumstances permitted.

"My dear sir," replied Pierre, temperately shaping my left sideburn, "if planners wish to sleep nights, they will not try to meddle in the millions of decisions made by businessmen every day. Instead, they will use gentle inducements like taxes and capital regulations to persuade management to play the game according to the rules.

"As for socialism, that is up to the public. But if I were a capitalist wanting to preserve the status quo, I would lobby for planning. Planning means an orderly economy. Planning means cooperation. Planning means more confidence in the future. Planning means less anxiety among workers. That is how I would see it if I were a capitalist.

"On the other hand, if I were a socialist wanting to change the status quo, I would still lobby for planning. Planning means a national debate about the future of the country. Planning means an open discussion about the allocation of resources and the distribution of income. Planning means making our economic goals explicit. Clearly, the public, so the socialist should reason, will be horrified to learn what objectives Big Business pursues and will want to change them. May the better arguments win."

I felt my fears ebbing away as the pleasant sensation of the electric massager spread throughout my shoulders. "Dictatorship?" Pierre mused. "Authoritarian governments engage in authoritarian planning. Democratic governments engage in democratic planning. Sleep in peace. Plans are subject to change at the next election."

"Must I swallow five-year plans, too?" I ventured. "They are so rigid."

"Plans are not plans without deadlines," came the ineluctable reply, as my hair was parted, the clock ticked away, and the next customer finished *Playboy* and started to fidget. "Take it from Peter F. Drucker: 'What do we have to do now to attain our objectives tomorrow?' 'Tomorrow' for me means cutting a head of hair in fifteen minutes. For a town planner it means building a new town in ten years. For a planner of mass transit it means constructing a national transportation system in twenty-five years. Plans are schedules, not straightjackets. If the unforeseen happens, if crops fail, if oil supplies are cut off, how much better is it to have a plan that can be adjusted than to have no plan at all."

"But," said I, as I rose from the chair, dug in my pocket for $3.50, and put on my jacket, "when planners make mistakes, heaven help us. They will be bigger mistakes."

"Bigger than what?" asked the astonished Pierre. "Here we are without planning, enjoying the worst shortages, the biggest inflation, and the deepest recession in forty years. Can planners do worse?

"My dear friend," concluded my friendly barber, walking to the door with his arm over my shoulders, "once fear is cast out, planning will become irresistibly appealing to the human sense of order, logic, and purposefulness. Think what a tribute it is to the persuasive talents of the economics profession that people have been convinced against all the testimony of their senses that the economy plans itself. Sadly, miracles happen only in economic theory, not in the workaday world. When fear stops, the illusion of the miracle will end. Then planning will not only become irresistible; it will become respectable."

March 1975

The Planning Bill

Senators Humphrey and Javits, joined by other members of Congress, will shortly announce their sponsorship of "The Balanced Growth and Economic Planning Act of 1975," a proposed piece of legislation that clearly has far-reaching implications. The bill was originally drafted by members of the Initiative Committee for National Economic Planning, of which Wassily Leontief and Leonard Woodcock are co-chairmen (and I am the coordinator). The final draft is the joint product of the Initiative Committee and the original Senate sponsors. A great deal of thinking went into the bill, and I should like to share it with the reader. It is always the case that each person who takes part in a project has a different emphasis when called upon to interpret it. I do not pretend that what follows is any but my own.

An attractive feature of the bill is that it is exceptionally neat and simple. It sets up an Office of Balanced Growth and Economic Planning in the Executive Office of the President. This office consists of a council, a director, a deputy director, and staff. The council has sixteen members: the director of the office, who acts as chairman; members of the cabinet; the chairman of the Federal Reserve Board; the chairman of the Council of Economic Advisers; the director of the Office of Management and Budget; and the chairman of an Advisory Committee. The Advisory Committee, reasonably balanced to represent various interests, will be formed to consult with the director on the work of the Office. Four of its twelve members will be chosen by the director; four by the speaker of the House; and four by the president of the Senate.

The director and deputy director of the office are appointed by the president with the advice and consent of the Senate. The director has cabinet rank and supervises the activities of the Office. He or she is directly responsible to the president and acts as chief officer for economic planning in the executive branch of government.

The functions of the Office of Balanced Growth and Economic Planning are:

1. To prepare a proposed Balanced Economic Growth Plan, to be approved by the council and then to be submitted to the president;
2. To monitor and report on the implementation and results of the plan;
3. To review the budgets of the departments and agencies of the federal

government, legislation proposed by the executive branch to Congress, legislation reported to the Senate or House by their committees, and major new programs or actions of the executive branch if they have an important bearing on the plan;

4. To make reports on the consistency of budgets, legislation, and new programs with the plan;
5. To conduct other activities pertaining to national economic planning as the president directs.

The bill provides that the Office contain a Bureau of Economic Information to supervise and coordinate the activities of the departments and agencies of the executive branch with respect to the collection and analysis of economic data and information. In order to ensure that the necessary detailed economic information is available to the Office as a foundation for its planning activities, the bureau is authorized to establish standards and methods for the acquisition, collation, analysis, and reporting of economic data by any department or agency of the executive branch and to initiate new programs for gathering and processing economic information essential to support the planning functions of the Office.

The director of the Office is empowered to employ a staff with the necessary qualifications to carry out the functions of the Office.

The Council of Economic Advisers will continue to advise the president directly on short-run economic problems and its staff will remain separate from the staff of the Office. The CEA will be required to include an analysis of the consistency of the Economic Report of the President with the Balanced Economic Growth Plan.

For the purpose of carrying out the act, the director of the Office is empowered to hold such hearings as he or she considers necessary.

The Office is given the authority to appoint advisory committees composed of representatives of labor, management, and the public to advise it on subjects in which committee members have specialized knowledge.

The bill requires the president to submit a proposed Balanced Economic Growth Plan to Congress biennially, prepared by the Office and approved by the council. The proposed plan will include:

1. An examination of long-run economic and social trends and objectives;
2. A recommended six-year economic and social plan, embodying coherent and realizable economic and social goals, including specific goals for each major sector of the economy;
3. Identification of the resources required for achieving the stated goals and objectives and a statement of the governmental policies and programs needed;

4. A review of economic and social goals contained in existing legislation, with analysis of the progress toward meeting such goals that can reasonably be expected in the six-year period;
5. Identification of the resources, policies, and programs necessary to achieve such progress, and the extent to which the achievement of such progress will compete with other goals and objectives that the president considers of equal or greater importance;
6. Pertinent data, estimates, and recommendations which the Office considers useful to the president, Congress, or the public.

After the proposed plan is submitted to Congress, the Joint Economic Committee will hold hearings to ensure comment, criticism, analysis, and reaction from interested groups, government agencies, officials, and the public. Chairmen of congressional committees will be asked to report on aspects of the plan that come within the competence of their committees. Within 90 days of receipt of the proposed plan, the Joint Economic Committee will make a report to Congress accompanied by concurrent resolutions (one for each house) recommending approval, disapproval, or modifications of the plan as submitted by the president.

The staff of the Joint Economic Committee is authorized to conduct a continuing, nonpartisan analysis of national economic goals and the policies necessary to achieve them, and to provide the Joint Economic Committee with the information and analyses necessary for enlightened decisions concerning proposed and existing plans.

The Congress will also be assisted by a Division of Balanced Growth and Economic Planning, to be set up in the Congressional Budget Office. This division, headed by a deputy director, will be responsible for the long-term budget planning that must be an integral part of the six-year plan.

After receiving the report of the Joint Economic Committee accompanied by concurrent resolutions, the Congress will debate the resolutions and vote on them, going on record as a body with respect to the plan. If approved, the proposed plan becomes the national economic plan. If not approved, it will be necessary for the president to submit a revised plan to Congress within 30 days.

The Office of Balanced Growth and Economic Planning is instructed to make a biennial report to the president and Congress evaluating the progress made toward fulfillment of the plan.

The president is authorized to ensure that departments and agencies subject to his direction conform as nearly as possible with the plan. The Congress, for its part, directs that United States laws, policies, and regulations be interpreted and administered as nearly as possible in accordance with the policies set forth in this act and with the plan then in effect.

The director of the Office of Balanced Growth and Economic Planning may ask any federal department or agency to submit a statement assessing the consistency of proposals or actions that have a significant impact on the fulfillment of the plan. The director will review the statements, and if he or she finds any serious inconsistency with the plan, he/she will inform the council, which then will report its views and recommendations to the president.

Finally, the bill requires that the national economic plan take account of regional, state, and local plans to the maximum extent feasible. It calls on the director to establish procedures for regular consultation with regional, state, and local planning agencies; if they request it, to review the consistency of their plans with the national economic plan and to recommend changes to bring such plans into conformity with the national plan; and to make grants to regional, state, and local planning agencies to improve their capability for long-range planning. In addition, the governor of each state may hold hearings on the proposed plan, and submit a report of findings and recommendations to the Joint Economic Committee. This report will include the views of state and local officials and private citizens.

So much by way of summary. Now to explain the considerations that shaped the bill.

The members of the Initiative Committee proceeded from two premises: to write a bill that would result in effective planning; and to do it in an American context, taking into account the realities of the U.S. political system and economy. The planning institutions proposed in the bill are built squarely on the presidency and the Congress. The Office of Balanced Growth and Economic Planning, the Joint Economic Committee, and the Division of Balanced Growth and Economic Planning in the Congressional Budget Office are the principal planning instruments of these branches of government. The president, through the Office, develops a planning program, including legislative recommendations, which he presents to Congress. The Joint Economic Committee examines the program in consultation with committee chairmen and the Budget Office, proposes alternatives where it sees fit, and recommends legislation to the appropriate congressional committees to carry out the plan. Congress passes the laws. The president executes them. If the president and Congress are of like mind, the concurrent resolutions and the legislation needed to implement the national economic plan will be passed. If they differ, they will have to seek a compromise.

Some who have given thought to this question and who fear an imperial presidency, would put the planning agency entirely in Congress. But this is impossible, since the president must carry out the laws that pertain to planning and must have the institutional means to do so. Moreover, the president, as the leader of the party in power, must have the staff to develop a planning program.

Others who fear that planning will fall into the hands of an elite, remote from the pressure of public opinion, would establish an independent Planning Commission somewhere between the Executive Branch and Congress, and select its directors—proportionally—from among representatives of labor, business, consumers, and other sectors of the public. The Initiative Committee rejected this idea. It is an illusion to think that the plans of any such commission can survive if they are contrary to the wishes of the president and Congress. The only way to get better plans is to elect better representatives. There is no shortcut.

The institutional arrangement proposed in the planning bill strengthens neither the president nor the Congress at the expense of the other, but allows them both to deal with economic problems more efficiently.

The Office of Balanced Growth and Economic Planning is located in the Executive Office of the President precisely so that it can be effective. The members of the cabinet, the chairman of the Federal Reserve Board, the chairman of the Council of Economic Advisers, and the director of the Office of Management and Budget are included in the leadership council so that they will be parties to the making of planning policy. Without their participation, planning cannot succeed and a plan will remain a scrap of paper, as we know by examining the experience of anemic planning councils that exist abroad. The director of the planning office is given the power to examine all proposed actions of the cabinet, of federal agencies, and of Congress, for their consistency with the national economic plan. This is an indispensable means to ensure the coherence of all economic and social programs of the federal government.

The bill provides that the president shall submit a proposed national economic plan to Congress. The Initiative Committee deliberately did not specify in this bill what the goals of the plan should be. We have received letters that say: start with the goals, then set up the planning mechanism. We profoundly disagree with this view. In a society as diverse as ours, we shall never reach permanent agreement on goals. Majority opinion changes over the years. But planning provides the intellectual and institutional framework within which to consider goals, to consider their feasibility, the cost of reaching them, and the alternatives we have to forego if we adopt them. The establishment of a framework for the rational consideration of goals is an immense step forward. The present method of government decision-making can best be described as a series of reactions to one emergency after another. Neither officials nor the public have a chance to consider goals in a systematic way. The process of planning will force us to think about the long run. It will also force us into a debate in which we will have to make our goals explicit. Anyone who recognizes the value of such a debate should welcome the prospect of setting up a planning system.

What will a plan be like?

The planning bill specifies that the proposed national economic plan include an examination of trends and general objectives covering a protracted period beyond six years. This provision implies scanning the distant horizon for possible dangers as well as opportunities that might be discerned, and devoting attention to undertakings that have a long gestation period— research on alternative sources of energy, for instance. But most of the planning staff will devote its time to working out a six-year plan embodying coherent and realizable economic and social goals, including specific goals for each major sector of the economy. It will identify the resources needed to achieve the goals. It will prepare a statement of the government policies and programs needed. And it will review progress toward achieving previously adopted goals.

This means that a plan will analyze the economy industry by industry and sector by sector. Of necessity it will have to deal with interindustry relations, using analytical techniques designed for this purpose. A great deal of detailed data will be required. The background material for the plan will undoubtedly fill several thick volumes, but its main features can and should be summarized in a small booklet. It will take a staff of perhaps 500 people to do the work and will cost possibly $50,000,000 a year. The plan will analyze and set general objectives for the allocation of resources, labor, and capital to specific sectors of the economy; and will set general objectives for the goods and services produced by those sectors. It will also analyze and set strategic objectives for the future structure of production and consumption. It will incorporate special projects for the development of energy, transportation, housing, health, research, and numerous other requirements of pressing importance. It will take into account "the quality of life" and the environment. And—what monetary and fiscal policy is supposed to do now—it will deal with such familiar matters as employment, GNP, and the price level.

No disparagement of monetary and fiscal policy is intended. The Council of Economic Advisers is preserved intact to advise the president on measures needed to influence the general level of economic activity. But the manipulation of monetary and fiscal aggregates is necessarily a short-run proposition, and deals with, clearly, aggregates, not component parts of the economy. Restrictive measures cannot, for example, stop inflation caused by shortages or by administered prices that occur in specific parts of the economy without destroying jobs and wasting billions in potential output. The planning bill will probably return monetary and fiscal policy to its proper function, since it requires that recommendations of the Council of Economic Advisers be consistent with the national economic plan. It is not likely that the plan will call for mass unemployment.

By contrast, a plan not only allows us to look at the general picture, but at its details. Plans are guides to the relationships between different parts of the economy and allow us to adopt coherent policies for the separate parts as required. The means to implement these policies are not specified in the bill. Just as in the case of goals, the bill provides a framework. A wide range of instruments can be used to accomplish specific, interrelated aims. These instruments are already familiar in nonplanning contexts or where the planning has been applied ad hoc: they are tax incentives and penalties; capital and credit allocation; laws requiring or prohibiting definite actions, such as those specifying how air, water, and land may be used; and projects within the public sector itself—the space program, for example. Incomes policy, now under a cloud, is also a possible planning instrument. Whether or not it is used depends, like everything else, on the circumstances.

Some who like neat definitions have asked what kind of model we have in mind. Is it indicative planning, like the French version? The fact is that the Initiative Committee didn't start with any foreign model at all, but tried to analyze American conditions and needs. Anyone who reads John Sheahan's article in the March/April [1975] issue of *Challenge* will see that French planning leaves much to be desired. The same may be said about Japanese planning, as one can learn by reading Ryutaro Komiya's article in the current issue. A planning commission that makes forecasts to which nobody pays attention is not what we have in mind. Nor do we have in mind a tug-of-war between planning technocrats, the Finance Ministry, and the prime minister. Nor yet a summary of the investment intentions of all the businesses in the country. Nor a planning system that is boycotted by unions because they are aligned with opposition parties. Least of all do we have in mind a pro forma planning procedure that is rubber-stamped by parliament and actually negotiated by chairmen of the boards of the largest corporations.

What we envisage is an effective planning agency, the Office of Balanced Growth and Economic Planning, that is the direct instrument of the president and that actually has the authority to plan. On the congressional side, we envisage a complementary and equally effective planning agency, the Joint Economic Committee, supported by an expanded staff, working with the Budget Office, able to recommend planning legislation to Congress. The bill also encourages and supports planning agencies at the regional, state, and local levels. It is therefore inevitable that a continuous public discussion will take place about what planning should be and how it is working.

We expect that the normal American political process, through which the president, Congress, and state and local officials are elected, through which issues are discussed, and through which labor, business, farmers, minorities, and other parts of the public are heard, will determine how we plan.

This kind of planning consists neither in making elaborate forecasts spiced with wishful thinking, nor in issuing detailed orders to businesses about how to run their affairs. The detailed decisions about purchases, sales, production, employment, prices, and investment remain private. All the virtues of decentralized decision-making are kept intact. Undoubtedly many sectors of the economy which are in a state of good health, where projections look favorable, will not call for any planning action at all. But in a modern industrial economy, a collection of private decisions does not necessarily guarantee that private and social needs are met automatically. The purpose of planning is to provide, where it is lacking, the mechanism to relate needs to available labor, plant, and materials. The plan is a guide to the market.

One last consideration. The president is required by this act to transmit to Congress biennially a six-year economic and social plan. What is the point of issuing six-year plans every two years? The answer is that as circumstances change, plans must change. The six-year plan is a rolling plan, subject to change as unforeseen difficulties or opportunities arise. Those skeptical of planning say that it is impossible to see a year ahead, much less six. That is true. Nevertheless, these same skeptics plan their businesses, their vacations, and their children's educations. If something unforeseen happens, the plan is changed. Still it provides a sense of direction. When you plan to drive from Boston to Washington, you cannot tell in advance which lights will be red and which green. You find that out when you come to them. If a bridge is washed out, you do not try to drive over it. You detour. The same kind of common sense that is useful in driving from Boston to Washington is also useful in planning a national economy.

May 1975

After re-reading this account of the Balanced Growth and Economic Planning Act of 1975, I concluded that it was suitable for the wastebasket since nothing came of it. Perhaps not quite nothing. The bill eventually became the toothless Full Employment and Balanced Growth Act of 1978, also known as the Humphrey-Hawkins Full Employment Act. The idea of planning disappeared and was replaced by exhortations to achieve full employment, defined as 4 percent unemployment, price stability, production growth, balanced trade, a balanced budget, and contingent public employment for low-skilled, low-paid workers who could not find jobs in the private sector. These lofty goals were largely entrusted to the Federal Reserve Board and then they mysteriously evaporated.

On further consideration, I decided to include the article in this collection on the grounds that it would save a great deal of time and effort for anyone who might be called upon to draw up a balanced growth and economic planning act in the future.

Reply to a Critic
of Planning

In the current issue there appears an article by Henry Hazlitt with which I thoroughly disagree. This should not be surprising, since *Challenge* runs a gamut of opinion. No one can agree with everything. But Mr. Hazlitt's article is a special case. It deals with planning. Planning is my subject. It would require a superhuman effort for me to remain silent.

Mr. Hazlitt discerns "a well-orchestrated campaign" launched by the Initiative Committee for National Economic Planning to attune the American public to planning. As a member of the committee, I take this as an open-handed compliment. Close inspection reveals no further gestures of conciliation.

Mr. Hazlitt detects three errors that "have led people to advocate the substitution of government for private planning." The first is that "there is very little private economic planning" and that "a free market is a chaos."

But my dear Hazlitt, no one is advocating the substitution of government for private planning. The idea is not to abolish private planning but to give it a better chance to succeed. Private planning is disrupted by inflation, unemployment, and shortages. Anyone who thinks well of private planning ought to welcome efforts to achieve a stable economy within which private planning can be more successful. I have not met a single person in the last two decades with the least pretension to economic literacy who believes that there is little private economic planning, particularly within large corporations. Corporations meticulously plan; they even attempt to manage consumers' preferences. It does not follow that a thousand private plans add up to a social plan. Even so, the market is not a chaos, certainly not all the time. It is an excellent means of decentralizing economic decision making. But the market we have is very far from the ideal version propounded by Adam Smith in 1776, in which many small firms sell uniform products to many small customers and in which labor and capital are easily and quickly transferable from one branch of industry to another as conditions of supply and demand dictate. The imperfect market that we have now is an imperfect allocator, and leaves many needs unmet. Planning stems from a recognition of the fact that the market must be given deliberate guidance where it fails to guide itself.

The second error detected by Mr. Hazlitt is that the planners fail to ask who plans for whom? He answers: the government will plan for the rest of us, and that means coercion. Let us not beat around the bush. Whenever the government passes a tax law, prohibits the dumping of toxic chemicals into a stream, or puts up a stop sign at a street intersection, these arrangements are coercive. Sanctions apply to those who ignore them. But the coercion here is accepted voluntarily, if reluctantly, because we elected the representatives who passed the laws. Suppose the next Democratic presidential candidate (or, far-fetched fable, Republican candidate) proposes to set up an Economic Planning Board in the White House responsible for making a sector-by-sector analysis of the economy and for proposing tax and credit policies to help those sectors—say energy production and consumption—balance better than they do now. Suppose that the candidate proposes that the Joint Economic Committee be empowered to hold hearings on such proposals and recommend to Congress (or not, as it sees fit) the legislation needed to enable the president to carry out the proposed program. Suppose further that the voters elect said candidate. The resulting planning will be no more coercive than the batch of disparate and incoherent proposals which are normally made in the absence of planning. But the results are likely to be a good deal more effective.

The third error detected by Mr. Hazlitt is that planners assume the production plans of government bureaucrats would be better than those of private industrialists. Would bureaucrats have developed the railroad, the automobile, the airplane, radio, or television? Would they have foreseen the Arab oil embargo a week sooner than the heads of private oil companies?

This question is so muddled that one doesn't know where to begin. The government is certainly making production plans without knowing it is making them. By building highways and neglecting rail lines, it unintentionally helped to shape not only our transportation system, but the distribution of population in rural, urban, and suburban areas, which, if done intentionally, would have been considered an act of malevolent insanity. Bureaucrats have had a big hand in determining the course of development of the railroad, the automobile, the airplane, radio, and television, to restrict oneself to Mr. Hazlitt's list. But no one asked what the consequences might be ten or twenty years later or whether we ought to have general social goals against which to measure particular policies. Heaven defend us against thinking about the kinds of health, housing, or energy systems we want in ten years because such thoughts will upset private production plans. But really, there are no production plans made by private firms on a society-wide scale, and only the public through its representatives can provide them. Does this mean telling General Motors what to do? If the public votes for candidates committed to high taxes on gas-inefficient cars and easy credit terms for municipalities that build better transit systems, we will indeed be telling General Motors what to do. But then its executives have never failed to express pride in being told what to do by consumers.

As to the Arab oil embargo, the general energy outlook was known to specialists, as was the fact that U.S. companies were not building refineries. But no consequential individual in any agency of government was responsible for giving thought to the problem and proposing action. The oil companies let us down—for meritorious reasons, of course. If we had had a public energy policy, instead of the Panglossian faith that a private energy policy was all we needed, a cutoff of marginal oil supplies would hardly have been the occasion for terror in Washington.

Mr. Hazlitt concludes by observing that "advocates of planning persistently ignore the frightful record of past failures and catastrophes." That comes as no small surprise. For the whole issue is that we have never planned (except in World War II, when we did it successfully). What failures and catastrophes do you have in mind, Mr. Hazlitt? They could only have been the results of actions that were unplanned, uncoordinated, incoherent, actions that were unrelated to other actions, actions for which the consequences were ignored. The author cites the poor results obtained by the Federal Power Commission in regulating natural gas prices and by the Federal Reserve Board in regulating currency. But these cases do not show the failure of planning. Instead they illustrate perfectly the damage done in trying to manage bits and pieces of the economy without an overall view.

It would be absurd to go to the other extreme and expect that planning will make everything perfect. But we have constructed a very complicated economic organization that is certainly not self-planning and certainly does not respond well to haphazard tinkering. We have no choice but to learn how to run that complex organization. The running of it requires seeing the relation of the parts to the whole; thinking in terms of actions over long periods of time instead of simply reacting to emergencies; and adopting general goals to guide our actions. We are all humble beginners when it comes to planning, and must learn by doing. But planning is a matter of pressing need in all technologically based societies and it is mischievous and misleading to depict it as the pernicious doctrine of fanatics or the preachment of the devil, though it may appear that way to those whose economic views are more germane to the eighteenth century.

A final word about Lionel Robbins, whom Mr. Hazlitt cites in the act of equating planning with socialism. Planning denotes central control of the means of production, and that is socialism, says Robbins. Contrast this version of planning with that of R.E. Pahl and J.T. Winkler, who in the last issue of *Challenge* equate planning with corporatism, and we have touched both extremes. Let us dispense with abstract arguments and simply say that planning has been practiced in such widely divergent societies as Norway and the Soviet Union. Planning does not determine the nature of society; rather, society determines the nature of planning. Robbins's confusion has to do with the degree of detail of planning and the method of implementation. If an Economic Planning Board finds that the energy industry must grow at a given rate if the transportation industry is to grow at another given rate, and Congress passes legislation to encourage this outcome, that is hardly incompatible with decentralized, private control of the means of production. If, on a different assumption, public opinion turns to the view that Exxon should be nationalized, that is quite another matter.

As to Pahl and Winkler, their attempt to define planning in Great Britain (and by extension, the United States) as a benign form of fascism—"fascism with a human face," as they put it—is an exercise in self-contradiction. Take away one-party tyranny, replace it with public debate and the election of representatives who engage in planning, and you don't have fascism. Facile phrases to the contrary, a peculiar kind of mental gymnastics is required to imagine benignity and fascism triumphantly united.

Planning will not usher in any more socialism or any more corporate domination than we already have. It will not abolish the Bill of Rights or private property. But it will provide a new framework for urgently debating competing visions of the future. That will shake us up much more than anything the detractors of planning have feared in their most feverish moments.

Changes in the Planning Bill

The editorial in the May/June issue of *Challenge* was printed a few days before Senators Humphrey and Javits announced their sponsorship of the Balanced Growth and Economic Planning Act of 1975. Several changes were made in the bill in that interval. The main ones should be noted.

Instead of an Office of Balanced Growth and Economic Planning with a director and a staff, there is now a three-member Economic Planning Board with a chairman and a staff.

The length of long-term plans is to be decided by the president and Congress. The specification of six-year periods has been deleted.

The administrator of the Federal Energy Administration is added to the Economic Planning Council.

The president rather than the director appoints four of the twelve members of the Advisory Committee.

July 1975

See my comment on page 58 on the law as passed, the Full Employment and Balanced Growth Act of 1978.

Recovery Without Recovery

Dear President Ford:

I read in the papers that you are against government intervention in the private economy. You are also against federal intervention in state and local affairs. These are sound conservative principles. As a conservative, I support them.

That is why I am alarmed at the horrendous contradiction between what you practice and what you preach. Since you took office over a year ago, you have given the economy the biggest battering it has received at the hands of any president on record save Herbert Hoover. You named inflation as the Number One enemy. With truly awesome *sangfroid*, you presided over the asphyxiation of the private and public economy by blocking the fiscal and monetary air supply. The resulting prostration separated some 10 million people from their jobs, put 32 percent of our industrial plant out of commission, wrecked the auto industry, brought construction to a standstill, piled the highest load of debt on businesses in history, and carried cities to the brink of bankruptcy. As a result of your deliberately engineered recession, we are losing some 230 billion dollars in potential production, which comes to one thousand dollars for every man, woman, and child in the country. When George McGovern proposed a demogrant of one thousand dollars per person in the presidential campaign of 1972, he was laughed off the stage as a harebrained dreamer. How are we to react when this same thousand dollars per head is thrown down the drain by deliberate calculation?

You have engaged—I am forced to say in all candor—in a squandering of national wealth that defies reason. You have taken it from private business. You have taken it from the cities. You have taken it from the states. You have taken it from rich and poor, from black and white. How, then, can we consider you a conservative when you have not conserved? A champion of private interests when you have brought those interests low? A believer in sturdy individualism when you deny jobs to a tenth of those who want to work? A supporter of independent cities when you strip them of police, fire, and sanitation services and force them to bear welfare costs which they haven't the means to pay for? What, precisely, are you conserving?

Now we are emerging from the recession. Do you propose to do all in your power to return free private enterprise to a state of healthy exuberance as quickly as possible? Not from what I read in the papers. The economy must grow at the rate of 8 percent a year for three years just to get unemployment down to 5 percent, to put that idle capacity back to work, and to provide business with enough customers to yield the profits for the large volume of new investments we will be needing. A tax cut of fifteen billion dollars in 1976 and a 10 percent increase in the money supply are essential to get us moving in this direction.

You will not do it. You are sponsoring a rate of recovery that will perpetuate the recession for the rest of the decade and possibly cause the recovery itself to abort. You will go on wasting potential wealth. You will interfere massively in every nook and cranny of the economy, tangling everyone who runs a business, a city, or a state, or works with hand or brain, with meddlesome monetary and fiscal restraints that will keep him from going about his proper business. And you will blame this gross interference on your fear of inflation—inflation caused by demand exceeding supply, which cannot possibly be the case when supply exceeds demand, as it most assuredly does now and will continue to do for the next several years.

You will hold the entire economy hostage to excess demand inflation which cannot possibly materialize, but you will do nothing about administered inflation, which is already beginning to manifest itself. The largest corporations have the power to set their own prices, regardless of the state of demand; and without public guideposts that are related to productivity, those prices will go up as soon as recovery gets under way. Wages in unionized industries will follow, and we will be shooting back up the wage-price spiral. Will you have the perspicacity to ask Congress to give the Council on Wage and Price Stability the power to set reasonable guideposts for industries in which the market fails to act as a price regulator?

As we recover, inflation may also be caused by bottlenecks in sectors where shortages occur. Will you ask Congress to set up the planning apparatus to make a sector by sector study of the economy in order to anticipate shortages of materials, labor, and capital before they arise?

To ask these questions is to answer them. You will not help the private economy and the state and local levels of government because you do not understand what they need. Instead of the minimum of intervention implied by planning and guideposts—sound conservative measures essential to the smooth operation of a modern market economy—you will go on espousing the maximum of intervention, disruption, and disorder: the stop-go political business cycle. With due respect, he who is willing to perpetuate that cycle is subverting the economy, not preserving it. This, despite the fact that your secretary of the Treasury, with all the irony of unintended innocence—speaking, I assume, for the administration—states that he believes the government should "play a more neutral role in the economy."

This subversiveness, I do not doubt for a moment, flows from the loftiest motives, from a desire to do what is good and right. But there is also a matter of intellectual unpreparedness. It must be faced. Late in July, you gave an interview to the *New York Times* and provided "a little postscript," as you called it, to the economic summit of September 1974. It amazed me. You said that "none of the economists who participated told us, whether they were on the left or middle or right, that we were going to have the precipitous drop, or precipitous increase in unemployment. . . ." You mentioned "the changed circumstances that nobody foresaw."

I happen to have retained a copy of the proceedings of the economic summit, and a casual perusal shows that you are in error.

Otto Eckstein. "[R]ecession looks almost inevitable and it is only a question of degree."

Arthur Okun: "I would expect unemployment to grow rather sharply."

Paul Samuelson: "The number one problem that the nation faces is stagflation."

Nat Goldfinger: "[T]he continuation of these policies . . . poses the threat of a deepening recession, the threat of widespread business failure and certainly the immediate threat and reality of high unemployment."

My amazement is compounded by the fact that you not only failed to note these warnings, as you admit in your "little postscript," but that in 1974 you espoused, proclaimed, and did your best to implement the restrictive monetary and fiscal policies that brought about the precipitous drop in production and employment in 1975. Granted that these measures were intended to stop inflation—wrongly diagnosed. But it is one thing quite deliberately, knowingly, and methodically to induce a recession and accept the responsibility for the consequences, and quite another to do it without knowing that you are doing it.

The question arises whether you know what you are doing now; whether you know that the rate of recovery in several previous recessions—8.6 percent in 1954–55, 9.2 percent in 1958–59, and 7.6 percent in 1960–61—allowed a reduction in unemployment twice as fast as you contemplate; whether you know that in the growth period of 1961–65, when wage-price guideposts were in place, the annual rate of inflation averaged just over 1 percent; whether you know that productivity goes up sharply when an economy recovers smartly from a recession; whether you know that all the concern of your administration about an impending capital shortage is so much prattle in view of the capital shortage being caused by a slow recovery—a recovery contrived to be slow.

On the evidence I must assume that you do not know. And if I am wrong, and you do know, on the evidence I do not see that it matters.

Sincerely,
M.E. Sharpe

September 1975

The Continued Existence of New York City Is Not Essential to National Security

By the time you read these words, they may be obsolete. New York City's financial situation is deteriorating by the hour. The only choices left are insolvency or federal aid. The administration could radically alter the fortunes of New York and all other cities and states without the expenditure of a penny. By the stroke of a pen, it could guarantee municipal and state bonds just as the Federal Deposit Insurance Corporation guarantees the safety of money in the bank. Stipulations could be made. Cities and states could be required to adhere to legitimate accounting practices in order to qualify. Management standards could be set up. With such assurances, investors would no longer need the inducement of tax-exempt status.

A second emergency step might be taken to give skittish investors time to conquer their fear of holding any negotiable piece of paper with the name New York on it. The Federal Reserve System could buy the securities of New York City, New York State, and their agencies. These are stop-gap solutions that will work. But for the long haul, declining cities like New York cannot continue to bear the costs of redistributional expenditures. The federal government will have to pay for welfare and Medicaid. These proposals have a unique virtue: there are no alternatives.

President Ford made a percipient remark to the mayor of Belgrade when he visited Yugoslavia earlier this year. Referring to New York City, he said: "They don't know how to handle money. All they know how to do is spend it." At about the same time, Chairman Arthur Burns delivered a similar judgment: "New York City has not been properly governed for many, many years now."

How true. New York City is no longer governable. It is too late. If the past could be changed, that might not be the case. With a slight effort, we can envisage Gerald Ford and Arthur Burns as mayors of New York instead of John Lindsay and Abraham Beame. We can then have the satisfaction of imagining that the city would not now be weighed down with a $3.3

billion deficit, that it would not be engaged in a frantic, daily search for money to pay bills, and that the press would not be bandying about the word "default." Ford and Burns—it is utterly simple—would have done what any prudent *paterfamilias* does: spend no more than is earned; borrow no more than can be repaid. If you do not have enough money to meet your needs, you do without. That is how cities, no less than families, live within their means. But this is a futile fantasy.

Mayor Beame, even though a former comptroller familiar with double entry bookkeeping, misunderstood this simple precept. So did Mayors Wagner and Lindsay, although they can be more easily excused on the grounds of not being accountants. The unforgivable sin of all three mayors is that they allowed their actions to be guided by the needs of the city rather than by the size of its revenues. They were seduced by the hope that the money would be found somewhere.

They fell into the habit of producing sham balanced budgets by overestimating future state and federal aid; by counting uncollectible property taxes as potential revenues; by putting current expenses into the capital budget; by pushing some of this year's expenses into next year and pulling some of next year's revenues into this year; and by going into the capital market and selling bonds and notes when all else failed. With the connivance of hundreds, the budget became the center of a vain, reckless conspiracy to do good.

The shameful facts are out. The perpetrators were in the hole, not a mere few hundred million, as Beame steadily maintained until the end, but over $3 billion. The conspiracy, durable as conspiracies go, since it lasted for ten years through the administrations of three mayors, was finally undone by the recession and the inflation. The sham balanced budget was knocked to pieces by the 12 percent rate of unemployment and by the 12 percent rise in prices. It became impossible for the city to up the ante to play the game, and for the banks to pretend that there really was no game, even when the inducement was 11 percent per annum, tax-free.

But the budget, the bonds, and the notes, about which there is great and prolonged agitation in the press, are only part of the story. The other part is that New York City has become the nation's leading poorhouse. You cannot run a poorhouse as you would run a manor house. In 1970, 56 percent of New York's population lived below the deprivation level and 14.6 percent lived below the poverty level, defined in part as income sufficient to provide enough food for a temporary, emergency diet. (The figures are from the Council on Municipal Performance.) Since 1969 the city lost 471,000 jobs. Moreover, out of a total labor force of 3.5 million, 605,000 live outside the city and therefore spend their money and pay their taxes elsewhere.

Allow me to give one instance of the reality behind these figures. I have an acquaintance who lives in Harlem. The streets around her apartment are alive day and night with addicts, drunks, and knots of sullen young men. Radios blare through the night, making it difficult to sleep. Derelicts wander into the hallways and doze on newspapers. They urinate and defecate on the floors. Couples have intercourse behind parked cars. Last summer two sizable riots took place in the neighborhood, news of which did not get beyond Harlem. A large radio and TV store was cleaned out overnight. My acquaintance saw and heard a woman run down the street screaming, pursued by a man with a long knife. He was arrested by two policemen whom he threatened to kill if he ended up in jail. He was released.

This is the kind of social distintegration and frightful, debased life that exists in some parts of New York City. Mayor Beame is the master of a poorhouse that is getting poorer. But Gerald Ford and his judicious advisers look at the books and see that they do not balance. They look at the city management and see that it is of poor quality. They look at the cost of garbage collection and see that it is collected more cheaply elsewhere. They look at municipal clerical salaries and see that they are 2.5 percent above salaries paid to workers in private industry. They look at skilled maintenance occupations and see that municipal pay scales are aligned with those in the building trades. They read that pensions provide affluent retirement for policemen, firemen, sanitation men, and clerks. They conclude that New York City must pay for its sins of poverty, extravagance, and pride by becoming a vast debtors' prison.

But debtors' prisons are out of fashion and, however wholesome for the inmates, have a certain odor of vindictiveness about them. No one denies that New Yorkers contributed to their own fiscal predicament. But it requires exceptional selectivity of facts to conclude that mismanagement is the only cause. Since New York is not part of a county, it must pay for services that are supplied by county governments elsewhere. Deducting these, its per capita expenditures are comparable to those of other cities. In fact, some cities pay higher wages and higher pension benefits, and have more employees per capita, than does New York. Then there are the needs of New York's poor, who cannot be asked to die in order to balance the budget. New Yorkers did not cause the recession which precipitated the crisis. That was managed in Washington. So much the more incongruous for the president, who took revenues out of New York's coffers, to lecture the victims on sound finance.

In the short run, the choice is clear: rescue New York or let it rot. But in the long run, aside from federalizing welfare and medical care, what else? There is not a chance that New York will spontaneously recover from its deep, demoralizing slide into the lower depths. Industry and the middle class are leaving. The tax base is eroding. The unions have been crippled. The banks are holding billions in dubious paper. The governor has been swept into the whirlpool. The schools are a disgrace. The blacks and Puerto Ricans have been abandoned.

The thing which strikes so many sound-thinking, high-minded public men as half ludicrous and half seditious must finally be done: the revival of New York City must be planned. And so must the revival of other cities. But the cities, the economies of which are shattered by shifts in population and industry, by unemployment and inflation, and by a lack of money and managerial talent, cannot go it alone. They must have the cooperation, rather than the enmity, of all other levels of public administration—state, regional, and national. Nothing less than a plan for the revival of all depressed cities, which is part of a larger plan for the revival of the country, can possibly open the exit out of the poorhouse.

There is a well-kept secret that has been hidden from the economics profession and the general public since the early sixties. Municipal, state, and regional planners exist and are working. They have long since resolved the question of whether to plan or not to plan. With various degrees of sophistication, they plan. But the odds are against them. The deep suspicion of national planning as a sure method for producing disasters—as if planning would routinely produce disasters greater than the one from which we are trying to extricate ourselves—undermines all other efforts. A state or a region may plan balanced growth for all it is worth, try to attract industries, develop natural resources, and entice trained workers to move in. Meanwhile, other states and regions are doing the same, with very little chance that their efforts will complement each other. Only a national effort can provide the coordination and the rational division of labor, not to mention the money, the know-how, the management training, and the incentives, to make local, state, and regional planning work.

In the past several weeks, mayors and financial experts across the country have described the widespread havoc entailed in a crash of New York City. Contrary to the experience of thirty years and in flagrant contradiction to opinion at the highest levels of government, this part of America is essential, after all, to national security. This is a fact of such novelty that it almost defies comprehension.

November 1975

In June 1975, the Mutual Assistance Corporation (MAC) was set up to save New York City from bankruptcy. Short-term debt was exchanged for long-term debt backed up by New York State and the federal government, the latter with the reluctant acquiescence of Gerald Ford. The heroes of the moment were Governor Hugh Carey and MAC director Felix Rohatyn, a banker from Lazard Freres known as Mr. Fix-it.

Ten Rules for Full Employment Without Inflation

Nineteen-seventy-six is a year of anniversaries, but few people are in a mood to celebrate. Official efforts to the contrary, the bicentennial festivities inevitably suggest the performance of last rites. Among economists, two hundred years after publication of *The Wealth of Nations,* cheerfulness about prospects for the free market must at best be muted. The same can be said of the Keynesian Revolution forty years after publication of *The General Theory.* And anyone who would raise three cheers for the Employment Act of 1946 can do so only while ruing its annulment.

But all is not lost. This is an election year. I don't know what odds Lloyds of London would give for electing a president who is willing to try to turn things around, but I suspect they are not worse than 50-50. I would therefore propose to prospective candidates that what needs turning around first is our policies on employment and inflation. To be blunt about it, they are fraudulent.

In the future, there will have to be as many policies as there are types of unemployment and inflation. Stop and go does not work. Six recessions should be enough to prove that. Traumatic as the thought may be to economists, it is time to move beyond the primitive stage of national economic management and use different techniques to deal with different problems.

Since this editorial is addressed to potential presidents who must have clear, unambiguous advice, I have cast my findings in the form of Ten Rules for Full Employment Without Inflation. Each rule is accompanied by an explanation for noncandidates.

I begin with Four Rules for Full Employment.

1. Do use monetary and fiscal tools to reach and maintain full employment of skilled workers. But do not try to bring about full employment of the unskilled this way. Through good years and bad, unemployment among unskilled workers is considerably higher than among the skilled. When all the trained workers who want jobs have them, any further increase in aggregate demand will bid up their wages, which in turn will bid up prices. Because of this fact, it is impossible to ensure jobs for all the unskilled who want to work just by increasing federal spending, cutting taxes, expanding the money supply, or

some combination of these without producing an intolerable rate of inflation.

2. Do use public employment to provide jobs for unskilled workers who cannot find jobs in private industry. This is logical, not only as the most direct way to provide work and training for men and women who are stuck in the basement of society, but also as a way of filling ever more demanding needs in transportation, housing, health, care of the young and old, conservation, crime prevention, and all the other items on the familiar list. The modest net cost in taxes (after deducting the savings in welfare, food stamps, unemployment insurance, and the like) to employ 3 million idle people is $20 billion a year, which, of course, can readily be obtained by closing unjust tax loopholes. The bonus to everyone is the removal of one source of inflation: the temptation to achieve full employment by increasing aggregate demand excessively.

3. Do link training programs to jobs. The irony of offering education as the means to escape poverty without also ensuring that suitable work is available has been much remarked. The impulse to remove the irony by removing the education should be resisted. If the Ten Rules are obeyed, the excuse that more jobs are inflationary will not be valid.

4. Do use incentives to get people and jobs to meet in the same geographic location. Again, an increase in demand is not the answer when perverse incentives move people away from jobs and jobs away from people. The aging city is the principal locale of an unpleasant drama in which the poor have moved in and the industries have moved out. The cities, desperately trying to make ends meet, only have the power to increase the perversity of the incentives by cutting services or increasing taxes or both. It is not only unwise, but also very dangerous, to turn a hundred centers of civilization into the habitats of a more or less permanently unemployed lumpenproletariat. The cities, states, and federal government together have the power to improve the urban environment, induce industry to return, and distribute the tax burden more equitably between the cities and the suburbs. The drama will not have a happy ending—as the Kerner Commission anticipated eight years ago—if we split into two separate societies, one rich and white living in the suburbs, the other poor and nonwhite living in the cities.

I continue with Five Rules for Price Stability.

5. Do use monetary and fiscal methods to prevent excess demand inflation. This rule is so well known that it requires no comment.

6. Do use wage-price controls to prevent administered inflation. This rule

is the hardest one to learn, but it cannot be bypassed. Administered prices and wages, it is clear, are set by hand rather than by the impersonal forces of the market. When profit margins are widened, or wages are increased, without a corresponding increase in output, the result is inflation. The only conceivable way of avoiding this type of inflation is through the use of public guidelines. They will work only if they are fair. This means that restraint on union claims has to be matched by restraint on upper income claims through control of prices where market power exists, and through rigorously progressive taxation. Interestingly, there are two other conditions for the success of guidelines: a stable price level and full employment. If corporations with market power face relentlessly increasing costs, the guidelines will not survive the pressure. Likewise, if the same corporations face declining markets and declining profits caused by unemployment, the pressure to recoup by increasing prices will be overwhelming. At the same time, without guidelines the temptation to use unemployment as the instrument of restraint will be irresistible. Therefore: workable guidelines depend on full employment and the containment of inflation; and full employment and the containment of inflation depend on workable guidelines.

Fortunately, the application of well-conceived guidelines is not beyond our administrative competence. They need apply only to a limited number of critical industries in which a handful of individuals already determine wage and price policies.

Curiously, most critics of guidelines are deeply concerned about the efficient allocation of resources but cast a blind eye on one of the chief benefits of guidelines—they help to remove the main contemporary causes of resource misallocation: unemployment and inflation.

7. Do monitor each sector of the economy to anticipate specific shortages. Shortages were responsible for much of the inflation of the past several years; because of resource depletion, environmental fragility, and global interdependence, they are likely to continue to nag us. Keeping track of interindustry supply and demand by means of input-output analysis can give us an early warning of prospective bottlenecks and allow time for remedial action. This action can take the form of tax incentives or favorable credit arrangements to stimulate the investment needed to eliminate the shortage, encourage research for substitutes, or make conservation an attractive alternative.

Still, unanticipated shortages will sometimes occur. No one foresaw the success of OPEC. If our aim is price stability, a temporary price ceiling and rationing are in order.

It will be argued that the price system can do the job. It cannot. It produces permanently higher prices. In today's economy, a rise in the price of a product in short supply induces most users to increase their prices or wages. These prices and wages will not be reduced even if the original shortage is eliminated and the price of the product in question declines. Dramatic price increases do not necessarily bring about the results wanted on the supply side, as witness health services. Moreover, the price system can very well price some consumers out of the market for essential goods+food, for example.

One further observation. Balancing interindustry supply and demand is not just a technical question. When such a project is undertaken, there are always alternatives. More investment or more consumption? More fuel or more conservation? More public services or more private goods? More weapons or more housing? The search for full employment and price stability will force us to choose other social goals as well.

8. Do not import or export inflation. Enter into multilateral agreements to check the flow of speculative funds from country to country and to limit fluctuations of commodity prices. This I take to be self-evident. It is only necessary to add that the stabilization of currencies will not be achieved through any known exchange rate formula, fixed or floating, but only through the attainment of full employment and price stability in the leading industrial countries.
9. Do not do anything about inflationary expectations. They will cease when there is no inflation to expect.

I conclude with One General Rule.

10. Do not use monetary and fiscal policies except as specified above. This negative injunction merits a separate rule because the temptation to take the easy way out will remain strong until the present generation of economists retires. Wrong policies are themselves highly mischievous because they complicate, compound, and create afresh the problems of unemployment and inflation.

These are the rules. They are undoubtedly frightening because they are new. But I find our present rules even more frightening. I do not expect anyone to run for president with these rules as his platform. If anyone does, he had better state them more circumspectly.

Needless to say, a president who follows the new rules must assemble a great deal of detailed information about the economy and coordinate federal, state, and local efforts in an unprecedented way. These are tasks far beyond the present capacities of government agencies. What is required is the ability to monitor the needs of individual industries, regions, and cities and draw up alternative sets of coherent policies which are considerably more detailed than those required by Keynesian aggregate demand management. Yet, paradoxically, this program will interfere far less with the market economy than the Keynesian program has in practice. Nothing interferes more with private decision making than unemployment and inflation, which have dogged Keynesian economics for the last twenty years. A distinction must be made, however, between interference and guidance. An economy characterized by a high degree of concentration does not guide itself in any acceptable way. I take this to be proven by events. It is wildly delusory to expect such an economy, in which the business of the thousand largest firms exceeds that of the remaining 12 million, and in which one-third of the gross national product passes through government, to be optimally self-regulating in the manner described by Adam Smith. Thus the guidance of the economy is no more a matter of interference than a pilot's actions are interference with the flying of a jetliner. The pilot sits in front of a console of dials and gauges that provide him with information about the performance of every part of the plane. He benignly neglects the systems that are working automatically, but turns knobs and pulls levers when action is required. The result is that the plane flies.

Of course, the analogy is just an analogy and must not be pressed too far. If it is jarring, the explanation is that we greatly prefer to believe in a pilotless economy steered by an invisible hand. But the luxury of such belief has become too costly. The political imperative of full employment without inflation will not permit it.

The Muse of History is full of tricks. It would be not unlike her to select this year of dour anniversaries for a refreshing change in the theory and practice of political economy which may perhaps make for happier celebrations in years to come.

January 1976

Contrary to what I wrote on page 73, I believe that an industrial country can attain full employment and price stability provided that an international clearinghouse keeps exchange rates from fluctuating beyond a narrow range. See page 278. Failing that, the only remedy is a tariff or embargo on cheap imports.

I should have made it clear that Keynesian demand management needs to be supplemented, not abandoned.

The Lost Papers of Jack Tanner

Few people realize that Jack Tanner was a real person. Most recognize him as the hero of Bernard Shaw's play *Man and Superman.* They therefore assume that Tanner is fiction. Not at all. He is fact. I know this to be so because Tanner's grandson was a classmate of mine at Swarthmore College and through him I came to know the elder Tanner. Jack and his wife Ann, whom Shaw adored and immortalized in his play, emigrated to the United States in 1910 and settled in Philadelphia.

All this is by way of preliminary to introduce the subject of Jack Tanner's lost papers. You will recall that Shaw appended a screed to *Man and Superman* entitled *The Revolutionist's Handbook,* allegedly written by Jack Tanner. Allegedly is what the public thought. But Tanner actually wrote it. Not only that, he wrote a sequel to it. That was many years later. He instructed his grandson to deposit the manuscript in the Swarthmore College Library, which was duly done. When I learned of this several years later, I was able to prevail upon Tanner to allow his work to be published. But in the meantime, a new library had been built on the campus, and when the contents were transferred from the old to the new, the manuscript was lost.

Last year I attended the twenty-fifth reunion of my graduating class, and went to the library to make sure that *Challenge* was on the shelves. By an extraordinary coincidence, I found that Tanner's manuscript had accidentally been bound into volume sixteen. I called Tanner with the good news, he added a few new observations to the collection, and here it is at last.

Ideas and Beliefs

Most scientific discoveries are made by the young before they have mastered existing doctrine.

What is counted as truth in one age is counted as myth in the next.

The character of each age is reflected in its miracles. Ancient Greece had Olympus; the Middle Ages had divine intervention; the modern world has the self-regulating market.

Two of the most pernicious influences on the modern world have been Adam Smith and Karl Marx. They spoke in parables which were mistaken by their followers for facts. Nothing is more dangerous than acting on parables as if they were facts.

The sickness of our age is not due to a lack of worthy causes, but to a lack of belief that worthy causes can be won.

Economics

The advantage of studying Greek and Latin instead of economics is that Greek and Latin improve style without impairing policy.

Nothing could discredit capitalism more than a decision by the Russians to try it.

Capitalism has performed the miracle of turning self-interest into self-less service to society. Economists have performed the miracle of getting people to believe it.

The detractors of wage and price controls are fond of citing the misguided efforts of Diocletian in 301 AD as a warning, implying that economics has been at a standstill for 1,675 years.

Politics

It is frequently said that politics is the art of the possible. So is everything else.

My first meeting with the New Socialist Man was on the streets of Moscow. He politely tipped his hat and said, *"Dobrii vecher. U menia bol'shoi vopros. Khotite li vy obmenit' dollary?"* That is, "Good evening. I have a big question. Do you want to exchange dollars?"

Italy and France, late 1970s. The Communist Parties come to power, faithful to the principles of free speech, press, and assembly. They inaugurate "socialism with a human face" and are protected from Soviet aggression by NATO.

Representative government with extremes of wealth and poverty resembles nothing so much as a corporation in which power is apportioned according to the number of shares held.

It is well to have the conservative's suspicion of the state and the liberal's suspicion of the conservative.

The trouble with participatory democracy is that the leaders will stay but the participants will go home.

Human Nature

People want to do good, but it is usually inconvenient.

Is human nature hopelessly depraved? How can anyone ask that question who has ever known a person well fed, tailored, and housed, doing the job he enjoys, working for causes he believes in, and living in sexual content-ment on $100,000 a year?

To thine own self be true. But it does not follow that thou canst not then be false to any man. Tact is still required.

Stray sayings

Fame is empty. But it is better to find that out afterward.

A person who does not cultivate certain faults in his character is insufferable and dangerous and should not be trusted.

Decide what you want to do and then find reasons for it. Otherwise you will not understand yourself.

The greatest creative work is done when we are asleep and dreaming.

We and the Universe

When God created the world, He said it was good. That was His second mistake.

In meeting either God or the devil, prudence dictates modesty.

Even the devil has good intentions by his own reckoning.

The greatest poet of our age was Albert Einstein, who wrote $E = MC^2$. From this poem an atom bomb was fashioned. Thus Einstein not only penetrated deeply into the secret life of the universe; he also penetrated into the secret nature of man, for Hamlet's question will finally be answered.

The source of comedy is the disparity between what people profess and what they do. The source of tragedy is the same. But the function of comedy is destruction, while the function of tragedy is consolation. That is why economics can be treated either way.

The impact of Smith, Marx, and Freud proves that style is more important than content.

A proper respect for the complexity of things makes one a skeptic among believers and a believer among skeptics.

William Lamb is said to have remarked, "I wish I were as sure of anything as Macaulay is of everything."

"This is the true joy of life, the being used for a purpose recognized by yourself as a mighty one; the being thoroughly worn out before you are thrown on the scrap heap; the being a force of Nature instead of a feverish little clod of ailments and grievances complaining that the world will not devote itself to making you happy." When I was young, I, Jack Tanner, took these words of Shaw as my motto. They still are. However, being advanced in years, I now believe that a small amount of complaining is permissible, as well as an occasional vacation.

An editor has no friends.

March 1976

Do Economists Discover Economic Laws or Are They Passed by Congress?

Not wishing to prejudice anyone for or against the Humphrey-Hawkins Bill, I will limit myself to a few casual remarks.

The reader will find the complete text and an interpretive interview with Senator Humphrey in this issue. It will be evident that the bill called the Full Employment and Balanced Growth Act of 1976 is the most consequential social legislation to come along since the Employment Act of 1946. The bill is a plan for planning, and first of all, for planning full employment without inflation. It is a large generalization about the objectives of this country and how to reach them. If it becomes law, we will, in effect, have reached agreement on an experiment and a compact that will take us on a long journey into uncharted territory. This will give economists plenty to do even though they may think the doing of it is impossible.

There is no need to rehearse the old arguments about how much easier it is to arrange to have unemployment, inflation, or both. Economists are past masters at these things. But it is always worth a reminder that the costs are intolerably high. The Joint Economic Committee has supplied us with some disquieting new figures. We have lost $500 billion in potential income and production in the late recession. We will lose another $800 to $900 billion between now and 1980. Federal, state, and local governments will have lost $400 billion by then if we fail to do better. You don't have to be a great champion of growthmanship to recognize how devastating all this is. It is small comfort that 90 percent of the labor force is still employed. We have turned onto a high-cost road. If we cannot or will not get off it, that is an admission of failure. The price will become higher, not lower, as we go on.

You cannot legislate intelligence, of course. But you can legislate objectives, and a framework and a procedure for reaching them. This is how the bill should be viewed. The vast reservoir of intellect among economists can then be tapped to make sure that the provisions are applied wisely.

It will be a great tonic to the morale of the reader to know that the AFL-CIO is supporting the Humphrey-Hawkins Bill. I hope that George Meany will not be embarrassed if I paraphrase Marx. Economists have interpreted the economy long enough. The point is to change it. That means less forecasting and more planning. This is the answer to the riddle in the title.

May 1976

See the comment on page 58.

How to Plan the Economy

Dear Jimmy Carter:

Several issues ago, I wrote to Gerald Ford. It didn't do much good. I am writing to you now because you may be the next president of the United States. I am told that you are open to constructive suggestions. If so, you are probably already thinking about planning. You will have an unparalleled opportunity to help us catch up with ideas that are taken for granted throughout the rest of the world. If we apply them with typical American enthusiasm, our descendants ought to have something to celebrate when the tricentennial arrives.

The purpose of planning is to coordinate the economy in order to reach economic and social objectives that we consider desirable. If we do not undertake the job of coordination, these desirable objectives are not likely to be achieved spontaneously. They certainly will not be achieved by accident. And the benign natural forces thought by some eighteenth-century thinkers to be abroad in the world are nowhere to be seen.

The ABCs of planning are: A. Establish planning institutions; B. Draw up a plan; C. Implement the plan.

We have discussed planning institutions before, and I refer you to previous issues of *Challenge*. Suffice it to say that the two aspects of planning must be taken into account: the technical and the political. An agency must exist whose personnel have the technical ability to draw up plans. Political bodies must be available to make a choice of objectives and methods of implementation, as well as to resolve conflicts. The president and Congress, together with the appropriate departments, agencies, and committees, are admirably suited to play the political roles.

As Wassily Leontief aptly says in this issue, there can be no planning without the making of plans. One begins with a model of the economy as it is now, in which everything, in principle, is known. This model shows in considerable detail the relations of various industries and sectors of the economy to each other. It is supplemented by regional models, state models, and even city models. All these encompass the classical trio—land, labor, and capital—as they are used in different parts of the economy. The next step is to look ahead to some future date, for instance five years hence, and to construct several model variations, each of which describes a possible future. Your choice will depend on your preferences. There can be choices among rates of growth of investment and consumption; among rates of growth of the public sector and the private sector; between the amount of spending for weapons and for social services; between investment at home and investment abroad; between a greater or lesser degree of equality in the distribution of income. Without too much additional trouble, each variation can have further variations. You might prefer to increase investment for a period, but then you have to decide whether you want it to go into highways or railroads.

From a technical point of view, each model variation must be coherent and depict a realizable future. You can't play the game if your variation doesn't pass that test. Then comes the debate over which narrative to choose. The politician who says that we must have national health insurance or a bigger navy will also be saying quite clearly that we will have to give up something else. This is a very sobering consideration, and not the least of the charms of planning. On the cheerful side, a model may show that we can do things that we thought we couldn't if we follow the right script.

The making of plans is obviously not the same thing as the making of forecasts. But you cannot plan without forecasting. Changes in technology, tastes, education, population, and the like push us in a certain direction. It is well to know in which direction we are being pushed and how fast. But the purpose of planning is to make things happen. The better the information about limits and possibilities, the better the plan. Since our perception of limits and possibilities, not to mention preferences, is constantly changing, a plan should never be sanctified. It should be regarded as a guide to action, subject to periodic amendment.

By the way, city, state, and regional models imply planning authorities at these levels, many of which already exist. The need for consistency and feasibility at the several levels requires continual consultation, through which local and national models inevitably have a mutual influence. In this process, initiative at lower levels of government can be treated with maximum respect at higher levels. At present it is treated with maximum disrespect. The efforts of mayors, governors, and private citizens are undone with appalling regularity by the primitive methods of economic management that are currently practiced in Washington.

Now allow me to pass on to implementation. We can speak of implementation by law and implementation by agreement. The federal government is routinely engaged in making and carrying out economic and social policies by means of legislation. It uses taxes, credits, rules and regulations, and public sector projects as the instruments to effect policies. None of this will differ under planning. None of this will differ, except that the president and Congress will have a coherent model to allow them to put together a set of policies that has a clear relationship to carefully defined objectives. Policies will not be made ad hoc, but within the framework of a plan of coordination. Just as every strategic question is a fair subject for economic and social policy, so it is for planning. Currently private decisions are made in the context of policies that are designed to influence them. The same situation prevails under planning, except that the influence is more systematic and is subordinated to long-range objectives.

Implementation of a plan—strictly speaking, parts of a plan—by agreement can be pictured as an extension of collective bargaining. It goes without saying that labor, management, consumers, and other interested parties ought to take part in the formulation of plans from the outset. Aspects of a plan dealing with a particular industry may well be the result of a compromise voluntarily arrived at by the organizations at interest and carried out according to agreement. A planning agreement in an industry is a tripartite arrangement (at least tripartite) by union, management, and government concerning real wages, productivity, investment, plant location, retraining of displaced workers, and any number of other subjects. I am under the impression that John Dunlop experimented with this type of bargaining—not in connection with planning, of course—when he was chairman of the Cost of Living Council and then secretary of labor. The extension of collective bargaining has seen its beginnings in the United States. It is but one further step to link this development to planning. In order not to be misunderstood, I should say explicitly that planning agreements must be consistent with the national plan.

Much has been said about corporate accountability and union responsibility. There is no better way to set standards against which corporate and union actions can be measured than through a plan arrived at after public debate. Nor is there a better way to obtain compliance than through agreement. Self-interest will not be overcome, nor should we expect it to be. But nothing is more conducive to an ecumenical view than having to look at the economy as a whole, now and in the future, as we must if we plan.

People are leery of government these days, Governor Carter, and you have become a potential president by associating yourself with that sentiment. Well, planning is a good issue because every other issue is connected with it, and it provides a way to make transparent what the government is doing and why. However, I am duty bound to warn you not to campaign for planning overtly because it is not popular, any more than Keynesian economics was popular when Truman or Kennedy were campaigning. People want the results of planning, not the planning itself. It is up to you to find a gentle way to break the news to the public that you can't have one without the other. Judging by your success so far, there can be no doubt that you know how to do it.

Being an optimist, I would like to think that economic discussion in the future will be quite different from what we have at present. Future debates will be conducted in terms of alternative plans, not impressionistic advocacy of isolated nostrums. The candidate who casts promises about like rose petals will be pulled up short by the citizen who asks to see his plan. You have the chance to lead the way. I hope you will.

Yours in good faith,
M.E. Sharpe

July 1976

Apologia Pro Vita Mea

Sorry, but I have no thoughts, opinions, or inspiration this time. Over the last three months, my horizons narrowed so far that the rest of the world virtually disappeared. First I moved; then I had an operation. Moving was much the more demanding event of the two. Actually, moving itself was not too bad. That took only a day. But the circumstances that preceded and followed moving almost did me in.

There was the matter of disaccumulation. My daughter and son never threw anything away. As packing time neared, they still possessed all the toys, games, drawings, clothes, furniture, and presents that they ever acquired. I am not blaming them. They faithfully followed the example of their parents, who never parted with a book, magazine, clipping, letter, manuscript, object of art, lamp, rug, or anything else that came their way. The incubus of unneeded things had to be unloaded before moving became at all practicable.

Then there was the matter of 350 linear feet of books that were simply indispensable for the continuation of a normal human existence. Unfortunately, I found just two books out of approximately 3,500 that I could bring myself to part with. Even those I regretted giving away afterward. There is no telling when a person might need the *Statistical Yearbook* of the United Nations for 1962 or a second copy of *Anna Karenina*. The other 3,498 books had to be packed and bookcases had to be built.

The new house was in almost perfect condition and only required that arrangements be made for taping, painting, papering, carpentering, plumbing, wiring, phones, burner inspection, water analysis, mail delivery, and refuse removal. We were undaunted by small difficulties (such as the recently discovered decorating principle that paint and paper never look the same on the wall as they do in the catalogue and therefore should be chosen at random); a thousand decisions were made and a thousand plans were laid. All lines relentlessly converged on moving day. The project was managed with single-minded passion. Only human frailty could cause a delay.

It did. The tapers, painters, paperers, carpenters, plumbers, electricians, phone installers, burner inspectors, water analyzers, mail deliverers, and refuse removers all miscalculated. No presentiment warned me that the cracks between the sheetrock panels were more extensive than anyone imagined. I did not anticipate that a philosophical difference of opinion with the painter would arise about the definition of the word *completed*. I could not know that a pipe would loosen and spread water uniformly throughout the basement on the day appointed to move in. It was impossible to foresee that a phone company crisis would result in the failure of phones to work properly until the sixth effort at installation. No one could guess that a conflict would arise among several technicians of the water company over the chemicals required to treat the well water. Consequently, the day after moving day, when everything should have been in perfect order, twelve dedicated men swarmed relentlessly through the house, in kitchen and bath, bedroom and hall; sawing in the study, nailing in the closet, mopping in the cellar. On moving day plus ten, they were still earnestly swarming. On moving day plus twenty, they were swarming further with good intent. On moving day plus thirty, they were swarming yet, with resolve. I have never had the privilege of living with a finer bunch of fellows.

Here nature intervened. After an annual checkup, my doctor advised me that the right side of thyroid had grown beyond all reasonable expectations and had to be removed. The news came as a great relief and I eagerly left for the hospital for peace and quiet. Upon returning home a few days later, I found that those whom I had come to regard as lifelong companions had stolen away.

Suddenly my horizons began to shift back to their previous positions. Gerald Ford reappeared. Ronald Reagan reappeared. *Challenge* reappeared. My books reappeared, now on new shelves. The great globe itself began to spin again. The time had come for me to justify my continued existence. What greater deed could I perform but to endorse Jimmy Carter? I reached for his economic position papers. It was too late. I didn't have enough stamina to read them. The editorial deadline flew by. Anyway, my doctor told me to relax. Very well, then. Here is my relaxed support for Jimmy Carter. Let me assure you that it is not founded on a whim. It is the product of conversations with friends who have spent time with him. They all had favorable gut reactions. These, as everyone knows, constitute by far the most reliable test of a man's character and ability. They prompted the same reaction in me. If you have not had one yet, you probably will. Perhaps you will also have time to read his position papers.

Getting back to the subject at hand, if you intend to move, it is well to practice a lot first.

September 1976

Carter did not live up to my relaxed expectations.

The Last Chronicle of Barset

Anthony Trollope was a living writing machine when he turned out *The Last Chronicle of Barset* in 1866, putting on paper a thousand words an hour for three-and-a-half hours every day. He got up at five in the morning, corrected the previous day's work from five-thirty to six, then wrote from six to nine-thirty. Afterward he had breakfast and went to his job with the British postal service, where he occupied one of the highest offices. At five he usually retired to the Garrick Club for a rubber of whist or a game of billiards. Unlike other postal officials, he took two days a week off to go hunting. This little idiosyncrasy was tolerated because of his eminence as an author and his unquestioned value to the post office as a civil servant. Records establish that it was he who invented the mailbox, a fact hard to credit because of our tendency to think that such a simple device didn't need inventing but always existed.

My dim memory of *The Warden* and *Barchester Towers* led me to think that this prodigality of energy and output was simply the peculiarity of a good second-rate writer. It is not so. Trollope is immensely great. *The Last Chronicle of Barset* was written by a master of the English language. I wonder that this is not generally known. It was known to Tolstoy, who read *The Prime Minister* with unstinting admiration and then wrote, "Trollope kills me, kills me with his excellence." I imagine that it will eventually become known to many. Trollope's champions are on the move. One of them, Galbraith, put me on to *Barset* in his September article in the *New York Times*, and on to a radical change in my estimate of Trollope.

In *The Last Chronicle of Barset,* England in the middle of the nineteenth century is laid before you. The story tells of an impoverished curate, Josiah Crawley, who is accused of stealing a check for twenty pounds. His case becomes a *cause célèbre* between two factions of the Church of England, and an ever widening number of people are placed in positions where they have to react to the allegations against Crawley. There is Crawley himself, who has some of the qualities of Lear. He is enraged by the accusation, defies the bishop's (but mainly the bishop's wife's) attempt to remove him pending the outcome of the trial, doubts his own memory of what he did but is—and knows that he is—fiercely scrupulous in all his dealings, stubbornly refuses to have a lawyer defend him, and considers it a point of honor to continue his duties until, in his judgment (to all appearances an unwarranted judgment), rising public criticism makes it impossible.

There is Mrs. Proudie, the bishop's wife and wielder of the bishop's power, a ruthless, overbearing woman of imposing presence, who has convinced herself of Crawley's guilt and is driven to remove him, as she thinks, for the good of his flock. There is Grace Crawley, the curate's daughter, poor as a churchmouse, but educated in the manner of a lady, who has a superb offer of marriage from a gentleman whom she loves, but who must decide if she is willing to taint the reputation of his wealthy family with the sin of her father. There is Major Grantly, the gentleman in question, who loves Grace in return, but faces the dilemma of marrying Grace and having his income terminated by an irate father, or of submitting to his father and losing Grace and his good conscience. There is Archdeacon Grantly, the very father, who is torn between affection for his son and his desire to rule his son, and to avoid what appears to be inevitable social disgrace.

In one of the great episodes of the English novel, the archdeacon goes to confront Grace Crawley with the intention of speaking his mind, only to change his mind in the course of the conversation and leave with his convictions amazingly altered. There is Septimus Harding, former warden of Hiram's Hospital, in the last days of his life, when one by one his naive pleasures are put aside under the incubus of increasing enfeeblement. He can no longer pluck the string of his cello, he can no longer take the few steps from his door to the cathedral, finally he cannot even play cat's cradle with his granddaughter and is confined to bed with his family ministering to him, protesting out of his own innocence a quiet conviction that Crawley cannot be guilty.

Barset develops through a series of stunning scenes. The characters, whose natures and preoccupations you know well, come to meet, and when they meet you find yourself on the edge of your chair wondering what will transpire between them. They all face ethical dilemmas and it is Trollope's greatness to be able to analyze these dilemmas. Not to resolve them, because everyone resolves them in his own way, but to show the duality of his people, all the subtle byplay that passes between them and within them as they are pulled in several directions at once, some trying to decide very hard what the honorable course is, others bent on their own interests above all.

Trollope's writing is unobtrusive and supple. He does not strike a pose. Perhaps he has been underrated because of his seeming unassertiveness. At first Trollope does not appear clever, but his characters do. You wonder if he is capable of broad joviality, and then you come across the attorney Thomas Toogood. You wonder if he knows anything of sordidness—then you encounter the stockbroker Dobbs Broughton in Hook Court. You wonder if he can muster a certain pungency of style—then you run into the incredibly manipulative, self-centered, ill-tempered Mrs. Van Siever. It gradually dawns on you that there is nothing of which Trollope is not capable. Then you suddenly realize that of course it is not just Trollope's characters who are clever, it is Trollope himself. He does not strike a pose. But he has a point of view, a mixture of skepticism and sympathy. This is just the right mixture to produce the illusion that his people are speaking and acting for themselves. It looks easy, but I don't suppose anyone will go home and write a Trollope novel. Behind the verisimilitude is insight, and this is not a thing that is readily transferrable.

Here I would like to make a far-fetched comparison. Trollope's approach is both narrative and analytical. That is nothing new. Every successful novelist must tell a story and at the same time make a systematic analysis of cause and effect among human beings. No economist ever analyzed the economic ramifications of a twenty-pound check more carefully than Trollope analyzed the social ramifications. I have never heard anyone reproach a novelist for using the narrative method while at the same time analyzing the people and events he is describing. Yet I have heard this reproach leveled at some economists by others who profess to see a contradiction between the two. But if we are going to discuss history, institutions, people, and policies—and we must—we need the narrative style just as much as it is needed in a novel. We know that in fiction a writer attempts to tell a convincing story about people. But so does an economist in economics. Economists like to think that economics can be more than a sequence of events torn from history. But then writers of novels like to think that there is some universality in the types of characters and situations that they write about, also torn from history. The novel has its constants just as economics has—birth, love, marriage, moral dilemma, death. The novelist isolates what he wants to study just as the economist does. But the formulas are always being shattered by the flow of events in a novel—just as they are in economics. Nevertheless, the idea that economics and fiction have anything in common is far-fetched, and I will not mention it again.

Toward the end of *Barset,* good old Johnny Eames is off to the Continent to track down the dean of Barchester's wife, Mrs. Arabin, who might know something about the twenty-pound check. When they meet in Florence you will probably be fairly sure about what is going to happen. And it is breathtakingly simple. But the cumulative effect of nearly 400,000 well-chosen words will knock you off your chair. When Lily Dale is trying to make up her mind what to do about Johnny's proposal of marriage, you will be anxiously hoping that she will make the right decision to please you! When Mr. Crawley is made a proposal of another sort, for all you know of him and his pride, you will be hard put to know what he will do. This is the same eccentric and unpredictable Crawley who refused to resign his curacy when intolerable pressure was put on him, but who resigned of his own volition when he felt that he could no longer carry out his duties effectively. Quite a refreshing thought after the elections.

November 1976

In retrospect, I believe that I liked Trollope from birth and was just having a memory lapse when I wrote this.

Advising Carter and Congress

The business of advising the president and Congress on economic strategy is virtually outmoded. Those who give the advice do not have the time, the will, or the way to take a long view of things and to weave separate strands of policy into one presentable fabric. To its credit, the Advisory Committee on National Growth Policy Processes has stated this simple truth and has offered remedies with which President Carter and Congress must reckon. The committee not only avoids the platitudes which are usually all that committees of businessmen, labor leaders, economists, and representatives of special interests can agree on; it actually has thought through the needs of policymaking more profoundly than any other study group set up by Congress has done before. Even further, the committee caused its report to be written (no committee ever writes a report itself) in a style singularly free from governmentalese, and the polishers and finishers are to be congratulated on creating almost a model of what a government report should be. The report deserves to be read by everyone interested in the making of economic policy; and must be read by everyone who makes it.

The committee originated in a warning by Senators Mansfield and Scott, issued at a time when the energy crisis was momentarily visible to everyone, that we had better look to our deficiencies before it was too late. A National Commission on Supplies and Shortages was set up in 1974, but the then president was dilatory in appointing his share of the members. When extending the life of the commission for another year in 1975, Congress added the Advisory Committee, presumably with the hope that the chances of getting a report would be doubled. As of the last week of December, the report of the commission was a deep secret, even to some of its members, and we shall have to content ourselves with reviewing the superior (until proved otherwise) report of the committee.

The first recommendation is to create a National Growth and Development Commission as an independent agency in the executive branch of government. Reduced to the simplest terms, the job of this commission is to think of the right questions to ask about the future and then to get the president, Congress, and the public to think about the questions too. The staff of the commission would be paid to do nothing but contemplate what might happen in the next five, ten, twenty-five, or fifty years and what we might do about it. They are to think about what choices we will have; what chances we will have; what resources we will have; what needs we will have.

Their job is to exercise imagination, not to make decisions. They are to look through the binoculars and operate the radar, not steer the ship. Sensibly, the committee suggests that Congress and the president be required to take notice of the commission's work so that it will have some tangible effect. It may be obvious that we should be doing this. But we are not doing it now. The penalty we pay is in poor advice to the president and Congress. No amount of brilliance on the part of their advisers can make up for it.

Next, the committee recommends expanding the Economic Report of the President so that it brings together monetary and fiscal, sectoral and regional, and long-range strategy considerations into one statement. This is an ingenious proposal. It requires no new legislation. The president has only to ask that it be done. The making of such a report, if it is done well, will force the Council of Economic Advisers to link up many things that are now considered separately or not at all. They will have to do much more sophisticated work than they have ever contemplated. They will have to think through the effectiveness and consistency of the entire range of national economic policies within one comprehensive intellectual framework. Some members of the committee would like to see this work done in a quantitative form. It cannot be done any other way. No doubt the very thought of such a comprehensive economic report, with all the preparation that must go into it, is staggering. The Council of Economic Advisers, however wise its members, cannot do it alone. But the president can no longer get along by receiving bits and pieces of advice from different people about different things without someone being responsible for seeing if it all fits together. Knowing the difficulties, the members of the committee have other proposals to advance.

They recommend that a sectoral analysis division be established in either the Council of Economic Advisers or the Office of Management and Budget. The logical place for it is the Council of Economic Advisers, but the committee shrank from being entirely logical in this instance because the council has been a small group preoccupied with the traditional Keynesian concerns. But it did not shrink from assigning the work of writing an expanded economic report to the Council. Never mind. It is more important that the sectoral analysis be done well than that it be done in any particular place. That place could just as well be the OMB as any other.

I referred to an intellectual framework which would serve the Council of Economic Advisers in putting together the much more complicated jigsaw puzzle that it would be playing with. The framework has to be more than a philosophical one. It has to be a complex, computer-based model of the U.S. economy that goes much beyond existing models, incorporating the sectoral and regional details essential for rational policy planning in the future. The Advisory Committee proposes the establishment of a Center for Statistical

Policy and Analysis in the executive branch to develop the model for use at all levels of government. This is the principal tool in the kit, and very little can be constructed without it. Very little can be done by the president, by the Congress, by the governors and mayors, by the contemplated National Growth and Development Commission, that is not already being done, without a model with which to analyze the direct and indirect effects of economic actions, real or contemplated, public or private, in much finer detail than we now are capable of. This is the technique, just as the cyclotron is the technique in physics. It will not tell us where every sparrow will fall before it has fallen, as Herbert Stein sagely observed, but it will provide the only way for the earnest adviser to begin to make sense of the welter of information that flows up to him and to bring our understanding of ends and means a bit further out of the realm of hunch and fantasy than it is now.

Before any such model can be put to use, the statistics must be timely, without gaping omissions, of good quality, and based on consistent assumptions. Though we are overwhelmed with data collected by over fifty federal agencies, these data do not all measure up to the standards that would be needed to run the center. For that matter, they do not measure up to the needs of public decision making without the center. Part of its essential work would be to rationalize federal statistical operations.

The expanded Economic Report will come to Congress. So will the reports of the National Growth and Development Commission. The services of the Center for Statistical Policy and Analysis will be available to it. However, Congress is not ready. Its committee system splits up issues into fractions, and senators and representatives in their hundreds are rugged individualists, each pulling in his own direction. Several recommendations are offered. The leadership and the caucuses can be centralizing influences. A multi-year budget can facilitate the taking of a longer view. The Joint Economic Committee, in considering the expanded Economic Report, with the assistance of additional staff specializing in sectoral and regional affairs, can cultivate an appreciation of the broader view. Concurrent resolutions, drafted by the JEC in response to the Economic Report, for consideration by the House and Senate, can be general guides for legislation, not legally binding, but useful as a way of seeing the interdependence of the world, and as declarations of intent that say what Congress hopes to achieve.

By now the reader will not be surprised to learn that the management of regional business is as disorderly as federal business is, or, by the lights of the committee, worse. Many regional organizations are deployed, either contributing to or deploring the tangle that has been made by our blithe manner of devising programs for regions, states, and cities without ever stopping (or being able to stop) to assess the consequences or even ask the right questions. The National Commission on Intergovernmental Relations comes closest to being an exception. This the committee would strengthen. It would also develop regional organizations—possibly ten—embracing all the states, to work together with the NCIR and all levels of government. Then the president in preparing the Economic Report, Congress in contemplating legislation, and the National Growth and Development Commission in deliberating on the future, would have someone to sit down with them and disaggregate.

These are impressive proposals, coming as they do from a solid, respectable committee that is not just sending up trial balloons but really must stand by what it says. There are others. I do not mean to slight any of them or do an injustice to the favorites of any committee member. Those that I have mentioned are connected to my theme: the economic consulting business, government as client, is hopelessly out of date and ready for a complete overhaul. It is not a matter of finding the best economist with the best intuition who also happens to be *simpático* to the chief executive. The answers cannot be divined by single economists, however able; they can only be reached by organized groups performing new functions in a new apparatus designed to bring the state of the art up to date.

The economics establishment does not have people who are qualified to run this new apparatus. They will need on-the-job training. Then they will have to go back to the colleges and universities and teach economics in a new way. No counsel promises a more startling change in the conception of what economists are supposed to do, and to teach, than that of the Advisory Committee on National Growth Policy Processes. Possibly the committee did not know this. Probably they should not be told.

January 1977

The Backward Art of Giving Advice

CHALLENGE OFFICE MEMO

The president has called for questions from the public which he has promised to answer truthfully. The following informal interrogation took place when the president visited the offices of *Challenge* and is not for publication.

Q. When do you expect to redeem your campaign pledge to bring about full employment?

A. When the public is ready.

Q. Isn't the public ready now?

A. No. There is no real call for full employment at the present time. Businessmen are content to live without it. Labor leaders don't want to face the inconvenience of fighting for it. The unemployed have no voice in the matter at all. And economists are mainly preoccupied with proving that full employment is dangerous.

Q. Then why did you make campaign promises?

A. Because there is solid agreement on all sides that full employment is a good thing. People wanted to hear this deeply held American value reaffirmed. But they didn't expect anything drastic to be done about it.

Q. Why does it have to be drastic?

A. We can't have full employment by the old methods and new methods always look drastic.

Q. Can you expand on that?

A. I can cite you an irony. We had mass unemployment in the Great Depression. The Keynesians came along with a prescription for full employment. Eventually they converted nearly everybody, because, as I said, we all want full employment. But sometime in the last ten years, Keynesianism evolved into a prescription for unemployment. Now you are really in a fix when you believe in a doctrine that tells you exactly how to do what you don't want to do. If you don't give it up, you soon find that you no longer do what you believe in but believe in what you do. Then the prospect of changing from comfortable, old, familiar methods to new ones, so that you can do what you want to do again, looks drastic and frightening. That is about the state of mind of the country today.

Q. Well, is the absence of real commitment to full employment due to technical difficulties or to a lack of will?

A. Both. If we could achieve full employment within the Keynesian frame of reference, we would. We are used to manipulating the money supply, the budget, and taxes. But there are technical difficulties, as you call them, that result in inflation long before there is full employment. You can do nothing about it by manipulating aggregates. When there is a conflict between what appears to be possible within your frame of reference and what you want to be possible, something has to give.

Q. In these matters, do you advise your advisers or do they advise you?

A. They tell me what I want to hear. But I want to hear what they tell me. You would be amazed how fast their story would change if public opinion changed.

Q. Do they tell you a story?

A. Exactly. Charles Schultze is an excellent technician, but when it comes to advice, all he or anyone else can do is to interpret events and suggest what to do next. As you know, events can be interpreted in various ways. There is no fixity in it. Giving advice is a backward art because the adviser does nothing more than try to tell a convincing story which blends together facts, theories, values, politics, economics, history, psychology, and anything else the adviser thinks is pertinent. He must tell part of the story because it is true. But he tells the other part of the story because he wants to lead up to a certain conclusion and must underline what is important to that conclusion.

Q. You are not getting economic science?

A. Of course I am not getting economic science. I am getting a frame of reference in which this or that proposition of economic science is brought in like a metaphor. If Schultze thinks it is appropriate, he tells me that too many cooks spoil the broth. If he thinks the opposite is appropriate, he tells me that many hands make light work.

Q. But you could get stories from Galbraith or Leontief or Lekachman or Keyserling.

A. I could. And when public opinion dictates it, I will.

Q. You do think that there is absolute truth in economics?

A. Yes, I do. The law of diminishing returns is true. The law of supply and demand is true. But what you do about them is another matter.

Q. If, God forbid, you should ever have to ask Galbraith, Leontief, Lekachman, or Keyserling for advice, do you have any idea what they would tell you?

A. They would say that unemployment is not inevitable. That is, there is nothing to prevent us from providing a useful job for everyone who wants to work, without inflation.

Q. Is the price too high?

A. It's too high for me until the public is ready for Galbraith et al.

Q. And the price of unemployment?

A. That's also too high. We wouldn't accept the argument that the free speech of 90 percent depends on its denial to 10 percent. It's just as objectionable to argue that the well-being of 90 percent depends on the joblessness of 10 percent.

Q. How will you resolve the dilemma?

A. Wait and see.

Q. But you have already shown that you are a man of courage and imagination by going to work without a tie.

A. An open collar is about as far as a president can go with courage and imagination these days. But maybe it can be considered a down payment for the future.

March 1977

JKG Versus the Angel

JKG lies asleep in his bed, snoring. An angel descends into the room.

ANGEL *(female).* Wake up, JKG. I've been sent to talk to you. *(Shakes him.)* Wake up.

JKG. *(Rubbing his eyes.)* Just say the word. I'm ready.

ANGEL. Ready for what?

JKG. To do another TV series.

ANGEL. If you'd look, you'd see I'm not a TV producer.

JKG. *(Sitting up and looking.)* Oh, Angelina. It's you again. Every time I write a book, you come to question me.

ANGEL. There's nothing wrong in writing a book. There's nothing wrong in doing a TV series. But the way you do it! You—

JKG. —commit the sin of pride. Don't scold. I know what you're going to say. But consider the facts.

ANGEL. I have considered the facts. The facts are that an economist is offered thirteen hours of prime time. He has a rare opportunity to sing the praises of his profession. But he just says a few words about Smith, Marx, Keynes, maybe one or two others, and nothing about Sismondi, Petty, Locke, Mill, Jevons, Menger, Wieser, Walras—

JKG. —which would bore people to tears. Please—

ANGEL. Please nothing. You refuse to talk about them because you prefer to talk about yourself.

JKG. *(Rises and strokes the angel's wings.)* Do calm yourself, Angelina, and let me call for some tea. *(Rings.)* You angels must try to see things in proper perspective. Almost everything that needs to be said can be said by discussing Smith, Marx, and Keynes. Smith is like Aeneas, founder of the Roman dynasty. There were those who came before and those who came after. But when you have told the story of Aeneas' travels from Troy to Italy, you have told all, especially if you tell it from the vantage of a later century as Virgil did. Aeneas was the center of a mythology; so is Smith. Those who believe myths don't regard them as myths. They are all the more powerful for that. If you look at economics as mythology, you will see that I was right to stick to Smith.

ANGEL. What about Marx?

JKG. A kind of countermyth. Like Goethe's Mephistopheles. He derides all that was previously thought sacred. Today we live under the myths of Smith and Marx, they share the world. Could I have done better than to use my thirteen hours to explain how things really are without the myths?

ANGEL. This is what I mean by pride, JKG. *(A knock at the door.)*

JKG. The tea has arrived. Come in.

Smith enters with tea followed by Marx with cake.

SMITH. Some devil shoved this tray into my hands as I came up.

MARX. *Irgend ein Teufel hat mir dieses Tablett Kuchen zu tragen gegeben.*

JKG. The myths have arrived. With tea and cake.

MARX. Do not be impertinent to your elders and betters. I founded the science of society and Smith laid the groundwork.

JKG. Forgive the joke. I always joke when startled. Great as you are, your claims are exaggerated. Let a thing happen; you have explained it. Let the opposite happen; you have explained that, too. Any explanation that appears valid regardless of what happens is no explanation. It is metaphysics. The theory of value is an example. It cannot be falsified by facts. Here's the best I can say for you. You made a reasonably honest but mainly unsuccessful attempt to get away from grand philosophical systems toward a science of society. That was a great accomplishment—for your time.

SMITH. Poppycock. It's perfectly clear that society breaks down if things are not done my way.

MARX. Worse than that. It's perfectly clear that society breaks down if things are not done *my* way.

JKG. The world is divided between you. That's why we're all going to the devil.

Mephistopheles enters through the open door.

MEPHISTO. I heard you mention my name. I should have come long ago. I'm a great admirer of yours.

JKG. Thank you. Words fail me.

MEPHISTO. Not at all. Do consider me a friend. As Faust did.

JKG. Oh, Faust. A humorless fellow. Something of a rat, too. I couldn't have been cruel to Gretchen for all the world. I would have made her happy. Faust was a bumbler with women. I'm not.

MEPHISTO. It was Gretchen who was a bumbler with Faust. But opinions differ in these matters.

JKG. Surely you didn't come to discuss Gretchen.

MEPHISTO. No. Of course not. I've come to discuss your book. I'm a compulsive reader, you know. Read everything of yours including *Indian Painting.* Now what I want to know is: when does the science of society really begin?

JKG. When we clear away the myths. There are bits and pieces of science in Smith and Marx. But science is just beginning. It really began with

Keynes if you want a name. He didn't attempt a whole system; just a few relationships.

Enter Keynes.

KEYNES. I don't know who I am.

JKG. (*Rushing to him.*) But you are Keynes. I recognized you at once. (*Enter Keynes Number Two.*) Good heavens!

KEYNES #2. My identity is not at all clear.

JKG. One of you is an impostor!

Enter Keynes Number Three.

KEYNES #3. Not at all. Not at all.

KEYNES #1. I am Aggregate Demand Keynes.

KEYNES #2. I am Financial Instability Keynes.

KEYNES #3. I am Cost-push Keynes.

KEYNES #1. Three in one.

KEYNES #2. One in three.

KEYNES #3. But terribly confused.

MEPHISTO. Come now, fellows. That's the result of not writing clearly. You must face it like a man—like men—like whatever the devil you are.

MARX. (*Stentorian.*) I demand to be heard. This queer triplet should not be welcome here. They are apologists for the status quo.

MEPHISTO. We are all apologists for one thing or another. No one is free of bias. The remedy for that is skepticism. Follow my example.

KEYNES #1. True. No one is free of—

KEYNES #2. —bias. The remedy for that is—

KEYNES #3. —to leave the bias out when you are doing science.

SMITH. No one is free of bias. The remedy for that is to know your bias. But I would rather call it commitment to an ideal.

JKG. All of you are right.

ANGEL. Straining for a paradox. Typical. It's enough to make an angel weep.

JKG. No, my dear Angelina. I am not straining. Take the law of diminishing returns. No matter what the bias of the person who believes it, it's a true statement, free of bias. Then take the theory of laissez faire. No matter how many true statements free of bias it may contain, the person who believes it sees the world with a bias or a commitment to an ideal, as Smith says. Finally, take both of the above. A person can be skeptical about whether the first applies to a particular situation and about whether the second is a valid means to reach the stated ideal. We must have bias, be free of bias, and be skeptical of bias all at once. Three in one. One in three.

SMITH, MARX, KEYNES NUMBERS 1, 2, AND 3 (*together*). Paradox! Paradox! Paradox! Paradox! (*They run around the room in a circle. Smith and Marx hurl their trays at JKG.*)

JKG. Get lost. You are apparitions from the past and cannot judge the present.

He picks up a cake knife from the floor and slices off their heads.

SMITH. Milton Friedman will hear of this!

MARX. I'm going where I'm wanted. To Paul Sweezy's house!

KEYNES 1, 2, AND 3. I must really try to get my heads on straight. (*Calling.*) Joan Robinson! Joan Robinson!

They leave with their heads tucked under their arms.

ANGEL. What a mess. Broken crockery and cake all over the room. (*Angelina, Mephisto, and JKG take brooms and sweep.*)

JKG. Most of my life I have been sweeping up the debris of the past.

MEPHISTO. You speak like a disciple of mine. Economics is rubbish from the past.

JKG. Do not misunderstand me. In my books and on television, I discuss the giant corporation, its symbiosis with government, the poor countries, the arms race. The present realities. These are the main subjects of economics today—or more accurately, of political economy today. If you go to Washington, London, Paris, Bonn, or Rome with theories from the past which conflict with realities of the present, you will be committing a sophisticated kind of fraud. It's not out of egotism that I gave my own views—not entirely anyway—but because no other view fits. No other view except for those of a few friends—they will know who they are.

ANGEL. Look here, old pal. You've made a pretty good case for yourself. But you fail to mention that you advocate socialism. You don't think that you can slip that through in a torrent of words when everybody's yawning and ready to go to bed, do you?

JKG. There is no acceptable rationale for the power that resides in the great corporation. Management is autonomous—uncontrolled by market forces, by government, by employees. It's a thoroughly undemocratic arrangement and I have only suggested that the present boards of directors be dismissed and new ones be made up entirely of public members, responsible to carry out public policy without interfering in details of management. My hope is that public policy can eventually be made to correspond to public interest.

MEPHISTO. Quite so. I myself am a socialist. Whenever I find myself in agreement with the majority, I hasten to reexamine my views. Why? Because the majority allows itself to be persuaded by the powerful, and the powerful are interested in finding justifications for their power.

JKG. When we have socialism, I presume the majority will have the power.

MEPHISTO. Then you will belong to me. (*Takes his hand and pulls.*)

ANGEL. No, to me. (*Takes his other hand and pulls.*)

MEPHISTO. You cannot serve God until you have served me. Self-interest first.

ANGEL. You cannot serve the devil if you want to serve me. Altruism first. (*Both pull harder.*)

JKG. I have much experience. Life is both giving and receiving. I have done my share of both. Smith be damned. Marx be damned. So stop pulling.

MEPHISTO. But tell us which one you will go with.

JKG. I didn't know I had a choice.

MEPHISTO. Heaven and hell are a matter of preference. People get whichever one they want.

JKG. I will keep that in mind. Meantime my preference is to go back to bed. But first I will kiss Angelina. (*Which he does. Mephisto goes through the floor with a bang and a puff of smoke. Angelina flaps her wings and floats through the ceiling in radiant light and to the accompaniment of heavenly music.*)

May 1977

What Is an Incomes Policy All About?

There is no chance of bringing inflation under control with the methods that are currently in use. The Labor-Management Group of eight labor leaders and eight corporate executives who advise the president are adamantly opposed to an incomes policy. The president has not given the slightest hint that he knows what to do. The economics profession in the main is only capable of deploring the fact that labor unions and large corporations do not allow the price system to work properly. There are shudders at the thought of wage-price controls. Nearly everyone knows that the present mode of operating is bad, but nearly everyone is averse to changing it.

Despite the almost unanimous opposition, I believe that an incomes policy has to be reconsidered. We are now witnessing the establishment of a wage pattern of 10 percent increases in basic industries where productivity is rising at the rate of 4 percent. The resulting 6 percent rise in costs will be passed on to the consumer in the form of higher prices as it has been in the past. A 6 percent per year wage-price spiral has virtually achieved the status of a law of nature. But it is not. It is simply the means by which unions and businesses in concentrated industries keep their relative income shares from falling behind. Everyone else follows suit as best he can. In essence, an incomes policy is an agreement by the parties to adjust their income shares without the inflation.

An incomes policy that is designed in the first instance to hold down wages and prices is bound to fail because it is based on a misconception. The relative income shares of labor and business are what the policy has to get at; then the wage-price spiral will take care of itself. Our present procedure for determining incomes occurs in two steps. First, wage bargaining takes place in a leading industry and a pattern is set for the rest of the economy. Then a major firm in the economy sets a new price level for its products, which serves as a precedent for other firms to follow. The price decision can undo the wage decision by raising the cost of living and the wage decision can undo the price decision by raising the cost of doing business. The trick is to bring these two types of decisions together so that they are made in concert.

Actually, a third type of decision has to be concerted with the other two. The administration's intention to speed up or slow down the economy has a direct bearing on relative income shares. If the economy is growing rapidly and sales and profits are increasing, labor will want increases to keep up with business gains. If the economy is sluggish and sales and profits are declining, businesses will make compensating price increases, the cost of living will rise, and labor will want compensating wage increases. So it is the wage, price, and monetary-fiscal decisions that have to be concerted.

Before going into that problem, I would like to say a few words about the way in which large corporations set their prices. I recommend to those who are trained to read economic analysis, Alfred S. Eichner's realistic and illuminating account, *Megacorp and Oligopoly.* The executives of the price leader in a concentrated industry set a price level so that members of the industry can meet their costs, including payments to their two chief constituencies, workers and stockholders. They of course do not stop at that but also take into account the need for retained earnings to carry out long-term investment plans. Two opposite pressures are at work on the price level: an upward pressure to obtain as large a fund as possible for investment; and a downward pressure to avoid three hazards—the use of substitutes by consumers; the entry of other firms into the industry; and intervention by the government. Thus executives do not set their price markup capriciously, but only after weighing the benefits and risks. The result is a flow of funds used for the maximum long-run growth of the corporation through investment, advertising, and research and development. Eichner calls the part of revenue used for these purposes the corporate levy, since it is comparable to a tax placed on the products of the corporation for its own use. About 90 percent of investment in concentrated industries, not including public utilities, is financed through this levy. Investment plans are primarily determined by its size, and once those plans are established they are jealously guarded by management against the incursions of inflation.

Eichner makes one other observation that is germane here. The corporation is the claimant of residual income; the stockholders are not. They are treated sympathetically, and dividend increases are not permitted to fall behind wage increases. But the stockholders are not treated *too* sympathetically and the increases are not *too* generous. Otherwise the funds for growth would be siphoned off.

Now we return to incomes policy. Here again, Eichner's book is helpful. What we need is a procedure to determine wages, prices, dividends, investment plans, and monetary-fiscal policy in relation to each other so that the separate decisions do not work at cross-purposes. The parties, then, must be brought together. The representatives of labor, management, government, and the consumer might form a council. What they would be asked to do is divide the growth of output in a noninflationary way. Theoretically, a group of experts could come up with a number of noninflationary proposals, including a high rate of economic growth at one extreme and a low rate at the other. The first would require that most of the increased output go into investment; the second, into wages. But in practice, a norm has already been set: a growth in wages and investment—averaging cyclical variations—in step with the long-run growth in productivity. The object of the representatives is not to lay down a general rule and hope that everybody will follow it, nor to set thousands of individual wages and prices. Rather it is to establish wage and price levels, leaving the parties or the market free to determine the details.

This arrangement has several implications. Dividends cannot be allowed to grow faster than wages. Unions, in return for accepting guidelines for wage levels, must have a say in setting the guidelines for price levels and investment. The president, Congress, and the Federal Reserve, for their part, should be free to cast aside the pretense that the wage-price spiral can be stopped by sedating the economy. The parties are expected to keep watch on the long-run trend of wages and investment, and make compensatory adjustments as needed. The process described here is not a restriction of collective bargaining; it is an extension of collective bargaining to include prices and investment. Agreement on relative shares comes first; wages, prices, and investment plans follow. Actually, nobody is giving up anything except inflation.

If this mechanism is used in concentrated industries, a pattern will be set for the rest of the economy and no further wage or price controls will be necessary. The aim cannot be 100 percent stable prices. In some parts of the economy a disparity between wage increases and productivity growth will cause inflation. But the rate will be slow. However, if the economy suffers from shortages, the rate of inflation will not be slow. Shortages will raise the consumer price level or business costs or both, and the incomes policy will fall apart. What is needed is a continuous study of each industry's capacity to supply the needs of the economy, given the rate of expansion that has been agreed upon. Indeed, the overall expansion must be made up of the expansion of separate industries at different rates. A monitoring of relations among the various sectors of the economy will indicate the different rates of investment required and facilitate the channeling of funds in the appropriate direction. Contrary to military doctrine, the doctrine of the new New Economics tells us that we must fight on all fronts at once to win the battle against inflation.

I assume that there is only a temporary freeze on considering alternatives to the current futile and harmful exercise that goes under the name of economic policy. An incomes policy cannot come about without the president taking the lead and winning consent. National leaders have for the moment immobilized themselves with fear and have nothing to offer but a 6 percent rate of inflation, a 7 percent rate of unemployment, and rueful wishes that it were not so. This is not a program with great public appeal. With the old way completely exhausted, we are not far from having to try an alternative, unlikely as that may seem.

I sometimes think that the complete disappearance of the economics profession would have no noticeable effect. The world would not be particularly better off or worse off. The little bag of tricks that economists carry around would be left behind. Presidents and congressmen have been well enough rehearsed to perform them without further instruction. No one would remonstrate that economists were essential for the perpetuation of inflation and unemployment. This thought is then banished by the pleasant expectation that economists soon will have some new and better tricks to teach.

July 1977

Little Red Riding Hood

Ms. Hood was fourteen when the incident occurred. It was to leave its mark on her psyche. Her psyche had already been badly scarred by that eccentric name. It made her brash and flamboyant. People have been known to change their entire personalities as a result of changing their shoe styles. When Ms. Hood changed her name to Rebecca, it calmed her down considerably. But that happened later.

It must be admitted that Mother was a big part of the problem. Mother was forty and the single head of a household. These facts depressed her. Living in Scarsdale depressed her. Working for the Fed depressed her. Grandmother's recent retirement to a house in the woods depressed her.

"Poor Grandmother, poor Grandmother. All alone in the woods." These words were addressed to no one in particular, but Ms. Hood chose to reply.

"Grandmother weighed the costs and benefits and opted for early retirement. She elected to take the lump-sum payout under her pension plan to make a down payment on a house. As for living in the woods, if you can call New Canaan the woods, there has been a marked population shift to the exurbs for at least a decade. Grandmother is following the trend."

Mother sighed. "Poor Grandmother, poor Grandmother. Alone in New Canaan." "I'll take Grandmother a picnic basket if it will make you feel better," offered Ms. Hood.

"Alas, we haven't got a picnic basket since we never go on picnics," sighed Mother. But at length a picnic lunch was placed in a brown paper bag. "Don't talk to strangers. Don't hitchhike." These were Mother's parting words.

Being brash and flamboyant, Ms. Hood did talk to strangers and did hitchhike. She was picked up by a character with singularly large ears, eyes, and teeth. He drove a 1974 Mercedes 250.

"What's your name?" he asked.

"Little Red Riding Hood. What's yours?"

"The Wolf," replied The Wolf.

They had a good laugh over that.

"Where to?" asked The Wolf.

"I'm taking this brown paper bag with a picnic lunch to my Grandmother's house deep in the woods of New Canaan. Grandmother had a high marginal propensity to save during her working life. She doesn't need picnic lunches in brown paper bags. But Mother is in a reactive depression and experiencing anhedonia. I'm doing this for her."

"Mother a bit sour, eh? But Grandmother is right as roast duck. Well, I'll drive you as far as I'm going. You can easily walk the rest of the way."

They had a good laugh over that, too.

The Wolf was in his mid-forties and hungry. He was one of those wolves who always has the things that money can buy without ever having any money. But life was passing him by.

"Can I take advantage of this girl's credulity?" he thought to himself as he stopped the car. The girl turned to him and asked, "Is this where I get out?"

"Yes," was his sardonic reply.

They laughed again.

The Wolf drove directly to Grandmother's house and knocked on the door. Grandmother was eating muffins and "Who's there?" sounded like two blasts on a muted trombone. Grandmother's forceful voice could not be stilled even by muffins.

"The Wolf," said The Wolf.

"Come in," said Grandmother, "and have some muffins. It's lonely in these woods, even if it is New Canaan, and I wouldn't mind having somebody to eat my muffins with. Mind you don't take more than your fair share."

"You are uncommonly kind," said The Wolf, wolfing down a muffin.

"Don't put me on," said Grandmother, eating another muffin.

"I must insist that you are uncommonly kind," replied The Wolf, wolfing down another muffin and breaking into tears all at once.

"Cripes, don't carry on. I can't stand maudlin scenes. Take a tissue."

The Wolf took a tissue and blew his nose. "Muffins always make me maudlin," he sobbed. "I once had a cafe that served muffins. It was taken over by creditors. That is why muffins always make me maudlin. When I meet someone who is generous, the shock of it and the cafe and the muffins bring tears to my eyes. I could eat you, you are so uncommonly kind," he added.

"You'd better stick to the muffins," remarked Grandmother.

Some time later, Little Red Riding Hood arrived at Grandmother's house after a long walk through the woods. Not hearing anyone stirring, she lifted the latch and walked in. There in Grandmother's bed she saw The Wolf. "My, what big eyes, ears, and teeth you have," was the first thought that ran through her mind. As The Wolf was thinking, "The better to—" Little Red Riding Hood cried out: "The Wolf has eaten Grandmother!"

A passing woodsman heard the cry and dashed into the house. He took a shot at The Wolf and missed. "Cripes," shouted Grandmother, poking her head out of the covers. "You've put a hole in my Chippendale headboard. Not since I retired as curator of the Detroit Museum of Paleontology have I met such a numskull. You meddlesome booby, you gawking blockhead, you interloping dunce, you fossilized herringbone, you—"

Just then, Mother, who had felt guilty about sending Little Red Riding Hood when she should have gone herself, drove into Grandmother's driveway. Hearing the shouting, she ran into Grandmother's bedroom.

"Grandmother, what are you doing?" asked Mother.

"Cripes, can't you see I'm eating muffins with The Wolf? Can't a body eat muffins in peace? Here, have some muffins. You have some too, Little Red Riding Hood. And you, you numskull," said Grandmother, alluding to the woodsman, "you might as well have some too."

At this, Mother looked at the woodsman. The woodsman looked at Mother. They felt involuntarily, irresistibly attracted to each other as they ate their muffins.

Little Red Riding Hood took it all in. "Mother said not to talk to strangers and not to hitch a ride," she thought. "Yet, if I hadn't disobeyed Mother, I would not have met The Wolf. If I had not met The Wolf, he would not have come here to eat muffins with Grandmother. If he had not come here to eat muffins with Grandmother, I would not have cried out. If I had not cried out, the woodsman would not have come in. If the woodsman had not come in, he and Mother would not have felt involuntarily, irresistibly attracted to each other as they ate their muffins. Life is uncertain and there are few rules that apply to all cases. By breaking the rule in this case, things turned out well. But probably this case should not be considered a precedent. It is hard to know when to obey Mother and when not to. One never has enough information to be sure."

Grandmother and The Wolf got married and bought a Burger King franchise, ending a long string of failures for The Wolf. Mother and the woodsman also got married, ending Mother's reactive depression. Little Red Riding Hood changed her name to Rebecca and bought stylish shoes. They all lived happily ever after.

September 1977

Searching for Homo sapiens

Is there anything that modern biology can tell us about the nature of *Homo sapiens*? When I was a boy, my aunt sang, "Ah, sweet mystery of life, at last I've found you," but she was a bit premature. Not until 1943 did Avery find out what genes are made of. He was able to turn one kind of bacterium into another by removing its DNA and substituting that of another strain. A decade later, Crick and Watson showed that the atoms of DNA are arranged in a double-helical structure which determines how that substance works. So it came to be known that strands of deoxyribonucleic acid molecules contain all the information necessary to make everything that is alive. DNA possesses the astonishing chemical property of replication: it makes exact copies of itself by serving as a template along which the appropriate constituents of new helical strands line up in the exactly correct order. This is accomplished with the assistance of catalysts that do the joining. The order is the information, just as the order of the letters in this sentence is the information.

But DNA not only makes copies of itself; it also serves as a template for the synthesis of RNA, ribonucleic acid. RNA, in turn, acts as a messenger of DNA, venturing into various parts of the cell to guide the synthesis of proteins. Proteins (you may know) make up much of the stuff of bodies, and also turn bodily processes on and off with precision. DNA is the lawgiver. It provides the instructions for building organisms and copies of the instructions which are carried by RNA. This is the chain of command through which it supervises the catalysts that actually build the organisms.

We cannot think our way back to the state of mind that existed before an insight burst upon us, but prior to Darwin, naturalists were faced with a staggering variety of life forms, from amoebas to elephants, with no satisfactory explanation of their relationship. The evolutionary hypothesis splendidly united the entire living world in a common framework of related lines of descent. While this conception never had a serious rival, not until a quarter-century ago was it provided with an unassailable foundation when the actual mechanism of heredity and variation was found. Then the elementary particles of biology came to play an explanatory role similar to that of the elementary particles of physics: one the common denominator of all life; the other of all matter.

The new story of creation starts from these premises plus one other: the tenacious durability and the sporadic mutability of DNA. Its impressive durability is reflected in the fact that species persist unchanged from generation to generation. Many contemporary insects are virtually the same today as they were in the Carboniferous period some 330 million years ago thanks to the faithful replication of the insect program contained in their DNA molecules. Yet once in several thousand generations a given gene may undergo a change due to a mistake in copying or an outside influence such as radiation. Once an error is made, it will be copied with fidelity, usually to the disadvantage of the individuals who carry the erring gene. But sometimes the error turns out to be useful.

In the beginning, about 5 billion years ago, the waters of the world were a hot thin soup (as Haldane described it), containing all the ingredients needed to make nucleic acids and proteins, the constituents of life. It has been demonstrated in the laboratory that lightning and sunshine were entirely sufficient to build these constituents up into prebiotic compounds. By sheer accident, it is surmised, at least one among the billions of molecules that must have been formed possessed the amazing property of assembling components of itself by itself. Once started, this singular molecule populated the sea. Over the eons in which this work could take place, some of the copies were inevitably defective, but only from the point of view of accurate copying. Thus several varieties of replicating molecules began to compete for their constituent compounds in the sea and, possibly, in each other. We should expect that those most successful in the competition survived and replicated, and that the rest came to grief. We must also assume that at some point in this ocean of time, one or several mutations produced a kind of chemical shell which enhanced the survival possibilities of its particular replicator, and the first step toward the development of a cell was taken. When two cells learned how to exchange genetic material, the range of variability was greatly enhanced. This hastened the rate of evolution; it also gave rise to that enduring phenomenon called sex.

Jacques Monod characterized the process we are describing by polar opposites: chance and necessity. Mutations occur at random. The probability of any particular mutation occurring is virtually zero. But once a mutation has taken place, the probability of its persisting thanks to the stability of DNA is virtually certain. Then the fate of the mutated gene will depend on the increased or diminished survival ability conferred on the individuals carrying it.

Among other things, Monod is saying that we are here by sheer fluke. That is an interesting fact, but one which requires no action on our part. Nor should it be a source of concern. But not everyone agrees. François Mauriac wrote, "What this professor says is far more incredible than what we poor Christians believe." It is certainly incredible, but the incredibility lies in our difficulty in imagining natural selection working through the law of large numbers. We are talking about billions of events taking place over the course of millions of years. Though the language is strange, it is not incomprehensible.

If *Homo sapiens* is the product of this ruthless process, must he be ruthless? True, the First Commandment of every gene is to be fruitful and multiply. Genetic success is defined as having the most, the toughest, and the stablest progeny. At first glance it appears that genes that dictate the most selfish traits to their bearers are the ones that survive together with their bearers. In effect, they have provided themselves with bodies programmed to win the competition in their particular niche in the environment. There seems to be no room for altruism, but the fact is that no one is the sole owner of his genes. Copies of the same gene are spread around among kin in a common fund known as a gene pool. An individual shares 50 percent of his genes with parents, brothers, and sisters; 25 percent with grandparents, aunts, and uncles; 12.5 percent with great-grandparents and cousins; and so on. When a Thomson's gazelle sees a predator, it runs away in a stiff-legged, bounding fashion called stotting, warning the pack of danger. When a nesting female nighthawk is approached, it distracts the intruder by flying conspicuously away from the nest, settling on the ground directly in front of the intruder with its wings extended. These actions reduce the probability of self-preservation, but the probability of preserving other individuals with some of the same genes is increased. If the net probability of survival of the several individuals is increased, the genes responsible for this behavior are positively selected. The question arises: how do animals distinguish between relatives and others? The answer is that they don't. But since kin among social animals tend to live in the same neighborhood, altruistic behavior is likely to apply to a relative. But it applies to others all the same. A bee sting is an extreme case. A bee commits suicide when it stings. This may not seem altruistic to the person who gets stung, but it is altruistic toward the bees in the hive being defended. Except for the extreme case, altruism and self-interest are not really opposites since they both increase the chances of an individual's survival: anyone may be a beneficiary of good deeds as well as their perpetrator. So the answer to the question at the beginning of the paragraph is at least the negative one that nothing in biology ineluctably decrees that *Homo sapiens* must be ruthless.

You may wonder how gazelles, nighthawks, and bees know what they are doing, and grow impatient with zoologists who presume to impute motives to them. Here the saving concept of teleonomy enters. When a program of behavior is inscribed in the genes, it appears that the animal is acting with a definite objective in mind even though this is not the case. The appearance of purpose is one of the consequences of natural selection, and every muta-tion is weighed according to its contribution to the teleonomic apparatus of the animal. It is due to the perfecting of this apparatus that every animal fits with precision into its natural habitat.

But if something in the habitat changes, the animal is out of luck unless it has the capacity to learn. A Sphex wasp prepares a burrow, finds and paralyzes a caterpillar, deposits it in front of the burrow, enters the burrow to make a last-minute inspection, then comes out to pull in the caterpillar for egg-laying. Sphex has but one theory about each phase of this operation. If you move the caterpillar a short distance when she is inspecting the burrow, she will drag it back to the same spot and go inside to inspect again. No matter how many times you move the caterpillar, Sphex will repeat the same sequence.

The connection between genes and invariant behavior is evidently direct, requiring only an environmental cue to set it going. An elegant example of genetic reasoning deals with two types of behavior of honey bees when confronted with foul brood, a disease that attacks grubs in their cells. One strain of bees prevents epidemics by throwing the infected grubs out of the hive; another does not. After the two strains were crossed, one group showed completely hygienic behavior; another showed no hygienic behavior; and a third uncapped the wax cells of the diseased grubs but did not throw them out. The experimenter surmised that two separate genes were involved, one for uncapping and one for throwing out. He supposed that a subgroup of nonhygienic bees had the throwing-out gene but not the uncapping gene. This was correct, because when he removed the caps himself, half the apparently nonhygienic bees performed the throwing-out sequence perfectly.

The story becomes more complicated when the source of information upon which an individual acts shifts from the genetic to the environmental. An animal which has the capacity to learn possesses genes which are saying, in effect, do what you think best, within, of course, the limits of your equipment. The limits for *Homo sapiens* are extremely wide, but let us not be in a hurry to get to such a difficult subject. Let us start with baboons. Even at this level of intelligence, genetic properties clearly affect behavior. Olive and hamadryas baboons are so closely related that they can interbreed, but the hamadryas male establishes a total and permanent attachment to females while the olive male seeks to appropriate females only at estrus. Through a multiplier effect, this trait alone results in profound differences in the social structure of baboon troops.

But as everyone knows, primates also possess an amazing degree of freedom from specific programs inscribed in their genes. Two case histories of invention and tradition among Japanese macaques are instructive. Japanese ethologists scattered sweet potatoes on a beach near a forest inhabited by macaques. The macaques accepted the gift, but found the job of removing the sand from the potatoes bothersome. One day an inspired two-year-old female named Imo walked to the water, dipped a potato in with one hand, and washed away the sand with the other. After a period, the habit spread to most of the troop. Two years after the first experiment, the ethologists scattered wheat grains on the beach. Picking grain from the sand was tedious work and Imo the monkey genius (as Edward Wilson calls her) conceived the idea of scooping up entire handfuls of grain and sand and throwing them on the water. When the sand sank, it was only necessary to skim the wheat off the water and eat it. After a time, most of the troop had institutionalized the practice, with the young members learning first, the adult females next, and the adult males lagging sadly behind (presumably because they stayed on the outskirts of the troop and had fewer chances to learn).

Even though friends who hear the story say that their brains are no match for Imo's, we know that this is false modesty. Imo had the power of simulation: she was able to imagine the result of throwing wheat on the water before she actually did so; but she did not have the power of language, which enlarges the scope of simulation incalculably. There are approximately 100,000 different genes in a human cell, but there are 260,000 words in the *Random House Dictionary of the English Language* (and it isn't the biggest dictionary). The information-carrying capacity of language is even greater than that of genes. Noam Chomsky has made the case that the deep structure of language is innate and does not have to be learned. A child, after incomplete and unsystematic exposure to a language, is able to construct a potentially infinite number of sentences with an infinite variety of meanings, and after a certain age, reaches a steady state in which language is "learned," with only marginal additions and refinements afterward. This view is compatible with other facts that are known about the nervous system, such as that of the transformation of upside-down, two-dimensional pictures on the retina into right-side up, three-dimensional objects in the brain. All this is completely consistent with genetic theory, which can easily account for the natural selection of brain structures that match the structures of reality with sufficient accuracy to promote survival. But we must withhold judgment, because the alternative is that we come by language by learning the rules just as we learn the rules of physics, and no decisive experiments have yet eliminated one view or the other.

Whatever the case, there is no doubt that the emergence of language turned evolution in an entirely new direction, no less novel than, shall we say, the decision of a fish (teleonomic) to walk on dry land. Once the first tentative steps are taken past such a turning point, the selective pressure of the environment promotes the development of new performances favorable to survival. Ten million years for the accelerating increases in brain capacity, accompanied by erect posture, bipedal locomotion, and precision-grip hands, is something of a record in the annals of natural selection. But then the pace increased exponentially beginning 100,000 years ago, when the brain and language reached a wholly new threshold and exosomatic evolution—the development of culture—began, which in turn reached another threshold 500 years ago when the accumulation of scientific and technological knowledge started to accelerate superexponentially.

This sequence is very heady stuff for *Homo sapiens,* who is always full of self-congratulation when it is discussed. I do not deny that I share that feeling. Yet there is nothing in it—going all the way back to DNA if you like—that tells us whether *Homo sapiens* will make it or not. We are not free from genetically determined systems: no one would want to tell his liver what to do; it knows how to do its job far better than we do. And yet, paradoxically, we possess a genetically determined system—the brain—part of which gives us an increasing array of choices based on what we learn from experience. Motive and purpose are absent from evolution, and yet, paradoxically, we possess motive and purpose. This duality of biologically generated equipment and experience-generated self, noted by Bronowski, is what *Homo sapiens* has to go on. Self-preservation is no longer the exclusive province of selfish or altruistic genes, but of imaginative representations in the brain of choices and their possible consequences. But there is a further duality, and that is between individual intentions and social results. In a kind of natural selection of social systems, technological society has smashed up all traditional societies. Can *Homo sapiens* react to the feedback in time? Possibly. Why not try? Meanwhile, the mystery mentioned at the beginning is still to be cleared up.

I have helped myself liberally to the ideas contained in several books read recently and commend them to you, only with the warning that their philosophical conclusions do not always flow from their factual premises.

The Genetic Code, Isaac Asimov; *The Identity of Man,* J. Bronowski; *Reflections on Language,* Noam Chomsky; *The Selfish Gene,* Richard Dawkins; *Life—The Unfinished Experiment,* S.E. Luria; *The Life Science,* P.B. Medawar and J.S. Medawar; *Chance and Necessity,* Jacques Monod; *The Lives of a Cell,* Lewis Thomas; *Sociobiology,* Edward O. Wilson.

November 1977

Current research indicates that anatomically, modern Homo sapiens *evolved about 200,000 years ago. Behaviorally, modern* Homo sapiens *evolved about 50,000 years ago, capable of language, music, and culture. Out of Africa migration took place about 70,000 years ago.*

Why a Tax-Based Incomes Policy Won't Work

Ten years ago I bought a violin made in 1761 and it is now worth four times the amount I paid for it. That is an example of a price determined by supply and demand. I am the inadvertent beneficiary, since I bought the violin with the intention of playing it, not of making a profit. In my activities as a publisher, nothing of the kind ever happens. If I make a profit (or manage to cover expenses), it is not due to the vagaries of supply and demand but to the markup above cost. Every two years the prices of books and periodicals must go up or we don't stay in business. The two-year pricing period is arbitrary; the regularity of price-raising is not. Of course there is always the question: will people pay more? And there is always the answer: apparently they will. A perusal of the *New York Review of Books* shows that other publishers are raising their prices. A visit to Altman's shows that the price of raincoats has gone up. It's hard to say how much; I don't keep track of that. I simply come away with the impression that prices are going up rapidly and that I am justified in raising mine too. The newspapers report an average increase of 6 percent a year. My own costs go up almost precisely at that rate. The result of these unscientific observations is that I raise my prices by about the same amount. And that, believe it or not, is how prices are set in most of the U.S. economy—not just by big operators, but by everybody except rare violin dealers and farmers. My staff also reads the papers and goes shopping. Inevitably it follows that a big part of my cost increase takes the form of higher salaries.

It warms my heart to see that a growing number of economists are coming around to the opinion that monetary and fiscal policies, short of extremes, don't greatly affect the way I and other businessmen make our prices and bargain our wages. It is always a pleasure when others get straight what you are doing, as long as what you are doing isn't crooked. That means that we are thrown back to a reconsideration of incomes policy. The version most widely discussed these days is TIP, which stands for tax-based incomes policy. The Wallich-Weintraub form of TIP uses a tax penalty against large firms that grant wage increases above a certain percentage, while the Okun form uses a tax rebate on profit and wage increases below a certain percentage. The aim, it is clear, is to arrest the wage-price spiral without resorting to wage-price controls or guideposts.

Much as I would like to support the initiative of Henry Wallich, Sidney Weintraub, and Arthur Okun, whom I respect, I am convinced that TIP suffers from the same weakness as wage-price controls and guideposts: it can be blasted to pieces by other types of inflation. If TIP had been law in 1966, it would have been undermined by Vietnam inflation just as the guideposts were. If it had been on the books in the early '70s, it would have been knocked down by the Russian grain deal, OPEC price increases, and the devaluation of the dollar. If TIP is enacted now, it will be discredited in a few years by the continued rise of prices, and we will be right back where we started from.

Stable wages and prices are simply beyond our reach until the day arrives on which we are willing to begin planning a set of coherent economic policies. It is futile to have an incomes policy if we do not also have a coordinate sectoral policy to deal with bottlenecks and shortages (which we don't face now but will face if we ever again approach the level of full resource use), a coordinate farm policy to deal with the food component in the cost of living, a coordinate foreign trade policy to deal with foreign demand and supply, and a coordinate monetary policy to deal with the cost of credit. The list could be lengthened on the slightest provocation. The point is that an incomes policy is only one element in what ought to be an anti-inflation plan. But we divide everything up in Washington. Numerous agencies and committees gather data, define problems, and make policies. We never bother to put things back together again. Is this asking for too much? If so, you and I will just go on raising our wages or prices to the extent that we have any say in the matter, TIP or no TIP, and we would use our time to better advantage reading a good novel rather than worrying about the state of the economy.

The advocates of TIP may justifiably reply: let us be more modest and begin by reducing inflation a couple of percentage points, that part attributable to wages and profits chasing one another. My answer is that we can do this for a short time, a year or two maybe, and then we will get swamped again. The real incomes of business and labor will go up (or possibly decline) at different rates. For example, TIP may allow a nominal increase (in the economic sense) of wages and prices, calculated to keep them in step, but an increase in doctors' fees will put them out of step, reducing the real increase in wages relative to prices. This imbalance in relative income shares, when it reaches an amount in excess of the tax rebate (or penalty), will result in a call for larger wage increases, which, when obtained, will raise business costs, inducing a rise in prices. We will ride up the spiral again. No formula is going to convince either side to accept a change for the worse in relative shares, but all kinds of forces in the economy are working for that change. Obviously it is not nominal wages and prices that we care about once the rate of inflation gets beyond 2 or 3 percent, but our real incomes. I have not traced the etymology of the phrase incomes policy but, fortuitously or not, it at least names the right problem: incomes.

The relative income shares of businessmen, workers, farmers, government employees, and professionals is the right problem to pay attention to because it leads us to a more comprehensive view of inflation than does single-minded concentration on wage-price guidelines, whatever the type. We must not delude ourselves into believing that we can improve the health of the patient by controlling the level of mercury in the thermometer. That was our frame of mind during the guidepost and control periods.

I have now been editor of *Challenge* for five years. Heaven forbid that I should ever contradict anything that I have written during those years. I am for an incomes policy, I have always been for an incomes policy, and I probably always will be for an incomes policy, rightly interpreted. But not in isolation. Inflation is a set of related problems and can only be dealt with by a set of related policies. I do not mean to be a naysayer but a realist when I argue that until we are ready to consider fiscal, monetary, incomes, sectoral, labor force, investment, agricultural, foreign trade, and natural resources policies together within one comprehensive system of analysis, we might as well whistle as try to control inflation.

January 1978

No need to worry about a wage-price spiral any more since unions have taken a beating and the bottom 80 percent of the gainfully employed have gained very little since 1980.

Anniversaries

After twenty years as a professional student, I sensed that the time had come to think about making a living. Since I had been a radical in the days of Joseph McCarthy, teaching was foreclosed. It became necessary for me to find an occupation which required no training, no experience, and little money. So I became a publisher. To become a publisher, a person need only publish something. Less. He need only have the intention of publishing something. On the first working day of January, twenty years ago, I opened a small office, or what might better be described as a large closet, in Manhattan. I bought second-hand a typewriter, a desk, two chairs, and an offset press. The last I installed on the premises of a printer. The desk and chairs were all right, but the typewriter and press were wrong for what I intended to do, which was publish a journal of economics translations from the Russian. By May, I had everything straightened out and published the first issue of *Problems of Economics*.

The first person I hired, as far as I can remember, was a translator. Victor Yakhontoff had been the youngest general in the tsarist army at the time of the Russian Revolution, was some fifty years older than I, and a man of imposing military bearing and regal presence. I was greatly in awe of him as he marched into my closet. I offered him the better of the two chairs. He, in turn, ignored the spartan surroundings and put me at ease. It seemed quite incongruous to me to be hiring a general before I had even reached thirty. I was aghast shortly later when I had to fire him. I had not known that a translator does best when he translates into his native language. General Yakhontoff used English words with authority, but they appeared in the order dictated by Russian syntax. After going through exquisite torture as I contemplated a deed which I classed with murder, arson, and rape, I summoned my courage and called in the general. Again he put me at ease, brushing off the whole business of his dismissal as insignificant. I am still grateful to him.

After I published *Problems of Economics*, Volume I, Number 1, the question arose, where is the money to come from to publish Number 2? I did not yet have enough subscriptions, and besides, I had made another mistake and set the subscription price too low. One possibility was to announce bankruptcy. Another was to announce a second journal and use the proceeds to publish the second issue of the first journal. This course appeared to offer a sporting chance, so I took it. I was thus able to publish the second issue of the first journal. But then the troublesome question presented itself of how to publish the first issue of the second journal and the third issue of the first journal. Obviously it was necessary to start a third journal. This I did. The process continued, first with Russian translations, then with Polish, Hungarian, Serbo-Croatian, Chinese, Japanese, French, Spanish, and German, punctuated by a few with original articles in English, until the total reached thirty. By then equilibrium had set in. The mad sprint to find money had finally subsided to a jog. It was possible to turn to other matters such as publishing books. (All the journals, by the way, are in the social sciences. Plenum and Pergamon had done the same thing in the physical sciences, perhaps not with the identical method of finance.)

All publishing houses carry on the same operations, but the degree of specialization depends on the size of the firm. In a tiny firm, the publisher edits manuscripts, worries over production schedules, fills orders, types correspondence, composes advertising copy, does something that passes for bookkeeping, makes packages, and takes them to the post office. As the firm gets bigger—if it gets bigger—the publisher sloughs off these functions one by one until there is nothing left for him to do. The test of a successful publisher is that he is not needed. To the extent that he is needed, he is not successful. The wise publisher appears once a week to collect his check and then leaves. This process of evolution fairly describes my working life for the first fifteen years. Then I made a dreadful blunder and became editor of *Challenge*.

That occurred five years ago. (*Challenge* had been published for a period of fifteen years prior to that—1952 to 1967—and so, on the theory that larger numbers are more impressive than smaller ones, we are celebrating its twentieth anniversary instead of its fifth.) The job of publisher, as I have implied, is the occupation of a gentleman. Editor—frankly, I can find no better way to describe it than that of a mad dog. Two months are required to write a carefully thought-out editorial, two months to prepare a well-planned interview, two months to select and edit the articles for an issue, and two months to fend off people who have been offended by what you have written, printed, or rejected. That is eight months' work for each issue with only two to do it in. Clearly not a decent way of life for the long haul. While the real publisher emerges at the end of the process when he has nothing to do, the real editor springs up full-grown at the beginning when he has everything to do. As he discards functions, to that extent he ceases to be editor. Only one consideration has stopped me from completing the discarding. The job of editor is second in importance only to that of president of the United States. The proof of this proposition is that it is believed by every editor in the country and possibly abroad as well. Like other editors, I have advanced solutions to all the major problems of our time. This cannot go on forever.

There is no point solving everything twice. Five years is a decently long period of time to inflict one's opinions on the world at regular intervals. I lay down that heavy commitment with this issue. (But for sentimental and honorific reasons I shall keep the title editor.)

I should not end without mentioning interviewing, an unusual art form in which I gained some experience. The first person I interviewed was Herbert Stein, then chairman of the Council of Economic Advisers. Being unsure of myself, I thought it best to attack frontally, and said, "This is my first interview. I hope you will say something brilliant." With characteristic aplomb, he replied, "That depends on the questions you ask me." Since I was a complete novice, I had written out in advance all the questions I intended to ask, in the exact order in which I intended to ask them. Herbert Stein speaks perfect prose. The result was a perfect interview which needed no editing whatsoever. After that, I gained enough confidence to write out a list of topics and possible questions, but to let the exact phrasing and sequence come spontaneously in the interview. My method was to learn the subject thoroughly and then act as devil's advocate, saying black if the person being interviewed said white and white if he said black. I wanted to get him to own up to the implications of his position, whatever those implications might be. The result, in Nat Goldfinger's case, was a terrible barrage of invectives, hurled in the general direction of my head. It was necessary to interrupt several times to explain that nothing personal was intended and that I really didn't dislike him. When I interviewed John Kenneth Galbraith, I referred to his views on the euthanasia of the stockholder. He exclaimed that he never used the word euthanasia, because it had overtones of what Hitler did to the Jews. I picked up a set of bound galleys of *Economics and the Public Purpose* and turned to the page with the offending word. After that Galbraith was suitably humble.

The interview with Leonard Woodcock led to a phone call from him several months later in which the following conversation occurred. Woodcock: "Something ought to be done about planning." I: "What do you have in mind?" Woodcock: "I don't know." I: "Do you want to make a study, issue a statement, start a committee, get a bill written, or what?" Woodcock: "What do you think?" I: "Let me think about it over the weekend." The following Monday, with Wassily Leontief's concurrence, I proposed that we start the Initiative Committee for National Economic Planning (the name was coined later by Galbraith). Woodcock agreed and we did.

Almost everyone I interviewed, no matter how seasoned a public figure, was slightly nervous while the interview was on. Every phrase had to be carefully turned, destined as it was to be preserved for all time. But as soon as the tape recorder was turned off at the end, usually a great stream of eloquence commenced which put the interview proper in the shadows. Unfortunately, I never could bring myself up to the necessary degree of deviousness to turn the tape recorder back on surreptitiously. I enjoyed interviewing and made many friends through it, but it was enormously time-consuming. Finally and reluctantly I gave it up.

Now I must apologize to all whom I have offended. To those who deplore the fact that I have written. To those who deplore the fact that I am stopping. To those whose articles I have declined to publish, a roster which includes the most distinguished economists of our age. (No one writes well every time.) To those who wanted their articles published in the front of the book but had them published in the back of the book. (Don't you realize that the back is the best part?) To those who want the subscription rate reduced. (Current projections show that the magazine will turn a profit in thirty years. I have laid aside the suggestion until then.)

One should resist stocktaking on anniversaries, but when three occur simultaneously, the temptation is irresistible. If anyone had told me as a student that I would become a businessman, the idea would have struck me as absurd, possibly vile. But no one knows who he is until the testing time comes. The world's work must get done and it turned out to my amazement that I liked doing it. A publisher, of course, is not just any businessman. He does not do anything so practical as make cars, cut hair, or even massage bodies. He simply moves words around. He is a practical organizer of the impractical, an activity that would strike any other member of the animal kingdom as lunatic. But *Homo sapiens* is compelled to live in the past, present, and future all at once, and that, among a vast assortment of other things, is the making of the publisher. Being impractical in a practical sort of way, I have found, is not an altogether nonsensical way to use one's time.

March 1978

Once More, Capitalism, Socialism, Democracy

These musings are provoked by a collection of twenty-six articles in April's *Commentary* in which the contributors discuss the theme "Capitalism, Socialism, and Democracy." I was not satisfied with any of the twenty-six, and so produce a twenty-seventh.

I would begin the discussion with the warning that capitalism and socialism are terms coined so long ago and under such different conditions from those that prevail today that they can have little value now and should be used with extreme caution. Still, despite the imprecise and often vague nature of the subject, it bears directly on what people believe in and therefore is extremely important.

Anyone who speculates about the nature of a good social order has to keep firmly in mind that we live in a technological society that sets the limits to anything that we possibly can do in the way of reform or even of revolution. To begin with, a society based on the application of science and technology cannot operate without a business class that stands for efficiency and productivity. Abolish this class and another must take its place. The ingenious discovery of new opportunities, the spirited launching of new projects, the timely mobilization of productive forces, the very act of being enterprising: these are not the tasks of engineers but of businessmen. It matters not whether they are called capitalist or socialist businessmen.

Further, a technological society cannot operate without a hierarchy of command in each enterprise. Management, whether elected or selected, must enjoy the authority to say what jobs have to be done or the jobs are not likely to be done. A business may be many things, but it is not a debating club. The proposition that the daily affairs of a business can be run by parliamentary methods is the best prescription for bringing those affairs to a standstill. Perhaps the organization of work can be made more congenial; perhaps some aspects of policy can be made through participatory democracy. But the act of management is by its very nature autocratic.

To continue with a widely accepted idea, a technological society cannot function well without observing the rule of decentralized decision making. Centralize the process and the top planners' ignorance of local requirements together with inevitable bureaucratic delays becomes intolerable. The Soviet economy is a brilliant example. Neither can a technological society function anywhere near its best without competition. I need only cite the U.S. Postal Service.

Now comes a more difficult argument: a technological society cannot function well without a division of labor between large and small firms. Suffice it to say that this division is partly dependent on the type of technology—a steel plant requires a bigger investment than a drug store; partly on the extent of the market—there is, for example, an international market for Coca-Cola; and partly on the fact that there is an irresistible drive for size to protect large investments from the vicissitudes of the market.

Finally, not a controversial point, a technological society cannot operate without some kind of coordination provided by the state. Even a monetarist will agree that the money supply should be planned. I would go further and assert that the balance between industries needs to be coordinated where the market fails. Perhaps I should make explicit what is implicit in each of these separate considerations: a technological society requires a set of interconnected markets as its underlying mode of organization.

What I have just described, except for the matter about coordination, must surely conjure up the picture of an unbearable social order. Add to the description a wealthy upper class which owns a disproportionate share of business and disposes of a disproportionate share of power, and the picture becomes positively outrageous. Much of the history of the last 200 years is an account of revolts against this order and of movements which have aimed to offset its hardships. It doesn't matter for present purposes whether the social legislation adopted to mitigate the effects of technological society is regarded as having been granted as concessions by the bourgeoisie or as having been wrung from them by the oppressed: the legislation exists. The best current depiction of business and upper-class power is contained in Charles E. Lindblom's *Politics and Markets*, where the influence of private power on government and public opinion is described in the most vivid and unmistakable terms that one could possibly want. Lindblom would agree that the influence does not run in one direction only: the welfare state is testimony to that. Nevertheless the concentration of power and privilege is still a stubborn fact to conjure with. This brings us to the ideal advanced by most of the twenty-six essayists in *Commentary*: whatever the type of society, the dispersion of power among many centers is an essential prerequisite of democracy. To what extent is this ideal realizable in a technological society?

Here my speculations about a good social order will take the form of some freely imaginative exercises in society building. I will consider various combinations of the following three factors, with all other things remaining the same (as much as is reasonable): the existence or nonexistence of an upper class; the prevalence of private or public ownership; the presence or absence of what I shall call public enlightenment. The terms can be briefly explained. Upper class is to mean a concentration of wealth in a relatively small number of hands. Public ownership refers only to ownership of large corporations, no more than a thousand. Public enlightenment means that various classes, strata, groups, or individuals outside the upper class can distinguish between their own interests and the interests of business when there is a distinction to be made, and that they are also able to muster some minimum level of public spirit. I also assume the existence of that much-maligned arrangement, bourgeois democracy. Let us see how it all turns out.

1. Unadulterated Capitalism. This is the capitalism criticized by Karl Marx and Friedrich Engels. The upper class is intact; all business is private; there is no general public enlightenment—business interests are supreme. In other words, power is concentrated in the hands of a small minority, notwithstanding the existence of formal democracy. We must agree with Marx and Engels in finding the situation intolerable.

2. Welfare State Capitalism. The upper class is intact; business is private (or largely private, even given a large public sector); there is public enlightenment—by reason of which the balance of power and of benefits is much more equitable than in the previous case, but by no means egalitarian. We in the United States, I think it is clear, stand somewhere between case (1) and case (2), possibly two-thirds of the way toward case (2). Those in Western Europe and Japan stand even closer to case (2). The ideal of dispersed power is far from realized, yet public enlightenment mobilizes a considerable measure of offsetting power.

3. Bastard Capitalism. In this case we assume that there is no upper class; that business is private; and that public enlightenment exists. I see no reason why almost everything that socialists ever wanted and that is achievable in the world as it exists, or can exist, within the bounds of a technological society, cannot be achieved here, despite the fact that we assume that business is privately owned. We have posited an egalitarian society, which means that the ownership of business is much more widely held than it is now; and public enlightenment, which means that the rules by which business operates must conform to the public interest (or interests) to a much greater extent than they do now.

4. Bastard Socialism. Here there is an upper class, but there is public ownership and public enlightenment. It is necessary to say that the only kind of public ownership consistent with the conditions laid down earlier for the best functioning of a technological society is a system of public holding companies in which the managers of enterprises remain independent decision-makers with only general policy handed down by the directors of the holding companies. This ownership setup is every bit as compatible (or incompatible) with the prescription of multiple centers of power as private ownership is. In both cases the degree of influence and privilege of the upper class (who under the public ownership assumption presumably own government bonds) will be the reciprocal of the degree of public enlightenment. The often cited bugbear that public ownership is necessarily the equivalent of centralized—and therefore extremely dangerous—power is ideological, not factual. We have legions of public agencies that are uncontrollable. The obvious ought to be added that public ownership per se is no indication whatsoever of how industry will be run.

5. *Slightly Tarnished Socialism.* There is no other kind. In this case there is no upper class; there is public ownership; and there is public enlightenment. It is Slightly Tarnished because, while we assume egalitarianism and a noncentralized form of public ownership of large corporations, we also assume what cannot be assumed away: a technological society with a business class (managers); a hierarchy of command within firms; and a large private sector of small entrepreneurs. (Why not public ownership of small business? No socialist in his right mind could want a public authority responsible for 12 million enterprises.) This is a possible socialism, but it is still a society of irreducible privilege, privilege inherent in the acts of management and entrepreneurship, privilege which cannot be abolished but only circumscribed.

6. *Confused Egalitarianism.* (There being eight possible combinations of three sets of alternatives, I must go on, but it is downhill the rest of the way.) As in the case of Bastard Capitalism, we assume no upper class, private ownership, but this time no enlightenment. This appears to be an unpleasant, grasping state of affairs.

7. *Confused Socialism.* Much worse than (5), for while we do not have an upper class and do have public ownership, public enlightenment is missing. This is an invitation to nastiness.

8. *The Soviet System.* Here we suspend our assumption of democracy and postulate an upper class (no one said it had to be a capitalist upper class), public ownership, but alas! no public enlightenment. Restore the assumption of democracy, and we have—the *British System.*

With this profusion of more or less distasteful possibilities, what can a person believe in? Is it possible to be passionately dedicated to Bastard Capitalism or to Slightly Tarnished Socialism? To work heart and soul for a slight improvement in an imperfectible system? To be an avid socialist and fight for a system that contains a large dose of capitalism, or a dedicated capitalist and defend one with a large dose of socialism? In the nineteenth century, it was possible to believe in systems. Socialism and millennialism were one and the same. From some pens, capitalism and millennialism were almost the same. The nineteenth century proposed; the twentieth disposed. It is no longer rational to believe in the millennium (perhaps it once was), but it is still rational, and even salutary, to think that a good social order is possible, though not inevitable, within the limits imposed by technological society. However, it is very awkward, as I have tried to suggest, to think about the issue as a contest between capitalism and socialism, since the underlying reality is incredibly more ambiguous than Marx could have imagined a hundred years ago and the problem of power incredibly more obstinate. In his book, Lindblom concludes: "The large private corporation fits oddly into democratic theory and vision. Indeed, it does not fit." I fear that his statement applies to large business, private and public, and that the best that we can do under any circumstances is to find an acceptable way of handling this indigestible anomaly without expecting that we can make it go away.

July 1978

We have moved far away from Welfare State Capitalism and are now one-third (or so) away from Unadulterated Capitalism. As for my announcement in the previous article that I would no longer write for Challenge, *I must have changed my mind.*

Is Inflation Inevitable in Post-Keynesian Capitalism?

I think not. But I think that we must deal with inflation in a way suitable to an economy where wages, prices, and business cycles are largely the results of direct decisions, rather than the resultants of impersonal market forces.

I doubt that the president's anti-inflation program is going to succeed. Inflation fever is so high that the people who make the decisions in businesses and unions are more likely to expect the current rate to continue than to expect the president's plan to work. They will act accordingly. Tremendous pressures from food, housing, energy, and medical care are certain (these increasing at the rate of 11.6 percent as of September). A tax rebate on wages and salaries is uncertain. Nobody is sure of anything, which means that the guidelines will be praised, and then disregarded. After that, possibly with that, ineluctably comes the decision to bring on the recession.

Almost everybody hates the thought of it; almost everybody knows it is no permanent solution; but if we want to stop inflation now there is only one way to do it, and that is by an across-the-board wage-price freeze. That is easy to say, if not to swallow. The real question is, what to do next? Can anything be done that hasn't been done before, during the six months or year of a freeze, that has the slightest chance of success?

The one arrangement that hasn't been tried is incomes policy by agreement, incomes policy by consent rather than by imposition. What does it mean? It means that leaders of government, business, and labor—they all contribute to inflation—sit down together and thrash out an agreement on a noninflationary policy for wages, prices, and taxes, as well as supply management in the inflationary sectors of the economy. It makes eminent good sense to ask the people who are supposed to carry out the program to help make the program, to help make the analysis, to help consider the alternatives, and finally, to make the commitment to what they had a hand in shaping.

How can it be done? In various ways, but the gist is this. Congress, in conjunction with the president, might set up a top-level, permanent, independent Anti-Inflation Council composed of representatives of Congress itself, the administration, business, and unions. The council should include chief executives of corporations that act as price leaders and presidents of unions that make the key wage bargains. It should have the support of a technical staff able to do the necessary econometric work, including the study of what to do in particular sectors that contribute heavily to inflation. Above all, the council should be instructed to deal with all major sources of inflation together in one analytical and policy framework, rather than piecemeal as we do now.

Can an Anti-Inflation Council do the job? We can specify on paper various ways to have price stability. The problem is not inherently or logically insoluble. What so far has proved intractable is finding a way to consider together the strategic, interacting decisions of business, unions, and government that produce—but do not have to produce—inflation. At best this is not easy. But two elements have been missing from previous and existing efforts, and some day we are going to have to include them. One is participation in a dialogue of those who now vie with each other to maintain or improve their income shares, and who in the process produce inflation which nullifies all the individual efforts. The other is comprehensiveness of view, which means that those who participate in the dialogue sit down and systematically consider the whole economy and discuss what each (including Congress and the president) can contribute to an overall anti-inflation program.

Is the great effort needed to set up an Anti-Inflation Council worthwhile? Yes, because the cost of failure is an engineered recession, a return to high unemployment, loss of hundreds of billions of dollars in potential output, and the decimation of social programs which we cannot blithely pretend are superfluous.

Though a social contract type of incomes policy is new to us, it is not alien to our preference for bargaining and compromise, with concessions made for concessions in return, or our practice of cooperation between government and the private economy. The fact is that in post-Keynesian capitalism, large corporations and unions have a lot of muscle, some of which they use to make inflation. It can only be unmade with a mechanism that takes into account this power, but that also reasserts the right of the majority who don't want inflation to rule.

January 1979

The president at the time was Jimmy Carter. In fact, a severe recession was engineered by Federal Reserve chairman Paul Volcker, who raised the federal funds interest rate from 11.2 percent in 1979 to 20 percent in 1981. The inflation rate came down from 12.5 percent in 1981 to 3.2 percent in 1983. As expected, stagflation was clubbed to death with a blunt instrument.

When Britain Ran
Out of Wood

Our energy crisis is not original. In the middle of the sixteenth century Britain began to run out of wood. By 1700 it had converted almost completely to coal. I learned this from an article by John U. Nef in *Civilization,* a collection from *Scientific American.* The effects of Britain's conversion to coal were immense. It is a little humbling to realize that we are not the first to live through such a transition, and encouraging to know that our predecessors somehow survived. They even flourished. The transition was not without costs, but who can doubt that we will do better this time since we have the earlier example before us.

People once scoffed at the idea that there could be a shortage of trees, but during the reigns of Elizabeth I and James I from 1558 to 1625 the shortage occurred and the price of wood outdistanced the price of everything else on the market in a general European inflation. Deforestation in all parts of the British Isles had been brought on by a pell-mell expansion of agriculture, industry, and trade, while the number of people living in England and Wales nearly doubled (3 million in the 1530s to nearly 6 million in the 1690s). A rush to the cities increased the demand for capital construction and transport. London grew almost tenfold from 1534 to 1696, ending the century with a population over 530,000.

Small quantities of coal had been burned in Europe since the twelfth century in areas where it had been accessible from outcropping seams. But medieval craftsmen turned up their noses at coal fires because the smoke and fumes tarnished their wares. Then all that changed. By the time of the civil war in the 1640s, Londoners depended on coal to heat their homes despite the grime. Coastal shipments grew twenty times between 1550 and 1700. At the end of the sixteenth century, Lord Buckhurst introduced a novel concept to the world by requiring customs officials to calculate the "rate of growth" of coal shipments from Newcastle. When it was found to be increasing rapidly, as the lord suspected, taxes were duly imposed.

The fumes of coal spoiled most products and this drawback had to be overcome. After 1610, glass began to be made in reverberatory furnaces, in which arched roofs reflected the heat, preventing contamination. As a further precaution, the raw materials, potash and sand, were held in clay crucibles. Both these methods served as prototypes for a large number of industrial processes. After long periods of experimentation, methods using coal became cheaper and more productive than those using wood. One industry after another converted. Here is a list given by Nef: brickmaking; nonferrous smelting; textile steaming and dyeing; manufacturing salt, alum, copperas, saltpeter, gunpowder, starch, candles, preserved foods, vinegar, Scotch whiskey, beer, sugar, soap, and finally, by the 1780s, pig and bar iron.

Nef relates that in the seventeenth century, not only were an increasing number of homes built with brick and stone instead of wood, but the mortar in the walls was made from coal-burned limestone; the glass in the windows was produced in coal furnaces; and the coal-burning fireplaces, the iron grates, and the chimneys themselves were made with coal.

By the 1660s, the price of wood had stopped rising. But the shortage persisted because wood was still used in increasing quantities for ships, carriages, and wagons, while forests were being replaced by farms, pastures, foundries, and mines. The deficiency was made up by imports from the American colonies and the Baltic.

The massive shift to coal created the worrisome problem of how to pump water out of the mines. The use of inefficient animal and water power began to drive down the rate of profit. In 1712, Thomas Newcomen installed an ingenious new device called a steam engine at a colliery in Staffordshire and the solution was at hand. And not only that. So was the railroad, mechanization, the age of iron and steel, the Industrial Revolution.

Is this a preview for us? The parallels are clear. They ran out of wood, its price soared, they substituted coal, they ran into severe technical problems. In solving them they created a whole new technology, the technology created new wealth, but it also created social havoc. Now the scale is much larger and we find ourselves at a much later moment in the same process of expanding population, dwindling resources, technical solutions, and social havoc. That's why I'm skeptical when advised that we should just let the market do its stuff. The technical virtuosity will be forthcoming but I doubt if we are about to do the Industrial Revolution all over again in utter disregard of its effects. I think that Robert Heilbroner is right when he says in *The End of Boom and Crash* that some kind of planning, or programming, or supply-side management (call it what you like) is inevitable with the kind of future we face.

But that's enough unpleasantness for now. Let's return to history. John U. Nef reminds us that in the tenth and eleventh centuries the Chinese also burned coal in many industries, but it came to nothing. That's the point.

We can't conclude that the Industrial Revolution happened just because the trees didn't grow fast enough in England. The same forces that depleted England's forests in the sixteenth century brought the English middle classes to power in the seventeenth. Oh well. It seems impossible to avoid politics even if one tries.

November 1979

Back to
Laissez Faire,
1988–1999

Thirty Years of Challenge

Thirty years of *Challenge*? Well, that is a cause for celebration. I lift my glass of orange juice to its success during the next thirty.

But I'm not quite sure what "success" is. A few months ago I read about a publisher who had achieved his lifetime goals in publishing and retired, or joined the navy, I forget which. That made me ponder my own lifetime goals as a publisher. I had to confess that I never had any.

It seemed impractical and unsportsmanlike to think some up retroactively. I reproached myself for a few days for this oversight, but then it occurred to me that at least I did have an implicit goal. I learned it from my father, who was a doctor: first do no harm.

I think that I can say with confidence that *Challenge* has done no harm, nor has anything else that I have published over the last thirty years. No one to my knowledge has ever been killed or maimed as a result of my publishing activities, although I do confess that I have met a few people who should have been slightly injured.

That raises the opposite question, which is whether *Challenge* has done any good. A much more difficult question. Certainly we cannot claim to have any influence with the current administration, since no one that I know of has advocated gargantuan twin deficits.

But I look at all the avowed and unavowed candidates in alarm. They are more terrified of revealing their economic commitments than they are of revealing their infidelities. If they have any economic commitments, these must be kept absolutely secret until after the election.

I can only conclude that the connection between private economic thoughts and public economic policy is a tenuous and unpredictable one that operates on the lottery principle. Perhaps the public will be lucky enough to elect a reader of *Challenge* as president within the next thirty years and the Age of the Lost Lottery will come to an end.

I agree with Chekhov that in the very long run people do finally learn something. But I wouldn't want to be held to my thirty-year forecast. Several centuries more of *Challenge* may be required to see concrete results.

One of my greatest satisfactions in dealing with economists came in 1974. I read a small article in the *New York Times* reporting that a friend and former UN economist, Henry Spetter, had been forced to return to Bulgaria, and had been tried and sentenced to death for espionage. I could not imagine

Henry Spetter as a spy. Even more difficult was to imagine any secrets that Bulgaria had that were worth anybody's life.

I called about thirty economists in the course of an afternoon and everyone to the last man and woman agreed to sign an appeal for clemency directed to the Bulgarian ambassadors to the United States and UN and to the Bulgarian prime minister. The *Times* cooperated and put the appeal in the paper the next day. Robert Lekachman and I went to see the deputy ambassador to the UN (or whatever he is called), delivered the appeal, sparred with him a little about U.S.-Bulgarian relations, but mainly asked for a humanitarian gesture.

Not long after, Henry Spetter was sent under guard to Israel and released, and his family soon followed. That was more than Bob Lekachman and I and all the others could have hoped for. Frankly, when I think of my opponents on economic issues, I also think about how they joined me to help Henry Spetter (I do not mean to imply that all thirty economists were opponents) and I am not entirely dismayed to be called an economist.

In 1975 and 1976 I worked as coordinator for the Initiative Committee for National Economic Planning, for which *Challenge* was not responsible. But I did meet Leonard Woodcock through an interview, and the friendship that followed led to the committee.

There was a great uproar in the press about planning, but all the committee wanted to do was to prod the federal government into coordinating its economic activities and projecting the consequences of these activities the same as any well-run business does.

In retrospect, I see how courageous it was, not to say foolhardy, for Senators Humphrey and Javits to sponsor a bill that called for setting up congressional and administration agencies to gather data, make alternative projections, and attempt to coordinate the federal government's disparate monetary and fiscal efforts and their impact on various sectors of the economy. Do you truly believe that such an effort would have produced a worse mess than we are in now?

At any rate, the final result was the ceremonial Humphrey-Hawkins Act, passed in October 1978 as a gesture to Senator Humphrey, who had died of cancer that January.

I suppose that, just as Senator Mondale was foolish to mention the word "taxes" in his election campaign, the Initiative Committee was foolish to mention "planning." Every presidential candidate has learned the lesson of Mondale and I have learned the lesson of the Initiative Committee. Never, never will I use the word "planning" again, although I may indulge myself to the extent of saying "programming," "projecting," or "budgeting."

As a publisher I plan my business with extreme care, even fanatically. But this kind of planning, as we know, is virtuous and we all hope that the Russians try it out. Nevertheless, I must confide to you that no matter how carefully its finances are planned, *Challenge* is subsidized by other publications.

If only I had conceived a lifetime goal when I started and defined "success," I would not have done anything as frivolous as publishing *Challenge.* But now *Challenge* must go on and I must ask indulgence for falling slightly short of being the ideal economic man, although I am trying to make up for it in other ways.

At this anniversary, I salute some of the contributors I have known. To Herb Stein, for his integrity as a conservative. To the memory of Walter Heller, for his cheerful can-do attitude. To Kenneth Boulding, who introduced economics to the social sciences and who showed so much tolerance to me as a student. To John Kenneth Galbraith, master detector of foolishness, as well as my friend and mentor. To Milton Friedman, with whom I enjoyed arguing. To the memory of Gunnar Myrdal, a gracious and unassuming giant. To Wassily Leontief, one of the few authentic geniuses of economics. To Murray Weidenbaum, the most considerate adversary known to me. To Robert Heilbroner, the polymath who has brought breadth and depth to economics.

To all the contributors and readers of *Challenge,* I again lift my glass of orange juice.

January 1988

The Speaker Speaks

A review of *To Renew America,* by Newt Gingrich. New York:
HarperCollins, 1995.

I approached the reading of the Speaker's book with considerable apprehension, expecting that I would have to write nasty things about it, and I
hate to write nasty things. Greatly to my relief, I find that I am in agreement
with much of what the Speaker has to say.

To Renew America is organized into twenty-nine chapters covering at least
twenty-nine subjects, ranging from the Third Wave Information Age to English as the American Language. Some of the chapters are three or four pages
long and at least one is a mere two pages. Since the Speaker is a discursive
writer, the amount of space per subject does not allow for close reasoning.
We have a series of assertions backed up by anecdotes. Jack Kemp said this,
Tom Kean said that. But no matter. We can find documentation elsewhere.

I could not and I would not, in a short review, comment on all twenty-nine
subjects, so I will limit myself to a handful that are of particular urgency.

Let us start with welfare. The Speaker doesn't like the welfare system,
partly because it is a barrier to work and partly because it promotes character flaws. With a little money and a little initiative, poor people can start
small businesses and they no longer will be poor. But since welfare support
by government kills initiative, tough love is needed and tough love means
largely removing the baleful influence of government support. Poor schools,
poor housing, inadequate medical care, broken homes, and the absence of
jobs certainly make life more difficult, but the Speaker personally knows
people who have overcome these obstacles.

Unfortunately, many poor people are unwilling to make the necessary effort.
These are the undeserving poor. The undeserving poor are the lazy, the alco-
holics, the crack addicts, the teenage out-of-wedlock mothers, the criminals.
They can be helped only by tough love; that is, by not helping them.

I should interject here that there is another point of view. A number of
sociologists compare the poor to troops who have been through a war. Some
survive with only bitter memories. But others suffer pathologies and need
psychiatric help, halfway houses, and other forms of rehabilitation. (See the
new book by Herbert Gans, *The War Against the Poor.*)

But let us contemplate the notion of the undeserving poor. Surely the

Speaker will agree that we cannot in all fairness restrict this idea to the poor. There must also be undeserving rich, undeserving office and factory workers, and even undeserving members of Congress. And surely the Speaker will agree that the American system of jurisprudence demands that due process be followed in identifying this possibly large group of individuals who are undeserving. You can't just go around pinning labels on people, can you? That smacks of trying to distance yourself from a significant part of the human race.

We will therefore have to set up Morality Courts all over the United States and establish objective standards by which to divide the deserving from the undeserving. The punishment is quite clear. No welfare for the undeserving poor. No mortgage tax deductions for undeserving middle-class homeowners. No subsidized grazing rights for undeserving ranchers. No tax advantages for undeserving takeover speculators who contribute nothing to productivity. No subsidies or tax breaks to undeserving corporations, which, according to the Cato Institute, come to $238 billion, compared to $47 billion for welfare and food stamps combined. Also, no eligibility for reelection for undeserving senators and congressmen, thereby eliminating the need for a term-limit amendment to the Constitution. A further benefit of Morality Courts is that they will require enormous numbers of people to run them, thus practically wiping out unemployment at a single stroke.

One final word on poverty. If the extent of poverty depends heavily on character or the lack of it, it follows that we need a Character Index to track its historical trends. I constructed such an index, and it amazed me to find how closely character fluctuates with the rate of employment. The higher the rate of employment, the higher the Character Index. Here is something for the Speaker to think about. Monetary, fiscal, and incomes policies that increase employment also tend to improve character and, by some as yet inexplicable process, actually diminish the number of the undeserving poor.

I can tell you as a certainty that the Speaker is against high interest rates because they produce recession (p. 67). Here is a place to start. How about some jaw-jaw with Alan Greenspan, Mr. Speaker? What the Speaker knows as well as I do is that if unemployment had been 5.5 percent in 1992 instead of 7.3 percent, the United States would have been $271 billion richer in gross domestic product, generating additional tax revenues to reduce the deficit or possibly even to spend on our decaying infrastructure or even on such exotic things as medical and scientific research or schools.

Another attribute of the Speaker that pleases me is that he is, in his own words, a cheap hawk. The Cold War is over, but now even greater dangers lurk in the shadows: terrorism; nuclear larceny; biological weapons; rogue states led by irrational men. Quite so. But our current military budget is $264 billion while the military budgets of all the other NATO members together amount to $147.6 billion. The combined military budgets of the putative rogue states Cuba, Libya, Syria, Iraq, Iran, and North Korea equal $9.64 billion (Seymour Melman, *New York Times,* June 26). A really cheap hawk—and I have no doubt that the Speaker is one—can afford to be absolutely breathtakingly cheap when you compare these numbers, can still be a genuine hawk, can reduce the deficit, can help the country become more competitive on the world market, and just simply be as pleased as the boy who found the cookie (p. 245).

Now a word about the American past. The American past is a great past and so the Speaker was taught when he was in school. And he was proud of that past and sees that pride being eroded by revisionists and multiculturalists who want to tarnish that past and tear down that pride. Perhaps the Speaker will some day write an inspiring account of the American past, but also an honest one that will not shrink from confronting the massacre and expropriation of the Indians, the enslavement of Africans, the expropriation of vast territories from Mexico, the impoverishment of millions in the crashes of the nineteenth century and in the Great Depression of the twentieth century, the racism, the anti-Semitism, the violence in the media, and—one must not be too delicate about this—the ruin that the liberals have brought upon this country. This book will be inspiring but honest. It will give all the facts, but it will show how this country is still the land of hope.

Next to last, I want to mention the vexed question of guns. "The Second Amendment is a political right written into our Constitution for the purpose of protecting individuals from their own government" (p. 202). The Speaker rightly takes President Clinton to task for foolishly thinking that the Second Amendment is for the purpose of protecting the right to hunt ducks. But apparently it means that if you don't like the government you can form a militia and take the law into your own hands. I hate to cavil with the Speaker, but if he is not contemplating future skirmishes between private militias and the U.S. armed forces, what is he contemplating? A recent article in the *New York Times* (July 20) by a judge in Montana described threats on her life by persons affiliated with the Militia of Montana over the appearance of a man in court in response to a summons for three traffic tickets. The man claimed he was not bound by the laws of Montana. Well, Mr. Speaker, we are faced with a dilemma here if we accept your interpretation of the right to bear arms. It is not possible to argue that the militias have the right to overthrow the government and the rest of us have the right to defend it and still be adjudged sane. Perhaps you will un-riddle this in future pronouncements.

Finally: "Unfortunately the federal government is going to remain a large system for the foreseeable future. Even a remarkably small federal government would spend well over $1 trillion a year and have well over a million civilian employees. There are still things that people expect from the government" (p. 224). Without quibbling about the exactitude of the millions and the trillions, we can see that this is a very hardheaded Speaker speaking. Government as a supplement to and a correction of the market system has always been, is, and will continue to be, an intrinsic part of capitalism. The real debate is not the shoddy one on the meretricious issue of whether the government is good or evil, but who will benefit from government policies. The constituency of the Republican Party is the well-off, and the well-off have been helped. The rich have gotten richer, everybody else has gotten poorer. No surprise here. The policies and practices of the 1920s prevail. Government as bold innovator, as guarantor of full employment, as supporter of the majority interest, has been ditched. The New Deal spirit of trial-and-error and trial once again to help the struggling has been denigrated and reviled. It is easy to distrust, even hate, a myopic government of the privileged. With sadness I am forced to confess that it is hard to believe that Newt Gingrich's jaunty, rear-looking fantasies, his breezy confidence in once-over-lightly nostrums, or his Never-Neverland schemes to reengineer the human soul, will be of much help.

But undoubtedly he is being ironic.

September 1995

The Rise and Fall of the New Deal

A review of *The End of Reform: New Deal Liberalism in Recession and War,* by Alan Brinkley. New York: Alfred A. Knopf, 1995.

I grew up during the Depression. I listened to the fireside chats. I saw Roosevelt on the Pathé News. I liked the man immensely. He was serious but cheerful. He spoke in words that I could understand. He radiated an optimism that was contagious. Under his guidance great projects were afoot. I knew the country was in good hands. And I argued the point repeatedly and vociferously with my parents and actually got them to vote for Roosevelt instead of Landon in 1936, even though they had voted for Hoover in the previous election. I had seen people lined up at soup kitchens in the movies and knew about the millions of unemployed. A few blocks from my house, I saw rows of unpainted, dilapidated shacks with black kids running around outside in tattered clothes without shoes. It seemed like a dirty deal to me.

But most of the businessmen I heard talking, and the ones I read about in the papers, hated Roosevelt's guts. They hated the PWA and the WPA, they hated the CCC and the TVA, but most of all they hated Social Security and the Wagner Act, which guaranteed unions the right to organize. Here's how businessmen saw it: The government was invading their turf. It was telling business what to do. It was violating the sacred right of the businessman and the worker to make a contract without outside interference. And the government was going into business for itself, competing with legitimate private interests. What, then, was the business program? Go away. Leave us alone. Stop undermining business confidence. The economy will come around when the meddling stops. And meanwhile, what about the unemployed? It's not my business.

So it appeared to me when I was growing up. The experience engendered a lifelong skepticism about the pronouncements of businessmen. Yet it is clear that Franklin Roosevelt failed in his main task, which was to end the Depression. This didn't happen until the beginning of the Second World War, when both military and civilian demand shot up, bringing about full employment and a great increase in production. Wage and price controls, supplemented by rationing, kept the rise in the retail price index within tolerable limits, a fact of some interest.

But how can we condemn Roosevelt's performance, since the management of demand was not in the conventional economics tool kit at the time? This is a difficult question to answer. Roosevelt was deeply committed to the classical arguments for a balanced budget and departed from his beliefs only out of the sheer necessity of providing relief to millions of unemployed and getting some reforms going that he thought were necessary for recovery. Even after the recession of 1937 (a euphemism referred to in the subtitle of Alan Brinkley's book), when Marriner Eccles and Leon Henderson finally convinced Roosevelt that deficit spending was essential in itself, not just as an adjunct of some special program, the amount of spending was still too small to bring about full recovery.

Meanwhile, the Depression in Hitler Germany was effectively over in 1936, much as we hate to acknowledge anything positive coming out of that regime. Sweden is a much more benign case, where the leading economists concluded early in the 1930s that government borrowing, public employment, support of farm prices, and a strong social security system would end the Depression. (See *A Journey Through Economic Time* by John Kenneth Galbraith.) Keynes had a lot of company, but Roosevelt was not among them. We had to wait until 1946 before demand management became part of the American political canon, when it was embodied in the Employment Act of that year.

Aside from providing relief and temporary jobs, Roosevelt was persuaded that the road to recovery lay in the reform of the capitalist system. If the leaders of banking and industry couldn't run the economy in the public interest, then let the rules be changed so that they could. Banking and industry had agglomerated into huge concentrations of wealth, prices and output were determined at management meetings, not by the impersonal forces of the market, and the public suffered the consequences. So why not let the public have a say in the matter? The whole system was at risk. Roosevelt was trying to save the hides as well as the assets of the masters of industry and finance, but they didn't get it.

Against accusations of communism, socialism, and fascism, Congress passed the National Industrial Recovery Act in 1933 in an effort to establish tripartite cooperation in industry and trade. The National Recovery Administration, under the flamboyant direction of General Hugh S. Johnson, set aside the antitrust laws and persuasively invited each industry to set up trade associations called code authorities. Under the watchful eye of Hugh Johnson and his staff, each code authority established industry-wide prices and output quotas in the fond hope that the downward spiral of prices, production, and employment would be arrested. Against the anguished cries of businessmen, workers were invited to form unions to bargain wages and hours under the notorious Section 7a of the act. Marvelous to behold, everyone flocked to sign up. Complying companies were allowed to display a blue eagle, thought up by Johnson and his cronies as a public relations ploy, and nobody wanted to be left out. I remember blue eagles sprouting up all over, on store fronts, on boxes in grocery stores, in ads in the papers. The blue eagle made everyone in the country feel good because it signified that something positive was being done.

But after two years the whole structure began to collapse because the big companies soon dominated the code authorities and labor was too weak to drag itself to the bargaining table. When the NIRA was declared unconstitutional by the Supreme Court in 1935, the administration let it die, relieved that it did not have to go on with this farce. But wait a minute. Government, business, and labor have achieved various degrees of constructive cooperation in postwar Germany, Japan, Sweden, and elsewhere. So the idea wasn't wholly perverse; the conditions just weren't right for it to succeed.

But Section 7a wasn't allowed to die. In 1935, conscience-driven by the relentless eloquence of Senator Robert Wagner, Congress passed the National Labor Relations Act, probably the most detested piece of legislation of all the detested legislation of the New Deal. Unions could organize and bargain collectively; it was the law. But the police were still called out and thugs were still hired to beat up workers and break strikes. If you want a first-person account, read eighty-year-old Genora Johnson Dollinger's description of the 1937 sit-down strike at the General Motors plant in Flint, Michigan. (See *Coming of Age* by Studs Turkel.) Nevertheless, a tremendous grassroots movement to organize unions sprang up in industry, culminating in the formation of the CIO under John L. Lewis, the next-most-hated man in America after Roosevelt. Without a doubt, the unions became a powerful counterweight to big business and led to a redistribution of income downward and the creation of a mass consumption society. How intriguing to think of the possibility of a repeat performance.

The twin and counterpart of the NIRA was the 1933 Agricultural Adjustment Act for farming. Paradoxically, the great corporate concentrations that prevented the market from working were found to be the cause of the Depression in the industrial sector, while the very success in the operation of the market was found to be the cause in the farm sector. The many small producers had no control over prices or output, so as unsold goods piled up, prices plummeted and farmers went broke in droves. The AAA made the federal government a partner of every farmer. The terms of the partnership were: limit output and we (the government) will support prices. In 1936 the Supreme Court, much to the dismay of Roosevelt and Secretary of Agriculture Henry Wallace, found the act unconstitutional. But it was soon reenacted with terms to bypass the objections and continues to this day as the modus operandi of the farm sector.

Now for a comic interlude. In 1937, a professor of law at Yale named Thurman Arnold wrote a fine book called *The Folklore of Capitalism*, in which he argued that society needed great corporate organizations but was not reconciled to them, and to salve its conscience, went through the ceremonial pretense of enforcing the antitrust laws. What could be more comical than to appoint Thurman Arnold to head the Antitrust Division of the Justice Department a year after his book was published? More absurd, he launched more antitrust suits than all his predecessors combined. But he was not against bigness; he was in favor of the Antitrust Division acting as a referee to maintain competition among the big players. More strange still was the fact that the administration had decided to abolish competition in 1933 and plan the economy under the NIRA, while in 1937 it decided to smite big business and restore competition. The explanation for this strange behavior is that Roosevelt had advisers on both sides of the issue and when one theory didn't work, he tried another. By the time Arnold resigned in 1943, the military-industrial establishment had come into existence as a result of wartime necessity and antitrust was consigned to the museum of antiquities.

In the long run, the piece of New Deal legislation that resulted in the greatest happiness for the greatest number came about through the persistence of the first woman to hold a cabinet post and the only woman in the Roosevelt cabinet, Secretary of Labor Frances Perkins. I refer to the Social Security Act of 1935. Belatedly and halfheartedly, since Congress watered down many provisions of the original bill, the United States joined the ranks of the European welfare states by providing for unemployment insurance, retirement and survivors' pensions, disability payments, and aid to families with dependent children. (Roosevelt used the ruse of calling Social Security "insurance" to keep future legislators from tampering with it.)

After all this feverish activity and more, the economy went into recession in 1937. Thereafter the legislative aspect of the New Deal was essentially over. The conservatives in Congress could no longer be prodded along under the goad of public wrath. Soon Roosevelt became preoccupied with the growing menace of war and had no time or energy to spare to fight for domestic programs. By the time the war began, he had completely dropped his antibusiness rhetoric. Big business and government cooperated with the acquiescence of labor. In Roosevelt's mind, this was the only way to achieve the prodigious feats of production that were needed to win the war.

Alan Brinkley, professor of American history at Columbia University and a contributing editor to *The American Prospect*, has retold the story of the New Deal for a definite reason, and that is to help in the project of constructing a robust contemporary version of liberalism. Given the performance of our economy and society, I am sure that no apology needs to be given for such an effort. *The End of Reform* is an investigation of New Deal liberalism, how it started out as a wide assortment of expedient and visionary programs and finally narrowed down after the Second World War to Keynesian monetary and fiscal activism aimed at full employment. Reform of capitalism was abandoned as difficult and unnecessary. In the last few paragraphs of his book, Alan Brinkley wonders out loud if the abandonment of reform didn't contribute to the present predicament of liberalism. The name of the book is *The End of Reform,* but the message of the book is: it is time for the beginning of reform.

November 1995

Ownership and Control

A review of *Rethinking Corporate Governance for the Twenty-First Century,*
by Margaret M. Blair. Washington, DC: Brookings Institution Press, 1995.

The *ancien régime* has returned. I do not refer to France before 1789, but to the United States before 1933. Unless you are old enough to have lived through the 1920s, you will not have seen a time when the few hundred largest corporations were as free of constraints as they are now. Federal regulations of corporate behavior to save the public from egregious injury have been lifted and unions have declined from their one-time status as muscular defenders against the depredations of big business to what they are now, an anemic nuisance.

The results are not in the least unexpected. The really rich upper half of 1 percent of the population have gotten majestically richer, the next half a percent have gotten moderately richer, while the bottom 99 percent have either barely held their own or have gotten poorer. Take-home pay of chief executive officers in the amount of ten million dollars or more per annum is regularly approved by boards of directors, appointed, of course, by the CEOs themselves. With such attractive prizes at stake, corporate raids by outsiders have become commonplace while leveraged buyouts by established management seeking to retain the prizes they already command are everyday news.

Meanwhile, the pension funds, mutual funds, and all the other funds that manage gigantic blocks of shares for their numerous, dispersed, and powerless shareholders demand the highest returns possible in the shortest time possible, and if they don't get them they switch rather than fight. CEOs are compelled under threat of oblivion to look to the short run and produce the expected profits. A whole new vocabulary has come into existence to describe the resulting practices: downsizing, outsourcing, temping, along with old-fashioned mergings, plant closings, and rapid removings to low-wage areas here and abroad. The long run no longer exists and the previous investments in plant, talent, and the services, conveniences, shops, roads, bridges, schools, homes, and the like of abandoned cities have become financially invisible if they don't show up on corporate balance sheets.

A peculiar, undeniable, and to some, embarrassing, fact is that the several hundred largest corporations have long been neither wholly private nor wholly public, but are a kind of hybrid, like a hugely overgrown centaur or satyr. No matter how hard the stagehands try to cover up the horse's end or the goat's feet of the corporate bodies, the quasi-private, quasi-public reality keeps protruding through the sheets for all to see.

If anyone deliberately designed such a system, he would be considered insane by any reputable psychiatrist and gently led off to a high-security facility and placed on antidelusional drugs until he came to his senses.

The subject of Margaret Blair's book is how to redesign this insane system to avoid the self-destructive results that we see all around us. We have the precedent of the New Deal: the creation of regulations in the public interest; the encouragement of collective bargaining to protect workers; the use of fiscal policy to bring about full employment. We could, if the electorate were so persuaded, restore these precedents and go beyond them by establishing an environment in which businesses gain by creating real wealth fairly distributed and lose by pursuing paper profits unfairly distributed. That would require reforming corporations from the outside. The alternative is reforming them from the inside, reforming corporate governance. "Corporate governance" is the discreet, academically correct way of referring to the struggle for corporate power and the uses to which it is put. Corporate power is a rough game, played by rough men who do not take kindly to advice from the outside. That is why it can only be reformed by a greater power than itself, and there is only one greater power, namely, the federal government. This is the reason that I am completely baffled by Blair's belief, if I understand that belief, that corporate power—governance, if you will—can be reformed by putting employees' representatives on corporate boards. I don't quarrel for one moment with her assertion that employees who have gained know-how by working long years in a company are stakeholders in the same sense that shareholders are: they have both made an investment. But who is going to be the enforcer to put workers on the boards?

The struggle for corporate power is a ruthless struggle engaged in by men and, not very often, women of single-minded, gargantuan ambition who are not going to change the rules unless they are forced to. I cannot easily imagine that Michael Eisner, the CEO at Disney, whose salary equals that of all 4,000 gardeners at Disney World and nearly equals the entire gross national product of Grenada, will voluntarily comply with a request to change the rules of corporate governance. (The salary calculations are borrowed from Anthony Sampson's new book, *Company Man.*) I have read that the employees at the theme parks must wear regulation outfits down to their underwear. I suppose that the representatives of these employees would be obliged to come to board meetings wearing their regulation underwear and perhaps would politely protest that they should have been consulted about Walt Disney's $19 billion acquisition of Capital Cities/ABC. This reminds me of a comment allegedly made by Charles de Gaulle to the effect that he would rather have one bad general than two good ones. I have no doubt that labor can serve on boards and make a contribution, but when it comes to strategic decisions, you are asking for trouble if you have two generals pulling in different directions.

It is not uncommon these days for economists to look at the economy as an abstract mechanism. The recent Nobel Prize winner, Robert E. Lucas, Jr., said after hearing of his award, "The U.S. economy is in excellent shape." I assume that it is just the people who are in poor shape. Take the 77,800 middle management employees of AT&T, who are being driven out with all the aplomb of sheep being herded by sheepdogs. Apparently it never occurred to them to organize an employee lobby, what with AT&T being so stable and paternal for so long. I am not so reactionary as to think that technology and reorganization will not reduce the workforce of industry just as it did in agriculture. But are we so impoverished in imagination and wealth that we cannot invent the means to help the redundant retrain and find equivalent jobs? Let us remember, when the time comes, to include this project in the new tasks of corporate governance.

Before the advent of the New Deal, it was not uncommon for respected public figures to speak bluntly about big business. Theodore Roosevelt referred brusquely to the "malefactor of great wealth," but such a comment would be considered in poor taste today. Woodrow Wilson remarked that "if there are men in this country big enough to own the government of the United States, they are going to own it," a statement that would now result in complete social ostracism. (The quotations are from the best and clearest concise history of the American economy, *The Economic Transformation of America: 1600 to the Present,* by Robert Heilbroner and Aaron Singer.) But it may just be possible that the restoration of the *ancien régime* will also bring about the restoration of the ancient rhetoric. We have talked a great deal about family values. It would be quite enlightening, would it not, to make a list of corporate values for our own edification and as a freely rendered public service.

The great shift in the balance between public and private power came in the 1930s when an angry electorate led by Franklin Roosevelt restrained an equally angry corporate power with a public, legal structure of guidelines and incentives to act in the public interest. A tacit pact emerged that resulted in an uneasy accommodation among government, business, and labor. The CEO's job description was expanded from maximizing his own income and satisfying shareholders to include some concession to workers, the public, natural resources, even the arts. It was imperfect, but it was not a bad accommodation. It was novel: we were all regarded as stakeholders, contemplated in the Constitution, but previously too inconvenient to put into effect.

The novelty arose in regarding citizens not only as political stakeholders but as economic stakeholders as well. Forty acres and a mule was a step in that direction but no longer did the job. The large public corporations could not function for a day without the social framework created by everyone who works. The corporations in return have incurred an obligation to create real as opposed to speculative wealth and to refrain from destroying anything that does not appear on their balance sheets. Too much has been made of Schumpeter's often repeated phrase "creative destruction," as if it were a law of nature. We do not absolutely have to be victims of the destruction brought on by business changes. We do not have to put up with it.

I am again puzzled by Margaret Blair's argument that we cannot expect corporate managers to take account of the public interest because the concept lacks theoretical rigor and fails to tell managers what the public interest is. Legislators daily decide what the public interest is and what it is not and provide incentives for us to act accordingly. The problem lies in the current mania to "leave it to business" and to expect everything to come up roses. As for theoretical rigor, it is not so much that accountants cannot count as the fact that we have not been willing to count the impact of corporations on society as a whole and therefore do not have a balance sheet on "creative destruction" for which the great corporations can be held accountable. If you have a large dog in your house and it chews the furniture, bites the children, and defecates on the living room carpet, your first thoughts do not run to theoretical rigor but how to restrain the dog.

It is hard to make historical comparisons, but the electorate may possibly be just as angry now as it was in the 1930s. To explain the accommodation that we need to restore will take a man with a mission or a woman with a will in the White House. Meanwhile we muckrakers have our work cut out for us. Once again capitalism has to be saved from being destroyed by the capitalists. We could do worse than suggest they start by adopting the physicians' maxim: First do no harm.

January 1996

Labor's Future

A review of *Report and Recommendations by the Commission on the Future of Worker-Management Relations,* by John T. Dunlop, Chairman. Washington, DC: U.S. Government Printing Office, December 1994.

I confess to being puzzled by the self-defeating behavior of my fellow capitalists. They have beaten organized labor nearly to death; they have restructured production, trade, and finance to their own liking; they have dictated the political agenda of the country; and they have propagated the creed of laissez faire without a single powerful voice to contradict them. How else do you describe this but total victory in the class war?

A reasonable person could reasonably expect that after such a complete victory the victors would immediately set about using their great power to raise the standard of living, improve working conditions, find jobs for the jobless, and earn the gratitude of the entire nation. But instead they have done the opposite. They have squandered their moment in history by foolishly taking as much of everything for themselves as they could. That was a blunder of the first magnitude. This is not ancient Rome, where an occasional slave revolt was put down by force, the slaves were nailed to crosses, and the ruling class went on ruling as before. Today people have rights. Under sufficient provocation they use them. My sadly retarded fellow capitalists have set the stage for a ferocious reaction. Unions will come back from near-death. Their business is to get people a raise. Word will get around.

The reaction has already begun. Little more than a year ago a blueprint for the revival of unions was released by a commission of businessmen, labor leaders, and academics appointed by the secretaries of Labor and Commerce, chaired by the distinguished authority on the labor movement and former Secretary of Labor John T. Dunlop. Last October, the militant, combative, contentious John J. Sweeney was elected president of the AFL-CIO.

John J. Sweeney and the labor movement are in a wrathful mood. They will organize no matter what it takes: money; civil disobedience; jail; and idealistic young people out of college, the kind who joined the civil rights movement in the 1960s, who are willing to go on a crusade because they believe in the rightness and justice of the unions' cause. They will block bridges if they need to, as Sweeney's service workers' union did in Washington last September as a last resort to call attention to the plight of janitors. You don't like the idea of blocking bridges? Neither do I. I would prefer that janitors get a better deal some other way. But what is a union blocking bridges to raise the standard of living compared with the Republican majority in Congress blocking the entire federal government on behalf of legislation to lower the standard of living?

The *Report and Recommendations* of the Dunlop Commission reflects well on the courage of the men and women who wrote it because they have mentioned the unmentionable: that employers should step aside and let their employees organize unions if that is what they want, without intimidation, without threats, without huge campaigns of obfuscation. They looked into the heart of darkness and wrote about what they saw, not with passion but with restraint, in the cool language of commission reports. Nevertheless they did look and they did write. Their recommendations would change the entire legal landscape of labor relations in the United States. Before discussing them, I offer a short primer to those who need one on the situation as it exists today.

* * *

Q. My first question is, what is so surprising about the decline of organized labor? Machines have replaced people in the industries where unions were strongest. The jobs have moved to the service sector. It's hard to organize people when they are scattered around in small groups.

A. True, unions have declined disastrously (for unions) from 36 percent of all nonagricultural workers in 1953 to 15.5 percent now. But not all those union jobs have been lost to automation. Millions have been lost as a result of plants moving to low-wage, nonunion locations in the South and Southwest and to low-wage, nonunion plants in foreign countries. A significant number have been lost as a result of firing union employees and then getting the same work done through nonunion contractors and contingent workers, temporary and part-time employees who don't belong to unions.

Q. It appears to be downhill for unions no matter how you look at it.

A. Not inevitably. Other industrialized countries are facing the same problems as the United States, but unions in those countries have held their own; some are even growing. Here is a sample of the union share of the workforce from a list of eighteen leading industrialized countries: 36 percent in Canada; 50 percent in the United Kingdom; 28 percent in France and Japan; 43 percent in Germany; and 96 percent in Sweden. The United States ranks last. (See the article by Ray Marshall in *Unions and Economic Competitiveness.*)

Q. Let's face it. American unions have a bad reputation. Most people don't want to have anything to do with them.

A. Sorry to contradict you, but surveys show that one-third of all nonunion employees would join a union today if they had the opportunity.

Q. Well then, why don't they join?

A. One reason is that people are afraid of losing their jobs. Pro-union employees are illegally fired in one out of four businesses where unions try to organize. Another reason is that union organizers can't just walk up to anyone they want to and talk about the advantages of joining a union. The Supreme Court has decided that union organizers don't have the right to enter the public areas of a nonunion company. They can't stand in the hallways, sit in the cafeterias, or even park in the parking lots. The law grants workers the right to organize but denies them the help of an organizer.

Q. But unions still keep trying, don't they?

A. Sure. About 40 percent of government workers belong to unions because the government doesn't do anything to stop them from joining. But only 10 percent in the private sector belong. Even when employees elect a union to represent them in spite of all the obstacles, one-third never get a first contract because management goes through the motions of bargaining without actually bargaining.

Q. I can't be wrong about everything. The Wagner Act is still on the books. The official, unequivocal, unambiguous policy of the United States is to encourage workers to organize and choose representatives to bargain about the terms and conditions of employment. The whole idea is to equalize the bargaining power of employers and employees, extend democratic political rights into the workplace, take labor out of competition, and raise the purchasing power of the workforce.

A. Yes, the Wagner Act is still the law, but it is so restricted in practice by Taft-Hartley, adverse Supreme Court rulings, one-sided NLRB interpretations, and scofflaw employers, that new legislation is needed to achieve the original intent. A law isn't much good if the prospective beneficiaries are denied the means to carry it out.

Q. You seem to specialize in horror stories. Don't you have anything favorable to say about labor relations in the United States?

A. Yes. The New United Motors Manufacturing Inc. (NUMMI) in Fremont, California, is a much-discussed example of union–management cooperation. The plant failed under GM and then reopened as a joint venture of GM and Toyota in 1984 with mostly the same equipment and the same UAW workers as it had before, but with a new management system. Even though NUMMI was less automated than GM's most modern plants, productivity rose 50 percent after workers were given a high level of job security and invited to establish work teams that set their own methods and standards. In 1989 NUMMI became the most productive GM plant in the United States. Since then other plants have done even better.

Q. How widespread is this approach?

A. Very widespread abroad but not here. In 1990, the Commission on the Skills of the American Workplace estimated that less than 10 percent of American firms are competing through high performance instead of low wages.

Q. If the cooperative approach is so successful, why don't more American employers try it?

A. We'll have to let readers answer that question for themselves. But the fact is that about two-thirds of all American companies that face union organizing drives hire anti-union consultants to plan and execute counterorganizing drives. A counterorganizing drive means daily company meetings, leaflets, and newsletters depicting the union as an outside business that enriches itself by collecting dues, fees, and fines from thousands of hapless employees. A counterorganizing drive deliberately delays a certification election for months by raising legal issues before the NLRB while management threatens utter disaster if any employee so much as thinks of joining a union. You can find all the details in *Confessions of a Union Buster* by Martin Jay Levitt. Here is what union busters do. Fire union activists under some pretext and pay a small fine several years later after the troublemakers are long gone, if the pretext doesn't hold up in court. Threaten supervisors with dismissal if they can't talk their supervisees out of joining a union. Compel employees to attend meetings where management threatens to move the company to the nonunion South or to a foreign country. Pry into police, credit, and medical records. Spread rumors, true or false, about union activists' personal lives. Pit family members against each other. After a while, most of the workforce just want everybody to go away, including the union, and leave them alone. The employees never get to decide whether the union will be good or bad for them. The answer to that question is lost in the confusion. And this is not just the work of the now repentant Martin Jay Levitt. Union busting is a two-billion-dollar business employing 7,000 lawyers and consultants. The biggest firms in the country use their services—effectively.

This is the reality that the Dunlop Commission had to face. If their program were adopted, U.S. labor law and its practical consequences would look radically different. The assault on labor would lose its legal foundation. Employers and unions would be steered away from class war toward peaceful coexistence. Here, briefly, are some of the commission's far-reaching recommendations:

Organizing and collective bargaining. Change the law to allow quick union elections, preferably within two weeks from the time a union notifies the National Labor Relations Board that it intends to seek an election. Postpone legal arguments about the scope of the bargaining unit until after the election to forestall months of recriminations and confrontational maneuvering. All the legal issues can then be resolved before the NLRB when the election is over. A majority card check system would be even simpler. The commission recommends its use when the two sides want to cooperate from the outset. The card check system works well in Canada and it worked well in the United States before it was outlawed by Taft-Hartley. We ought to pick the simplest way of resolving the representation issue and legalize it again.

Employee access to union representatives. Change the law to overturn Supreme Court decisions prohibiting employees from meeting union organizers in the public areas of private companies. Employers have the right to express their opinions to their employees every day. The commission's recommendation would restore free speech equality by allowing employees to hear the union point of view where they work instead of on a bus or in a bar.

Penalties for firing pro-union workers. Change the law to require immediate injunctions against firing union supporters. I would go further and require companies that break the law to pay substantial fines. Unions face injunctions and severe fines for engaging in secondary boycotts (picketing firms not involved in a dispute). The law is very effective. I expect it would be equally effective against firms that contemplate illegal discharges.

First contract bargaining. Change the law to require an employer and a newly certified union that fail to reach a first contract after a specified time to use mediation or, as a last resort, arbitration.

Contingent workers. Placing workers in a contingent relation has become a common subterfuge for employing them while avoiding the responsibilities of an employer. The commission recommends changing the law so that the real employer is responsible for Social Security coverage, working conditions, civil rights, taxes, and applicable union contracts of contingent workers, whether they are part-time, temporary, seasonal, leased, or independent contractors. In the garment industry, for example, a department store chain might contract work to jobbers who contract work to manufacturers who run sweatshops no different from those that existed a hundred years ago. The woman doing the sewing may be three times removed from the management of the department store chain but she is still effectively its employee, working under a dodge that wipes out all responsibility of the department store for pay, benefits, and working conditions. (I owe this example to Gus Tyler, who describes it in his excellent book, *Look for the Union Label.*) By redefining "employer" and "employee," the commission would put an end to this kind of exploitation.

The commission made other valuable proposals, such as changing the vast, aptly named "command and control" system of workplace regulations so that they can be applied locally through negotiated agreements between management and labor to fit local conditions, rather than trying to make one set of rules fit every situation. I might also mention the commission's recommendation for the local resolution of disputes. At present, grievances can drag through the courts for years, costing tens of thousands of dollars to adjudicate, forcing unions to use triage just to decide which grievances to pursue. I recommend reading the extraordinary book, *Which Side Are You On?* by Thomas Geoghegan, with the rueful subtitle, *Trying to Be for Labor When It's Flat on Its Back,* to anyone who wants to understand the slow, tortuous, dirty, thankless, exasperating grind of litigating grievances.

My main regret is that the commission did not discuss the Supreme Court ruling in the *Mackay* case, which goes all the way back to 1938. The law granted workers the right to strike, but the Supreme Court granted employers the right to hire permanent replacements—in effect, to fire strikers for striking. This catch-22 in the law lay waiting until unions weakened, and now it is destroying them. If unions are legitimate American institutions, then they cannot be forced through a legal sieve that breaks them up. Only a few rogue employers used the Mackay doctrine until Ronald Reagan gave the signal for attack in 1981 when he fired 11,500 members of PATCO (the Professional Air Traffic Controllers Organization) and hired permanent replacements. If the employer, government or private, can destroy a union, then the right to belong to a union is nothing but a fiction. (Thanks to Stephen Schlossberg, former general counsel of the UAW, for explaining the *Mackay* case to me.)

* * *

I was brought up with the comforting idea, eloquently propounded by John Kenneth Galbraith, that we live in a country where the enormous power of corporations is roughly balanced by the countervailing power of unions. We could expect some kind of fair distribution of wealth under this premise and even a modicum of fairness about the conditions of work—an imperfect but perfectible expansion of democracy into the shop and office. This world has vanished before our eyes.

It sounds ludicrous, there must be some logical explanation, but the titans of business have conquered their own fellow American workforce and exacted tribute from them as if they were senators in ancient Rome. All the gains in national income over the last twenty-five years have gone to the top titans while the bottom 80 percent of the quietly desperate who helped make those gains possible are poorer now that the country is richer than they were when the country was poorer. Maybe there is a better word for it, but it used to be called tribute.

The quietly desperate sometimes have a way of making themselves heard, but who is listening besides a few old-fashioned liberals and the unions? Can you name anyone else at all who cares most about, and is single-mindedly working for, higher wages, full employment, a living minimum wage, and a secure safety net? Not those engaged in fantasy discussions about the global economy and the deficit while ignoring the fact that most people are barely making ends meet. Maybe we have to learn all over again what was obvious fifty years ago: that unions are not optional; they are not disposable; they are not outmoded; they are not evil: they are an indispensable part of a country whose citizens want to call themselves humane.

*   *   *

Q. Before finishing this review, please tell me, what ever happened to patriotism?

A. It has become the last refuge of the decent.

March 1996

The obstacles inside and outside the AFL-CIO were too great for John J. Sweeney to overcome. Unions never recovered as I thought they might at the time.

What's Wrong with Economists?

A review of *The Crisis of Vision in Modern Economic Thought,* by Robert Heilbroner and William Milberg. New York: Cambridge University Press, 1995.

My task in reviewing this book will be made much easier if we agree at the outset that economics can be divided into two varieties: fiction and nonfiction. Economists who have a talent for fiction assume the existence of a self-regulating market mechanism that allocates the factors of production—land, labor, and capital—optimally among various possible uses, to produce an assortment of goods and services that best conforms to the preferences of consumers. Economists with this vision before them are deeply concerned about the efficient use of resources, the rational distribution of income, and maximum consumer satisfaction, all of which result from the operations of the self-regulating market. They are ready to sound the alarm at any inclination of government to improve things in the private sector. Nothing can be improved; government can only make matters worse.

We should not be surprised to find that economists of this persuasion dominate the profession. Economic ideas, like goods and services, are subject to the laws of supply and demand. Given a strong demand for theories that prove the superiority of unfettered capitalism, the supply will be forthcoming.

Robert Heilbroner and William Milberg have provided us with a survey of these theories: the monetarist view; the rational expectations hypothesis; the New Classical Economics; and, finally, the New Keynesian Economics. They all have in common a sense of the superiority of the invisible hand to any alternative. Monetarism, primarily the work of Milton Friedman, would restrict government's role in the economy to the tight management of the money supply in order to control the general price level. But in the 1970s, the actual relation between the quantity of money, prices, and incomes proved to be highly unstable and therefore unpredictable. A more enduring contribution of monetarism—regarded as incontrovertible by most of the profession—was the discovery of the natural rate of unemployment. Expansionary monetary and fiscal efforts that attempt to push unemployment below the natural level can only result in an accelerating rate of inflation. Consequently, all the major governments of the world have abandoned expansionary policies and have accepted slow growth, massive unemployment, and a decline of real wages as the inevitable result of an inviolable economic law.

Next comes the work of Robert Lucas on rational expectations. This work is an elaboration of rational choice theory, to be found under the section on microeconomics in every introductory economics textbook. Rational expectations proves that market participants do what they do because they expect what they expect, which in turn depends on what they think others expect. If they expect that others expect that prices will go up, they will act accordingly, and prices will go up. This is a soundly logical proposition, but occasionally prices go down, jobs disappear, and people are ruined anyway. As Lucas so rightly observed, "To explain why people allocate time to unemployment we need to [know] why they prefer it to all other activities" (p. 116).

Particularly notable is Lucas's assertion that monetary and fiscal moves by the government will be annulled by private-market countermoves—the Policy Ineffectiveness Proposition. Any attempt to influence the economy is doomed to failure. For example, expansionary fiscal policy is offset by the increased savings of private parties against anticipated future increases in taxes (p. 77). But if everyone thinks that everyone else thinks that the country will be better off, including themselves, perhaps people will spend more instead of saving more. Or perhaps people will wait to see what happens. A study of economic history since the 1930s might be helpful.

Rational expectations merged into the New Classical Economics, which shows how all markets automatically interact and bring about general equilibrium in the economy. Random fluctuations caused by the introduction of new technology will result in corresponding fluctuations in the relative prices of goods and services. Individuals will then change their patterns of consumption and move from job to job as the demand for labor changes. The consequent business cycles are simply the manifestation of markets efficiently responding to changes in technology. The interaction among markets causes all of them to clear: prices and wages will adjust so that they accurately reflect the forces of supply and demand. The word "classical" in the designation refers to the complete, triumphant restoration of the pre-Keynesian postulates that reigned up to and through the Great Depression, incorporating proof that state attempts to steer the economy along smoother paths are both unnecessary and harmful.

The New Keynesian Economics differs from the classical version only in acknowledging that prices and wages do not adjust immediately, and what is called the supply side can benefit from government initiatives in education, job training, portable medical benefits, and, in the belief of its more radical adherents, an increase in the minimum wage. But demand stimulus to increase the rate of growth and reduce unemployment is dangerously inflationary and unthinkable except in major recessions—hence the ghost of Keynes that remains in the machine. Here we have a fair description of macroeconomic minimalism as we find it in the Clinton administration.

Conservatives are only too happy to share "visions" of the best of all possible economies, in which government interference inevitably causes mischief, except in those few public activities sanctioned by Adam Smith.

A sense of fairness prompts me to acknowledge that economists on the whole are reasonable and occasionally brilliant members of society. But economics, unlike the other social sciences, is at its core a deductive discipline. Every would-be economist is indoctrinated in the powerful theory of logical choice that explains the economy without reference to empirical evidence. Once you acquire the habit of thinking about firms and consumers that optimize their behavior according to innate psychological laws, the actual economy where class and power strongly influence prices and incomes disappears and is replaced by a fantasy economy. You are then placed in the hapless position of recommending fantasy policies. These can be harmful. The "crisis of vision" that Heilbroner and Milberg refer to is the direct result of trained incompetence, except in the case of those few rare individuals who were not paying close attention during this part of the course. (See the masterful essay by Alfred Eichner, "Why Economics Is Not Yet a Science," in the book of the same name.)

The nonfiction view of the economy, shared by Heilbroner and Milberg, is that we live in a highly unstable capitalist market economy characterized by a litany of ills that most of us can repeat in our sleep, including extremes of wealth and poverty, a high rate of unemployment, a dependent labor force, slow growth, massive child neglect, and giant corporations with the power to pursue their own short-run interests to the detriment of everyone else. In the last two decades, to repeat some now well-known statistics, real gross domestic product rose 36 percent while real hourly wages for the vast majority of workers declined 14 percent. In the 1980s, 64 percent of all gains in earnings went to the top 1 percent. (Cited by Lester Thurow in *The Future of Capitalism,* p. 2.) We are witnessing what Marx called immiserization, a dead and buried idea that has been brought back from the grave by Marx's worst enemies. Prestigious economists are now asked every day of the week what can be done, and the answers reported in the press are always the same: not very much.

This is not the answer that you will find in *The Crisis of Vision in Modern Economic Thought.* Foremost is the need to recognize that the modern capitalist order is made up of two sectors: the public and the private. The role of the public sector in directing and coordinating the economy is essential to protect the capitalist system from self-destruction. The failure of the economics profession to recognize the legitimacy of the public sector—at the very least to carry on the work of Keynes—is the central cause of the crisis of vision. Economics conceived as the study of the "natural" course of events reduces the profession to the status of onlookers, much as sailors who refuse to take hold of the wheel in a storm.

During the cataclysm of World War I, Shaw wrote his tragicomedy, *Heartbreak House,* in which his stage persona, Captain Shotover, accuses an imaginary crew—the sophisticated citizens of the world—of lying in their bunks drinking while the ship heads for the rocks. What is our business, a visitor asks? Shotover: To learn navigation. "Navigation. Learn it and live; or leave it and be damned."

What is the business of economists? Navigation. The steering requirements are not a mystery. They have been discussed at length by institutionalists and Post Keynesians (not to be confused with New Keynesians). They include an espousal of strong fiscal measures to stimulate growth and full employment; an incomes policy to prevent inflation; legal reform to restore the countervailing power of labor as an offset to the power of corporations; and a return to the civilized concept of corporate responsibility. That is navigation. We will learn it and live; or leave it and be damned.

One of the most carelessly considered questions in the annals of modern economic navigation is variously known as incomes policy, guidelines, the social compact, or more bluntly, wage and price controls. Without notice, in complete secrecy, a committee of bankers within the Federal Reserve System sets the price of credit and can at will cause a radical redistribution of income between debtors and creditors as well as the grossest inefficiency imaginable in squelching investment and employment. But not a murmur of dissent is heard among economists. However, let there be a suggestion that incomes policy be used as a tool to facilitate full employment without inflation, and the loudest protestations are heard about distortions in the price mechanism that will cause misallocation, shortages, etc., etc. One of the most constructive projects that economists could undertake is to study this question more diligently, because incomes policy is the inevitable accompaniment of full employment.

Today, all is disarray. Heilbroner and Milberg, borrowing a term from Schumpeter, look forward to a new "classical situation" where there is general consensus among economists about what economics is. Those "classical situations" of the past, captured in the works of John Stuart Mill, Alfred Marshall, and John Maynard Keynes, whatever their shortcomings, at least maintained a healthy connection between economics and reality and an empirical breadth that did not shun political, social, and ethical concerns. The great irony of modern conservatism is in abetting ruthless capitalism while extolling civic virtue under the name of family values. Economic theorists have been too hasty to accept this artificial dichotomy. The presumed rules of business are crowding out the rules of civic society. And yet capitalism depends on noncapitalist values in the surrounding society to survive. Without cooperation, solidarity, sympathy, fairness, and responsibility, civil society will be destroyed and capitalism with it. The New Deal introduced the ethics of civil society into the workplace and they are now being driven out in the name of supposedly better ones—the ones that were tried before repeatedly and failed repeatedly. (For more on this subject, see *They Only Look Dead: Why Progressives Will Dominate the Next Political Era*, by E.J. Dionne, Jr.)

The economist Lorie Tarshis was a young student when he heard Keynes lecture at Cambridge between 1932 and 1935 as he was writing the *General Theory*. Tarshis recalls what Keynes supplied, aside from a startling new way of looking at the economy. Excitement, impatience, hope. What is wrong with economists? Today they offer no excitement, no impatience, no hope. Heilbroner and Milberg have pointed the way to restore these necessities of life.

May 1996

The Good Society and Its Enemies

A review of *The Good Society: The Humane Agenda,* by John Kenneth Galbraith. Boston and New York: Houghton Mifflin, 1996.

The writing of a book on the good society is a subversive act. It invites comparison with the society that we actually have. And yet the material components of the good society are within reach. We are prodigiously productive: a few percent of the working population grows all the food that we need and we are moving rapidly to the time when a few percent more will be able to make all the other necessities and conveniences that we may need or want, and no small share of the extravagances. Everyone else available for work will be free to perform services of increasing variety and possibly even usefulness. We will have a superabundance of labor to do what needs to be done: the workweek will inevitably grow shorter while private time grows longer.

The good society is not difficult to define. As Galbraith writes, every citizen must have the opportunity for a rewarding life. No child will be forced to live in poverty, endure neglect, or attend an inferior school. No adult will have to go without a job, sufficient income, or support in old age. No one will be denied decent living space or medical care. Nor will anyone be denied equal treatment because of sex, color, or religion.

Is the good society possible in the United States? No one could effectively claim that technological obstacles stand in the way. The obstacles lie in the realm of economics and politics.

We have paid a high price for the view that the public sector is harmful and a burden. The public sector makes up for deficiencies of the private sector; neither business nor labor could survive without it. We have also paid a high price for cynicism about political democracy. But only the harassed majority, which stands to gain most from the combined action of the private and public sectors, can bring about the necessary changes in policy by recognizing and voting for candidates who are willing to carry them out.

The rich, except for those whose consciences dictate otherwise, are not going to be in the vanguard of that movement. It is convenient for them to believe that the good society will emerge from the market as a by-product of the goods and services—some day in the future—when the poor reform. But it is difficult to reform when there is one job for every ten people looking for work, which is the case in New York City.

Neither will those like House majority leader Dick Armey lead us to the good society. "Behind our New Deals and New Frontiers and Great Societies," writes Dick Armey, "you will find, with a difference only in power and nerve, the same sort of person who gave the world its Five Year Plans and Great Leaps Forward—the Soviet and Chinese counterparts" (quoted by E.J. Dionne in *They Only Look Dead,* p. 286). I have no reason to believe that Representative Armey is other than a public-spirited man who has been so dazzled by the utopian vision of free-market capitalism that he has been blinded to the distinction between democracy and dictatorship. I wish only to reassure him that the humane agenda faces many obstacles and that he will have numerous opportunities to turn it back.

That agenda requires the reversal of tenets that have gained the status of unassailable wisdom. First, the commitment to unemployment. It is the deliberate policy of the president, the Congress, and the Federal Reserve to keep employment below the maximum level attainable because they believe the use of monetary and fiscal policy to promote high economic growth is inconceivably dangerous and irresponsible. They wrack their brains about stagnant wages, inadequate investment, unsatisfactory improvements in productivity, frightening international competition, insolvency of the Social Security system, and even the lack of jobs—while by far the single most effective action to deal with these problems lies at hand: increase aggregate demand and reduce interest rates. Sluggish economies exacerbate all problems. Fully employed economies—it falls to Galbraith to teach the same lesson over and over again—perform better all around. They increase earnings and tax receipts; they provide the funds that no one can now find to pay for the programs we must have to qualify as the good society.

But politicians in office have done everything in their power to dodge this truth because of their paralyzing fear of inflation and increasing deficits. We put aside the awkward fact that major contributors to campaign funds have prospered greatly and are content to leave things as they are. In the good society the unemployed cannot be used as sacrificial victims to prevent inflation. A moderate rate of inflation must be accepted as far less harmful. This was the case after World War II. The danger of destructive, runaway inflation in a well-managed economy is not real. A wage-price spiral such as we witnessed in the 1970s does not have to be repeated. International competition now operates against it. Still, businesses and unions have a critical part to play by keeping the rise of wages and productivity in step and prices stable. Certainly the most highly trained professional economists in the world can help educate the public on this issue. Indexing bonds and annuities would protect interest income. Secretary of the Treasury Robert Rubin recently announced such a step for government bonds, perhaps anticipating the adoption of Galbraith's agenda by the Clinton administration.

At the risk of sounding eccentric or worse, a hazard noted by Galbraith, it is necessary to say that no economic principle requires a balanced budget. If we have a severe recession that necessitates deficit spending, and at the same time have a law, or worse, a constitutional amendment, that prohibits deficit spending, what then? The presiding precept is to keep the cost of the debt within the means to service it. If the economy is growing, the debt can grow. A provident businessperson divides the business budget into operating expenses and investment, pays for operating expenses out of current revenue, and may borrow for investment that promises a future return. Most governments—not ours—do the same. There is no logic in refraining from investing in education, health, and the welfare of children, which enrich the country in the future, because we erroneously call the expenditure for such investments a current expense. Education, health, pleasant cities, parks, and safe transportation are not a burden on our grandchildren.

The good society also requires rules for conducting business, commonly called regulation. My teacher Kenneth Boulding used to say that the market produced both goods and bads. The purpose of regulation is to keep the bads to a minimum. It is true that we do not expect our dinner from the benevolence of the butcher, the brewer, or the baker, but from their regard to their own interest. But if their self-love leads them to provide not only our dinner but also toxic discharges into the air and water, sweatshops for their employees, harmful additives to the beef, beer, and bread that they produce, or ruinous speculation in S&Ls that threatens the savings of trusting investors, then the self-love among the rest of us calls for rules to protect our well-being. Here we must invoke the Market Ineffectiveness Proposition. If the market does not accommodate, then we must regulate.

What are the political prospects for the humane agenda? The well-to-do have shifted life's chances so far in their favor that a reaction is not out of the question. That will have to include clarifying the goals of the majority—Galbraith's purpose—and organizing the majority to vote for representatives who stand for their interests, possibly even chastened Democrats. The awakening of the unions from a long sleep will, if they succeed, help to reestablish an offsetting power to the near-monopoly control of politics by the affluent. The majority must quickly move to raise the level of education. The deprived need the hope that they can get ahead and enjoy life. Ignorance and self-rule are an explosive mixture.

The guiding thought behind *The Good Society* is that the distress, anxiety, and want of the nonaffluent majority are avoidable, but only if they themselves make their needs heard within the political system. The affluent will still be affluent and influential, but democracy will no longer resemble an exclusive club with benefits restricted to members who can afford the fee to join. In this effort the majority has a staunch supporter—John Kenneth Galbraith. Adam Smith wrote, "He is certainly not a good citizen who does not wish to promote, by every means in his power, the welfare of the whole society of his fellow-citizens" (quoted in *Adam Smith in His Time and Ours* by Jerry Z. Muller). I perceive that Galbraith and Smith are in complete accord.

July 1996

Adam Smith: Right and Wrong

A review of *Adam Smith in His Time and Ours,* by Jerry Z. Muller. Princeton: Princeton University Press, 1995.

Even though more than 200 years have passed and the world has changed radically, a version of Adam Smith's ideas is revered by millions of prosperous and influential individuals who don't know what Smith's ideas were. Jerry Z. Muller's book is an exercise in historical excavation and as an excavator he succeeds very well. But I am dubious about Muller's claim that Smith is still the most cogent defender of capitalism. Too much has changed in the last 200 years for that to be the case. He—Muller—must be absolved from responsibility for the opinions expressed here; they are mine, not his.

We start with the excavation of the first of Adam Smith's two books, *The Theory of Moral Sentiments,* published in 1759, to Smith's evident dissatisfaction, since he revised it six times until his death in 1790. The subject is the unraveling of a mystery: What holds society together? Why do innately self-seeking humans usually act decently to one another? Our credulity is strained to think that the fear of punishment explains it all. The police would have to be everywhere. The question is about nothing less than the origin of morality.

Smith observed that each normal person is born with the capacity to imagine how it feels to be in someone else's place. He or she also feels a need for the approval of others. This need is directly related to the passion (as Smith called it) to seek one's self-interest. A normal child learns to mold his behavior in a way that will win recognition and approval and avoid scorn and disapproval. The molding starts in the family, extends to the neighborhood, church, and school, and ultimately to the wider society.

In the course of this tutelage, a human being internalizes social norms and develops a conscience—an impartial observer which is able to measure the behavior of the person observing himself and the behavior of others by the same standards. A social being emerges from this hitherto mysterious process as one who possesses self-command: who is able to rule his or her own passions and thus be fit to live with others.

Some indeterminate number of men and women, due to exceptional endowment or circumstances, are able to take a further step and, rather than guiding their actions according to the praise of others, guide them by standards they themselves consider praiseworthy. Among these moral exemplars is a small party concerned with improving the institutions that serve the general interest. As a man of the Enlightenment who placed hope in the power of reason to sweep unreason before it, Smith looked to this small party to gain the attention of statesmen and in due time enlighten them. In this capacity he himself was unexcelled.

There is a strange inversion here. Smith believed that it was not reason that ruled but human passions. Yet it was necessary for reason to discover and support the institutions that directed the passions to universally beneficial ends. Probably nothing further needs to be said about this as long as we keep clearly in mind whether the subject is the invisible hand or the visible hand.

The only question that Smith could not answer was *why* people are moral, other than assuming that God made us that way. In *The Descent of Man* (1871), Charles Darwin provided the most widely accepted explanation: cooperation is adaptive in social species; cognitively advanced social species take pleasure in the company of others; and language gives *Homo sapiens* the ability to generalize from shared experiences about fairness and duty. This degree of intelligence makes it *possible* to extend moral behavior from kin to non-kin; to a village, a religion, a class, a nation, or the entire world. The history of social institutions, a subject on which Smith wrote with erudition, shows that exclusion or inclusion of those for whom we feel moral sentiments is not fixed once and for all but depends on how we define "us and them." Nothing in Darwin contradicts Smith.

We can be sure that Smith was aware of this issue because of his comments on the conflict between the British establishment and the American colonies, about which he learned a great deal from his friend Benjamin Franklin. Smith considered taxation of the colonists without representation in Parliament folly. The outcome leaves no doubt that Smith knew moral sentiments cannot survive the effects of alienation.

Now we come to Jerry Z. Muller's excavation of Adam Smith's great unread book, *The Wealth of Nations,* published in 1776. Many readers may think this excavation unnecessary, the ideas of that treatise being so well known. Perhaps. The invisible hand ranks as one of the most successful academic metaphors of all time. In the market, people are strangers to one another. They may be acquainted or even friendly. But their interests are opposed. Self-interest rather than moral interest prevails except on the rules of the game: no coercion, fraud, contracting away third parties' rights, and so forth. But the single-minded pursuit of self-interest nevertheless results in the general good, as we all know, because free competition forces prices to the lowest level compatible with the cost of land, labor, and capital. It induces enterprisers to move their resources out of markets where supply exceeds demand into markets where demand exceeds supply, so that the goods and services they produce correspond to the wants of consumers. No one planned these results, and no one intended them to come to pass: free competition is self-regulating.

The mercantilists, against whom Smith polemicized, believed that the wealth of nations depended on the accumulation of gold and silver obtained by countries which export more than they import, a result enhanced by monopolies in trade bestowed by the state. The rise in the standard of living during the eighteenth century underlined Smith's counterargument that the wealth of nations depends on the growth of the market, which encourages an increasing division of labor, more specialization, and consequently greater productivity. Monopolies increase the wealth of monopolies; free competition increases the wealth of the entire country.

Many of Smith's present-day epigones, who have not followed Professor Muller's excavation deeper, conclude that Smith was a particular friend of business. He was not. He scorned the frequent practice of merchants who conspire behind closed doors to raise prices and depress wages and warned that they bear watching. He was no more a friend of workers who combined to raise wages, although he recognized that the repetitiveness of manufacturing jobs made factory hands as dull as they possibly could be. But he expected the salutary effects of commerce to raise wages in the long run, increase leisure time, and create revenues for public elementary education to offset the misery of simple-minded, numbing work.

Does Smith's championship of free markets mean that he was hostile to the state? It does not. He expected the responsibilities and size of the state to grow as commerical society grew and the revenues of the state to increase commensurately, contrary to the views of his modern apostles. The state must spend for defense; for public works; for the enforcement of law; for public education; and for creating a structure to protect every member of society from the oppression of every other member by, as he wrote, "promoting the prosperity of the commonwealth, by establishing good discipline, and by discouraging every sort of vice and impropriety; [it] may prescribe rules, therefore, which not only prohibit mutual injuries among fellow-citizens, but command mutual good offices to a certain degree" (quoted on p. 148).

But Smith had no illusions about the impartiality of government. He did not trust the landowners, the capitalists, or the workers. He recognized that laws reflect the power of those who make them and codify the shared standards of the dominant orders of society. Universal suffrage was not even a topic of conversation, and deference to the higher orders was taken for granted.

Like most men of the Enlightenment, he was dazzled by Newton's model of a self-regulating universe, which astonished the world in 1687, and used it as an inspiration to create a self-regulating social universe where class power is controlled by an invisible hand much as the heavenly bodies are controlled by gravity.

Looking back, we can see that Smith was both right and wrong. He was right about the power of moral sentiments in civilizing society, but he knew the limits to the impartiality of the impartial observer and he knew that moral sentiments stop at many borders unless the strongest incentives exist to extend them.

He was right about the effectiveness of the free market in prodigiously increasing the wealth of nations, but he knew that men were constantly trying to find ways to circumvent it. He could know nothing of the inventions that brought about the Industrial Revolution, the huge concentrations of business, the emergence of trade unions, the periodic waves of unemployment, and the bads produced along with the goods—externalities as Arthur Pigou called them—the costs of which had to be paid for by somebody. With all these exacerbating tensions of the nineteenth and twentieth centuries, it was too much to expect that lawmakers, prime ministers, and presidents could understand, much less agree on, how to contain this explosive mixture.

Almost everything that could go wrong with Smith's civilizing project did go wrong. We can no more expect Smith to be right about the 200 years between his time and ours than we can expect ourselves to be right about the next 200 years. The great problem with Smith's system is that it is riven down the middle by two invisible hands at war with one another. One invisible hand guides the moral sentiments of civil society; the other guides the self-interest of commercial society. And many visible hands are grasping at their wrists to turn them in this direction or that. The two invisible hands are ghostly apparitions of the two spheres they represent: the capitalist market and the civil society. The separation of the two is the fatal flaw of modern conservatism. How to bring morality into the market is the central issue of capitalism.

As I said at the beginning, Smith is not the most cogent defender of capitalism; we live in a different capitalism. If I wanted to sketch a defense of modern capitalism, and it is the only practical thing to do, I would start with the fact that we live in a society of conflicting interests, and that the only alternative to going to hell together is compromise between the conflicting interests. The best defense of modern capitalism is a social contract between the two classes that matter most, business and labor. But no contract can exist between two classes of markedly unequal power. Only the reorganization of countervailing power by labor and its supporters can lead to a compromise of mutual benefit.

I say reorganization because countervailing power and a social contract existed after World War II. But in the last twenty-five years we and Europe have decivilized into high unemployment, rising poverty, and an increasingly unequal distribution of income.

I am describing a *possible* capitalism, one where there is concurrence on minimum standards of life for all and concern for the common good. Those who write about the free market triumphant and social democracy in the dust are premature. A one-class society—pluralistic, democratic, with common rather than antagonistic interests: let us not be too hasty to say *finis* as the present situation becomes increasingly untenable.

The greatest unforeseen and unintended consequence of Adam Smith's doctrine is its use as an ideology of the privileged. His means are naively or hypocritically supported, for we have no free market in the sense that Smith defined it. But the ends of fairness, for which he proposed the means, are ignored.

We have it on the authority of Sir Walter Scott that when Adam Smith and Samuel Johnson first met, they fell into an argument, with Johnson saying to Smith, "You lie!" and Smith replying, "You are a son of a bitch!" This colloquy seems out of character, since Smith was widely respected for his learning and humanity by contemporaries as diverse as Edmund Burke and Voltaire, both of whom he counted as friends. But it does give us an idea of what he would have to say to some of his present-day admirers.

September 1996

Short Takes: Pleasant and Unpleasant Reviews

A review of *The Tyranny of the Bottom Line: Why Corporations Make Good People Do Bad Things,* by Ralph Estes. San Francisco: Berrett-Koehler, 1996.

Nothing could be more obvious: the bottom line of a financial statement does not measure the total effect of a corporation's activities on everybody. The bottom line may look good, but employees may be trading their health for their jobs. Customers may be buying products that will cause an early death. Suppliers may invest in a plant suddenly worth nothing but its value in scrap if a big purchaser goes elsewhere. Communities may provide roads, sewers, schools, only to see their work wasted when a large corporation moves out. The nation may pay more for the "services" of a corporation than it gets back—the health cost of smoking, say. Managers can even graciously increase their emoluments while stockholders' stakes go down. Only the last item is reflected in the bottom line and managers can always justify their salaries by arguing that a bad situation would have been even worse without their efforts.

Why should we continue to mismeasure? Let's make a corporate scorecard that really keeps the score on all six stakeholders enumerated above—stock owners, employees, customers, suppliers, communities, the nation. Let corporations make a comprehensive annual report to one agency. They are supposedly chartered for the public good. Let them prove it.

But are the managers held hostage to the bottom line, or is the bottom line held hostage to managers? Mr. Estes asks in his subtitle why corporations make good people do bad things. Possibly because they gain by it and then interpret the bad things as good things. Mr. Estes, do you really believe that people who are making a fortune using the present accounting system will change it because yours is self-evidently better? It would be nice to hang a bell around the cat's neck, but which mouse is going to approach the cat and hang the bell?

A review of *The Loyalty Effect: The Hidden Force Behind Growth, Profits, and Lasting Value,* by Frederick F. Reichheld. Boston: Harvard Business School Press, 1996.

Loyalty pays; but disloyalty pays even more. The rich have gotten richer. Managers are making millions. Only a fool would switch the formula when the present one is working so well.

But, says the author—and who can deny it?—repeat customers cost less to get through the door than new ones. Experienced employees produce more than novices. Steady investors provide cash that doesn't have to be replaced in the market every year.

Here's the point. If company *Alpha* keeps 95 percent of its customers and company *Beta* keeps 90 percent, and each attracts 10 percent new customers a year, company *Beta* is just replacing old customers with new ones and will stand still while company *Alpha* will double in size in fourteen years. But typically 10 to 30 percent of the average firm's customers are defecting each year; employee turnover of 15 to 20 percent is common; and the annual replacement rate of investors exceeds 50 percent.

We all know that the much-favored short-run view of draconian cost-cutting is a mirage. Fewer than half the firms that downsized in the last five years have increased their profits, and after six months, earnings of downsized companies fell 24 percent behind the Standard & Poor's 500 average.

Mr. Reichheld has his favorite firms that do well by practicing loyalty and he extols them. But great is the seductiveness of ready money. The really rich are converting disloyalty into large bags of cash and making their way to the bank as you read this sentence.

A review of ***Mean Business: How I Save Bad Companies and Make Good Companies Great,*** by Albert J. Dunlap with Bob Andelman. New York: Times Business/Random House, 1996.

Such sentimental trash has been written about how terrible a man Albert Dunlap is because he fires thousands of people, ruins communities, drives ruthless bargains with suppliers, refuses to donate corporate money to charity, frightens high-minded men and women off corporate boards, and makes millions for himself in the course of all these depredations.

His best-known exploit was saving Scott Paper from inevitable doom by firing 11,200 employees, selling off nonessential assets to reduce debt by $2.5 billion, merging Scott with Kimberly-Clark, moving corporate headquarters from Philadelphia to Boca Raton, increasing shareholder value from $2.5 billion to $9 billion, and making $100 million in the eighteen months that it took him to do all this.

Dunlap is blunt about it: "My $100 million was less than 2 percent of the wealth I created for all Scott shareholders. Did I earn it? Damn right I did. I'm a superstar in my field, much like Michael Jordan in basketball and Bruce Springsteen in rock 'n' roll" (p. 21).

He is blunt about his job: to make money for stockholders; not to save jobs; not to serve the community; not to give stockholder money to charity; not to serve "stakeholders," a word he loathes. Stakeholders have risked nothing. Stockholders have risked their money. Serve them and you must necessarily serve the consumer. If you want to be liked, buy a dog. If you want to support charity, give your own money.

It would be sheer obstinacy to refuse to recognize that Dunlap has figured out how the system works. He started out as a poor kid from Hoboken whose bedroom was so small that he constantly bruised his knees on the furniture and he ended up a rich man. He merely recognized and accepted the fact that the world is offered on certain terms: mansions; yachts; villas-by-the-sea; fame; the means to collect art and politicians: if you want to be rich, you must accept the terms.

Certainly he is wrong about stakeholders. Employees invest their time and lifeblood in their jobs; cities and towns invest in infrastructure that makes it possible for corporations to operate in the first place. And they pay the price when businesses are mismanaged and must be reorganized and don't get any of the benefits when the job is done. A large part of reality is simply invisible to the CEO because the system has defined his reality to make it invisible. All those stakeholders—the fired workers, the city Fathers and Mothers of Philadelphia, the outraged citizens—are in complicity with Albert J. Dunlap because they, not he, have allowed the terms that define business success to be what they are. If those deeply outraged citizens don't carry out their first duty, which is to insist on having reasonable terms for the act of making a living, then they have nobody to blame but themselves, and Dunlap cannot be charged with doing anything except what he was set up to do, which is the normal, natural, and expected thing that any sane, ambitious, and talented man or woman would do under the same circumstances.

A review of **We're Right, They're Wrong: A Handbook for Spirited Progressives,** by James Carville. New York: Random House, 1996.

Scene 1: A Republican barbecue on the Fourth of July. Mary Matelin can't go. James Carville has to face it alone. He fills up his plate and heads for an empty table in the corner of the yard. After him come Newt Gingrich, Rush Limbaugh, William Bennett, Bill Kristol, Pat Buchanan, Phil Gramm, Pat Robertson, and twenty others who are about to blast him for crime, drugs, taxes, big government, and everything else. Then Mary wakes Jim up from his nightmare.

Interlude: Top Five Tips on Potato Salad.

Introduction: Jim got support and a good example from his mamma and daddy, and he got opportunity from the government. Like most other people. And he admits it, even savors it.

An army doctor delivered him at Fort Benning, Georgia. Three generations of Carvilles served as postmaster in Carville, Louisiana. The federal government kept his feet dry by building a levee system to stop the Mississippi River from flooding in the spring. It built a disease-control center in Carville to take care of people with leprosy. It sent black kids to school with white kids, which Jim thought was bad until a government librarian handed him *To Kill a Mockingbird.* He read it. Then he said, "They're right and we're wrong." He got government loans and the G.I. Bill to finance his way through Louisiana State University, and the government paid his salary when he taught eighth-grade science at a public school in Vacherie, Louisiana.

The rest of the book: Carville's Rapid Responses; Extended Versions; More Things the Government Does Right; A Recipe for Your Backyard Barbecue.

Some of the things government got right: Earned Income Tax Credit (1975); Head Start (1966); Americorps (1993); Clean Water Act (1972); Centers for Disease Control and Prevention (1946); Medicare (1965); Ban on Leaded Gasoline (first stage: 1975); Consumer Product Safety Commission (1972); Food Labeling (1990); G.I. Bill (1944); Interstate Highway System (1956); Meals-On-Wheels (1972); Peace Corps (1961); School Lunches and Breakfasts (1946); Social Security (1935).

Carville: Who are you kidding? We need this stuff. (This is not a direct quote. It's an approximation of Cajun English.)

Rapid Responses to Republican Myths: Example: "In the early 1980s we set out to create conditions that would expand the U.S. economy. We passed tax cuts across the board for every taxpayer."—Ronald Reagan, July 8, 1993.

Rapid Response (by Carville): "Sorry to rain on your parade, but at least 40 percent of American taxpayers had a bigger bite taken out of their payroll checks at the end of the 1980s than they did when Reagan took office." Followed by Extended Version.

And lots more of these Rapid Responses followed by Extended Versions.

You get the picture? This is a book of facts to contradict the myths by a political pro who floats like a butterfly and stings like a bee.

A review of *Teachings from the Worldly Philosophy,* by Robert Heilbroner. New York and London: W.W. Norton, 1996.

After forty-three years, *The Worldly Philosophers* has gained a companion, a book of readings from the works of those self-same philosophers. This is no ordinary compendium of Smith, Mill, Marx, Marshall, Keynes, and a dozen more. It is a guided tour of the summits, conducted by the man most qualified to lead the tour, Robert Heilbroner. By ingenious selections and knowing comments, we are led in the shortest possible space and time to comprehend the personalities, preoccupations, and passions of the worldly sages, whose names we know, but whose works we may not have read.

It is an audacious scheme, to make the perfect selection of passages, and to interpolate precisely the right comments, which provide the connections to hold the entire enterprise together. Here is the main story line, and here is how the plot developed.

You don't need eccentric tastes to enjoy reading this book. The great worldly philosophers have urgent things to say to us and they say them powerfully. If you are an old hand at economics, this volume will bring with it a long train of associations. If you are new at it, you will be provoked to think anew about matters you assumed settled. Perhaps you will think anew even if you are an old hand. In either case, buy the book.

November 1996

The Labor Movement and Black Ghettos: Two Reviews

A review of *America Needs a Raise,* by John J. Sweeney with David Kusnet. Boston and New York: Houghton Mifflin, 1996.

The mild-mannered Mr. Sweeney is into far-reaching projects. When he was elected president of the AFL-CIO in October 1996, the labor movement turned away from business-as-usual to face the considerable problem of rebuilding its membership and restoring its clout. In the early 1950s, a third of the labor force belonged to unions, but now the total is down to about 16 percent. Unions have fallen on hard times in other advanced countries as well, but the fall has not been nearly as catastrophic as this.

America Needs a Raise can be summarized in one sentence: Organize the unorganized and seek affirmative action for the 80 percent of jobholders and jobless whose real incomes have declined since 1973, declined even though productivity has increased about 25 percent in the same time. All the gains, to the dismay of the unfavored four-fifths, have been diverted to the upper 20 percent, a disproportionate share to the upper 1 percent, and by far the most disproportionate share to the upper one-half of 1 percent. The current blip at the top of the business cycle has had little effect on the long-run trend.

This increasing inequality in income distribution has been solemnly, even ruefully, attributed to impersonal forces beyond human control by business leaders, politicians, commentators, and especially economists. But increasing inequality is really not the result of changing technology, or shifts of jobs from basic industry to services, or increasing global competition. These developments brought on real problems. No one argues otherwise, certainly not Sweeney. But it was how the problems were met by American business that caused the radical redistribution of income, not the problems themselves.

As Sweeney writes, American corporate leaders chose a low-wage solution, not spontaneously, but through an organized anti-union campaign led by the Business Roundtable, composed of CEOs of the largest corporations. They fought the dubious fight to delegitimize unions and undermine their rights under U.S. labor law. The somnolence of the AFL-CIO leadership over the past thirty years, despite this barrage, did not help either.

After the terrible alarm of the Great Depression and a dozen years of cajoling by Franklin Roosevelt, business and labor entered the postwar era with the unprecedented understanding that they would work together for full employment and a fair sharing of the benefits. The era of shared prosperity lasted for more than a quarter of a century. But when the balance of power shifted from rough parity between unions and businesses to the present, much-celebrated supremacy of business, that understanding was replaced by unilateral corporate decision making. The good old days had returned. (The November–December 1996 issue of *Harvard Magazine* wryly describes how Roosevelt was considered a traitor to the class of 1904.)

America Needs a Raise is Sweeney's credo: Restore parity between labor and business; restore the social compact; restore government that is concerned with the needs of the 80 percent who have lost out in the past twenty-five years.

Can it be done? Polls show that a third of those working in private industry would join a union if they had the opportunity. Sweeney himself led the Service Employees International Union from 625,000 to 1.1 million members while most other unions declined. In his Justice for Janitors campaigns, Sweeney turned contract battles into political battles which appealed to the public's sense of fairness (as well as their liking for alliteration), spent a lot of money to organize, and won.

Sweeney calls on the AFL-CIO to be a social movement again, in the spirit of the New Deal, not just a narrow-gauge labor movement that does not care about productivity, quality, competitiveness, or the divisions between blacks and whites, men and women, or cities and suburbs. *America Needs a Raise* is by far the most audacious labor statement in decades; it must be taken seriously.

In *A Reporter's Life,* Walter Cronkite calls the late elections "an unconscionable fraud" because the candidates dodged all the basic issues. You cannot say that about John Sweeney. And so bashing labor bosses is back. But if the labor bosses put together a really big parade, I'm confident that President Clinton would be happy to march in front of it. That's why we have politicians, isn't it?

A review of **When Work Disappears: The World of the New Urban Poor,** by William Julius Wilson. New York: Alfred A. Knopf, 1996.

William Julius Wilson, now professor of social policy at Harvard, not only discusses what happens when work disappears from inner-city black ghettos, but also why work disappears. Work disappears because large factories and distribution centers move to the suburbs or the South or abroad or shut down altogether. Hundreds of small neighborhood businesses then go broke and even more work disappears. Blacks who have the education and the resources move to the suburbs where the jobs are, and those who can't move commute. Those who can't commute fall into dire poverty. They can't commute for various reasons. They don't know where the jobs are. They don't have the education to do the jobs. They won't be hired even if they do. Or the cost in time and money is so great compared to the wages that it makes commuting futile.

The result is an intense concentration of desperately poor unemployed people living in central city pockets where the social and economic system has broken down. That means that the schools, day-care centers, clinics, hospitals, apartment buildings, and transportation facilities are falling apart and are primarily holding zones of human misery. The two-parent family, already battered from other directions, is even more battered. Children are mere jetsam with neither the framework of daily life that work provides nor the prospect of making a living from legitimate work themselves. *Cherchez le monnai,* as Milton Friedman said, so enterprising young blacks go into the drug trade. In that trade guns are standard equipment.

Add to this the conservative belief that individuals are responsible for their own plight, and old-fashioned American racism, and the welfare phaseout that will turn thousands of women and children into beggars, and you have a fair understanding of how work disappears and what happens when it does. (Wilson commented on the end of welfare after his book was published.)

Let us put all this in the perspective of numbers before we review Professor Wilson's proposals. A quarter of African Americans are doing well; a quarter are just getting by; 20 percent are at the margin of poverty; and just under 30 percent are below the official poverty line. The greatest density of poverty is in the older, larger cities, such as Chicago, Philadelphia, and Detroit, which for one reason or another have failed to annex their suburbs, inexorably segregating wealth and poverty into different jurisdictions.

The author proposes a way out, if only we will take it. It is a way out for all the poor, not just the black poor (and of the 39 million poor, whites outnumber blacks by more than two-to-one). It means establishing and financing national performance standards in all public schools, providing day care, health care, and a national program of school-to-work transition (the U.S. is in last place among developed countries in this regard). It also means setting up a federal infrastucture program like the WPA that will provide work for everybody who wants a job and can't find one in the private economy.

This is affirmative action for all who need it, and it cannot be stigmatized as preferential treatment for one group at the expense of another (although our society is riddled with preferential treatment for whites with wealth and connections, so we should be used to the idea. And for heaven's sake, the ghetto blacks are glued to the bottom of the bag. Doesn't that alone justify affirmative action?).

Professor Wilson ends with a word of hope for ghetto children, who swim in a vast sea of child poverty. No decent person can blink at the fact that in wealthy, righteous, self-congratulatory America, 14.7 million children—20.8 percent—live in poverty: 16.2 percent of all white children; 40.0 percent of all Hispanic children; and 41.9 percent of all black children. It is hard to say which is the greater crime, that of the drug pushers, or that of the politicians who turn their backs on children. The application of the same jail sentences and fines to the pushers and the politicians is certainly worth thinking about.

January 1997

The Short Twentieth Century

A review of *The Age of Extremes: A History of the World, 1914–1991,* by Eric Hobsbawm. New York: Pantheon Books, 1994.

The Age of Extremes is written both as history and memory. The author lived through it, it is his age as it is ours who are old enough to make the claim, and he avowedly feels deeply about it, even as a spectator or minor participant. History and memory, as he says, are correctives of each other. You can look something up. But you can also remember, "No, it wasn't like that at all." You can't do this with the Peloponnesian War. Yet the Peloponnesian War took place in an era that is finished, so we can understand that war in its entire context. Our era isn't over. We do not even know if we are at its beginning, middle, or end. That, of course, never stopped anyone from having strong opinions on the subject. As observers of our own times we have both advantages and disadvantages.

Hobsbawm writes about the Short Twentieth Century, 1914 to 1991, because it has a real beginning and end, the First World War and the collapse of the Soviet Union. He divides the Short Twentieth Century into three parts, the Age of Catastrophe, from 1914 to just after the Second World War; the Golden Age, about twenty-five years that lasted into the 1970s; and the Landslide, which we are still experiencing.

We who did not live through the First World War must try to imagine what a shocking break it was from the past for those who did live through it. The educated, cultivated inhabitants of industrialized Europe and its English-speaking outliers accepted science, technology, peace, progress, and their rulership over the rest of the world as a matter of course. At the same time, a large section of the working class believed as gospel truth that the brotherhood of man—socialism—was within their grasp. An arms race was on and the guns were loaded, but a kind of complacency lulled the public into the view that civilized nations did not go to war, at least with each other. Then a horrible reciprocity of slaughter awakened cultivated men and women and earnest socialists to their real situation. High culture was to no avail and the workers of the world did not unite.

Instead they threw themselves at each others' throats in a delirious fever of patriotism that made all previous thoughts of internationalism appear to be utopian fantasy. That fever cost about 8 million dead and 21 million wounded, the breakup of the Austro-Hungarian and Ottoman empires, seething revenge-seeking resentment in Germany, and the loss of the tsarist empire to Bolshevism. I remember arguing with my father when I was an adolescent that the war was nothing more than a battle between two pirate ships and that he took our side because he found himself on our ship instead of the other one. I never convinced him.

What had happened was that the balance of power that had kept the peace among the great states of Europe for 100 years, save for the Franco-Prussian War of 1870, had become too rigid to balance: it became frozen with Britain, France, and Russia on one side, and Germany, Austro-Hungary, and the Ottoman Empire on the other. All the empires were in danger of disintegrating into separate national entities, or in Britain's case, losing first place to Germany. Any minor incident could start a war. And it did.

This was an imperialist war, just as Lenin said. But let us make some distinctions. Imperialist wars have taken place since Sargon I of Akkad conquered Sumer. That is to say, as soon as states came into existence 5,500 years ago, they have had to resort to alliances and wars for self-preservation. The capitalists as a class inherited a pre-existing political order and added a new element, the inherent drive of capital to expand as a condition of survival. Long before the Great War, the competition of capitals had become global. The possession of colonies for their raw materials and for profitable investment in facilities such as railroads and ports was now part of the game. Hence the first *world war.*

An immediate outcome of the war was the disintegration of the Russian Empire for a brief interval until it was reintegrated as the Union of Soviet Socialist Republics. We often read that Lenin seized power, but there was little power to seize since Russia was in a state of near anarchy. The "party of a new type," an invention of Lenin's under tsarist restrictions on speech and assembly, was ideally suited to pick up the power that was lying in the gutter, since the Communist Party was a quasi-military, quasi-evangelical organization whose members were absolutely certain of their mission. Shortly before, Rosa Luxemburg, co-leader of the German Sparticists, predicted that Bolshevism would start with the dictatorship of the proletariat, lead to the dictatorship of the party, and end up as the dictatorship of one man. She was prescient. It is fashionable these days to excoriate Lenin as ruthless, and so he was. But so was Abraham Lincoln, who was willing to preside over the deaths of 650,000 men in order to preserve the Union. Let us at least be clear about our standards of judgment. Yet the current attempt to equate Lenin with Stalin blurs all distinctions. Stalin not only was ruthless but also imagined that enemies lurked in every shadow and in broad daylight as well, so the twenty-year forced march to industrialize Russia took place at the highest conceivable cost in lives and grief. Nevertheless, in the beginning was Lenin, who charted a disastrous course for Russia and misery for the rest of the world.

I remember hearing Roosevelt's speech on the radio during the Great Depression of the 1930s in which he said that one-third of the nation was ill-fed, ill-clothed, and ill-housed. Later I learned that an earlier draft contained the more accurate figure of two-thirds, changed in the final draft because, in Roosevelt's opinion, the higher figure was too frightening to acknowledge.

The New Deal in the United States and social democracy in Western Europe were improvised responses to the collapse of free-market capitalism, driven by the recognition that the intervention of the state was mandatory if capitalism was to survive at all. A period of class collaboration began which lasted until the early 1970s, advantageous to both capital and labor. The most that can be said for our contemporary neoconservative proponents of pre-1930s laissez-faire capitalism is that they suffer from historical amnesia. The small part that I played as a precocious child in advancing the cause of the welfare state consisted in convincing my conservative parents to vote for Roosevelt instead of Landon on purely humanitarian grounds.

Eric Hobsbawm rightly speaks of the Thirty-One-Year War because the Second World War was the resumption of the first after an armed truce. Two conditions cleared the way for the rise of Hitler—the Versailles Treaty and the Depression. Hitler could never have come to power if there had not been a punitive peace recklessly imposed on Germany by the short-sighted leaders of the Allies, or a severe world depression which was wholly a capitalist phenomenon. Hitler quickly restored capitalist German prosperity by totally disregarding economic orthodoxy, and proceeded to wipe out German humiliation through a megalomaniacal plan to dominate the world. *Deutschland über alles* was not just a catch phrase, but, in modern terms, a mission statement. To accomplish this end, Hitler needed the German capitalists and, once he was in power, they needed him. The relationship proved to be a thoroughly bad bargain for the capitalists; nevertheless it contradicts the repeated assertion that there is a necessary connection between capitalism and democracy.

The Allied populations had acquired a horror of war so overwhelming that appeasement was the order of the day until the last possible moment. But Hitler, thinking that Russia was weak and the U.S. was indecisive, maniacally chose to fight on two fronts at once and declare war on the United States. If he had defeated Russia and Britain in a blitzkrieg of three months, fascist historians would now be writing the history of the twentieth century, as Hobsbawm observes, but failing that, the preponderance of economic and therefore military power turned against him. Paradoxically, as Hobsbawm also astutely observes, the Soviet Union saved liberal capitalism from destruction. I should add that the reverse is also true. The liberal democracies saved the Soviet Union from destruction as well.

My main impression of World War II, I being just under military age, was acute daily suffering for those millions who were being killed or maimed, an absolute conviction that our side would win, and a sense that there existed a fervent solidarity among hundreds of millions of people in the world who shared the belief that they were fighting the greatest evil that ever existed. I have never before or since had so intense a feeling that I was part of a vast sea of humanity which would sweep away all obstacles before it.

World War II let loose a second wave of revolutions, and one-third of mankind came to live under communism. The exhaustion of the colonial powers and the clean sweep of the colonial liberation movements put an end to the Age of Empire, which lasted no longer than the lifetime of a single individual, say, Winston Churchill, to cite Hobsbawm's example, who lived from 1874 to 1965.

Two types of bastard socialism were abroad in the world: communism and social democracy. Lenin made a horrendous, even fatal mistake in 1919 by splitting international socialism into two movements, insisting that the social democrats were enemies of the "vanguard." This move relegated communists in the developed countries to the status of despised outcasts and by the time Stalin called for a united front against fascism, the damage had been done. Milovan Djilas observed that this "vanguard" had converted itself into a new class in the Soviet Union and Eastern Europe, operating a command economy and a command state, which was as far from social, political, and economic democracy as it was possible to get. While this command class produced some remarkable results, such as the first Sputnik, the most it could accomplish, as Hobsbawm notes, was to construct the best nineteenth-century economy of the mid-twentieth century. The conflict between the new class and all the rest of the multi-ethnic population, papered over by socialist slogans, probably explains better than anything else why the Soviet Union disintegrated overnight as soon as the grip of the Party was loosened. Bertolt Brecht did not exaggerate much when he remarked at one point in East Germany that the government was dissatisfied with the people and had decided to elect a new one.

The social democrats in the West, on the other hand, accommodated themselves to the continuation of capitalist private ownership and were content to tack on a welfare appendage. Since the capitalist structure of society remained intact, the representatives of capital retained the power to malign and then start to sweep away the welfare excrescences when these were found no longer suitable. Both communism and social democracy are the heirs of a great nineteenth-century movement and the best that can be said of them is that they are its illegitimate offspring. Since the Chinese are now trying a New Economic Policy, a market economy and private enterprise under party dictatorship, we can add them as a third.

My own observation of the worldwide communist movement, which I did not get out of a book, is that it had two distinct sides. On one side were tens of millions of men and women who truly longed for peace, equality, a decent livelihood, and a tolerant, democratic commonwealth; on the other were ruthless dictatorships that went against every decent instinct of the millions they purported to lead. My own close friends in the Soviet and Chinese Communist parties were well aware of this horrible contradiction and worked within their parties to change them. There were millions of less influential Khrushchevs and Gorbachevs and their Chinese counterparts and I doubt if we have heard the last of them.

The years between 1947 and 1973 (approximately) Hobsbawm calls the Golden Age—the age, in other words, of the welfare state, the social compact between business and labor, the astonishing growth of all industrialized economies, the rapid rise of the standard of living, the pell-mell introduction of new gadgets that sprang from the brains of scientists and technicians, the introduction of the green revolution in the Third World, a significant rise in the average lifespan as a result of the widespread use of antibiotics, and, of incalculable significance, the end of the peasantry as the majority of the world population after six millennia.

I must confess that as editor of *Challenge* between 1973 and 1978, I did not notice that the Golden Age had come to an end. I conceived my assignment as how to make things better, not how to keep them from getting worse. Not for a moment did I think that we would have to fight just to hold onto the gains that had already been won.

The Golden Age began with the impetus of universal intoxication and exultation felt in defeating fascist Germany, Italy, and Japan. It was constructed of diverse materials: the wondrous scientific advances made during the war; the colossal demand to rebuild war-ruined Europe and Asia; the new means of transportation and communication that turned the statesman's political slogan of one world into actuality; and the widely accepted view that governments must play a role in directing the market economy, which had fared so poorly in the interwar years. The subjective side of all this was the unity of purpose that the masses of men and women valiantly tried to carry over from wartime to peacetime and their irresistible insistence on fair treatment in return for the sacrifices they had made.

But the Golden Age was not all golden. The conflict between capitalism and communism resumed and came to dominate almost every aspect of life. The wars in China, Korea, and Vietnam, actually three of the many wars of national liberation, were seen in the West as part of a Soviet plot to dominate the world, while NATO was seen in the Soviet Union as part of an

American plot to do the same. A mutual escalation of hysteria developed, together with the atom bombs and missiles to go with it. While the threat of mutually assured destruction brought forty-five years of world peace, not counting local wars, the small probability of atomic war always hung over us. During the naming ceremony of my newborn son in October 1962, Soviet missile–laden ships were steaming toward Cuba and our small group of celebrants didn't know if we would be alive the following week. But for the last-minute sobriety of Kennedy and Khrushchev, we might not have been.

After this somewhat tarnished Golden Age, we are now experiencing the Landslide. In a landslide you are on a slope with rocks and earth moving rapidly downward and you risk being buried alive—or dead. The situation is out of control. This is a pretty good description of the situation in which the majority in the industrialized countries find themselves. They cannot do anything about the high rates of unemployment, declining living standards, increasing inequality, runaway global finance and investment, or the moral pollution that surrounds them like smog. The same is true in the former Soviet Empire, only worse by several orders of magnitude. We rejoice that Gorbachev brought the former Soviet citizens freedom, but have nothing to offer concerning the misery, poverty, and gangster capitalism that came with it except the hope that it will go away. U.S. politicians on both sides routinely commit perjury in the course of a day's work because the majority is not their constituency and cannot be told the truth, which is that government is of, by, and for the highest bidders—in the United States, according to the *New York Times,* now $250,000 per contributor.

Altogether a number on the order of 187 million men, women, and children have been killed intentionally or by deliberate neglect in the twentieth century, civilians have again become legitimate targets of war, and torture has been raised to new levels of sophistication. Weapons, including the atomic bomb, have reached an advanced degree of perfection, and the destruction of 100,000 people at the single push of a button, out of sight of the button-pusher, can be accomplished with the greatest of ease.

It would be pleasant to cry reprieved! reprieved! as the twentieth century comes to an end. But that remains to be seen. The Landslide will surely raise doubts about capitalism just as the catastrophes of 1914 to 1945 did. If we must endure thirty-one years of catastrophes to enjoy twenty-five years of reform, no one in his right mind will pay the price. We do not know if the Golden Age was an unrepeatable episode or is achievable again in the twenty-first century. A repeat performance does not seem implausible. But capitalism has been wracked by instability for 200 years and does not show promise that reforms can be any more than episodic in the future as they have been in the past, followed by their partial or complete dismantling.

Will there be Socialism II in the twenty-first century? At the present moment the very asking of the question seems absurd if not downright perverse. But strange to say, the failure of capitalism to meet the needs of human society is the best guarantee that socialism will survive the crimes and stupidities of its bastard incarnations of the twentieth century. And yet the legitimacy of capitalism is so deeply rooted that its own crimes and stupidities evoke merely cynicism rather than a desire to change it. This is the case at the moment. But since humans are hoping animals, as Hobsbawm puts it, the egalitarian organization of society where wealth, class, or position do not purchase privilege, where merely being human purchases privilege, is an ideal which may be lost in the past for the moment, but the past is not lost. Someone is sure to find it. Then there again will be a struggle for the mantle of legitimacy. If you are young enough, you will live to see what happens.

The author of *The Age of Extremes* tells the story of a bright student who came up to him after class one day and asked if the designation Second World War did not imply that there was also a First World War. Without historians like Eric Hobsbawm to remind us what happened in the past, we would be utterly lost.

March 1997

The Theft of Russia

A review of *Resurrection: The Struggle for a New Russia,* by David Remnick. New York: Random House, 1997.

David Remnick's two books, *Lenin's Tomb* (that is, the Soviet Union) and *Resurrection* (of what, remains to be seen), were written by a correspondent who met most of the celebrities, heard most of the stories, and witnessed most of the main events during the last days of the Soviet Union and the first days of the presumably resurrected Russia. A kind of immediacy is conveyed by Remnick's account of who was drunk and who was sober, who was wise and who was a fool, among those who ran the Soviet Union and then Russia from 1985 to 1996. When Prime Minister Chernomyrdin drank to a friend on his birthday with the toast, *"Za vas, za nas, i za gaz"* (To you, to us, and to gas), you get a good idea of where the former comrade in charge of the Soviet gas and oil industry, now prime minister, is coming from. And possibly where he is going, with Russia in tow.

In 1994 the present deputy prime minister Anatoly Chubais said, "They are stealing practically everything." Who are "they"? Mainly the former magnates of Soviet government and business who took off the drab suits of commissars one evening and put on the well-tailored attire of the *haute bourgeoisie* the next morning. (I speak metaphorically. Actually it took some time to learn what clothes, jewelry, and shoes to wear and what resorts to visit, but a glossy magazine soon appeared that gave helpful instructions on these matters.) The Soviet Union disappeared but the Soviet elite remained. Perhaps congratulations are not in order, but neither is blame. They had no choice. Few men and women who value a nice apartment, a Mercedes, a bank account in Frankfurt or Zurich would willingly join the pitiful rump of losers led by Gennady Zyuganov, head of the resurrected Communist Party, whose book *My Russia* I have published in English and which you must read to find out how it is possible to combine Bolshevism, chauvinism, and revanchism in one nostalgic movement. The short answer is contained in a joke that made the rounds in Moscow: "What has one year of capitalism in Russia done that seventy years of communism was unable to accomplish?" The answer: "It has made communism look good" (repeated in the excellent book *Revolution from Above* by David Kotz and Fred Weir).

On January 2, 1992, Boris Yeltsin's young acting prime minister, Egor

Gaidar, administered the largest voltage of "shock therapy" ever attempted, expecting to transform the decrepit Soviet economy into a vigorous, free-market economy in an instant of time. Gaidar, a resolutely self-confident theoretician with deep book knowledge of laissez faire, a great admirer of Milton Friedman, and a man with a strong distaste for state intervention in the economy, intervened to free prices, allow the ruble to float against other currencies, and put state property up for sale to the highest bidder. Never before did Milton Friedman have so much influence.

Later that year, the same Anatoly Chubais whose lament on theft we quoted above, issued vouchers to all Russian citizens to buy shares in state-owned businesses. What could be nobler than every Ivan and Tanya a capitalist? But unfortunately Chubais neglected to index the vouchers against prices in a year when inflation was running at 2,500 percent. The vouchers quickly became worthless. No, not worthless; they were good for a bottle of vodka.

The Soviet nomenklatura, the men who ran the government, the banks, and the industries, bought the vouchers at a kopek on the ruble, with bank loans on preferred terms, granted by banks controlled or formed by themselves, and then with vouchers in hand, bought up the natural resources, factories, trading companies, and remaining financial institutions of the former Soviet Union, frequently at auctions held at secret locations in which the principals of the enterprises on the block were the only bidders.

In fact these astute purchases were subsidiary to the direct appropriation of abandoned assets by generals, factory managers, bank directors, and administrators of natural resources, with some legerdemain of paperwork to make it all acceptable to those poor bookkeepers who received handsome bonuses for the neatness of their work. These acquisitions were complemented by the transactions of men with banks who lent the government money collateralized by stock in public enterprises, on which they promptly foreclosed when the government defaulted on the due date—an inevitable occurrence since tax evasion is endemic, leaving the treasury without the funds to conduct its normal business.

Behind-the-scenes deals depend on a partnership between the purchaser and a patron in government who signs the necessary documents in return for a share in the enterprise, or a payment, normally called a bribe, against a schedule of tariffs which is calibrated according to the size of the deal. It works the other way around as well. An official appoints a worthy acquaintance to head such-and-such a business, making him a millionaire in the course of a morning. In gratitude the worthy acquaintance assigns the official a share of the business. Or the official leases state premises at very reasonable rates, with similar results.

It is self-evident that the top communist managers, party, and government bureaucrats nationally, regionally, and locally were the only ones, except for a talented minority shrewd enough to muscle its way in, with the know-how, connections, experience, and therefore power to run the country, the joint ventures, the big businesses, and the state monopolies. At a lower level, the same applies to the managers of the retail shops, the cooperatives, and the state or collective farms, many of whom had practice converting them to personal property, ostensibly running them for their fellow workers under cover of the Enterprise Law of 1987. The rest of the population was taught to take orders for seventy years, not excluding special obedience training for union officials. By 1992, the only way to stay ahead was through grand larceny at the top, petty larceny at the bottom, and moderate larceny in the middle. The result is that three-quarters of Boris Yeltsin's staff, three-quarters of the central government, and three-quarters of the business elite and near elite are converted communists, with comparable or greater proportions at lower levels of government and business.

Almost every transaction in Russia is in some way illegal, but at least each party to a deal acts with a clear conscience, knowing that there is no other way to do business if business is to be done at all. But in the underworld beneath the semi-criminal upper world is the outright criminal, the mafioso, a member of one of the 8,000 gangs that reach into every branch of business and department of government, whose modus operandi is extortion, pure and simple. The mafia is a second government that extracts payoffs much more effectively than the first government extracts taxes. It succeeds by shooting people who do not comply. Those who do not comply and want to live surround themselves with private bodyguards. Vladimir Gusinsky, once a mediocre theater director, now owner of the biggest TV network in Russia and director of the MOST bank, apparently the bank with the most money, deploys an army of 1,100 men, and still finds it desirable to take frequent vacations in London, Paris, and New York. Any policeman who seriously investigates a crime is well-advised to plan his own funeral.

The best up-to-date book on the economic consequences of Boris Yeltsin is *New Rich, New Poor, New Russia,* by Bertram Silverman and Murray Yanowitch, which I have just published, with no credit due me save my good fortune in knowing such well-informed authors. Those who want the data behind the arguments should turn to this book. Kotz and Weir's *Revolution from Above* is also rich in detail. Suffice to say that if the top 10 percent of Russian society was resurrected, the rest was damned. Between 1991 and 1996 the gross domestic product dropped 40 percent, compared with 31 percent during the entire decade of the Great Depression in the United States. In 1995 capital investment was down to 35 percent of its 1991 level and wages were down 55 percent in addition to delays in payment, forced leaves, and shorter hours. Only the legacy of management paternalism kept unemployment from going higher than 9.1 percent, not counting dropouts from the labor force. Estimates of those living in poverty vary from 25 to 85 percent, depending on the time of measurement and the yardstick used.

The poverty rate for doctors, teachers, journalists, engineers, and technical personnel—the intelligentsia that so fervently supported Yeltsin's reforms at the beginning—was 49 percent. The life expectancy of men dropped six years and that of women three, while infant mortality went up 42 percent—because of a catastrophic breakdown of medical services, rampant disease, and the sheer stress of living under intolerable conditions.

Of course all these data are suspect; they are measurements of chaos, with strong motives on the part of both rich and poor to lie because confiscatory taxes and illegal activities make it impossible to tell the truth. They can only be considered the best approximations under the circumstances.

The anticipated Yeltsin paradise turned into the Yeltsin hell partly because a simple Keynesian rule was violated. If the state reduces consumer demand, investment demand, and government demand all at once, the economy is going to sink. The enrichment of the elite and the impoverishment of the rest was the consequence of trashing the state economy while failing to see that the industrialized countries of the world have both a private sector and a state sector, the latter necessary to ensure a fair distribution of social services and income or, at bottom, merely to assure that such services and income exist.

All of the steps leading up to this tragedy are traced in Remnick's two books. The Soviet Union fell without the consent of the governed. Deep flaws there were, and the governed chafed under them. But how these flaws were dealt with depended on the decisions of individuals and, as everyone knows, the two men who possessed the greatest power to make decisions were Gorbachev and Yeltsin.

Very few of Gorbachev's closest associates knew what this able and persuasive man actually believed before he was elected general secretary of the Communist Party in 1985. Gorbachev and his wife Raisa spoke their true thoughts to one another only while taking walks, far from eavesdropping equipment. Once in power, he made his thoughts known, and they resonated with the public. They fell into three categories: replace the oppressive regime with a democracy; remodel the lumbering economy; end the military confrontation with the West. In his *Memoirs,* Gorbachev makes clear that he considered these issues so entangled that they had to be tackled all at once.

He succeeded in ending the Cold War partly by making reasonable proposals for arms reduction to his Western counterparts and partly by making unilateral reductions to show that he meant business. He succeeded in opening Soviet society to free discussion by flatly condemning the Stalinist terror and by breaking the grip of censorship. A torrent of truthtelling by the public and the media made glasnost unstoppable. (I once met Foreign Minister Andrei Gromyko at a reception in New York in pre-glasnost times and jokingly said, "Tell me some secrets." This request was met with a look that suggested that I should be rounded up.)

But with perestroika, political and economic restructuring, Gorbachev lost his way.

1. Gorbachev avowedly favored a system of democratic market socialism, but he never advanced a straightforward plan to achieve it. He might have opened up a private sector, side by side with the state economy, gradually marketizing or reforming the latter while buying off displaced members of the Old Guard with sinecures or dachas on the Black Sea. This he never proposed, much less attempted, and as the economy worsened, the reformers, now led by Yeltsin, gave up on any kind of socialism at all, democratic or otherwise, and headed straight for the exit marked "normal society" not mentioning the alarming word "capitalism" in public.

2. Gorbachev was oblivious to the centrifugal forces thrusting the Soviet republics apart once the grip of the Communist Party was loosened. Eastern Europe set the example. By the time he realized what was happening it was too late. Each republic leader wanted his own fiefdom free from the dictates of Moscow. That these fiefdoms would be ravaged by civil war and dictatorship seemed to be of little concern to any but Gorbachev and his intimates. All he could do was propose weaker and weaker forms of union at least to preserve internal peace and common citizenship, defense, currency, transportation, and communications within a common market. But the attempted Old Guard coup of August 1991 removed Gorbachev's last shred of authority and made it impossible for him to do anything at all except watch the Soviet Union go to pieces.

3. He never had a clear idea of the political situation or the tempo of change. By 1991 the Communist Party had broken up into three factions: the conservatives under the Old Guard who wanted to do a little tinkering at most; the reformers under Gorbachev who wanted to move to market socialism; and the neoliberals under Yeltsin who wanted to dispense with the labels socialism and capitalism as outdated and just move to a free market with no strings attached. Until as late as 1990, the divisions among these factions were not hermetically sealed. Party members shifted position according to their convictions, if any, and self-interest. But the bandwagon was going Yeltsin's way and the majority joined the bandwagon when that became clear. And since by then Yeltsin was chairman of the Russian congress, the faction on the bandwagon became the ruling faction. I do not see any evidence for the thesis propounded in *Revolution from Above* that the Party elite made a deliberate choice of the capitalist road before all the other roads were blocked. The people I met were worried about where they would end up. Changing systems is perilous and uncertain at best, even for the powerful. Not many do so voluntarily.

As general secretary, then president, Gorbachev had enormous power and prestige. The bandwagon was moving toward reform; he started it rolling himself; yet Gorbachev got on and off until it rolled away from him. In 1987 he drove Yeltsin from the Politburo, making an enemy of an ally, and late in 1990 he appointed reactionaries to the key ministries of government, making allies of enemies. These same men launched the last-ditch coup against him in August 1991.

At least one could say that Gorbachev was a good man fallen among communists. Unfortunately power did not corrupt him. In Yeltsin's case, the communists had an adage that is relevant: It is impossible to make an omelet without breaking eggs. Yeltsin has shown proficiency in breaking eggs but seems to lack the talent to make an omelet.

By 1990 Yeltsin's public support surpassed Gorbachev's as the man who would finally get something done. In June 1991 he became the first democratically elected president of Russia and as such the first popularly chosen leader in Russian history. In August he was the cynosure of all democrats as he stood on a tank and faced down a coup. But this was not enough. In December he made a coup of his own against Gorbachev as president of the Soviet Union and against the Soviet Union as a state.

Yeltsin, together with Kravchuk of Ukraine and Shushkevich of Belarus, made their coup at a secret meeting in Belovezh Forest outside Minsk on December 8 without thinking two steps ahead about the consequences. Remnick reports that Yeltsin was drunk. But not everyone was drunk. Being drunk, one might fall down, one might slur one's words, but one does not destroy a state because of inebriation. The Soviet public had voted for a reformed union in a referendum on March 17. The leaders of nine republics plus Gorbachev had agreed on a new union treaty that was scheduled to be signed August 20—the day after the coup that Yeltsin faced down; the signing never took place. But these were merely expressions of opinions and intentions, no longer of sufficient weight to block the dismemberment of the Soviet Union. That dismemberment resulted in the splintering of the Soviet economy, tens of thousands of casualties in Transcaucasian civil wars, hundreds of thousands of refugees, dictatorships in Central Asia, 25 million Russians living in non-Russian republics, and 80,000 deaths in Chechnya after Yeltsin and his defense minister Grachev finally realized that Chechen independence could not be suppressed in half an hour as Grachev originally believed.

We have already discussed the economic reform and its catastrophic outcome. The Yeltsin brain-trust embraced the catch-phrase: You can't traverse a chasm in two jumps. A compelling thought when you are trying to jump over a chasm, but more to the point is that Moscow wasn't built in a day; you don't tear down your old house until you build a new one. The economic problems pushed Yeltsin and the legislature further and further apart. By the end of 1992 the parliament forced Yeltsin to drop Egor Gaidar as prime minister. By September 1993, relying more on brawn than brain, Yeltsin decreed the intransigent parliament dissolved. The parliament in return deposed Yeltsin as president. In October Khasbulatov and Rutskoi, leader of the parliament and deposed vice president, invited a gang of reds, browns, and unaffiliated felons gathered around the White House to march on the centers of communication in Moscow in a deadly imitation of Lenin's actions in Petrograd, October 1917. In reply, Yeltsin convinced Grachev to send tanks to shell the parliament building, the White House, and beat back the putsch. The two sides matched crime for crime. One-hundred-and-fifty people—legislators, aides, journalists, supporters, and onlookers—were killed in this battle between a democratically elected president and a democratically elected parliament.

Long before the presidential elections of 1996 Boris Yeltsin was a walking corpse both politically and physically. But since the alternative to Yeltsin was Zyuganov, a summit of billionaires undertook Yeltsin's political resurrection through their virtual monopoly of the media and a campaign of extraordinary largesse, including dispersal of enormous amounts of cash to pay back wages and pensions, and promises that Yeltsin would personally hug every granny in the country and throw out all the bad men in the Kremlin who had done all the bad things during his term in office, none of which he approved of or even knew anything about. After Yeltsin was hidden away in a well-furnished morgue between the first and second rounds of the election, and the election was won, a small group of heart specialists undertook his physical resurrection through bypass surgery. Anyone who reads the papers can see the results. The doctors went home but the billionaires stayed on. It is hard to say if Yeltsin is their prisoner or they are his. In practice it doesn't matter. The man who stood for a separation of the state and the economy now sits at the apex of a state-economic complex as closely interlocked as it was under the Soviet dictatorship.

The *Nation* of February 17, 1997, reported that "Deputy Security Council Secretary Boris Berezovsky [risen from a car dealership] announced proudly that he and six other businessmen control 50 percent of the Russian economy. 'Russia is undergoing a redistribution of property on a scale unprecedented in history.'" Of course this is braggadocio. But what truth lies in this braggadocio? When Chubais said, "They are stealing absolutely everything," he added, "They will become owners and decent administrators of their property" (quoted by Silverman and Yanowitch). This may be so, but how will it help the rest of Russia? Perhaps David Remnick knows, since he titled his book *Resurrection*. But he has kept the answer a secret. Could it be that he has in mind the reaction to the reaction?

September 1997

Forty-Thousand Years of History

A review of *Guns, Germs, and Steel: The Fates of Human Societies,* by Jared Diamond. New York and London: W.W. Norton, 1997.

In his work as an ornithologist observing birds in New Guinea, Jared Diamond also observed people. Seeing how hazardous tribal life was there, he concluded that New Guineans had to be more intelligent than most other people in order to survive. That conclusion set red lights flashing in my brain. I wondered if Jared Diamond had ever thought about the hazards of life in inner-city ghettos of the United States while observing birds there, or observing birds while trying to cross the street in Rome.

I have started with a digression. The subject of *Guns, Germs, and Steel* is the broad patterns of world history. Over thirty years ago, when I became skeptical about the broad patterns of world history according to Marx and Engels, and everyone else for that matter, I decided to find out about the patterns for myself by reading history from the beginning to the end, or at least until the present.

By that time—thirty years ago—archaeologists and anthropologists, treating the surface of the earth as a great palimpsest, had scraped layer after layer away, back to the beginning of time for *Homo sapiens sapiens,* which is now recognized to be about 150,000 years ago. All of our ancestors everywhere were foragers living in small groups of extended families for most of those 150,000 years. They solved the problem of surplus population by slowly fanning out from Africa to all the hospitable places in the world. Fire and furs made even Norway, Sweden, and Siberia tolerable.

Then about 40,000 years ago, something extraordinary happened in Europe. That layer of the palimpsest reveals a sudden profusion of new tools and weapons, including lethal bows and arrows, and somewhat later, the evocative cave paintings of Lascaux and Altamira. By 40,000 years ago we recognize human beings who could have done anything we can do—surf the Web, cross the street in Rome, or manage a portfolio of stocks, bonds, and Treasury bills. Around that time we bid goodbye to *Homo sapiens neanderthalensis,* who was totally outclassed.

Beginning 11,000 years ago, humans made the most far-reaching change in history, with consequences that are still being played out. Starting in the Fertile Crescent of the Middle East and then independently in China,

Mesoamerica, the Andes, eastern North America, and possibly several other places, they invented agriculture. But not all at once, and not knowing they were doing it. It came piecemeal by selecting seeds, weeding, watering, fertilizing, harvesting, and storing the products of a few valuable plants. Around the same time they began managing several species of animals and breeding them for what they wanted: better meat, skin, fur, fleece, and a willingness to pull a cart. Only after a period of time when all these separate operations were performed in concert can we speak of a system of production, the parts of which have long seemed to fit together naturally.

Why would hunter-gatherers go to the trouble of doing all the extra work? The answer must be that the benefits of producing food came to exceed the benefits of gathering and hunting compared to the work required to get the results.

Why did the transition to agriculture take place in several independent locations within a few thousand years, after tens of thousands of years of hunting and gathering? Or if you include preceding hominids, after millions of years of hunting-gathering? And why did agriculture spread from those few points of origin to replace foraging almost everywhere?

Our ancestral hunter-gatherers regulated their numbers stringently to avoid exceeding the carrying capacity of their habitats. But a small increase in numbers was accommodated by migration to new territories. Eventually bands were everywhere that bands could be; they reached the Americas 13,000 years ago. Suddenly—in the long sweep of history suddenly means several thousand years—the line of greatest advantage changed from migrating for sustenance to settling in villages and helping along the useful plants and animals. Our ancestors did not know what they had done: they had brought about autocatalysis. That is to say, food production led to the reproduction of more people who had to reproduce more plants and animals which led to the reproduction of more people who had to reproduce more plants and animals.

All this reproducing of plants, animals, and people set off one of the greatest bursts of creativity in history, which led directly to a second great transformation, the invention of cities. I use the word invention retrospectively, since the Sumerians 5,700 years ago, and subsequently the Chinese, Mesoamericans, and Peruvians, were unaware that they were inventing cities until they were on the threshold of inventing them. That is, they were engaged in a process with consequences they could not foresee. This process runs through a sequence of bands, tribes, chiefdoms, and states. Everywhere that cities appeared, this sequence repeats itself, even in places where agriculture was borrowed from elsewhere, such as Harappa in the Indus Valley or Egypt in North Africa. When a sequence repeats itself with regularity, it cannot be accidental.

The simplest explanation is that people adapted in similar ways to similar circumstances. In tribal villages, where less than a hundred people lived together and belonged to related families, the management of affairs required no more than the informal supervision of a head man who had only the power of persuasion. Why it was not a woman is a whole other story. When villages grew larger, and several villages of a thousand or more people of unrelated lineages began working together, the management of affairs became much more demanding. The unpresuming head man now stepped forward as a chief, altogether a superior man, dressed in resplendent clothing and attended by warriors ready to exact obedience to his commands. This was necessary. A thousand or ten thousand people cannot regulate their affairs in the same manner as a hundred. Along with farming, material property of some magnitude had come into the world. It had to be apportioned according to rules. Disputes had to be settled. Raids on enemies had to be undertaken or repulsed, lest one be slaughtered or taken into slavery. Spirits had to be invoked, quite out of the competence of the common run of men. A world-historic event took place as tribes imperceptibly became transformed into chiefdoms: the division of men and women into rulers and the ruled.

We should have some notion of time. Chiefdoms prevailed in Mesopotamia from 5500 to 3700 BCE, 1,800 years. Then the great panoply of civilization came into being: Cities with classes of slaves, craftsmen, merchants, warriors, artists, scribes, landlords, bureaucrats, priests. States ruled by kings, mightier than chiefs. States supported by the surplus of farming extracted as tribute or taxes. Irrigation canals built by conscripted labor, monumental public buildings, so necessary to impress the masses with the brilliancy of their godlike priests and kings. With the physical manifestation came the spiritual, the gods who blessed the status quo, and as it is related in some ancient scripts, the rulers themselves, not only godlike but gods, sent down to direct the affairs of ordinary men. As to whether cynical doubts crept into the thoughts of any man or woman god who walked the earth, the scripts are silent.

Although we can safely say that the great majority of city dwellers and farmers living at the time entertained only rumors and fantasies about distant lands, by 1000 BCE four civilizations dominated Eurasia and North Africa: the Middle Eastern, the Mediterranean, the Indian, and the Chinese. Even as late as the thirteenth century, Marco Polo was considered an incorrigible liar in describing the accomplishments of the Chinese and the magnificence of their cities. Nevertheless, behind the backs of the low and mighty alike, these four centers of power promoted their mutual growth through the borrowing of crops, livestock, inventions, religions, arts, and the techniques of statescraft and war from each other. Empires rose and fell and frontiers changed, but the achievements of civilization knew no borders. Neither did trade. A network of exchange by land and by sea reached across Eurasia. The best practices of each center gradually moved to all the others, with one or another civilization taking the lead at different times.

Even so, the seemingly impregnable urban empires lived on a seesaw balance with the nomadic chiefdoms and proto-states of the Central Asian steppes. When disease or political crisis wracked the cities, they became irresistible targets to archers on horseback from the steppes, who could concentrate their forces and move on the cities with devastating suddenness. Not until artillery came into regular use in the middle of the fourteenth century could the city dwellers defend themselves adequately, and only then was the great terror of invasion out of nowhere lifted.

Jared Diamond enters the subject of world history with a series of questions. Why did Europeans conquer Americans instead of the other way around? Why did the Europeans have guns, steel swords, and seaworthy ships, while the Americans had none? Why did European germs kill Americans and not the Europeans? Why did Europeans have such a long head start on Americans in 1492?

The ultimate answer lies in the biogeographical differences between Eurasia and the Americas. The people of the Fertile Crescent, and of China as well, were simply fortunate enough to be endowed with better resources than the people of the Andes and Mesoamerica. Barley and wheat were easier to domesticate than maize. More important, the people of the Fertile Crescent had wild cattle, sheep, goats, and pigs suitable for domestication, while the people of the Andes had only llamas and alpacas, not much good for pulling carts or riding, while the people of Mesoamerica had no large animals at all. Eventually the civilizations of Eurasia obtained horses from Central Asia, domesticated around 4000 BCE, while the horses of North America, together with hundreds of other large animals, became extinct at the end of the Pleistocene about 13,000 years ago. The superior collection of plants and animals in Eurasia gave the people living there a clear advantage.

Next was the relative ease with which agriculture spread from the Middle East to adjacent areas. The Mediterranean climate that stretched 3,000 miles from Mesopotamia to the Iberian Peninsula was hospitable to the founder plants and animals of western Asia. The Mediterranean was a God-given—or geologically given—conduit. The same can be said about the spread of millet and rice along the Yangtze and Yellow rivers in China. By the time of Jesus and Hillel, all the founder crops and animals of Eurasia had spread to wherever they could be grown or cared for, as far north and west as Ireland, as far east as Japan, and as far south as Ethiopia.

Along with all these presumably good things came disaster. Diseases little known to hunter-gatherers spread from animals to people living cheek by jowl on farms and then erupted in that excellent culture medium, the city.

A new demographic norm grew up together with civilization: children died and were replaced with new ones. The survivors became immunized adults. A cycle of infection, death, and survival repeated itself every generation for 6,000 years until recent methods of hygiene and the discovery of antibiotics broke the cycle. Each time trade was restored across Eurasia after intervals of interruption by the nomadic herders of the steppes, exotic pathogens were tapped and carried from one end of the continent to the other and delivered to populations without immunities along with the products of commerce. The stability brought to Central Asia by Genghis Khan, to quote the best known example, permitted the unrestricted passage of goods and germs. One-hundred-and-fifty years passed after the Black Death of the fourteenth century before the populations of Europe and China were restored to their pre-bubonic plague levels.

When Europeans and Americans met, the Europeans came with guns and steel, but also with smallpox, measles, influenza, typhus, and bubonic plague, to which they had degrees of immunities and to which the Americans did not. The outcome was predetermined: the Europeans came as conquerors.

When Jared Diamond asserts all of the above, he is right. But then he adds to these quite reasonable observations a dubious one: the cause of causes of Eurasia's superiority over the Americas at the time of contact was its east-west axis. The Americas unfortunately are lined up along a north-south axis. A north-south axis inhibits the spread of agriculture and civilization because variations in climatic zones act as barriers. Differences in climatic zones do act as barriers. But placing the orientation of continents at the pinnacle of causation is certainly false and contradicts everything else that Jared Diamond has written.

The reasons are many. Nature was generous in providing superior plants and animals in the Middle East and China and niggardly in providing inferior ones in the Americas. This fact has nothing to do with the axes of these continents. North America stretches 3,000 miles from east to west. Why should we suppose that the North Americans would not have evolved along the lines of Eurasians if the resources had been available, despite the north-south axis of the continent? We need only ask ourselves what would have happened if the Middle East and China had not been favorably endowed.

If we take an atlas in our hands, we will see that Saharan Africa also stretches 3,000 miles east-west, but the fact that it became a desert at the end of the Pleistocene epoch is unrelated to the north-south axis of Africa. The atlas will show us that Australia stretches east-west, in accordance with the Diamond hypothesis, but unfortunately, the outback, which occupies almost the entire interior of the continent, is one of the hottest and driest places on Earth.

Our atlas will also show us that the three centers of civilization in Mesoamerica—the Yucatan Peninsula, the Oaxaca Valley, and the Valley of

Mexico—are all in the Tropics. The Tropics did not ipso facto inhibit the rise of agriculture. The relatively small area of these centers and their limited natural resources had more to do with their level of civilization than the north-south axis of North America. The fact that the African Tropics developed differently follows from the dearth of domesticable plants and the total absence of large domesticable animals rather than from the orientation of that continent. Rhinoceroses cannot be ridden. Zebras are unmanagable.

If we look at our atlas again, we will see that Eurasia stretches 10,000 miles east-west; but it is fragmented into many climatic and topographical zones: cropland, forests, deserts, mountains, and steppes, ranging from extremely hot to extremely cold, and very moist to very dry. That is why it took 8,500 years for Fertile Crescent cereals to reach all of Eurasia. Yet the interaction of zones with substantially different environments gave scope to all the fruitful borrowings that we have discussed.

After this short excursion over the map, I arrive where I was before I read *Guns, Germs, and Steel,* namely, that humans adapt to their entire environment, natural and social, and their entire environment is not solely or even mainly determined by the axis of the continent they happen to live on.

Given the Eurasian advantage, we should say at least a word about the last great transformation that is not at the center of Jared Diamond's attention: capitalism. Columbus, after all, came to the Americas looking for a route to the East Indies. His voyage was not taken on a whim or because of an axis but because European merchants were engaged in an increasingly profitable trade with eastern and southern Asia and were feverishly looking for an easier and cheaper way to get there. The enticement of cold cash led to the Americas, and the incorporation of the Americas into the rest of the world led to an expansion of trade beyond anyone's calculation. The gold and silver of Mexico and Peru multiplied this trade, not only to the Indies, but to everywhere. In a world doubled in size overnight, markets widened, specialties increased in number, products cheapened in price, and the merchants, financiers, and princes of Europe, masterminding the projections and sending out the fleets, rose to the apex of a world system that had never before existed. This was not just one more churning of the 7,000-year-old order of tribute and submission, but its subversion in a mere 200 years.

While I think that the axis theory is an aberration, Jared Diamond's probings into a general theory of world history are not to be waved away. History is full of contingencies; contingencies are what most historians study. Most historians are quite shocked to hear anyone propose that history is anything but one damned thing after another. I hope they are quite shocked by Jared Diamond. He has looked for regularities, and regularities are what turn a mere compilation into a science.

The person to look to here is Charles Darwin. The parallel sequences from bands, tribes, chiefdoms, and states indicate that, with all the randomness, trials, errors, and miseries, human societies adapt in the same manner that organisms adapt. But the means are not changes in genes but changes in know-how, acted on by men and women as best as they can. As for the prevailing view of the late twentieth century that the crooked timber of humanity cannot be straightened, we all know people who are not crooked and circumstances in which people are decent. If humanity is hopelessly depraved, we will continue to go from bad to worse and back again. But it strains credulity to believe that a system that makes greed its guiding principle is the final human destination.

March 1998

See my note on page 114 on current estimates for the evolution of anatomically and behaviorally modern Homo sapiens.

We do not yet know when Homo sapiens *reached the Americas. The estimates range from 40,000 years ago to 16,500 years ago.* Homo sapiens *might have traveled across the Beringian land bridge when the sea level was low, or by boat close to the pacific shoreline. Another hypothesis posits the arrival from Europe along the edge of an ice sheet across the Atlantic.*

The Past and Future of Socialism: The Communist Manifesto *at 150*

A review of ***The Communist Manifesto: A Modern Edition,*** by Karl Marx and Frederick Engels. With an introduction by Eric Hobsbawm. London and New York: Verso, 1998.

I had the good fortune of meeting Eric Hobsbawm in London while I was writing this review. He gave me a copy of the edition cited above with his striking introduction. It is one of several pieces that I have come across commemorating the hundred-and-fiftieth anniversary of *The Communist Manifesto.* Probably there are many more.

Marx and Engels were thirty and twenty-eight when the *Manifesto* was published in an infinitesimal German edition in February 1848. A tiny group of workers and intellectuals, the League of the Communists, had commissioned a statement of principles late in 1847. It was approved at a meeting in London a few months later. These small beginnings were no measure of the later impact of the *Manifesto.* By the 1870s it had become the most influential revolutionary document written in the nineteenth century.

The reasons for its impact are self-evident. The explosive force of the prose, the concision, the sweeping indictment of exploitation, the near eschatological promise of a humane future for mankind—these elements combine in a statement of messianic conviction.

The *Manifesto* reflects Marx and Engels's historical conception of capitalism as the most recent in a succession of societies that create the conditions for their own replacement. It also reflects the mindset of the moment. The authors had grounds to think that a proletarian revolution was imminent. A depression, unemployment, hunger, and fear swept the working classes throughout Europe and pushed them into open revolt almost as the *Manifesto* was being published. Most of the governments on that continent, cobbled together in 1815, were overthrown. Within eighteen months, except for the monarchy of Louis Philippe in France, every one of them was restored. Marx and Engels had witnessed the first and last Europe-wide revolution, although the expectation of another one gained mythical force. But instead of opening Europe to socialism, the insurrections of 1848 led to a vast expansion of capitalism and ultimately to limited liberal democracy.

We are all 150 years older than Marx and Engels in 1848, so we can review the *Manifesto* with the accumulated knowledge of those years. Both truth and error are mercilessly revealed to us as a kind of unearned income just for showing up during Act II after Act I is over.

The celebrated characterization of mid-century capitalism as an enormously expansive but unstable system of production can be accepted by every reasonable person, regardless of political persuasion. Marx and Engels's description of a global market created by railroads, steamships, the telegraph, and cheap goods is a bravura performance, and uncannily familiar. Substitute jet planes, the fax, e-mail, and overnight delivery by FedEx, and we are talking about today's headlines.

Previous ruling classes thrived on stability and calm. But the bourgeoisie are constantly driven by competition to find new, more productive machinery to replace the machinery already in their factories; new, more productive industries to replace the old ones; and to race around the world frenetically looking for new markets.

But all this amazing expansion is too powerful for the narrow confines of the bourgeois social system. Crises of overproduction break out. Capital destroys the wealth it has already created, only to rise from each period of destruction with even more prodigious feats of production.

I can attest as a capitalist publisher that in the course of forty years I have progressed from using now antique Linotype machines to the latest desktop computers, any one of which can outperform the entire array of processors used at Los Alamos in the early 1940s to make the atomic bomb. Correspondingly I have had to find ever more sophisticated methods of selling the increasing number of books and journals that we are capable of producing, reaching out to every country in the world, only to be faced with the need to put all those millions of words on CD-ROMs and the Internet and find a way to get paid for doing so.

Along with capital came the proletariat, the factory wage-laborers, men, women, and children, without property, desperately ill-paid, overworked, used up, and cast out when they were maimed, sick, or became redundant.

These sullen work-slaves found themselves thrown together in increasingly large numbers in the factories of the cities and towns and began to form unions and political parties in self-defense. As in all previous societies, two classes stood opposed to each other. The bourgeoisie had created its own nemesis: the proletariat. The middle strata—the petty capitalists, shopkeepers, and professionals—fought to survive but were increasingly pushed into the ranks of the proletariat. Out of desperation, the great mass of workers, finally understanding that there was no alternative, would have to rise up and overthrow the few remaining masters of capital and convert their private property into the property of all, administered by a public authority in the interests of all.

After the passage of 150 years, we know that there are a lot of things wrong with these declarations. Marx and Engels did not so much as consider the possibility that the conditions of the working class could be improved within the prevailing system, even though they understood and extolled the astonishing productive powers of capitalism. They did not consider that capitalists as a class might prefer to compromise on such issues as wages and working conditions rather than fight to the death. They did not envisage a capitalist state providing pensions, sickness insurance, and other measures of social support. Nor did they consider the plausible case that the middle classes of shopkeepers, salespeople, teachers, doctors, and bureaucrats would grow as the powers of production increased.

In the end, as Eric Hobsbawm observes, the propositions that the proletariat would overthrow capitalism and establish communism did not flow from Marx and Engels's actual analysis, but from a philosophical tenet that was smuggled into their pages as a hope. They deduced that history proceeds as a contradiction of opposites followed by a resolution, a deduction borrowed from Hegelian dialectics. The outlook of Marx and Engels in the 1840s seemed to be confirmed by the French Revolution, a violent break with the past. The prospect of gradual change of a fundamental sort was beyond their ken.

The assumption that workers of the world would unite unjustifiably ignores the fact that workers have other, often conflicting, identities. One is not only a worker or a capitalist, but also a Frenchman, a German, or an Italian; a Christian, a Muslim, or a Jew; a conservative, a liberal, or a radical; a citizen of a state or a subject of a sovereign; a holder of ethical opinions; and a man or a woman. It is hard for people to sort out what their self-interest is and harder to act on it. We are not entitled to the presumption that membership in a class is the ultimate reality that will dominate all the others. Only an examination of specific circumstances will tell us which identity takes precedence at a given moment. Successful modern politicians instinctively know this.

I am reminded of my short-lived experience as an industrial worker in the late 1940s when I was shocked to hear the white workers abuse the black workers behind their backs, and women, of whom there were none on the shop floor, spoken of in disrespectful language. I had been somewhat misled about what to expect.

In spite of a widespread belief to the contrary, Marx and Engels did not assert that a socialist revolution was inevitable. A revolution would come about only by the political activity of the working class. The authors of the

Manifesto considered the possibility of what they called "the ruin of the contending parties." This fact is noted by Hobsbawm in his introduction. The world wars of the twentieth century, the Great Depression, fascism, and Soviet communism are ample illustrations of this point. The workers of the world had more than their chains to lose. They had their lives to lose. And they did.

Further on in the *Manifesto,* Marx and Engels discuss the relations of workers and communists. The communists are not a separate party, they declare, and have no separate interests. Their role is to point out the common concerns of the workers and to represent the interests of the movement as a whole.

This is a far cry from Lenin and Stalin. Which brings up the inevitable question: How far are Marx and Engels responsible for the blunders and crimes committed in their names? Everyone must judge for himself. A reasonable answer might be: as far as Jesus was responsible for Torquemada and Moses was responsible for Netanyahu.

Marx and Engels also discuss utopian socialism, which they dismiss as small-scale, middle-class, do-good, fantastic. We are entitled to ask whether the views put forth in *The Communist Manifesto* are not also a fantasy. We would have to say that the effort to predict the future from the past, with the degree of confidence implied in the language of the *Manifesto,* is itself a fantasy. As much so the idealization of the working class as a class with a mission to liberate humanity from several thousand years of oppression.

But that is not the last word. Their understanding of capitalism as an epoch in history that is both expansive and unstable is the foundation for any realistic discussion of the system in which we live. Socialist and reform parties have challenged capitalism, have even administered it at times, and have taken off some of its raw edges. Even today, after all their failures in the twentieth century, social democratic parties are either in power or form the main opposition in most countries of Europe. With all their doctrinal changes, they are still carriers of a secular ideal.

Ironically, capitalism has turned back on itself over the last twenty-five years and in 1998 looks more like the capitalism of the *Manifesto* than it did in 1948, 1958, or 1968. Eighteen million workers are unemployed in Europe. The gap between rich and poor has grown everywhere. The welfare state is under assault. The sweatshops of 1998 look like those of 1898. International financial manipulations are beyond the control of sovereign states. We have suffered a Sisyphus syndrome, pushing the stone of reform up the hill from 1945 to 1973, only to see it roll back down again. Eric Hobsbawm puts it bluntly: at the beginning of the new millennium, triumphant capitalism is out of control.

What of socialism in the future? It will be premised on the failure of the socialist and communist parties of the twentieth century. It must be different. It may not even be called socialism, which is immaterial. If capitalism is reformed to the point where majorities truly control the political, social, and economic policies of state and superstate organizations, the system will no longer be capitalism. It will be postcapitalism under some name that we or our grandchildren choose to give it.

The collapse of the Soviet Union has opened the way to a hitherto impossible convergence of socialist, labor, and reformist movements. This point was impressed on me by Donald Sassoon, author of a masterly book on the European Left, *One Hundred Years of Socialism*. Everyone is speaking to everyone else in civil tones again. The self-defeating split between social democrats and communists has passed into history. They are prepared to present friendly socialism, friendly Labourism (British), and friendly reformism (U.S.) to the electorate. They are prepared to experiment with many different forms of social organization, much along the lines that Alec Nove pointed out in his 1991 book, *The Economics of Feasible Socialism Revisited*. People do not want to be scared out of their wits. They want feasibility, not apocalypse.

For skeptics who doubt the possibility of change for the good, I would like to point out that the sense of what is legitimate and what is not is subject to change. It was once acceptable to spit on the sidewalk, blow your nose in the air, break wind in public, perform surgery without handwashing, smoke in crowded rooms, drive drunk, subordinate women, own slaves, and exclude citizens from voting. None of these practices any longer makes sense. Is it too much to believe that desperately poor children, sick people without adequate care, poor people who live in dilapidated houses and send their children to dilapidated schools, people who hold jobs that leave them in poverty, and involuntary joblessness itself will some day be viewed as an intolerable social blight? Won't the day come when the present indecent disparities in wealth and power will appear as outmoded and unacceptable as the medieval disparities between lord and serf appear to us today?

The point of *The Communist Manifesto* is not that preconceived historical changes are inevitable, but that they are brought about by political movements within the conditions available to them. On this subject the last laugh has not yet been laughed.

May 1998

The Truman Show

When I was about five years old, I entertained the fantasy that my mother, father, aunts, uncles, and acquaintances were actors who performed their parts in my presence and then reverted to their natural non-acting selves when they were out of sight. Unfortunately, I never found out if I was right or wrong.

I was not surprised to discover that a movie was made out of the likes of my childhood angst. In this comedy of exquisite sadism, written by Andrew Niccol, Truman Burbank is adopted at birth by a giant television company—novel, but of doubtful legality—and everyone around him is an actor: his mother, father, best friend, wife, coworkers at a spurious insurance agency that sells spurious insurance to spurious individuals, shopkeepers, street-sweepers, etc., etc., etc. This whole monstrous fabrication is paid for by corporate advertising. To drive the artificiality of this conceit into the heads of the most obtuse, all the actors overact: the mother is oh too-too motherly; the best friend is so awfully true blue; the wife is ever so wifely; and the father, well, he drowns early in the story and returns later as a der-elict: there has to be some concession to reality. As to his not-to-be college sweetheart we'll come back to her later. I must retract what I said about the obtuse. The effect was designed for the obtuse and observant alike.

Everyone who watches *The Truman Show* on television—and it is the most popular show in the history of shows—knows that Truman's whole life is a fake. Only Truman himself is not a fake. But he is hoodwinked, bamboozled, and hornswoggled about living in a world created by someone else.

That person is Christof, ironically named, a master of deception who directs the show from a control room in a huge dome that covers the pris-tine town of Seahaven, built on an island inside the largest television set in the world. Even the sun, moon, stars, clouds, and sky are fake, more dazzlingly real than real, all composed of painted scenery and light show put on within the dome. (If I remember correctly, a half-moon is shown fifteen to twenty degrees away from the setting sun, an optical impossibil-ity.) Five thousand cameras allow the audience to see Truman twenty-four hours a day.

The premise of *The Truman Show*—the portrayal of duplicity—is realized by the clever merging of illusion and reality as well as illusion within illusion. Everything that we see has several meanings. We see events—fiction to begin with—but we know the events are telling several stories simultaneously, one perceived by Truman, one perceived by the staff of the studio, one perceived by the spectators watching television in the movie, and one perceived by us sitting in the theater. We are flooded with perceptual dissonance, which stoops or rises to get our attention; it's hard to say which. We see actors acting as actors (Shakespeare, Pirandello), actors acting as non-actors (ditto), and actors acting as directors (also ditto). The real spectators (you and I) are set up for an evening of loathing. The screenwriter has found a perfect metaphor for manipulation.

No sham, however elaborate, can be without flaws. Truman begins to notice them when he is about thirty. A spotlight falls out of the sky onto the street a few yards from Truman with the curious label "Serius." As he drives to work, an actor-newscaster attempts to cover up the mishap by announcing that debris has fallen from a plane. (The set is bigger than any of us imagined.)

Truman's car radio jams and, with characteristic American ingenuity, he kicks it several times and hears that he, Truman, is turning a corner: he has accidentally tuned in a radio frequency directed to the actors.

He notices that several people circle the block repeatedly in the same sequence. His "wife" Meryl brushes off this observation as the result of an overactive imagination.

He conceives a desire to go to Fiji, as far away from Seahaven as it is possible to get. Meryl suggests that they conceive a baby instead: what actresses will do for a living these days is truly remarkable.

As the affable Truman becomes more and more suspicious, he loudly claps his hands in a supermarket as a test. Nobody looks up; Christof has evidently failed to coach his actors in spontaneity.

Now while they are driving he confides in Meryl that he is the center of some kind of gigantic conspiracy and they must get off the island immediately. But, since every word of his is heard in the control center, a traffic jam suddenly materializes on previously empty streets and he can't move his car.

It's not as though Truman wasn't warned about the conspiracy. One member of the cast and only one cannot stomach the fraud. Lauren, his not-to-be sweetheart in college, blurted out the truth one night on the beach, but she was hustled off the set by her actor-"father," who hastily explained that Lauren was a little mental and was given to blurting out nonsense on a regular basis. Subsequently, the camera intermittently cuts to Lauren, now Sylvia—her real name—sitting in her room somewhere in America watching *The Truman Show* in a state of righteous indignation. Strategically placed behind her for us to see if we look carefully is a poster announcing a Free Truman Rally. A few people out there are not just spectators after all.

Jim Carrey shows us that a really serious actor was hiding behind the exaggerated facial contortions of his previous roles. He makes the transition from insouciant insurance salesman to terrified fugitive with honor to his not always distinguished profession. Laura Linney is an effective complement as his excessively smiling and reassuring actress-nurse "wife." One of her most incongruous scenes shows her pitching a commercial for cocoa to a television camera with her broad faux smile while she is at the same time offering to make Truman a cup of the same cocoa; he stands incredulous at her artificiality. Ed Harris—Christof—plays an impenetrably self-confident executive whose words and demeanor make the case for a leader who is ruthless for the good of others.

Later we see Truman, leafing through his wedding album, notice with consternation that Meryl's fingers are crossed in a photograph of their post-nuptial embrace. Even the wedding was a fraud.

Of course Truman has to escape. In alarm at the thought of the longest-running and most-watched TV show coming to an abrupt halt, Christof cues the sun in the middle of the night—a startling sight even in a movie—and sees Truman sailing away toward the horizon. The horizon, you recall, is the inside of a dome. But I have said enough. All of which I assume you will have forgotten when you see the movie, if you haven't already.

The Truman Show is a treacherous metaphor for America in the last quarter of the twentieth century that somehow managed to make its way out of Hollywood and say something true and significant. We are living *The Truman Show*. We are passive spectators watching Truman—millions of Trumans who are in a predicament—and we have lost the knack of doing anything about it. A small number of us are Christof, manipulating Truman and everyone else, buying the acquiescence of politicians who are strangely silent about the plight of Truman. Some of us are Meryl and the other actors and crew who have talked themselves into thinking that Truman doesn't need help. A few of us are running corporations that sponsor the program that torments Truman. A minority of us are Sylvia, who organizes rallies to protest the treatment of Truman to no avail.

Christof himself announces: "We accept the reality of the world with which we're presented; it's as simple as that." (I owe this quote to Janet Maslin of the *New York Times,* who must have brought a penlight so that she could take notes.)

The quote is quite right up to a point. Truman is trapped in his culture and we are trapped in ours. And yet a movie like *The Truman Show* could not have been made in the 1930s or 1940s when millions of us or our parents or grandparents were active participants instead of spectators, even if we or they only pulled the lever for Roosevelt or bought War Bonds. No one would have thought of making a movie showing spectators sitting at home doing nothing about hardships that affected three-quarters of the country. Sometimes we don't accept reality; we do something about it.

Perhaps Truman escapes all by himself without help from any of us in the end. It only happens that way in the movies.

September 1998

World Development for the Few

A review of *Human Development Report 1998.* New York, Oxford: Oxford University Press for the United Nations Development Programme, 1998.

The long and the short of it is that in the last century world production and consumption have grown prodigiously while distribution has been grotesquely unequal and is getting worse. The standard of living of a minority of the world's population has risen, but up to 2.5 billion people lack adequate food, clean water, sanitation, housing, medical care, education, transportation, and energy sources. The upper 20 percent consumes 86 percent of the world's output while the poorest 20 percent consumes 1.3 percent.

I do not intend to impose on the reader even a fraction of the masses of statistics in the *Human Development Report* that prove the contention of the previous paragraph in the most exhaustive manner imaginable. I would not even know how to go about such an enterprise without duplicating the entire book. But there are a few primal facts that should be of interest to every literate person and that strain comprehension even after they have been memorized and impressed indelibly on the brain.

We would scoff in disbelief if this were fiction, but in reality the 225 richest people in the world own assets worth over $1 trillion, an amount equal to the annual income of the poorest 47 percent of the world's population—2.5 billion people. (Box 1.3, page 30.)

"The three richest people have assets that exceed the GDP of the 48 least developed countries." (Continuing to read Box 1.3.)

"The 15 richest have assets that exceed the total GDP of Sub-Saharan Africa.

"The wealth of the 32 richest people exceeds the total GDP of South Asia.

"The assets of the 84 richest exceed the GDP of China, the most populous country with 1.2 billion inhabitants."

Since we are Americans, let us not leave out the United States. (Well, we haven't really, since 60 of the 225 richest individuals in the world are Americans, more than those from any other place.) The United States has the highest per capita income among 17 developed countries, yet has the highest rate of poverty. The assets of the richest man in the world, Bill Gates, equal the assets of the bottom 40 percent of Americans, that is, 106 million people. I owe this observation to Lester Thurow, and I think it is about right.

Returning to Box 1.3, I continue to quote because I can't say it any better or shorter.

"It is estimated that the additional cost of achieving and maintaining universal access to basic education for all, basic health care for all, reproductive health care for women, adequate food for all and safe water and sanitation for all is roughly $40 billion a year. This is less than 4% of the combined wealth of the 225 richest people in the world."

For the sake of comparison, Table 1.12 on page 37, called "The World's Priorities?" indicates that in a recent year (not given) $400 billion was spent on narcotic drugs and $780 billion on the world's armies and their equipment. More modestly, $35 billion was spent on business entertainment in Japan and $50 billion on cigarettes in Europe. I heard on television a few weeks ago that Americans spent $55 billion on soft drinks in 1997 (and confirmed this figure through an article in *Ad Week* of May 18, 1998).

What does all this mean? The UNDP team that wrote the report does not suggest that the 225 richest people in the world transfer part of their wealth to the poorest or that the Japanese stop entertaining or the Europeans stop smoking. Actually, they do not say what all this means. They present a high-minded "Agenda for Action," such as "ensure minimum consumption requirements for all as an explicit policy objective in all countries." Of course. This is self-evident. So why haven't we done it before?

The answer, which the team did not aspire to give, is that capitalism is working splendidly, producing an ever-growing cornucopia of good things and services while concentrating the wealth to acquire those good things and services in fewer and fewer hands, as it usually does. (See page 29 for the statistics.) No surprise at all: everyone knows that the last 25 years have seen the triumph of free-market ideology; that the results reported by the UNDP are the results of the free market at work; and that the transnational corporations, the world's financial institutions, the world's governments, and the syllogisms propounded by most economists and reverently accepted by most beneficiaries, as one accepts the laws of nature, have done their job.

I begrudge the 225 nothing. But the world of the capitalist cornucopia is not a world that I care for, even though I am one of the beneficiaries. Yet after a century, the efforts of progressives, reformers, liberals, and socialists have come to nothing. No, not quite nothing. But everywhere reforms are under attack. In the industrialized countries alone, 37 million people are out of work. What seemed to be countervailing power, celebrated by John Kenneth Galbraith almost fifty years ago, has proved to be exceedingly precarious. Should we be surprised that under capitalism the capitalists hold the commanding heights and that redistribution, to use John Stuart Mill's concept, is a sometime thing? This has been the case since the much noted global market began when Americans encountered Europeans in 1492 and has since floresced in all its splendor.

No sane person can believe that the extreme degree of inequality described in the *Human Development Report* is anything but a mockery of political democracy or, more fundamentally, of elementary decency. I suppose I must take back those words, since seemingly sane people who presently control the House and Senate swear by the system as it exists. The power of righteous belief works wonders. But I suppose that no one can argue with the proposition that all capitalism is crony capitalism, not just Indonesian or Malaysian, as long as politics is a marketable service.

It could be that reformers, progressives, social democrats, or whatever they choose to call themselves in the future, will learn something from the near-futile wrestling match with capitalism in the twentieth century and tame it in the twenty-first century. But then, if it is tamed, it will no longer be capitalism.

January 1999

Remembering Wassily Leontief, 1905–1999

He frequently used the expression "You see, my dear . . ." in his melodious Russian accent, and then launched into a pyrotechnical commentary on the subject we happened to be talking about. If the discussion touched on Japan, he would say, "Last week when I spoke to the prime minister in Tokyo . . ." Or if it touched on Europe, he would say, "When I was in Vienna two weeks ago, the finance minister told me that . . ." Wassily Leontief had more firsthand information than anybody else I have ever known. That information was assimilated and classified and interpreted by one of the best brains of this century. After I met Wassily in 1974 to do an interview for *Challenge,* the same phrase came to mind over and over again: authentic genius, one of the few.

I once asked Wassily if he was a Keynesian. At that time, almost everyone was, even Nixon. His answer was "No." I should have known better. I detected a slight condescension toward Keynes. After all, input-output deals with both the supply side and the demand side. He didn't like aggregates if he didn't know exactly what they were made up of. He battled a lifetime to convince economists and politicians that we needed an industry-by-industry picture of the flows of goods, services, and money. The only way to get this was with data, data, and more data. He was an empiricist in a nonempirical profession. The common attitude was: If everything turns out for the best through the workings of the free market, who needs masses of data? But what if everything does not work out for the best?

It was obvious that things were not working out for the best in the 1970s, with the oil-price shocks and the wage-price spiral. By 1974, even congressmen were alarmed and sent a bill to President Ford to establish a Commission on Supplies and Shortages. He actually signed it. The commission was called on to "perform the basic indicative planning function until Congress acts on its recommendation as to a permanent facility." Really! In plain English, if the data on industry supplies, prices, and demand had been publicly visible, we would have had a greater chance to do something before it was too late. Exactly Wassily's point.

When Congress extended the life of the commission in 1975, it added an Advisory Committee; Wassily was duly appointed. I recall going to a meeting in Washington where one of the members made a somewhat incoherent statement. Wassily was a kindly man, but in debate he was ruthless. He wielded a scalpel like a good surgeon, made an incision, removed the dead tissue, and sewed up the hapless man without benefit of anesthesia.

Sometime in the summer of 1974, Leonard Woodcock phoned me after we had gotten acquainted during an interview. You will remember, or will have read, that he was president of the UAW. My notes record the following conversation: Woodcock: "Something ought to be done about planning." I: "What do you have in mind?" Woodcock: "I don't know." I: "Do you want to make a study, issue a statement, start a committee, get a bill written, or what?" Woodcock: "What do you think?" I: "Let me think about it over the weekend." The following Monday, with Wassily's concurrence, I proposed that we start the Initiative Committee for National Economic Planning. (The name was coined later by John Kenneth Galbraith.) Woodcock agreed, and we did.

Using ideas already developed by Wassily, and with strong support from Senators Humphrey and Javits, we drew up a bill to establish a board to coordinate national economic policy, along the lines already envisaged by the House and Senate. Not unexpectedly, there was a tremendous hullabaloo in the press about planning. Most economists thought that the coordination of government economic policy was wrong, assuming that one mess would cancel out another, or something along those lines, and, in any case, coordination of policy was one step away from socialism. As often happens, more water was added to each successive draft of the bill until the tepid Full Employment and Balanced Growth Act emerged in 1978. Even so, not a single president has paid the slightest attention to this law since its passage. Both Republicans and Democrats have ample grounds to impeach all of them.

During the election campaign of 1975, Leonard Woodcock met and became enamored of a candidate named Jimmy Carter, not suspecting that Carter could stick all the economics he knew in his right eye. That was the end of the Initiative Committee. It was a simple case of alienation of affection, and where affection went, UAW money went. Looking back, a good case can be made that the Initiative Committee and all it stood for was the last hurrah of the New Deal. Wassily Leontief played a central role. Then came Ronald Reagan and the dawn of a new age.

Wassily was an elitist, but a good elitist. Maybe he brought this tradition over from Europe, I don't know, but he conducted a dinner salon of savants and students for the benefit of the students. Any person known to be brilliant and who was passing through Cambridge was fair game for an invitation. I got in by virtue of being there on the right day. At least I wasn't told otherwise. I remember Wassily's comments fairly well. "My students come from many different backgrounds. Yes, I want them to master charts and graphs. But I also want them to learn to become cultivated ladies and gentlemen, observe the proper way to use a knife and fork, where to put their napkins if they don't already know, recognize what a good wine tastes like, and learn the art of conversation."

Although input-output analysis is fraught with mathematics, Wassily also taught with the simple analogy. If one good analogy is worth an entire textbook, then here are some of Wassily's lessons:

On our way of making economic policy: A car is driven by three people. One person steers, another person presses the accelerator, and the third person steps on the brakes.

On the free market and public policy: Private enterprise is the wind that fills the sails and public policy is the hand that steers the ship. Without a hand on the tiller and a good chart, the ship is going to end up on the rocks.

Again on the free market and public policy: The market is a giant computer that gets very good results. But think how often you have to call the repairman.

Wassily Leontief died in February at the age of 93, undoubtedly knowing that the science of economics is still in its adolescence.

May 1999

Social Health and Social Illth

A review of *The Social Health of the Nation: How America Is Really Doing,* by Marc Miringoff and Marque-Luisa Miringoff. New York, Oxford: Oxford University Press, 1999.

We now have Republicans who call themselves New Democrats in the United States, New Labour in Great Britain, and Social Democrats in Germany. Tony Blair and Gerhard Schroeder recently issued a joint statement saying that they would like their economies to look more like the American economy and their policies to look more like American policies. They want to emulate that robust American GDP, roaring stock market, and low rate of unemployment.

They are operating under a disastrous delusion. The United States has the highest rate of poverty among seventeen industrialized countries; the greatest gaps of income and wealth between rich and poor; while Americans take first place in the number of hours worked per person per year among all industrialized countries, with very little to show for it in improved real income in the bottom 80 percent of the workforce.

The husband and wife Miringoff and Miringoff, director of the Fordham Institute for Innovation in Social Policy and professor of sociology at Vassar College, have compiled an Index of Social Health, which measures how people are doing instead of how business is doing. It is a compilation of 16 separate indicators such as infant mortality, child poverty, health-care coverage, affordable housing, and unemployment. The index, using comparable data from 1970 to 1996, shows stagnation in the 1980s and 1990s, down from 76.9 in 1993 to 43 in 1996. These numbers are compared to the best performance possible, 100. Some component indicators are improving; most are worsening or fluctuating.

If the index is compared with the GDP, using nine components available from 1959 to 1996, we see that it kept in step with GDP until the mid-1970s, when the two types of measurement began to diverge like an open scissors.

These results may not be the results that Mr. Blair and Herr Schroeder are aiming for, but they are what they are going to get if they emulate the American system. They are what Bill Clinton got by appropriating Republican policies.

Miringoff and Miringoff point out that newspapers have sports sections and business sections and fashion sections, but they don't have a section on "How are we doing?" Same for TV coverage. Yes, that would be helpful, but most European countries issue national social reports, which haven't helped them reduce their average 10 percent rate of unemployment over the last decade or so. You can look at social indices all you want to, but without a social movement and a political party to do something about them, they are just inert jottings on pieces of paper. When the richest 1 percent of the population owns more wealth than the bottom 90 percent, and when government officials can be bought and sold like shares on the stock market, then a plutocracy-government complex is the unastonishing outcome.

But shaming the shameless is good and proper. The Miringoffs are shining a light on disaster. So please keep on indexing.

November 1999

For more recent data on the Index of Social Health, see the review on page 260.

Further Down the Downward Spiral, 2005–2011

Robert Heilbroner, 1919–2005

L unch with Bob Heilbroner was always an intellectual feast. Everybody who knew him will say in one way or another that he was a man of infinite imagination and infinite hope. The subject of his imagination was the vast historical enterprise of capitalism, its origins, its progression, its locale, its politics, its economics, its ruling and subordinate ideas, its clashes, the covert and overt drives of the men and women locked in this great matrix, and how that matrix might some day be shattered. The subject of his hope was the possible attenuation of the cruelties, the injustices, the deprivations, and the destructiveness of capitalism by surpassing its limits and moving into a future that used to be called socialism.

You are aware that we are not talking about economics 101. Heilbroner disdained "economics" cut out of history. That economics is a dead specimen laid on a dissecting table. Bob Heilbroner's economics is a living regime, always moving and permutating, not susceptible to definitive declarations about eternal maximizing behavior.

Bob Heilbroner's thinking had an experimental, probing feel to it. First he would set out a breathtaking subject, then make some disarming remark about the need to pursue this subject whether we wanted to or not, and thus charm us into letting down our guard. After getting past our defenses, he would proceed with his investigation.

Bob's hope sprang from a deep concern for human beings and an absolute need to believe that some genius in us is capable of more than strife. For 200 years the secular name of that hope has been socialism—not Soviet despotism, not a command economy, not a one-party system, but a democratic socialism that preserved what we have achieved but also crossed the far boundary of capitalism. Short of that, Bob Heilbroner speculated about a slightly imaginary Sweden, as he liked to call it, taking Sweden in the heyday of its welfare state embodiment, and imagining a Sweden not bargaining with a few wealthy families, but one in which the state was irretrievably in the service of the public. That is really another way of saying feasible socialism, market socialism if you like, just beyond our current imaginations and just beyond our current reach. In Heilbroner's imagination, this need not be forever so.

He was a disciple of Adam Smith, Karl Marx, Sigmund Freud, and John Maynard Keynes. But he was never the acolyte of any of them. The great gift of Bob Heilbroner is that he is relevant.

March 2005

The Biography of John Kenneth Galbraith

A review of *John Kenneth Galbraith: His Life, His Politics, His Economics,* by Richard Parker. New York: Farrar, Straus and Giroux, 2005.

For most of his public life, John Kenneth Galbraith has been a sane man on a ship of fools. When he was in charge of price controls during World War II, he kept the economy from going into inflationary overdrive. Instead of thanking him for performing a necessary wartime service, a substantial number of business and congressional leaders named him a communist and extremist. One business association headed its monthly newsletter with the banner "Galbraith Must Go," and eventually he did go. When he was responsible for assessing the effect of Allied bombing in Germany after the war, he found that the massive bombing of cities and factories had little effect on production. The equipment in bombed factories was moved to schools, churches, and hospitals, and production rose to its peak in the last year of the war under the direction of Albert Speer. Galbraith learned in conversations with Speer how badly the German economy had been organized. The Nazi leaders were a gang of inept mobsters who had taken over a country and had no idea how to run it. The U.S. Air Force generals did not want to hear that the massive bombing raids had little effect on the German war effort, and they did all they could to keep the truth from coming out. Galbraith remarked to Orvil Anderson, deputy chief of the Army Air Force in Europe, "General, this is just a matter of intellectual honesty." The general replied, "Goddamn it, Ken, you carry intellectual honesty to extremes." Galbraith did carry intellectual honesty to extremes, and the published report had a large element of truth in it. He then went to Japan and found that the Japanese had decided to surrender two weeks before atomic bombs were dropped on Hiroshima and Nagasaki, but the high command was determined to demonstrate the effects of its new weapons. These incidents instructed Galbraith about the terrific struggles for power going on in public life, which did not exclude mendacity when mendacity served a higher purpose, namely, one's own interest.

Ken Galbraith has the good fortune of having a biographer who knows everything and has had the patience to write it down. There will never be a bigger or better or more reverential biography of Galbraith. I say this with the confidence of foresight. The subtitle, *His Life, His Politics, His Economics,* is too modest. The book is also an account of the politics and economics of the United States from the New Deal to the present; the personalities, the diplomatic history, and the history of economic thought in Gaibraith's time, because Galbraith either counseled or opposed everybody in the upper spheres of public life and polemicized in the lower spheres for what passes as economic thought.

I came across just one fact unawares. Galbraith wrote for *Fortune* from 1943 to 1948 with two absences for government assignments—by invitation of Henry Luce, who had become a Keynesian and found in Galbraith an adroit expositor of Keynesianism. At the same time that Henry Luce became a disciple of Keynes, so did I. In those days I read every issue of *Fortune* from cover to cover and thereby also became converted. What I had forgotten or never knew was who was writing the Keynesian articles for *Fortune.* At the same time, I was writing Keynesian articles for my high school civics class. My connection with Galbraith, then, to my current amazement, goes back to the 1940s. My regard for Galbraith has been more steadfast than Henry Luce's, who wrote to President Kennedy, "I taught Kenneth Galbraith to write and I can tell you I've certainly regretted it ever since."

Galbraith went back to Harvard in 1948 after an absence of nine years. The first time around, his appointment was not renewed because he had signed a petition against firing two popular and competent instructors whose sin was being too far left for the board of trustees. By some mysterious operation of chance the first time around, one of his students was named John Fitzgerald Kennedy. A fast friendship developed between master and pupil. When Kennedy became president in 1961, he turned to Galbraith for advice, some of which was taken. One gets the impression from Richard Parker's account that Kennedy's relation to his officials and generals was like that of a man trying to drive a herd of wild elephants in a straight line. One elephant went off into the Bay of Pigs, a terrible disaster, since Cuba under Castro was no more than a flea on an elephant's back. But the flea on the elephant's back almost caused the end of the world in the Cuban Missile Crisis. Galbraith was off as ambassador to India at the time and couldn't have much influence on the course of events. For a few weeks in October 1962, we didn't know if we were going to live or die. I would not be writing this now if Kennedy and Khrushchev had not been cool poker players who ignored the advice of their own hotheads and decided that we would live. This outcome illustrates a profound point: at crucial moments, the course of history is decided by a handful of men and women. I happen to have met both Castro and Khrushchev. They were both amiable men in person, at least in my presence.

Galbraith's time as ambassador to India is an instructive period in private diplomacy. His advice was sought by both Nehru and Kennedy. The channel of communications was evidently shorter to the former than to the latter. Dean Rusk at the State Department was not one of Ken Galbraith's admirers, and Galbraith's briefings to Kennedy frequently got stuck somewhere in the maw of that great institution. His really serious correspondence with Kennedy bypassed Rusk and was sent directly to the White House. Galbraith was led to write to Kennedy, "Mr. President, trying to get a message to you through the State Department is like fornicating through a mattress." Rusk, however, did express appreciation to Galbraith for helping to end the Sino-Indian war of 1962, although Galbraith had nothing to do with it except counseling restraint on the Indian side.

By the time of the Kennedy administration, Keynesian fiscal policy had become an accepted juncture between economic theory and practice. When Kennedy had to decide how to keep the postwar boom going, Walter Heller, the chairman of the Council of Economic Advisers, a cheerful and committed man whom I interviewed for *Challenge* around that time, proposed a tax-cut stimulus to Kennedy. That was a good move, but Galbraith had a better one: increase spending on public needs like schools, housing, and health care, a neglected side of society that received attention in *The Affluent Society* in 1958. The business pressures were all on the side of the tax cut. I preferred Galbraith's way, but my attitude was: Thank the Lord for small favors. I did not imagine that in a decade Keynesian economics would be abandoned because the effort to curtail inflation was bungled and Keynesians would be blamed. It was as if an experiment in chemistry had been botched and the chemistry profession decided to abandon chemistry and go back to alchemy. That is why I look back with nostalgia on the deliberate tax cut made with a deliberate objective in mind and why I have a warm spot in my bosom for Walter Heller.

The dogs of war were the undoing of the Keynesian interregnum. The generals and diplomats pressed Kennedy to replace the French in Indochina and stop the spread of communism in Vietnam. Galbraith was much concerned, and he advised Kennedy to just say no. What happened in Vietnam would not change the world much one way or the other. Since the end of World War II, Galbraith has consistently been for negotiations instead of confrontation, including negotiations with the Soviet Union instead of Cold War. The logic of confrontation leads to more confrontation and the logic of negotiations leads to more negotiations. But the Cold War mindset created its own reality and required otherwise presumably sane men and women to see the world as a titanic confrontation between communism and capitalism or dictatorship and democracy and in its current incarnation as between good and evil. Now comes the speculation about the course that Kennedy would have taken had he not been killed in Dallas on November 22, 1963. I have no idea, and neither does anyone else.

Lyndon Johnson sought out Galbraith, who continued to advise against getting in deeper in Vietnam. But the close personal relationship with a president and the level of influence that goes with it was at an end. Johnson's record on civil rights, Medicare, Medicaid, Head Start, and the like was revolutionary: Like any good businessman, he threw money at problems, an unpopular procedure since then unless it is the Pentagon doing the throwing. Johnson's undoing was getting ever more deeply mired in an unnecessary and unwinnable war without enough money to throw at military and domestic problems at the same time and without the will to raise taxes. The whole welfare state enterprise crashed with the unleashing of inflation.

For some reason, Richard Parker missed an episode in Ken Galbraith's life in which I was involved. In 1975, Leonard Woodcock, president of the United Automobile Workers, called me and said, "I would like to do something about planning." I asked him, "What?" He answered, "I don't know." I responded, "Give me a few days to think about it." I then called Ken Galbraith, Wassily Leontief, Bob Heilbroner, Bob Lekachman, and a few others, and we decided to form a committee to draft legislation for the purpose of coordinating government programs, programs that would support a high level of employment without inflation. Woodcock agreed. We recruited a few bankers, businessmen, and government officials. Galbraith suggested that we call ourselves the Initiative Committee for National Economic Planning. At that time even President Ford was talking about economic planning. But we got it hot and heavy from the press and in retrospect the name was a mistake. Nevertheless, I worked with Senators Humphrey and Javits to write the first draft of what became the Humphrey-Hawkins Bill, subsequently enacted as the Full Employment and Balanced Growth Act of 1978. Humphrey and Javits were two of the most intelligent and best informed men I ever knew, proving that what you see in public is not necessarily what you get. The act was 90 percent watered down from the original draft and Galbraith didn't like it. Richard Parker says that Galbraith didn't like Humphrey-Hawkins from the start. That depends on when the start started, since Galbraith was in at the start. I was not so critical. The act set the goal of 4 percent unemployment and 3 percent inflation. I have said, and I admit that I have said it lightheartedly, that every president since Ford could be impeached retroactively for failing to reach 4 percent unemployment except Clinton, and he has already been impeached.

One other small cavil with Richard Parker. He quotes me as saying that *American Capitalism: The Concept of Countervailing Power* "was the only one of Galbraith's major books that had about it an aura of complacency." I did say that in *John Kenneth Galbraith and the Lower Economics*. The issue was his theory of countervailing power. Instead of the market as regulator, in the modern economy countervailing organizations arise: unions against large corporations; retail chains against manufacturers; farmers' cooperatives against their suppliers. In the first edition of *American Capitalism,* Galbraith presents this process as a fait accompli. Mr. Parker does not think that Galbraith was complacent. But Galbraith thinks that he was. In 1952, he wrote in *A Life in Our Times,* "I made it far more inevitable and rather more equalizing than, in practice, it ever is. Countervailing power often does not emerge. Numerous groups—the ghetto young, the rural poor, textile workers, many consumers—remain weak and helpless." Again: "There was an erroneous implication in the title and a euphoric tendency in the text." Do we need countervailing power? More than ever. Do we have it? It is very much battered.

Well, Richard Parker, I hope that you will not be angry with me for caviling with you and for making the following suggestion. *John Kenneth Galbraith* is so massive that it needs Cliffs Notes. Short of Cliffs Notes, it needs a chronology and a bibliography, and you have the most complete chronology and the largest bibliography on Galbraith of anyone in the world. If Farrar, Straus and Giroux won't publish them in the next edition, I offer my services.

I have known Ken Galbraith for over thirty years. His main fault is telling each publisher that he knows that he or she is the best in the world; each teacher that he or she is the best; each writer that he or she is the best. I doubt if this applies to economists. I have spoken with him, I have exchanged letters with him, and I have read him. I can say with confidence that his two main beliefs are, "Thou shalt not kill" and "Love thy neighbor as thyself." What is wrong with him? Very few people have such extreme views.

May 2005

The Way Out of Iraq

The Bush administration has lost almost all influence on the political situation in Iraq. Kurdish autonomy in the north is a longstanding fact. A Shiite autonomous region in the south has become enshrined in the draft constitution. The Sunnis in central Iraq, shut out of the constitutional process, have no alternatives but to vote down the constitution in their provinces and continue the insurrection. The possibility for a united Iraq has vanished.

American troops are present, but the Shiites, who constitute 60 percent of the population, are establishing Shariah, or Muslim religious law, under the noses of the Americans and will strip women of their rights in marriage, divorce, child custody, and public life. Their main ally and mentor is not the United States but Iran. The Shiites control about 80 percent of Iraq's oil reserves, and their disposition will come under the control of mullahs and allies of Iran, like Vice Premier Ahmed Chalabi.

The only bargaining power left to the United States is to get some concessions in return for reparations and leaving Iraq. The most obvious are equality for women, acceptance of the Sunni area as an autonomous region, and per capita distribution of oil reserves. Very problematic is a limited Iraqi state in which the three regions are equally represented in matters of defense, diplomacy, and finance.

If we don't get the concessions with the little bargaining power we have left, we stay in the Iraqi cauldron for no reason at all. I wonder why a single woman, Cindy Sheehan, must bear the brunt of the antiwar movement without any help from American political leaders.

September 2005

One President, Five Disasters

One disaster per administration, such as dalliance with an intern, can be considered an anomaly. Five disasters are a matter of concern.

Disaster 1. Seven-and-a-half months before the attacks on New York and Washington, the counterintelligence chief Richard Clarke wrote a memo to Condoleezza Rice to say, "We *urgently* need . . . a Principals level review on the al Qida [as spelled] network" (January 25, 2001). Nothing came of it until September 12. We cannot know what would have happened, or not have happened, if the principals had paid attention. On September 12—that's a day after September 11, you remember—George W. Bush said to Clarke, "See if Saddam did this." Clarke rejoined, "But Mr. President, Al Qaeda did this" (see his *Against All Enemies*). "'Look into Saddam,' the president said testily and left us" (pp. 30–32). Four years later we are still wide open to further attack. Such an obvious precaution as securing all the nuclear material in Russia will not be finished until 2022. We haven't experienced an atomic attack, so we can't count it as a disaster yet.

Disaster 2. The administration stirred itself into action and scoured Afghanistan for Osama bin Laden and the al Qaeda leadership. Our troops drove the Taliban out of Kabul. They located bin Laden in the Tora Bora mountains. Then somebody very high up contracted out the capture of Osama bin Laden to local warlords. The warlords went to Tora Bora. They came back from Tora Bora. Bin Laden remained in Tora Bora. Or he went someplace else. Then the president got tired of looking for Osama bin Laden and turned his attention away from the sideshow in Afghanistan toward the main event, Iraq.

Disaster 3. The question about Iraq has come to this: What is the best way to lose? The war accomplished nothing. We have no control over events. Our troops are preoccupied with ways to avoid getting killed. Our presence inflames passions and recruits terrorists. Our chance of extracting any concessions in return for leaving is slipping away. Nothing will have been accomplished in the future unless we can master the obsession with oil, and work on finding an alternative, and leave the Middle East altogether. Then al Qaeda will wither away. If we are not wise, the price of oil will go up to the sky, and then we will have to do under the threat of another disaster what we can do now before it is too late. (Do not even mention greenhouse gases. *Global Warming for Dummies* hasn't been written yet.)

Disaster 4. In September, lo and behold, New Orleans was wiped out by a hurricane and we had disaster number four. But in the United States of Make Believe, levees are not destroyed by storms and 450,000 people do not have to be evacuated, although some eggheads in the Federal Emergency Management Agency considered the destruction of New Orleans one of the three largest possible disasters, the other two being an earthquake in San Francisco and an atomic attack on New York.

Disaster 5. Yes, the middle class and the well-to-do got out because they had cars, cash, and credit cards. As in the sinking of the *Titanic,* first-class passengers got into the lifeboats. Steerage passengers were locked in the hold. But these facts didn't come to the world's attention until the ship went down. Who knew that the poor, the black, and the sick were locked in the hold in New Orleans? Disaster number five took the form of a revelation, like a landscape suddenly lit by a stroke of lightning. Suddenly it was revealed that we have poor, black, and sick people who are locked in the hold in New Orleans, in Detroit, in New York, in Los Angeles—everywhere. George W. Bush is going to do something about it. I have no idea what that will be. We have three years to find out.

November 2005

New Orleans:
A Modest Proposal

Think for a moment how you would feel if your hometown had been wiped out and you could only go back to the wreckage. More than that, your hometown was an extraordinary place. A good friend of mine—a woman who was born and raised in New Orleans, grew up in a house that has been in her family for 200 years, attended an exclusive Catholic girls' school in the city, and then graduated from Tulane University—went down from Greenwich to the wreckage. After she managed to get to her house and look through the windows, she found that the first level had been flooded and that the floor, the furniture, the pictures, and all the valuables that make a house were beyond recovery. The claims adjuster came and looked over the property, and some time later the insurance company sent her a letter stating that the damage wasn't covered. My friend is a not a pushover, and I suspect that she will file an appeal. All that aside, she has not been able to get into the house yet because it is now inhabited by alligators, which are eating the rodents that accidentally wander in. Probably the Society for the Prevention of Cruelty to Animals or some other agency will lure the alligators out some day.

I read a story on the Internet—sorry, I misplaced the name of the blog—about a man whose house in New Orleans was damaged beyond repair. Logically he called the Federal Emergency Management Agency, but for hours on end he got the same recording and never was able to speak to a live person. He faxed and didn't get a response. He e-mailed and didn't get a response. After making what might be called a serious attempt to reach FEMA, he turned into a raving maniac.

Today I read an article in the *New York Times* reporting that 30,000 households in Jackson, Mississippi, 150 miles from the Gulf Coast, received $62 million in aid, although, according to the *Times,* "the worst damage suffered was spoiled food in the freezer." The payments "set off a spending spree on jewelry, guns, and electronics."

It appears that insurance payments or FEMA money cannot be counted on to rebuild New Orleans. Will the Bush administration allocate funds to rebuild New Orleans? The answer is doubtful, as the funds are tied up elsewhere. What are we to do?

Private money is the easiest to come by if the terms are attractive. I'm reasonably confident that George W. Bush has a crony who is willing to construct a theme park in what was once New Orleans. This theme park could be called Gumboland or Big Easy USA. I see gleaming new hotels and dioramas showing the founding of New Orleans in 1518, Andrew Jackson's gallant stand in the War of 1812, Lincoln watching a slave auction in 1831, lynchings after the Civil War, and the final destruction of New Orleans in 2005. There will also be rides and a daily Mardi Gras parade for tourists, as well as restaurants with gourmet cooking and mellow jazz entertainment. The French Quarter will be restored just as it was.

The attractiveness of this plan is that all the poor, black refugees who fled New Orleans will be able to come back as laborers to construct the theme park and then service the tourists when they arrive. Housing and schools of a high quality can be provided in Gretna, now a mostly white town across the Mississippi from New Orleans. The integration of Gretna will allow the Gretnians to atone for the action of their police officers, who blocked the bridge to Gretna, which was the main escape route for tens of thousands of New Orleanians trapped in the city during the flood.

January 2006

The Country Left the Man

K urt Vonnegut calls his notification that the world is coming to an end *A Man Without a Country,* by which he means that the country left him, not the other way around. Mr. Vonnegut is quite hilarious in contemplating the impending disaster. I semi-quote: Humor is a way of protecting yourself from how awful life can be and next to the last step before giving up altogether. Here's how life is really awful. The country is led by psychopathic personalities without consciences but with enormous power. These psychopathic personalities are "persuasive guessers" who guess disastrously about the future. We go along, we trust authority, we are patriotic, we are ignorant, and we are gullible. We can't even identify the people who know something about the world that we are tearing apart. Not the country into which Vonnegut thought he was born.

Psychopathic personalities muck up the environment, but guess the consequences of the mucking up is just a scientific hypothesis, so why bother doing anything about it? They play with soldiers like toys but guess the world will be much better off sometime in the future. They are deeply religious, but they rarely mention the Sermon on the Mount.

Vonnegut knows something about Dresden. When advance scout Vonnegut was held in an underground meatlocker on the outskirts of the city as a prisoner of war, the U.S. and British air forces incinerated or asphyxiated several tens of thousands of civilians, nobody knows the exact number; and twenty-three years later, after mulling it over, he wrote *Slaughterhouse Five.* Killing several tens of thousands of civilians did not shorten World War II by a single day. Kurt Vonnegut thus began to entertain dark thoughts at an early age.

Here is a constructive idea. Back in the 1940s, George Bernard Shaw wrote about the need for an anthropometric test to measure the qualifications of all would-be national leaders or, to put it differently, to disqualify psychopathic personalities. No one could rationally oppose a constitutional amendment requiring such a test for the president, members of Congress, Supreme Court justices, and leaders of large corporations who keep them in spending money. I guess I'm entitled to a modest guess that Kurt Vonnegut would want to know why I think the issue would be decided rationally. I would say the capacities to fear and reason may not be as far apart as we think. Since he is guessing about our impending self-destruction, to which most of the evidence points, I guess further that at 11:59:59 we will wake up and see that we are about to extinguish ourselves. The Europeans after 5,000 years of war did. Why not the rest of us? If the future turns out better than expected, then the country can rejoin Kurt Vonnegut. Not a bad outcome.

March 2006

Garbage

A review of *The Disposable American: Layoffs and Their Consequences,* by Louis Uchitelle. New York: Alfred A. Knopf, 2006.

Disposable means something you use once and then throw away. You blow your nose into a tissue and then throw it away. Your child pees into a disposable diaper and then you throw it away. You eat your dinner and then throw away the leftovers. That's garbage. Large corporations hire workers and when they decide to move south or outsource to India, they throw the workers away. Tissues, diapers, garbage, and workers are in the same category. That is why Lou Uchitelle calls his book *The Disposable American: Layoffs and Their Consequences.*

He starts by describing the plight of employees of the Stanley Works, with headquarters in New Britain, Connecticut, where he interviewed three consecutive CEOs. They made hand tools in plants concentrated in the Northeast and Midwest. The tools were very good and were widely admired and bought by people who use hand tools. Then in the late 1970s, really good hand tools started to arrive in the United States from Asia. They sold for much less than the Stanley hand tools because the workers who made them were paid much less than the Stanley workers. The Stanley CEO was brought up with the belief that you don't fire workers en masse, so he tried attrition and then some layoffs. This CEO, who liked the Stanley Works workers and was used to walking around the shop floor of plants chatting with them, could not bring himself to think of them as disposable, so with his back to the wall, he retired.

His successor was more attuned to layoffs, outsourcing, and moving south. Even he tried to save a plant in New Britain that made retractable measuring tapes by automating the assembly line. But it broke down too often, so basically the plan failed. He didn't lay off, outsource, and move fast enough, so the board hired a third CEO who got the job done, and when it was done the plant in New Britain was empty except for the headquarters staff.

Unfortunately, the fate of the Stanley Works can be multiplied a thousand times. From 1984 to 2004, about 30 million American workers were laid off and their work was moved somewhere else where it is done at a fraction of the previous cost to the corporation.

If I may reminisce for a moment, I remember the time between the late 1940s and the middle 1970s when steady work at a company was taken for granted and a certain mutual loyalty existed between employees and management. Costs were regularly reduced by using the most advanced technology in the world, which made it possible to raise wages across the board from the lowest to the highest. Much of the basic research was financed by the government, in science and engineering, for example. The airlines, trucking, banking, railroads, and utilities were regulated so that the interests of the workers, owners, and consumers were in some way fairly balanced. At the time, I thought there was nowhere to go but up. I had no expectation that the accepted idea of social responsibility would give way to the idea of every man and woman for himself and herself, and that we would go back to where we were at the end of the nineteenth century when workers had precious few rights in fact or in law.

It's sad but true that the advocates of the unfettered free market won the battle by the end of the 1970s with the myth that everybody would be better off if large corporations could compete in the global market on their own terms. The pressure to increase productivity through R&D was off and the pressure to lower costs through layoffs was on. You have high labor costs? Move production someplace where they are one-tenth your present costs. The era of the disposable American returned.

Ah, but skilled workers can always find work. You don't have the right skills? Retrain. That's a bitter joke. "Knowledge workers," as Peter Drucker called them, have the same knowledge in Bangalore, Singapore, and Hong Kong as they do in Cambridge or Seattle and provide it for one-tenth the cost. The result is a layoff crisis, in Lou Uchitelle's precise words. That is only a fraction of the problem. Very few of the skilled or unskilled laid-off ever make as much as they did before they were laid off. And they can be laid off again and again. No matter what the cause, self-reproach of the laid-off is almost inevitable and the blow to their families almost always manifests itself in shame. The downward pressure on wages affects the entire workforce. So we end up with a nation in a massive state of anxiety.

We have not only the disposable American, we have the disposable town when a large plant closes and the disposable region when a whole industry moves somewhere else. If corporations had to count the costs of wasting towns and regions, small shops going out of business, the wasted skills of teams of workers dispersed, and the new technologies forgone because they didn't have to develop them, they would have saved nothing. They don't have to absorb these costs. The public does.

Joseph Schumpeter perfectly captured Karl Marx's description of capitalism as a process of creative destruction. New technologies come along and destroy older ones. He thought the process could be managed, and it can, if not his way. Yet we need to ask: In the disposable economy, what is being created and what is being destroyed? Great wealth among a few is being created, opportunity among the many is being destroyed. This is no longer creative destruction. It is destructive destruction.

"Globalization made me do it" is a poor excuse. We could manage globalization and regionalization in the spirit of mutual accommodation, but the present beneficiaries would not be happy. Disposable Americans are disposable because they are deceived, disunited, and leaderless. They are disposable workers, disposable soldiers, disposable minorities, and disposable majorities. They are quiet Americans, disposable. Garbage.

May 2006

John Kenneth Galbraith, 1908–2006

I am impressed most by John Kenneth Galbraith's courage. During World War II, he successfully controlled prices despite the howls of businessmen and politicians until the howls finally forced him to resign. As the war came to an end, he led a team to assess the effects of fire-bombing German cities and concluded, over the strong objections of Army Air Force generals, that the mass murder of civilians did not shorten the war by a single day.

In 1962, when liberal economists called for tax cuts to prevent an economic slowdown, Galbraith advocated an increase in public spending instead, true to his argument in *The Affluent Society* that America was a country of private wealth and public poverty. Today, we can go into a supermarket and choose from 400 types of breakfast cereal or go into a hospital and die for lack of trained personnel. The same neglect of the public purpose, which was the leitmotif of Galbraith's intellectual life, is still evident.

In 1996, he summed up his preoccupation in *The Good Society,* which some critics said was superfluous, since everybody believes in the good society without another book on the subject. We are still waiting for "everybody" to deliver adequate medical care and remedy a few other deficiencies.

Twenty-three years before writing *The Good Society,* Galbraith stated quite explicitly what steps were required to realize a good society in *Economics and the Public Purpose.* We need public control of health care, mass transit, and housing; public ownership of military contractors; public ownership of the largest corporations; planning of overall production to meet public needs; and government support of small business and labor.

This is the necessary program in order for the majority interest to prevail over the minority interest, a very small, privileged minority. Galbraith used the phrase "the five socialisms" to characterize it, over the objection of close friends. He could have called the program economic democracy, compassionate liberalism, or the New New Deal. What is the point? He wasn't running for office. He was being honest.

As to who is going to accomplish all this, Galbraith had the same conviction as the founders of the British Fabian Society: enlightened men and women of all ranks who needed to organize themselves into a public force.

When I visited Galbraith in 2004, he handed me bound galleys of *The*

Economics of Innocent Fraud, his last book, which restates his contention that the well-off always find ways to justify their narrow self-interest as the overriding social interest. The free market as we know it is for the best, and all that. After he scrawled his iconic "JKG" on the front page, he looked up and said, a little mischievously, "This is my best book." As I left, I thought, how refreshing for a writer to think that his most recent book is his best, even if a little mischievously.

July 2006

See page 16 for a note on the origin of the phrase "the five socialisms."

The Heavy Burden of Wealth

A review of *Who Rules America?* by G. William Domhoff. New York: McGraw-Hill, 2006.

The American public, in its collective wisdom, has for many years turned over responsibility for running the country to a handful of men and a few women. Unfortunately, with self-interest as their guiding star, this handful has run the country for their own benefit. The public has been innocently trusting and distracted by ostensibly personal concerns. This unfortunate state of affairs is laid out with utmost clarity by Bill Domhoff—G. William Domhoff—in the fifth edition of *Who Rules America?* published this year.

Who Rules America? is an analysis of power, and so it begins with an examination of the most powerful private organizations in the United States and why they are powerful. These are the great corporations and banks. The chief officers and directors of the largest American corporations and banks form an interwoven group of friends and acquaintances, or acquaintances of acquaintances, who know each other as members of boards of directors, business associations, policy groups, country clubs, neighborhoods, or as graduates of a select list of boarding schools and universities that attract the wealthy. Domhoff calls them the corporate community. They are a community because their backgrounds, organizational connections, and similar beliefs bind them together.

Any decision about how many of the largest corporations are the "largest" is arbitrary, but the Fortune 500 is as reasonable a measure as any other. In 2005 their combined revenues made up 73.4 percent of the country's gross domestic product. The other 23 million businesses made up the rest. Of the more than 12,000 American banks, the 25 largest commanded more than 50 percent of the assets. Compared to these immense global organizations, small and medium-sized businesses are puny and scattered and have no real national presence or power.

"Corporate community" does not mean that everybody in it agrees on everything. Some businesses are growing, some are declining, some are in fierce competition. At the inter-firm level their interests might diverge or converge in alliances. But at the general level of policy, especially labor policy, tax policy, and regulation policy, their interests are remarkably similar, ranging from conservative to very conservative. There are also a few Warren Buffets.

Most of the top corporate and bank officials come from the wealthiest 1 percent of the American population, which owned 57.3 percent of all business equity in 2001, while the bottom 90 percent owned 10.4 percent. For all practical purposes, the wealthiest 1 percent is an upper class. Of course the dividing line between the lower upper class and the upper middle class is also arbitrary, but the fact that there is a wealthy American upper class is not. It doesn't matter whether Jones is in one category or the other. What matters is that there is a locus of wealth. Pundits who argue that it doesn't matter because families are entering and leaving the upper class all the time miss the point. The same could be said of the old aristocracies of Europe, but the aristocracies themselves endured as an institution. The American upper class also endures as an institution. It wields power by supplying the most powerful American organizations—the largest corporations and banks, the most influential policymaking groups, and the federal government—with a disproportionate number of top officials. And many families remain in the upper class for generations, just as did members of the old aristocracies.

Within the upper class is a social upper class whose members form overlapping circles of men and women who know each other, or who know others who know others, who have gone to the same prestigious boarding schools and universities and are members of a limited number of corporate boards, policymaking organizations, who frequent certain clubs and resorts, and who live in recognizably affluent communities: very similar to the circles of the corporate community. From this group, many have served as high officials in the federal government. The social upper class is also fuzzy around the edges. The Clintons may not make it on financial grounds, but they are no doubt welcome in social upper-class settings. At the same time, failures, addicts, and corporate felons may be dropped. If the social upper class is for the most part the richest of the rich, we are talking about the upper 0.1 percent or 300,000 people. (This year the U.S. population will reach 300 million.) Most of the men and some of the women are active in business, foundations, policy groups, government, or in more than one of these. The rest are busy, or indolent, living their personal lives.

The policy-planning network, which exercises power in the area of opinion making, as Domhoff describes it, examines necessary changes in policy that will serve the interests of the upper class. Informal discussions take place in corporate boardrooms. Foundations give grants to think tanks and policy discussion groups. Experts do research and write papers. The leaders of these institutions then pass along recommendations to federal, state, and local governments. By far most of the corporate and individual contributions go to conservative organizations in the policy-planning network. Liberal counterparts operate, financed by unions and affluent progressives, but on much smaller budgets. The 161 members of the Business Roundtable, for example, are CEOs of the largest corporations. The Council on Foreign Relations is the largest and most influential policy discussion group in this area and is controlled by corporate officials.

Domhoff calls those members of the upper class who are the controlling officials of the largest corporations or of the most influential policy-planning organizations or both, as well as their senior administrators, the power elite, a term used by C. Wright Mills to denote those who control America—or any other country. How do we know that the power elite really possess power? Domhoff, a sociologist and a social psychologist, by the way, proposes these tests: 1. Who benefits? 2. Who governs? 3. Who wins on issues? By all these tests, the upper 1 percent come out far ahead, followed by the next 9 percent, followed by the next 10 percent, leaving the bottom 80 percent possessing little wealth and stagnating with respect to wages since the 1970s. By contrast, the wealth and income of the upper 20 percent have grown moderately, and the wealth of the upper 1 percent has grown astronomically in the last thirty-five years. The salaries and stock options of the *Fortune* 500 CEOs put them in the upper 1 percent, if not the upper 0.5 percent, if they were not already in those brackets when they started. The issue of the alleged separation of ownership and control can hardly exist when corporate officials not already in the upper class are absorbed into it.

With respect to the power elite, I differ with Domhoff on one important issue. True, the power elite as he defines it attempts to dominate the federal government to serve its own interests. But the power elite already runs the federal government from within, allowing for the exception of a number of liberals in Congress and on the Supreme Court. I would include the presidency, Congress, and the Supreme Court as the third, and even at times effective, circle of the power elite.

A new point in the fifth edition of *Who Rules America?* is Domhoff's rejection of the existence of a military-industrial complex as defined by Dwight Eisenhower. I confess that I had taken this structure for granted. It is a fact that the largest military contractors are diversified corporations with extensive lines of products and services for civilian consumption. It is also a fact that most large nonmilitary corporations do extensive business with the military establishment. These observations leave us with the conclusion that the entire corporate community is a military-industrial complex. The upper class is not only a ruling class—it is a class of military adventurers.

Two groups take part in elections: the corporate-conservative coalition and the labor-liberal coalition. These coalitions make contributions to candidates and parties and gather around themselves members of the general public. By far most of the contributions come from the corporate-conservative coalition, which supports both the Republican and Democratic parties, the former with considerably more largesse. When we consider that the primary goal of the corporate-conservative coalition has been to control the labor market and with it the distribution of wealth and income, generally helped by the public consensus that the best government is the least government, we have to conclude that the corporate-conservative coalition has gotten its way no matter which party was in power. Never mind that it is impossible to disentangle the public sector from the private sector. Lobbyists, mostly corporate, move back and forth between private and government jobs with the greatest of ease.

It is now a bit far-fetched even to speak of a labor-liberal coalition. Not only have unions declined from one-third of the labor force in the 1950s to 12.5 percent of America's total workforce and only 7.8 percent of the private sector workforce today, but "labor" is diverted by issues that have nothing to do with Who Benefits. Abortion, gun ownership, the death penalty, gay rights, drugs, porn, and religion have nothing to do with power in corporate America other than to keep people's minds off the fact that they are getting swindled.

Nothing in Bill Domhoff's analysis leads him to believe that we are a closed society. Liberals pushed through the National Labor Relations Act, the Social Security Act, the Equal Pay Act, the Civil Rights Act, and the Occupational Safety and Health Act, albeit as written by conservatives when they had to compromise on these issues. The civil rights movement, the women's movement, the gay rights movement, even with all their unfinished business, show that the promise of American life, as Herbert Crowly put it, has a strong hold on us. The ultraconservatives charging heedlessly into an unnecessary and unwinnable war in Iraq have split the corporate-conservative coalition, alienated public opinion, and antagonized the rest of the world. We don't know how the next chapter or the chapter after that will turn out, but the upper class has placed a heavy burden on itself. It has to live on the same planet as everybody else does. Losing the world and losing the competence to repair even one city, New Orleans, are merely symptoms of a power in the process of destroying itself.

September 2006

Although corporate managers almost always own substantial shares in the corporations they control, I was wrong to deny the separation of ownership and control. The great majority of stockholders—"owners"—have next to nothing to say about the management of large corporations. The sixth edition of Who Rules America? *was published in 2010.*

He's Got the Whole World in His Hands

Since the present administration thinks that we are in charge of the world, it might be interesting to see how that state of mind came about. In the beginning, a few planters and merchants signed on to a document that proclaimed all men to be equal, with the rights to life, liberty, and the pursuit of happiness. This document has ever since caused no end of confusion because it excluded Indians, blacks, women, and foreigners, but these people didn't know it. They believed the document, but the planters and merchants didn't. Most of them, anyway. Thomas Jefferson was so confused about its meaning that he allowed some of his children to be free and kept others in slavery. He bought the Louisiana Territory from France, doubling the size of the United States, without even consulting the Indians who lived there. They didn't count among those who had been created equal.

The Indians didn't like it. The blacks didn't like being brought over from Africa as slaves, either. And by the way, as of 1820, five times as many blacks had come to the Americas as whites. From the beginning, the white North Europeans, now Americans, had come with a sense of superiority, entitlement, and righteousness because they could. Their adversaries were weaker than they were.

In the 1830s, Andrew Jackson pushed the Indians out of their eastern homeland to the west of the Mississippi, to the extremity of death and despair among the Indians. The Anglo-Texans took Texas from Mexico in 1836 and it became a state in 1845. The white Oregonians got the upper hand in 1846, and then in 1848 James K. Polk took the northern half of Mexico from the Mexicans but didn't take all of Mexico because he didn't want the United States to be overrun with Mexicans. Then California joined in and the United States became an empire from sea to sea—"an empire of liberty," as Jefferson called it before it actually happened.

The final bill for the empire of liberty had yet to be paid. The stench of slavery hung over the West. When I was a boy, a ubiquitous billboard proclaimed, "The wages of sin is death." The wages of slavery was death to the sinners and non-sinners without distinction, 620,000 of them. Together with their grieving families and friends, the total was greater than all the slaves in the United States in 1860: 4,000,000. In 1864, the bill was marked "paid," but not in full.

That's not the end of the story. In 1867 Secretary of State William H. Seward bought Alaska from the Russians, not from the native Alaskans to whom it belonged. Then we had nowhere to go but overseas, so in 1898 William McKinley took Puerto Rico and the Philippines from Spain, and Cuba as a protectorate, turning against the liberation movements in these countries, which had been our allies, and then took on as our clients the rest of the southern Americas. And Hawaii and Guam for good measure. The main reason for conquering an overseas empire, aside from our desire to help them, is that we could. Not to mention the trade and investments. That is to say, Spain and the other countries involved were weak and we were strong.

In 1991 the United States stood invincible in the world. During the previous seventy-three years all the other empires had throttled themselves to death: the British, French, Dutch, Russian, Ottoman, German, Nazi, Japanese, Italian, and Soviet. What a grand opportunity to show the world who we were. And we did, we did. We imposed our rules of trade, investment, finance, democracy, military power, and benevolent American rule almost everywhere.

This history, and the overthrow of governments in Nicaragua, Honduras, South Vietnam, Iran, Guatemala, Chile, Grenada, and Panama, led directly to the invasion of Afghanistan and Iraq after September 11, 2001. Being a superpower, or an empire as numerous current books call it, with 725 military bases in over 100 countries, we (meaning the administration) invaded Afghanistan and Iraq because we could, not because we were clever. Being clever would have meant understanding al Qaeda, understanding its tactics, understanding its strengths and weaknesses, understanding potential divisions in its ranks, and mobilizing the police and intelligence services of virtually the entire world to isolate and immobilize it. Instead the administration let the supreme moment of world unity pass and turned unity into enmity.

What kind of superpower or empire, we need to ask, attacks weak powers and cannot win? This superpower lost in Korea and Iran. It lost in Vietnam. It cannot negotiate peace between the Israelis and Palestinians. It cannot win in Afghanistan or Iraq. This superpower is overstretched because it relies on military and economic power alone, which results in blowback, a CIA term that denotes retaliation against incursions abroad and, I might add, hatred. It's too late for Niall Ferguson's benign liberal empire policing the world for the world's own good. A liberal empire is just a euphemism for a megalomaniac colossus that pits the United States against the rest of the world. Why don't we contemplate the alternative to a frightful war without end against "terrorism" and possible nuclear annihilation—the alternative of a global alliance of states guided by international law. Never tried before, but the world has not been faced with total destruction before either.

Recommended Reading

Bacevich, Andrew J. *The New American Militarism: How Americans Are Seduced by War.* Oxford: Oxford University Press, 2005.

Bender, Thomas. *A Nation Among Nations: America's Place in World History.* New York: Hill and Wang, 2006.

Brown, Sherrod. *Myths of Free Trade: How and Why America's Trade Policy Has Failed.* New York: Free Press, 2004.

Faux, Jeff. *The Global Class War: How America's Bipartisan Elite Lost Our Future—And What It Will Take to Win It Back.* Hoboken, NJ: Wiley, 2006.

Ferguson, Niall. *Colossus: The Rise and Fall of the American Empire.* London: Penguin, 2004.

Galbraith, Peter. *The End of Iraq: How American Incompetence Created War Without End.* New York: Simon & Schuster, 2006.

Johnson, Chalmers. *Blowback: The Costs and Consequences of American Empire.* New York: Owl Books, 2000; with a New Introduction, 2004.

——. *The Sorrows of Empire: Militarism, Secrecy, and the End of the Republic.* New York: Owl Books, 2004.

Kinzer, Stephen. *Overthrow: America's Century of Regime Change from Hawaii to Iraq.* New York: Times Books, 2006.

Mann, Michael. *Incoherent Empire.* London: Verso, 2003.

Odom, William, and Robert Dujarric. *America's Inadvertent Empire.* New Haven: Yale University Press, 2004.

Richardson, Louise. *What Terrorists Want: Understanding the Enemy, Containing the Threat.* New York: Random House, 2006.

Soros, George. *George Soros on Globalization.* New York: Public Affairs, 2002.

Stiglitz, Joseph E. *Globalization and Its Discontents.* New York: W.W. Norton, 2002; with a new Afterword, 2003.

——. *Making Globalization Work.* New York: W.W. Norton, 2006.

Todd, Emmanuel. *After the Empire: The Breakdown of American Order.* New York: Columbia University Press, 2003.

November 2006

Iraqonomics

The war in Iraq is lost. George Bush can do handstands, but nothing can change the fact that the war is lost. Every penny spent on that war is lost, and every penny that will be spent is lost. If we accept David Leonhardt's assumption (*New York Times,* January 17, 2007) that the cost is $1.2 trillion, that $1.2 trillion is gone without a trace, like rainwater in a desert. That's $200 billion a year and "includes $120 billion in annual military expenses plus the cost of veteran medical care and disability payments, the cost of rebuilding the military after the war, and the increased cost of oil as a result of the war." If we accept the assumptions of Linda Bilmes and Joseph Stiglitz, the cost is $2 trillion. They include the forgone economic effect of spending the money in the U.S. If we take my assumptions, add the cost of reconstructing Iraq, which will come to more.

David Leonhardt tries to overcome our feeble comprehension of $1.2 trillion by making comparisons. One hundred billion dollars would buy complete health care for all Americans who don't have it. Thirty-five billion dollars would buy universal preschooling, "half-days for 3-year-olds and full-days for 4-year-olds." Ten billion dollars would pay for all the security recommendations of the 9/11 Commission. Five billion dollars would pay the annual budget of the National Cancer Institute. And—oh, enough of this sentimentality, Mr. Leonhardt—$0.6 billion would pay the annual cost of immunization against measles, whooping cough, tetanus, tuberculosis, polio, and diphtheria *for all the children in the world.*

Then there's New Orleans, which I would add to my "to do" list. I have seen construction estimates of *$200 billion*, a horrendous amount of money; we can't afford it; so much will go to waste; New Orleans will never be the same again; and all that. Well, neither will Iraq, which is being destroyed at a cost of—*$200 billion a year.*

Let's stick to hard numbers. Let's not bother to put a price on lives or on world public opinion, which turned against Bush in March 2003, when he ordered the occupation of Iraq, and then against Americans when they reelected Bush in 2004. See *America Against the World: How Americans Are Different and Why We Are Disliked* by Andrew Kohut and Bruce Stokes, who quote the headline from the British *Daily Mirror* of November 4, 2004, that wonders: "How can 59,054,087 people be so DUMB?" For $1.2 trillion to $2 trillion we have bought—well you know as well as I do what we have bought.

Let's not go into WMD, ties to al Qaeda, and Saddam Hussein, either. Let's just ask why our generals were so DUMB. It's because they were prepared to fight World War II, an "industrial war," not a "war amongst the people." General Rupert Smith, a top British army commander during the First Gulf War, Bosnia, Kosovo, and Northern Ireland, makes this distinction in *The Utility of Force,* which I recommend to all generals, armchair and otherwise. An industrial war is a war between two or more states that deploy massive armies and that control large manufacturing capacities and a large pool of manpower that can sustain a prolonged fight that ends in a massive deciding event. Napoléon was the initiator of industrial war, and he was brilliant at it throughout most of Europe, but got bogged down in a guerrilla war on the Iberian Peninsula and then in a protracted march on the Russian steppes, where Kutuzov traded Moscow for space, sparing his army a decisive battle, after which freezing weather gave the coup de grâce. The American Civil War was the next big industrial war, in which the North far outmatched the South in financial resources, industrial capacity (by nearly ten times), railway mileage, munitions making, and manpower. In spite of initial tactical victories by the South, the North had multiple advantages, noted during the course of the war by no less a personage than Karl Marx, who expected the North to win. So did Abraham Lincoln.

General Smith tells us categorically that war in the old sense no longer exists and is not likely to exist again because it is no longer practical to use huge armored formations. What we have seen for the last thirty years or so are wars amongst the people. A war amongst the people is a war fought by irregulars, militias, gangs, zealots; men who can adapt guns and explosives to new purposes; men who change uniforms as easily as they change underwear; men who can withdraw into the population and emerge again somewhere else; men who fight within a state or between states that do not have the power to suppress violence. In a war amongst the people, the issue is, who are the people with? To know that, you must have intelligence, information, know who's who. If you don't win the people, you can't win the war. Military considerations are secondary to political considerations. You need a strategic aim that isn't just clobbering the other side with your mailed fist. If you are not prepared to provide order and security, you lose. If, say, you disband the Baathist army and police force along with its leadership, fire the heads of ministries, hospitals, schools, and museums, and don't replace them immediately, you have wrecked order and stability and you lose. If you engage in torture at Abu Ghraib and hold prisoners incommunicado at Guantánamo, you lose. If you thumb your nose at International Humanitarian Law starting with the Geneva Conventions, you lose. You have given a propaganda victory to the enemy. On this, here is General Smith: "The people are not the enemy. The enemy is amongst the people" (p. 408). You cannot terrorize the people with your industrial and technological advantage without having them turn against you.

Never mind Vietnam. What about the Soviet disaster in Afghanistan between 1979 and 1989? Eighty to 100,000 Soviet soldiers occupied Afghanistan at any given time, but they lost and left. They didn't win the hearts and minds of Afghans by blasting them to Kingdom Come. Instead, the drain of lives lost in the mountains and valleys of Afghanistan lost the hearts and minds of the Russians. Now we follow in the footsteps of the Russians, inserting ourselves in a war amongst the people. No one seems to have noticed that we have lost.

I will conclude with the topic of oil, not our official reason for occupying Iraq. ("My boy died so we'd have enough oil for our cars and trucks" doesn't quite have the right ring to it.) In April 2001, a paper was prepared at the James A. Baker Institute of Public Policy called "Strategic Energy Policy: Challenges for the 21st Century." It asserted, while dwelling on the looming world shortage of energy, "The United States remains a prisoner of its energy dilemma. Iraq remains a destabilizing force to . . . the flow of oil to international markets from the Middle East." In the same year, the Cheney Energy Task Force, composed mainly of oil executives, drew up a list of "Foreign Suitors for Iraq Oilfield Contracts." In 2003, the State Department Oil and Energy Working Group stated that Iraq "should be opened to international oil companies as quickly as possible after the war" using production-sharing agreements, although, thank God, the oil would be government-owned. Now I have just read that global warming is "unequivocal" and caused by people. But ExxonMobil will pay $10,000 to any scientist who can prove that wrong.

You want me to end with a moral. Don't start wars amongst the people. A war amongst the people is not a war on terrorism. The war on terrorism is not a war. It is an intelligence operation. Find out who the terrorists are. Find out where they are. Find out who is on our side. Use bribes. Use diplomacy. Use threats. Use surgical strikes against terrorists if necessary. Use surgical strikes for humanitarian reasons if there is no alternative. See Darfur. Close our bases around the world, and bring our troops home. They are useless in wars amongst the people. They are useless in the fight against terrorists. They are a hangover from the confrontation with the Soviet Union, which is finished, and from a military mindset that hasn't changed since the war with the Axis, which ended sixty-two years ago. But we know how to do industrial war, and we don't know how to do war amongst the people. So we will just go on doing industrial war and just go on losing. But that cannot be. We are by far the strongest military power in the world, so we should be winning. Wait, wait. Something is amiss. I have a splitting headache. Doctor, where are you taking me?

March 2007

How to Become a Friend of the Next President

L et's be fair and admit that George W. Bush single-handedly won the 2006 congressional elections for the Democratic Party. Maybe not entirely single-handedly. Some credit ought to be given to his supporting cast. If all goes as it is going now, and there is no reason to expect that it will not go as it is going now, George W. Bush will also singlehandedly win the 2008 presidential election for the Democratic candidate, whoever that might be, with the same qualification that some credit must be given to his supporting cast.

At the same time, in the interest of a balanced assessment, the president has beaten the Republican Party almost to death and it will be staying at the Walter Reed Medical Center convalescing for the foreseeable future. Neoconservatism, as distinguished from the Republican Party itself, which includes old conservatives as well as neo, is also standing at death's door and I am afraid it will pass through.

Turning now to the voters. The voters have grievances. The voters always have grievances. But rarely do grievances rise to a level of frustration sufficient to change the tranquil course of American history. You can name the Great Depression, the Korean War, the Vietnam War, double-digit inflation, times when frustration mattered more than jollying the folks along. We are at one of those times.

That brings us back to the 2008 presidential election. We do not need to have an election. A poll will do. The candidates don't need to raise any money. They can go on talk shows or give speeches and get paid. But the parties are doing the only thing they know how to do, which is to raise money. Money-raising is like an arms race. Neither side can let the other side get ahead. The chairman of the Federal Election Commission made an estimate. He estimated that the 2008 presidential election would cost $1 billion, about $500 million per candidate. This will be the highest-priced voter-bidding in history, so preposterous when the outcome will be decided by frustration, not money.

What happened to the McCain-Feingold Bipartisan Campaign Reform Act of 2002, which was supposed to make elections cheaper, I mused? Businesses and unions can't give money to political parties. That's good. Individuals can give $2,300 for the primary and $2,300 for the election. That's good. These contributions are called "hard money."

But there's "soft money." Anybody can start a political action committee. PACs cannot support a candidate. But they can support causes that happen to correspond to the causes that their candidate supports and they can be against causes that the candidate they don't support supports (America Coming Together; Swift Boat Veterans for Truth). A 527, named after a section of the tax code, can raise *unlimited amounts of money* to advocate something or mobilize voter turnout. (I suspect some tilt as to which voters are mobilized, but nobody can stop Republicans from looking at www.MoveOn.org.)

Then there's "bundling," a scheme said to have been devised by Karl Rove for the 2004 elections but perfectly legal. You collect hard money from your friends. Limited amount from each friend; unlimited amount of friends. Before you know it, you have an envelope containing $200,000, $300,000, who knows how many thousands, depending on how many friends you have. Some people tend to have more friends. Then you hand the envelope to your candidate, and if he or she wins the election, there's no telling what good things will come your way.

But as I said, money will have nothing to do with the outcome of the next election.

May 2007

The 2008 presidential election actually cost $2.4 billion. The total for federal elections was $5.3 billion.

America's Suicide Pact with George W. Bush

We are stuck with a war that we don't want because our political institutions don't work under the present circumstances. One man has the power to assert his will over the will of the majority.

He is commander-in-chief. The commander-in-chief possesses plenary power to prosecute a war—two wars—any way he sees fit. So he says. That power is claimed under the newly discussed theory of the unitary executive. Nobody is the executive except the executive.

He can abrogate treaties, suspend habeas corpus, order torture, arrange extraordinary rendition, monitor phone calls, intercept e-mail, declare surges, make signing statements, send carrier groups off any coast, and keep the public from seeing caskets. It's the war on terror.

The commander-in-chief as Caesar? In his new book, *Nemesis: The Last Days of the Republic,* Chalmers Johnson speculates that the American president, as commander-in-chief, with the wind of war behind him, could become a Caesar and replace democracy with one-man rule. Please allow me to make a correction. The current president already is a Caesar *pro tem,* and will remain one until his term expires or a veto-proof majority against the war or wars emerges in Congress.

When the commander-in-chief sees the world as a battlefield, every nation capable of developing nuclear weapons is prodded to develop them. The more nuclear weapons in the world, the greater the danger of proliferation. The greater the danger of proliferation, the more chance that nonstate entities—terrorists—will get their hands on them.

When the commander-in-chief proposes to build a ballistic missile shield in Central Europe, other states are forced to take countermeasures, Russia, for example.

When the commander-in-chief is favored with a budget that allows him to proceed along the military path, and he wants to proceed along the military path, he does. The American military budget is equal to or exceeds that of all other countries in the world together. Whether it is "equal to or exceeds" depends on whose estimates you read. The commander-in-chief also benefits from near-sacred weapons industries whose owners and employees desperately need contracts. A great cry of pain goes up when the Pentagon talks about closing a base or terminating a weapons system. A senator or representative in the affected state or district is always ready to make the case that immeasurable harm will come if the base is closed or the weapons system is terminated.

The commander-in-chief is supported by an archipelago of 737 military bases in over 130 foreign countries, according the 2005 *Base Structure Report,* which fails to mention those in Afghanistan, Iraq, Israel, Kyrgyzstan, Uzbekistan, Qatar, and Britain, and numerous others that would bring the total to more than 1,000 (Johnson, p. 140). These bases help us keep order in the world. I mean our order in the world. The American burden, as Kipling almost said.

The commander-in-chief inherits a sixty-six-year history of military Keynesianism (starting from 1941, the year that we entered the Second World War). I had the fortune or misfortune of studying economics, and I can say with confidence that military spending has a multiplier effect on all kinds of economic activity, and though politicians eschew Keynesianism as they would exposure of illicit sex, it is nevertheless the undercover mode of operation. "Military spending" is not just the Department of Defense budget, currently at $585 billion. It is also supplementals, Homeland Security, veterans' benefits, 80 percent or so of the interest on the national debt, and numerous other items that you can find online or in *Nemesis,* all of which come to $1 trillion, give or take a few billion.

It is an open secret that the war in Iraq has something to do with oil as well as spreading the blessings of American democracy. The use of oil is related to the greenhouse effect. Now comes the brilliant plan of our domestic coal companies for converting coal into liquid fuel. As I write, these companies are lobbying Congress to free us from reliance on Middle Eastern oil and solve the problem of global warming by converting to carbon-emitting coal.

Here's the American suicide pact with George W. Bush that we are trying to get out of. The commander-in-chief pushes the world; the world pushes back. The commander-in-chief occupies Afghanistan and Iraq; a crop of terrorists springs up. The experts say global warming; the commander-in-chief says let's wait and see. The commander-in-chief says the world is a battlefield; the world says nuclear proliferation.

Sometimes the sponsors of a president-cum-commander-in-chief lose control of him. Say, for instance, he is a psychopath, a theory of the late sage Kurt Vonnegut. Or an ignoramus. Or someone who had trouble with his father. Then the public must order Congress to go over to the White House with a straitjacket.

A friend of mine asked, in effect, why don't I recognize and accept realpolitik: every nation acts in its own interest, not in the interest of some airy sense of global morality.

My answer is that the world has come to the point where it can destroy itself, or most of itself, in several different ways, and there is no longer any difference between realpolitik and morality.

Kurt Vonnegut died believing that mankind was hopeless and what was the point of trying to do anything about it except voice our protest in articles and books. We shall see.

July 2007

Poor People

A review of *Ending Poverty in America: How to Restore the American Dream,* ed. John Edwards, Marion Crain, and Arne L. Kalleberg. New York: New Press, 2007.

John Edwards is the lead editor of *Ending Poverty in America,* a collection of nineteen essays by well-known experts. This is not a campaign-style book dealing in generalities. It is a very serious book dealing with the precariousness of life in the lower depths that reaches well up into the middle class. It is a product of the University of North Carolina Center on Poverty, Work and Opportunity, established by Edwards in February 2005.

Let me first address the canard that you cannot live in a 13,000-square-foot house and really care about poverty. You do not have to live in a shack to care about poverty. You can have a conscience whether you are rich, poor, or middle class. The accusation of hypocrisy against Edwards is a cheap way to avoid the subject.

The official definition of poverty was established in 1960. It is out of date because it doesn't encompass what is needed to escape poverty now. Even more, it doesn't encompass relative poverty, usually defined as some percentage of median income—60 percent of the median in the European Union. Relative poverty means relative to the standard of living that people are accustomed to expect in a given country. John Edwards, through *Ending Poverty in America,* makes clear that abject poverty grades into intermittent poverty, which grades into middle-class insecurity through the loss of a job, maxing out a credit card, defaulting on a mortgage, or dealing with an illness that wipes out your health insurance and leaves you broke after you use up your savings. You can face a catastrophe at any level of income in America today unless you are rich enough to tide yourself over in an emergency.

Most poor people bequeath poverty to their children through habits imposed by circumstances. Poor nutrition and inadequate medical care of mothers affect newborns who live in substandard apartments and often violent neighborhoods. Then the children reach five or six, only to attend substandard schools and never acquire the knowledge and skills—the know-how, know-what, know-when, know-why, and know-who—to get anything but a poverty-wage job or any job at all. Poor people's circumstances are a mirror image of the circumstances of the affluent: they bequeath the know-how, know-what, know-when, know-why, and know-who to their children who are equipped to get ahead and stay ahead. (I learned the "know-hows" from my teacher Kenneth Boulding.) Since the 1980s an increasing number of American adults and their children stay in the income quintile into which they are born. The unlucky ones learn the wrong know-hows. They grow up in dysfunctional networks.

In several respects, the poor and the middle class are in this together. The cost of clothes, food, appliances, and per-person transportation has gone down while the cost of housing, medical insurance, child care, taxes, and two-earner family transportation has gone up. These expenses cannot be dodged. The median household is only several months away from bankruptcy even when one parent is still working—even closer with a single mother–headed household and a black or Hispanic household.

The issue of living near the cliff of bankruptcy makes it clear that poverty is not just a matter of income but also of assets or positive net worth. A family can fall back on assets to get through a time of unemployment or sickness and can get ahead with assets that can be used to buy a house or pay tuition for college. The traditional definition of poverty was perverse: if you had assets, you were off welfare. So you could never get anywhere. Today the poorest 25 percent of households have a negative net worth. So they can't get anywhere.

All the authors in Edwards's volume, whose ideas I have ransacked, have answers to the question: What is to be done? Let me make amends by crediting some of the authors with their proposals.

Jacob S. Hacker calls our attention to "the great risk shift" from business and government to families that puts households across all income groups on an economic roller coaster. (I assume that Bill Gates et al. are excepted.) We've switched from a "security and opportunity society"—we're all in this together—to a "go it alone worldview"—nobody gives a damn. We need universal insurance, under which all the government-sponsored insurance that we have now would be supplemented by insurance that we have discussed for decades but have not implemented. Professor Hacker presented the same view in the May–June 2007 issue of *Challenge*.

Michael Sherraden, who established the concept of "assets for the poor" in a book by the same name, which I had the privilege of publishing in 1991, writes about the complementarity of social insurance and guaranteed assets through Children's Development and Individual Development accounts, in which every child and family has the resources for a minimum standard of living and the chance to improve on it. (I, for example, could not have become a publisher if my father had not put up the cash I needed over the first two years of my efforts. No bank would have come anywhere near me, since I knew absolutely nothing about publishing.)

I should also mention Elizabeth Warren's proposal for a Financial Product Safety Commission to protect consumers against out-of-control usury on variable and subprime mortgages, late credit card payments, corner-store check cashing, and so on.

Then there is the question of good jobs and bad jobs, discussed by Beth Shulman. There are no good jobs and bad jobs as such. What makes them good or bad is the way we, and employers, perceive them. Once factory jobs were bad. Then they were unionized, wages became living wages, and substantial benefits were added. The same can be said about many service jobs today: childcare worker; elder-care aide; medical technician; janitor; hotel worker. What if we underwent cognitive restructuring and the pay and benefits were raised to some minimum household level? Service worker jobs wouldn't be bad any more. The question is not good or bad, but necessary or unnecessary. One essential thing about these jobs is that they can't be sent overseas, just like the dirty job of surgeon. He or she has to be within arm's reach of you.

The most comprehensive proposals come from William Julius Wilson in discussing "America's Ghetto Poor." A change in strategy to tight labor markets that benefit low-skilled workers through fiscal, monetary, and trade policies, and, necessarily, a green light to unions, also benefits everybody else. So does a strategy aimed specifically at revitalizing poor urban neighborhoods with a surge of schooling, training, jobs, and reconstruction.

My apologies to all other contributors for not mentioning them by name. If you buy the book you will have a comprehensive examination of poverty, near-poverty, insecurity, and injustice in your hands—and see who all the eminent contributors are, each applauded in a final essay by John Edwards.

I can add only one thought. Not even John Edwards, if he were to become president, could accomplish all these tasks alone. It will take a movement bigger than anything we've seen since the 1930s. Against whom or what the authors don't say. But they all have opinions on the subject.

September 2007

In spite of John Edwards's subsequent personal problems, Ending Poverty in America *is a serious contribution to the subject that deserves serious attention.*

With respect to a surgeon's need to be within arm's reach of you, the situation has changed. The surgeon can use remote-controlled endoscopic technology together with remote imaging and can be in Los Angeles while you are in New York.

The New New Deal

A review of *The Conscience of a Liberal,* by Paul Krugman. New York: W.W. Norton, 2007.

About half a century ago the distinguished sociologist Erving Goffman wrote: "Society is an insane asylum run by the inmates." He did not reckon with George W. Bush. The asylum is no longer run by the inmates. It is run by the director against the wishes of the inmates. But then they elected him. To paraphrase an old saw: elect in haste; repent at leisure.

In fact, if we go back to the 1870s, as Paul Krugman does in *The Conscience of a Liberal,* we find that a wealthy minority ran the insane asylum in their own interest until the onset of the Great Depression. He calls this extended period the Long Gilded Age. It includes the Populist and Progressive eras. Then from the 1930s to the 1970s, the inmates got control of some of the levers of power and compressed the distribution of income and wealth. Krugman calls this period the Great Compression, otherwise known as the New Deal followed by the Great Society. The blows of double-digit inflation and double-digit interest rates, the Vietnam War, and most of all, the Civil Rights Act and the Voting Rights Act, which alienated the white South from the Democratic Party, did in the Great Compression. The demise of the Great Compression was helped along by free-market fundamentalists ready with chapter and verse to convince the inmates to restore the Gilded Age. And they did. The new period Professor Krugman designates as the Great Divergence: the distribution of income and wealth restored to their Gilded Age disparities, diminished only by some New Deal leftovers like Social Security. We are now living in the waning days of that dispensation.

What next? It appears that the gullibility of the inmates has been pushed as far as possible and that they are restive. They are ready for a redress of grievances, or a change in the relation of forces, as occurred during the Long New Deal, if I may coin a phrase. (I seem to remember that Marxists use the locution "relation of forces." It is a good designation for class conflict when used with discretion.) That would be, according to Paul Krugman, a new New Deal. A new New Deal means restoring the countervailing power, progressive ideas, progressive movement, and progressive wing of the Democratic Party, against the powers that be: ultraconservative business; ultraconservative preconceptions; and ultraconservative movements.

This is Krugman's argument: At critical moments, prevailing beliefs can be changed. The balance of economic power between business and labor can be changed. And the balance of political power between the upper few percent and everybody else can be changed. At critical moments, people decide to make these changes; they are not made by impersonal forces beyond human control.

I sometimes read that the Democrats have no new ideas. What could be more novel than restoring the idea of working for the well-being of everybody? Krugman remembers the old days when the idea was commonplace in politics. So do I, and thought at the time that the future was upward from the New Deal. It is, but the future was delayed a whole electoral era, some thirty-five years, by the Great Divergence.

Electoral eras—I assume it is clear that I mean the Long Gilded Age, the Age of Compression, the Age of Divergence, and the possible new New Deal— are marked by long-lasting electoral coalitions that arise out of political-economic crisis and end after the next crisis begins. The electoral coalition that formed during the Great Depression—the familiar list of workers, farmers, part of the middle class, blacks to the extent that they could vote, and the pragmatic wing of corporate business—created the familiar social compact, with the federal government as an essential player, committed to the much excoriated program of full employment, regulation of business, progressive taxes, aid to farmers, and the right to join a union. The New Deal, denounced by its critics as socialist ruin, but accepted at the time by moderate Republicans as good sense, never pressed beyond the limits of capitalism for all the fear that it inspired among its enemies. Regulation of business; but no participation of unions or government in running business. Progressive taxes; but no euthanasia of the rentier. Fiscal policy; but little direct allocation of resources by government until the demands of World War II overwhelmed all other considerations.

Then came the aforementioned crisis of the 1970s and the dissolution of the New Deal order. In the Great Divergence, the era of polarized wealth and income *redux,* the inmates of the asylum were promised unswerving war on abortion, homosexuality, big government, taxes, and un-Christian morals. Yet abortion, homosexuality, big government, taxes, and secular morality are here to stay, not to mention big business. The question is, how to get big government, big business, and taxes to work in the interest of the public, as the New Deal reformers tried to do, instead of against it.

Now we are at the crisis of the Great Divergence, intensified by gratuitous war, when a new New Deal order can be created through a new electoral coalition similar to the electoral coalition of the first New Deal. I use the word *created* in the same sense that Paul Krugman does. Economic and political conditions may be auspicious, but nothing happens by itself. We have to *act* to create the new. The idea of universal health insurance epitomizes the way we have to act, and Paul Krugman's chapter on universal health insurance is the best thing written on the subject. It is not a bad idea to see the whole social problem in light of government as the insurer of last resort. That is why government was invented. It doesn't clarify much to call social insurance "socialized insurance," although I have no objection.

For the purpose of acting to create the new, *The Conscience of a Liberal* is the right book at the right time. Inmates of the asylum, rebel! You have nothing to lose but your illusions.

November 2007

A Sick Society

A review of *America's Social Health: Putting Social Issues Back on the Public Agenda,* by Marque-Luisa Miringoff and Sandra Opdyke. Armonk, NY: M.E. Sharpe, 2007.

It might just as well be called "America's Social Sickness," but the book I have just published is called *America's Social Health,* with the subtitle *Putting Social Issues Back on the Public Agenda.* The implication is that we might do something about our sick society if the facts were drummed into our heads by a periodic social report.

The authors, Marque-Luisa Miringoff and Sandra Opdyke, carry on the work started by the late Marc Miringoff, founder of the Institute for Innovation in Social Policy. They have assembled in one book the damning information that every social scientist should be able to recite in his or her sleep.

They start with an "Index of Social Health of the United States, 1970–2005," based on sixteen components as follows:

- Children: infant mortality; child poverty; child abuse;
- Youth: teenage suicide; teenage drug abuse; high school dropouts;
- Adults: unemployment; wages; health insurance coverage;
- The elderly: poverty, ages sixty-five and over; out-of-pocket health costs, ages sixty-five and over;
- All ages: homicides; alcohol-related traffic fatalities; food stamp coverage; affordable housing; income inequality. (Index components, p. 70.)

This index (see Figure 4.1 below, from p. 71) shows a decline in social health of 19.7 percent from 1970 to 2005, and five years of consecutive decline during the most recent years. Each bar measures the average of the sixteen indicators against the best possible performance, 100.

Within the index, some components have been improving while others have been worsening:

- Improving: alcohol-related fatalities; high school dropouts; homicides; infant mortality; poverty, ages sixty-five and over; teenage drug abuse.

4.1 Index of Social Health of the United States, 1970–2005

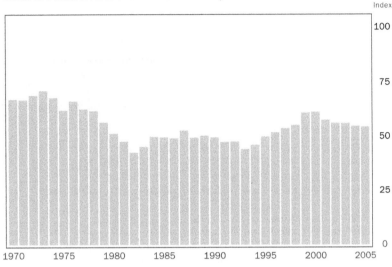

Source: Institute for Innovation in Social Policy

4.3 Index of Social Health and Gross Domestic Product, 1970–2005

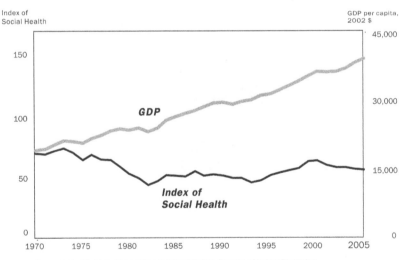

Sources: Institute for Innovation in Social Policy, Bureau of Labor Statistics

- Worsening: affordable housing; child abuse; child poverty; food stamp coverage; health insurance coverage; income inequality; out-of-pocket health costs, ages sixty-five and over; teenage suicide; unemployment; wages (p. 73).

A graph called "Index of Social Health and Gross Domestic Product, 1970–2005" shows an increasing divergence between the social health index and GDP over a thirty-six-year period (see Figure 4.3, from p. 74).

4.4   Key deficits

Percent responding yes, strongly/somewhat agree

	During the past 12 months . . .
	Income
32	*had to cut down on important food items such as meat, fruit, or vegetables*
39	*had to work extra hours or an extra job to make ends meet*
42	*found their rent, mortgage, or utilities difficult to pay*
54	*expect their retirement income will not be sufficient to cover needs*
	Health Care
23	*did not get health care because could not afford it or too difficult to get*
34	*worried about paying for the cost of medications*
37	*worried about paying for the cost of dental care*
38	*worried they would not be able to cover health care costs*
	Safety
34	*decided not to go somewhere at night because of concerns over safety*
65	*worried about the safety of family and friends*
69	*felt uneasy opening the door to strangers*
76	*kept doors locked when at home*

Source: Institute for Innovation in Social Policy

4.5   How hard/easy is it for average Americans to provide for themselves and their families?

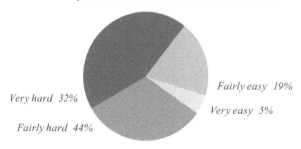

Very hard 32%
Fairly hard 44%
Fairly easy 19%
Very easy 5%

Source: Institute for Innovation in Social Policy

During the past twelve months, the key deficits are depicted in Figure 4.4, from p. 77.

The authors present another view of national deprivation in a chart called "How hard/easy is it for average Americans to provide for themselves and their families?" (see Figure 4.5, from p. 78).

A closer look at the scissors graph of gross domestic product and the Social Health Index for the years 2000–2005 is telling. The authors ask: A social recession? If two years' decline in the Index of Social Health is a social recession, as the authors suggest, then six years is a national tragedy (see Figure 4.12, from p. 85).

Except for five categories, the graph that follows gives a disheartening look at the Social Indicator performance of 2005 (p. 93).

4.12 A social recession?
Index of Social Health and GDP, 2000–2005

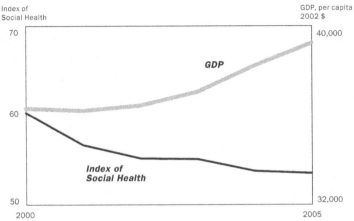

Sources: Institute for Innovation in Social Policy, Bureau of Labor Statistics

Social indicator performance, 2005

Rated against the best level achieved from 1970–2005
Top performance = 100

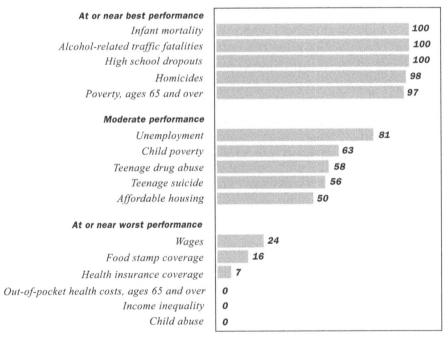

At or near best performance
- *Infant mortality* — 100
- *Alcohol-related traffic fatalities* — 100
- *High school dropouts* — 100
- *Homicides* — 98
- *Poverty, ages 65 and over* — 97

Moderate performance
- *Unemployment* — 81
- *Child poverty* — 63
- *Teenage drug abuse* — 58
- *Teenage suicide* — 56
- *Affordable housing* — 50

At or near worst performance
- *Wages* — 24
- *Food stamp coverage* — 16
- *Health insurance coverage* — 7
- *Out-of-pocket health costs, ages 65 and over* — 0
- *Income inequality* — 0
- *Child abuse* — 0

Source: Institute for Innovation in Social Policy

Several graphs indicate a differential between ethnic groups. Infant mortality during the first year of life out of 1,000 live births was 5.7 among whites in 2004, 13.6 among blacks (p. 97). Poverty among female-headed households with children between 1996 and 2005 was 29.2 percent for whites, 45.2 percent for Hispanics, and 42 percent for blacks (p. 103).

International comparisons are an indication of American social policy disasters:

- Infant mortality among twenty selected industrial countries, estimated for 2006: United States ranks last (p. 99).

- Child poverty among twenty-five selected industrial countries, data ranging from 1997 to 2001: United States ranks next to last, just above Mexico (p. 105).

- Graduation rates from upper secondary schools, twenty-one selected industrial countries, 2004: United States ranks nineteenth. (The Russian Federation ranks tenth [p. 125].)

Just one more country ranking: Homicides, twenty-four selected industrial countries, 1999–2001—the United States ranks last (p. 160).

I will finish this statistical review with some data about income inequality. (Please see the book for the authors' methodology in collecting and interpreting all the information.)

- The share of income of the top one-fifth of American households in 2005: 50.4 percent. The share of the bottom four-fifths: 49.6 percent. The numbers have steadily converged since 1970 from 56.7 percent for the bottom four-fifths and 43.3 percent for the top (p. 177).

- The pay ratio of the average top executive to the average production worker, 2004: 431. The ratio was 107 in 1990 (p. 178).

- The share of household wealth of the top 10 percent in thirteen selected industrial countries, in available dates ranging from 1997 to 2002: the United States at 69.8 percent ranks next to the highest, which is Switzerland, leaving 30.2 percent of the wealth to the bottom 90 percent of the households (p. 179).

Are all of the above the result of inevitable, necessary, ineluctable natural law? I don't think so.

January 2008

Hard Times

The economy is a roller coaster on which we all ride. When it goes up, the magnates of business and finance are geniuses. When it goes down, they are dunces. But they are in fact neither. They are riding the roller coaster with the rest of us. The ups and downs are properties of the roller coaster, not the people who ride it, not even the magnates. It is operated by an Invisible Hand.

We all know that the roller coaster is going down at present because it had previously gone up. It went up on the rails of the housing boom and the subprime mortgage spree; it went up on the rails of credit card debt and home equity borrowing. Why it should have gone up can be explained by crowd behavior. A cartoon shows one person looking up. Another person comes along, sees the first person looking up, and looks up. Soon a crowd of people comes along and looks up. In our case, people get on the roller coaster because they see other people getting on, and people continue getting on until someone becomes dizzy from the height and wants to get off. The roller coaster goes down. It's a case where the actions of people make the roller coaster go up and down, not the other way around. In the rush to get on and off, the crowd inevitably jostles the Invisible Hand.

This phenomenon has become increasingly global, with trillions of dollars sloshing around the world, so that the geniuses-become-dunces at Merrill Lynch, Morgan Stanley, and Citigroup, who didn't know that they were buying subprime mortgages in an AAA certified mix, can terrify every banking center in the world by their poor judgment. Just how interdependent the global corporate and financial system is, is explained by David Rothkopf in his new book called *Superclass: The Global Power Elite and the World They Are Making*. Twenty to fifty leaders in any given field, who know or have access to each other, decide through e-mail, phone calls, and stratospheric meetings how, when, and why to shift capital, resources, and jobs from one place to another anywhere in the world. They meet informally at the World Economic Forum at Davos, at events sponsored by the William J. Clinton Foundation, at world summits, and at various venues where networking, access, exclusivity, and, above all, power define the mode of operation.

Does Mr. Rothkopf know what he's talking about? I think so. He is on speaking terms with several hundred members of the superclass, goes to Davos regularly, networks, has access and exclusivity, and was a managing director of Kissinger Associates.

There are some 6,000 world elite—the superclass, says David Rothkopf, an order of magnitude, not an exact number, a daily changing group—who make decisions that affect everybody in the world without anybody in the world having anything to say about it except the superclass itself. And, I might add, the decisions are made while they are on the roller coaster that they don't control.

Who are the members of the world superclass? Here is a thumbnail sketch (from pages 299–300):

- The superwealthy: 946 billionaires, who make up less than 0.000015 percent of the population of the world and have almost twice as much wealth as the poorest 50 percent;

- The financiers: The highest officers of 100 financial institutions, who manage nearly $43 trillion, about one-third of the world's financial assets; for example, the chairman, CEO, and board members of Fidelity, with assets of $1.9 trillion, which owns more than 10 percent of America's largest businesses;

- The corporate moguls: They manage the 250 biggest companies in the world, which have more than $13 trillion in annual sales, about one-fifth of world GDP;

- The generals: The United States and NATO generals, who preside over more than 80 percent of global military expenditures;

- The politicians: A few people, the president of the United States foremost, and the prime ministers or presidents of a handful of other countries, who hold the commanding heights in the dominant political, financial, and military organizations of the world;

- The religious leaders: Christianity and Islam each has more than a billion adherents, or one-third of the world's population:

- Total: About 6,000 men and a few women.

I fear that the constituents of the aforementioned superclass are riding the roller coaster along with the rest of us, sharing and nursing the illusion that they somehow control it. What sane coterie would engineer a financial catastrophe? As usual the private and public members of the superclass are too late with their remedies. After John Maynard Keynes, it's not as if the remedies are unknown. Enough effective demand, preferably through standby monetary and fiscal measures that are triggered by predetermined downturn indicator, is what it takes. But you could say of the present superclass: that is not their thing.

March 2008

Racism and Polite Conversation

The Reverend Jeremiah Wright is angry about racism, intemperate in his remarks about blacks in America, even wrathful about the killing in Iraq. I gather that some public figures want a calm, polite discussion of kidnapping in Africa, forced passage across the Atlantic, coerced labor in the New World, cotton picking, beatings, lynchings, separate black and white drinking fountains, seating in the back of the bus, jail for miscegenation, segregation in the army, Marian Anderson barred from the front door of the hotel, and similar embarrassments.

That's history, of course. But I gather that some public figures abhor intemperate remarks about current irritants as well, say the black infant mortality rate (13.6 out of 1,000 live births in the first year of life compared with 5.7 for whites), the poverty of black female-headed households with children (42 percent compared with 29.2 percent for whites), the incarceration rate of young black men (one in nine of those age twenty to thirty-four: that's more than 10 percent, you know), joblessness (50 percent of black men in their twenties, including high school graduates); about the lack of marketable skills, drug addiction, inner-city gangs, children who are fatherless; humiliation, failure, and not a clue about the way out of hell.

So tut, tut, Reverend Wright. You are out of bounds. Let's discuss this calmly.

April 9, 2008

One minute before press time: In speeches before the NAACP and the National Press Club, at the wrong time, in the wrong place, Jeremiah Wright shows so great a self-regard as not to care a damn about the impression he makes. Or not to understand it. Justifies the caricature of his worst enemies. Turns himself into a caricature of his message. Attacks Barack Obama to save himself. Becomes a bitter enemy of what he values most. "He never said a mumblin' word," goes the gospel song. The reverend did not heed.

May 2008

Super-Bubble

A review of *The New Paradigm for Financial Markets: The Credit Crisis of 2008 and What It Means,* by George Soros. New York: Public Affairs, 2008.

In this book, George Soros discusses reflexivity, his failure as a philosopher, reflexivity, reflexivity, the super-bubble, his success as a speculator, and his current outlook on reflexivity. Let us start with the super-bubble.

The super-bubble began in the early 1980s under Ronald Reagan and Margaret Thatcher with increasing credit expansion, increasing globalization of financial markets, and decreasing regulation of the same. The latest inflation of the super-bubble came with the housing crisis, followed by a near meltdown of the international financial system, including credit, banking, and foreign exchange, and complicated by rising prices for food, commodities, and energy. Probably we are at the end of an era.

Market fundamentalism is the underlying assumption of the world power elite that manages the financial system; that is, markets are self-regulating, keeping up-and-down swings within tolerable limits. That is not the case at all. Markets, particularly financial markets, continue upswings beyond reasonable limits because investors look at the market and see it going up because other investors look at the market and see it going up, and they all invest. This is reflexivity. The very act of investors investing changes the market. Then someone sees an unsustainable bubble and liquidates, causing a stampede by the mass of investors to the liquidation counter.

Soros calls overshooting followed by undershooting reflexivity. In systems language it is called positive feedback, which happens, for example, in an arms race, when an increase in arms by one country results in an increase in arms by another country, which results in a further increase in arms by the first country, and so on. The process of disarmament is reciprocity in the other direction. Negative feedback can be illustrated by the operation of a thermostat, which turns the furnace off when the room gets too hot and turns it on when the room gets too cold.

The idea of reflexivity is elementary to anyone with the slightest familiarity with systems theory. I am puzzled by George Soros's insistence these past twenty years that reflexivity is original and by his vexation that he does not receive accolades from the economics profession for his originality. (Chapter

2: "Autobiography of a Failed Philosopher.") Soros regards the economics profession with disdain; it is a cult of market equilibrium theorists. But he frets that the very cult he disdains does not honor him for reflexivity, which is not original to begin with.

His son Robert has the best insight on this subject. "My father will sit down and give you theories to explain why he does this or that. But I remember seeing it as a kid and thinking, Jesus Christ, at least half of this is bullshit. I mean, you know the reason he changes his position on the market or whatever is because his back starts killing him. It has nothing to do with reason. He literally goes into a spasm, and it's this early warning sign" (pp. 21–22).

If Soros would just stop going around saying "I don't get no respect" and espouse the Backache Theory of Financial Markets, the economics profession would soon award him the prize for Best Achievement of an Economist over Forty.

Let us be serious. His backaches have made him billions. (Chapter 6: "Autobiography of a Successful Speculator.") And he is right about reflexivity. He is right about not allowing banks to sell off subprime mortgages into a mish-mash of derivatives instead of policing their investments themselves. He is right about the need to revivify financial regulatory agencies (the thermostat). He is right about the agencies not approving financial arrangements that they don't understand. He is right about trillions of dollars sloshing around the world at the behest of a world financial power elite who don't know what they are doing and are not responsible to anyone for doing it. And he is probably right about the bursting of the super-bubble as the end of an era.

But given the truth of reflexivity, we shall have to wait and see.

September 2008

The Case for Government

Jeff Madrick has written a fine book called *The Case for Big Government,* published by Princeton University Press. My purpose in writing this article is more modest. I would simply like to make the case for the very idea of government itself. The advocates of the free market have been busily privatizing everything from the military to the Congress by contracting out work to mercenaries and lobbyists. There is hardly anything that they have not tried to privatize, including the purchase of elections. But let me remind you that the United States would not exist at all but for a government that gained independence from Britain, purchased Louisiana from the French, stole Texas, California, and the Wild West from the Mexicans, and bought Alaska from the Russians, notwithstanding the fact that the entire continent was stolen from the Indians and the Eskimos to begin with. Pierre Joseph Proudhon wrote that "property is theft." But then the Indians and the Eskimos did not share our concept of property.

The U.S. government then sponsored or created banks, money, credit, the post office, schools, business contracts, slavery, the settlement of Western lands, laws of incorporation, scientific and medical research including the invention of the Internet, and the building of roads, bridges, canals, railroads, airports, the military-industrial complex, and prisons, all of which support the private market.

Were it not for government we would still be living in a state of nature described by Thomas Hobbes as "solitary, poor, nasty, brutish and short," although he did not anticipate the subprime mortgage crisis. So the problem is that we did not have *enough* government to prevent the subprime mortgage crisis.

Most people like public schools, Social Security, Medicare, Medicaid, and laws to ensure that our food, water, and medicine will not kill us. Would most people like a government-sponsored right to a well-paying job, affordable medical care, a stable economy, and a chance to go to college? You betcha.

But taxes to pay for these? Oh, no. Taxes take away what rightfully belongs to *us.* Take away *our property.* But wouldn't most people be willing to pay for the right to a well-paying job, affordable medical care, a stable economy, and a chance to go to college? If you could go out in the market and could afford to buy them, wouldn't you? But you can't unless you're rich, and even then you can't buy a stable economy. The only way for the majority to buy this package is through taxes.

One more thought about your property. *Your property* is what we collectively say is your property. If we collectively say that *your property* is what you have left *after* taxes, then that's your property. Contrary to what John Locke thought, there is no natural law sanctifying your property. Property is what we decide it is. If you are rich, you are rich because you live in a country with the physical and mental assets, the laws and the customs, of the United States. You, rich person, were born into this culture and enjoy all its benefits and did not create them. You would be somebody else if you had been born in a place with the physical and mental assets, the laws and customs, of Waziristan.

All these ruminations take me back to Jeff Madrick's new book, *The Case for Big Government*. Government, local, state, and federal, now costs us about 36 percent of our gross domestic product. That's already big government. If we bought ourselves a much healthier, better run, more equitable, and highly educated society for another 10 percent, we would be getting an excellent bargain *through our taxes.*

But first we have to disenthrall ourselves from the deception that majority rule and minority rule can coexist. We cannot have democratic government and market dictatorship at the same time.

November 2008

Barack Obama and the Revolution of November 4, 2008

Our election of Barack Obama is the singular culmination of several great trajectories in American history, beginning with the introduction of slavery to the Americas and continuing through the great fight up from slavery to the very day we elected a black man president. A long sector of that arc was determined by the contradictory acts of the men who wrote a constitution and a bill of rights that endorsed slavery and freedom at the same time. The election of Barack Obama is not an incremental step away from the heritage of slavery; it is a social revolution.

A second trajectory ended in the decisive rejection of the dominant view through American history, with the exception of the New Deal Era, that a self-acting economy is best, in favor of an economy socially guided, coming after our second experience in seventy-nine years of depression and now near depression. A third is the political rejection of a small minority, the business leaders and their retainers, who act as pirates on their own ships. A fourth trajectory ends with the rejection of a blustering stance toward the rest of the world and the beginning of collaborative diplomacy.

In all this we see decades and centuries of accumulating changes seeming to burst forth in a single day. I am paraphrasing Karl Marx, who wrote: "In such great developments twenty years are but as one day—and there may come days which are the concentrated essence of twenty years."

Why now? Because we have finally learned to say "enough!" to the unnecessary racial, economic, political, and global disasters; and because Barack Obama happened to come along at the right time to lead a party and a movement that prevailed on November 4, 2008.

And by the way, the outcome wasn't all so pure. Before the election, I made light of a constituency that I called "racists for Obama." After the election, polls showed that there is a constituency of "racists for Obama." They just had to subordinate their racism enough to see that he is cool, calm, collected, and smart, and that the election of a black president was preferable to the continuation of a disaster. (I cringe at the terms "black" and "white" with regard to people; the words have no connection to reality.)

I have no doubt that circumstances, if not book learning, have made Obama a Keynesian. He has chosen the Keynesian model of deficit finance and regulation over the alternative model of market fundamentalism and deregulation. Some sows' ears among his economic advisers have been miraculously turned into Keynesian silk purses. If they turn back into sows' ears, I assume that he will throw them out.

Let me recommend to the economic team Paul Davidson's magnificent book *John Maynard Keynes,* in which he strips away the palimpsest of neo-Keynesian writings that have built up over the last sixty years, covering up the original Keynes, and lets Keynes shine through. Keynes's message is straightforward: capitalism is an unstable system. It does not have to be an unstable system. The government can stabilize it by increasing demand through deficits to prevent joblessness and by reducing demand through increased taxes to prevent inflation. Full employment can be maintained by the timely alternation of budget deficits and surpluses. All the rest is commentary. For the commentary—by which I mean Keynes's animal spirits, liquidity preference, future uncertainty, and paying people to dig holes and fill them up instead of doing nothing, as Keynes wrote to make his point clear even to numbskulls—see Paul Davidson.

And let me recommend James K. Galbraith's excellent book *The Predator State,* in which he makes the case for an economy of well-paid workers, not only because it is morally right, but because we simply need people with money to buy what we are able to produce. We need the countervailing power of unions so that workers are well paid, as Galbraith *père* argued. We need rules and regulations to prevent buccaneer CEOs from running the corporate and financial system for themselves alone in collusion with a predator state, where everybody else is left on his own and too bad for the hindmost. We need to treat the hundred or so largest corporations as public utilities that must perform in the interest of the public because there is no such thing as a private giant corporation. We need planning, known in American parlance as industrial policy, to guide the market, and, where necessary, replace the market, for full employment, universal health care, the best education from preschool through college, and all the other items on the familiar list. We need trade policies that avoid our present system of winners and losers—see Keynes's proposals for Bretton Woods, discussed in both aforementioned books.

How can we afford all this? We can afford a great deal when everybody who wants to work can work—at a well-paying job. The cost of well-paying jobs is known to be a marvelous force that drives businesses to invest in ever more productive technology.

We are already deep into planning: What are the Pentagon, the Federal Reserve and the Treasury, overcrowded public schools, clogged roads and airports, the trade deficit, if not the result of public planning? It's just the wrong planning. The revolution of November 4 is about changing the political model of public planning.

The foreign policy revolution that took place on November 4 lies in the fact that Barack Obama is regarded as the first President of the World, even if metaphorically. We have all read that greater majorities supported Obama in Germany, France, Italy, England, Russia, India, and elsewhere than in the United States. They couldn't vote for Obama with their ballots, but they did vote for him with their yearnings for a sane, calm, intelligent, and fair world leader.

So there is much room for disappointment. Affairs move both forward and backward after revolution.

Written December 7, 2008, sixty-seven years after Pearl Harbor and forty-four days before the inauguration.

January 2009

I saw the icing on the cake, but I didn't see the cake until several months into the Obama presidency. He's the one who made the cake and he's the one who put the icing on it. Most of the public saw the icing and voted for him. He became the leader of an incipient progressive movement and then abandoned it. I prematurely spoke of four revolutions. The election of a black man is an astonishing departure from past political practice. Blacks are proud. Many whites are proud. But most blacks are now worse off by all social measurements because the administration has not helped them get out of the recession, much less helped them get out of the basement of society.

As for the other three "revolutions" which I thought I saw, Obama's performance has proven my vision to be hallucinatory. He is not a New Dealer planning our way out of a great recession. He is hardly half a Keynesian. He has not rejected business leaders and their retainers; he has embraced them. He has in fact rejected blustering diplomacy and signed an agreement with the Russians to reduce our nuclear stockpiles, but he continues to shed blood in a hopeless war in Afghanistan and hopeless nation building in Iraq.

The branding of Obama as a "socialist" is one of the more ridiculous manifestations of the ridiculous side of American history. For a sober reassesment of Obama the president, see my article "Obama's Failures" on page 294.

What Keynes Knew

John Maynard Keynes was chief Treasury representative of the British delegation at the Versailles Conference in 1919 and was horrified to witness the triumphalist Lloyd George and Georges Clemenceau demand punitive reparations from Germany and its allies, which they could never pay. They jollied along Woodrow Wilson by assuring him that his idealistic League of Nations would be included in the deal. But the deal left Europe hungry, ruined, and prostrate, all for the short-term political gain of Lloyd George and Clemenceau. Keynes left the British delegation in anger and wrote *The Economic Consequences of the Peace,* in which he denounced the Versailles Treaty as a nightmare for Central Europe and therefore all Europe. The widespread shock of Keynes's denunciation guaranteed that his voice would be heard for the rest of his short life; he was sixty-two when he died in 1946.

Unlike his American colleagues, who found themselves in the midst of seemingly endless good times, Keynes had to worry about a depression immediately after a short bout of postwar inflation. The Bank of England hiked interest rates to 10 percent. Prices, output, and employment plunged. By 1923 unemployment got stuck at 10 percent until 1930, when it rose to 20 percent, only to be ended by the onset of World War II.

The British Labour Party had no prescription for restoring employment; it was capitalism or socialism, and nothing in between. The Conservative Party endorsed the Treasury position along the lines of classical political economy: a balanced budget and a reduction of wages and prices as the way back to prosperity. Only the diminished Liberal Party, a minority in Parliament, and a few dissidents across the political spectrum, supported public works as the way out. In the Liberal Party Keynes found a home. A home that housed dreams of diversity and liberty; a free market of enterprise, invention, science, and art; a home to men and women of unbounded imagination. Bolshevism was despicable, killer of all he believed in. The trade unionists herded by the Labour Party were a flock of sheep. The way out lay in finding the means to save the middle class from the extremes of labor dictatorship on the Left and Tory dictatorship on the Right.

All the while Keynes was trying to liberate himself from the dogmas of his teacher Alfred Marshall and Marshall's predecessors, Say, Ricardo, and Mill. The liberation came with the publication of *The General Theory of Employment, Interest and Money* in 1936. Against the classical theory of capitalist stability, Keynes perceived capitalism as *inherently unstable.* Investment decisions were made against an uncertain future. They were driven by "animal spirits," the confidence of businessmen that they had considered the risks of investment and had accounted for them. In tranquil times, these were usually good, solid decisions. What they supplied in the aggregate matched demand in the aggregate: the demand of consumers, businesses, government, and foreign buyers. Then the leveraging ability of the financial sector led businessmen to extend investment further. If all major indices were going up, it seemed that all risks had been accounted for. The capitalist system had no internal signals to keep the financial sector from expanding with no apparent limit. The moment of euphoria had come. Then came a moment when the railroads could not pay; real estate in Florida could not pay; the stock market could not pay; the savings and loans could not pay; the dot-coms could not pay; the subprime borrowers could not pay: the moment of crisis had come. The flood of liquidity suddenly drained away as families, businesses, and banks wanted nothing but cash.

Keynes came to realize that Say's Law was wrong. As Say and the classical economists saw it, every sale is a purchase and every purchase is a sale, so all the gears of the economy mesh nicely. Only outside perturbations like overproduction, underconsumption, a mismanaged bank, excessively good or bad harvests could cause a temporary crisis. Keynes's predecessors had treated money as neutral, a unit of account and a means of exchange, a facilitator. But Keynes saw that money was also a store of value that was saved and invested, but not always: at critical moments money was withdrawn from circulation and held for the sake of safety, a cause of crisis *internal* to the capitalist system. In a crisis, every family, business, and bank tries to hold on to as much money as it can, blocking the cash flow of society as a whole. What was good for the individual was not good for the mass. Keynes had made a distinction between the workings of the microeconomy and the macroeconomy.

We all know that the majority of economists and politicians embraced Keynes's insights after World War II, with as many interpretations as there were Keynesians. But no Keynesian that I know of doubted Keynes's prescription of government as investor of last resort as the private economic engine started to sputter. Large-scale deficit spending was the only way to resuscitate employment and bring the economy back to health. Anti-Keynesians have always worried about the burden that deficit finance puts on our children and grandchildren, not recognizing the worse burden of continued unemployment for our children and grandchildren or the fact that the restoration of employment means an increase in the number of taxpayers to pay off the deficit.

Then came the eclipse of Keynes in the 1970s and a period of some thirty years in which Keynesians were sent into the wilderness to recite Keynesian-isms to each other. Monetarists and supply-siders took over and brought us the wreckage that we see before us and around us. But now when we need him, Keynes is back, with a strange assortment of economists and politicians supporting a huge stimulus package. Even more, this strange assortment of economists and politicians recognizes Keynes's observation that the "real" economy of production and services is separate from but related to the financial sector, each of which required separate bailout packages. Some even recognized that a bloated financial sector doesn't produce anything and that millions and billions and trillions have been invested for naught but the enrichment of wealthy investors and the unfortunate subsequent disenrichment of many of them.

Keynes also understood the dangers of inflation. In 1940 he wrote a pamphlet called "How to Finance the War," in which he recommended steep progressive taxes and enforced savings. The savings would be returned after the war, when the inflationary pressure of military spending ended. His understanding of inflation would have served us well during the era of wage-price hikes of the 1970s if the excess demand over the growth of productivity had been taxed away. The well-known Keynesian and origina-tor of the *Journal of Post Keynesian Economics* Sidney Weintraub proposed a variant of Keynesian tax policy in 1970 called TIP, tax-based incomes policy, in which the largest U.S. firms would be taxed by the amount of the aver-age annual wage increases conceded in union bargaining above the average annual rate of productivity increases—a circuit-breaker for the inflationary wage-price spiral that would tamp down wage and price increases through-out the economy.

The co-founder of the *Journal of Post Keynesian Economics* and author of the comprehensive *John Maynard Keynes,* Paul Davidson, suggested, in the Keynesian spirit, the maintenance of commodity buffer stocks ready to be put on the market at times of inflationary shortages. A strategic petroleum reserve was established in 1975, too late to affect OPEC's radical oil price increases of 1973 and 1979, but our economists and politicians learned nothing about the addiction to Middle Eastern oil. Even in the oil price inflation of 2008 the reserves were too low to have an impact. Nevertheless, rationing and an anti-inflationary tax, offset by subsidies to low-income families, could have avoided the oil-price contribution to double-digit inflation. Instead double-digit inflation was fought by the Federal Reserve under Paul Volcker with double-digit interest rates that ended in the recession of 1981. Since then the world's standard for fighting inflation has been to increase unemployment.

High interest rates inhibit investment. The side effects are reduced em-ployment, consumption, and prices. Hence the end of inflation. But zero interest rates or near-zero interest rates, as we have now, cannot induce businesses to resume investing; that is, demand is too low to make investment worthwhile.

In 1944 Keynes led the British delegation to the Bretton Woods Conference to set up a postwar system of international trade and payments. Keynes proposed an international clearing system or world bank, in which the national banks of each member nation would have an account whose size would vary in line with the size of its national economy. Keynes suggested that a fixed exchange rate be established through negotiations, adjustable within limits above and below, as a way to keep world trade and payments in balance. He recommended that the world bank create a monetary unit called the bancor to record international assets and liabilities of national banks and provide liquidity for international transactions, with limits on both debit rights and surplus rights and penalties for exceeding either. He suggested that the burden of international trade and finance fall on the surplus countries by helping debit countries with investments or by giving them outright assistance to keep credit and debit accounts within reasonable limits. Keynes wanted to promote internal investment by poor countries and discourage export-led investment as the Chinese have practiced at great cost to both China and the United States. He also wanted an international system that would discourage any country from devaluing its currency to steal a trade advantage. A country that unreasonably devalued its currency would be penalized by an unfavorable adjustment of its bancor account.

But the United States, which had by far the strongest economy after the war, had the strongest bargaining position at Bretton Woods, and the U.S. negotiator, Harry Dexter White, prevailed in making the U.S. dollar the unit of account at the newly minted World Bank, while limiting U.S. aid to Europe well below Keynes's proposed level. In the event, the United States shortly caught up with Keynes's proposal through the Marshall Plan, which not only helped Europe recover but also created strong demand in Europe for U.S. products, proving Keynes's point that aid from better-off to worse-off countries pays. Keynes's proposal for substantial aid to poor countries was soon replaced by loans from the rich countries with the disastrous proviso that the poor countries tighten their belts in order to pay back the loans. In other words, become poorer.

How well it would be now for the Obama administration to reconsider Keynes's proposals at Bretton Woods and in particular extricate the United States from the mutually damaging trade and deficit-surplus relationship with China.

The Keynesian understanding was ignored from the mid-1970s until 2008, with the onset of the worldwide financial collapse brought on by the bursting of the subprime housing bubble. The first order of business was to arrest the free fall of the banks and banklike entities, whose collapse was tearing apart the entire world economy. The Bush administration began with the muddled TARP (Troubled Asset Relief Program) rescue of the biggest financial malefactors under the supervision of the muddled Henry Paulson, then secretary of the Treasury. What Mr. Paulson failed to realize is that the banks and near-banks preferred to hold onto their money: Private banks cannot assume the risk of lending anywhere near the scale required. So the rescue package sat in the banks. Keynes called this liquidity preference. Muddled or not, we are all Keynesians again under our Keynesian-in-chief, President Barack Obama.

In the final chapter of *The General Theory,* Keynes reflected on his long-term views or, as he wrote, his social philosophy. The main faults of capitalism, as he saw them, were its failure to provide full employment and its arbitrary and inequitable distribution of income and wealth. Capitalism depends on the savings of the rich. But full employment depends on a high propensity to consume, while the rich have a high propensity to save. As Keynes saw it, full employment and a high propensity to consume were the best route to a reasonable rate of economic growth.

Nevertheless, valuable activities require an environment of private wealth ownership. But the ownership of wealth needs to be spread more evenly throughout society. This thought leads to Keynes's famous phrase, the euthanasia of the rentier, by which he meant the gradual elimination of the small wealthy class that makes its living mainly through its financial investments. The concentration of wealth gives the wealthy oppressive power to exploit the scarcity value of capital as a reward for no genuine sacrifice. Keynes clearly envisioned a society with minimum and maximum levels of incomes and every level between. Only such a society would provide for the large variety of work that men and women prefer, offering a wide range of remuneration, while eliminating unforgivable poverty and antisocial wealth.

Keynes summed up: "I conceive, therefore, [that] a somewhat comprehensive socialization of investment will prove the only means of securing an approximation to full employment." This imagined state of affairs requires public and private cooperation. Only full employment will provide the general public with the means to invest, in conjunction with public investment, designed to eliminate the swings toward inflation and depression. The government's responsibility, Keynes's point, is to adjust the propensity to consume and the inducement to invest to each other. "The central controls necessary to ensure full employment will, of course, involve a large extension of the traditional functions of government."

Keynes called these views moderately conservative. Indeed in the 1930s they were moderately conservative, but today they appear radical. Keynes is really talking about capitalism without the extreme concentration of wealth. He is talking about-middle class capitalism; one-class capitalism. The profit motive would be a means to an end, not an end in itself. Keynes notwithstanding, this is really postcapitalism: both political democracy *and* economic democracy. Socialism, democratic socialism, to those who prefer to use an epithet. Perhaps Keynes's phrase the "socialization of investment" says it best after all.

In his essay "Economic Possibilities for Our Grandchildren," written in 1930, Keynes foresaw a future with a much shorter workweek, in which leisure would be the permanent problem of mankind, not work. This was a bit of dreaming of an Edwardian gentleman, because we all now need washers and dryers, TVs, computers, cell phones, cars, credit cards, and mortgages, for which we have to work. But we consume much of what we consume not because we need it but because other people have it. Is there really any necessity for hundreds of models of cars and hundreds of varieties of cereal? The cost of each would be much lower if the production lines of a much smaller number of items were much longer. And we would all be much richer with much less work.

If we had realized Keynes's program, we would be far beyond where we are now. More than half a century later, a good society, or even a good enough society, goes beyond Keynes. We now have the environment to save and toxic fuels to eliminate. A good enough society provides health care to everyone and provides every child and young person with equal and adequate training and education from preschool through college. It eliminates inequalities of race and sex. A good enough society manages the largest corporations and financial institutions as public utilities that follow rules that serve the public. A good enough society recognizes that the largest banks and corporations are not private. They dominate politics and control the fate of the country and the world. Adam Smith wrote *The Theory of Moral Sentiments.* Now we must consider the theory of immoral sentiments, which dominate the largest private and government institutions, save for the pushback of the public. We must consider Joseph Schumpeter's "creative destruction," in which a company can leave a town without taking any responsibility for the havoc it has left behind. We need to supplement the short horizons of private business, which plans for the short run, with the long horizons of the entire society, which needs to plan for the long run.

I think that all these suggestions are in the Keynesian spirit. It took 2,000 years for Europeans to realize that war doesn't pay. Will it take us 2,000 years to realize that laissez faire doesn't pay either?

March 2009

Postscript on the G20 Summit: What Members Can Learn from the WPA

I am writing this note a few hours after the Group of 20 meeting concluded. By the time you read it, all the decisions and nondecisions they made or failed to make will have been thoroughly investigated. I therefore confine myself to impressions that will linger.

The leaders of the largest economies in the world are now politely talking with one another, thanks to the good offices of President Barack Obama. A fact that we already knew was confirmed: Barack Obama is an eloquent, likable, steel-spined scholar-president with a world constituency. The long-run effect of talking politely should not be underestimated.

The G20 leaders put many commendable measures on paper. But thanks to the economic illiteracy of Nicolas Sarkozy and Angela Merkel, the leaders failed to agree on a financial stimulus large enough to move the world—and their own countries—out of the slump. Both France and Germany are suffering from an unemployment rate over 8.5 percent. The Organization for Economic Cooperation and Development (OECD) forecasts European unemployment of around 10 percent by the end of the year. But who can blame the confused leaders when their own economic advisers suffer from confusion themselves?

Perhaps more effective will be financial help promised to income-poor countries; clear regulations for private financial organizations, including the shadow banking system that has run amok, operating with no regulations at all; and a commitment to moderate remuneration to business leaders consistent with long-run results instead of inflated annual statements that justify multimillion-dollar bonuses. We shall see how the G20 follows through on their constructive but minimal decisions.

Of immeasurable good is the willingness of Barack Obama, Dmitri Anatolievich Medvedev, and Hu Jintao to talk among themselves politely.

Here are two suggestions for the members to consider.

The state shall become employer of last resort, providing jobs to all who want them. Banks and businesses must be rescued and state and local governments must be rescued. But the unemployed must be rescued directly and immediately. The most direct way for governments to get unemployed workers employed is to employ them. We don't have to wait until the banks and businesses recover. Between 1935 and 1943, the Works Progress Administration, under the direction of Harry Hopkins, created 8.5 million jobs; it became the largest employer in the United States. The WPA, as it was called, worked on 1.4 million projects, including building or repairing 1,000 airports, 2,500 hospitals, 2,500 sports stadiums, 3,900 schools, 8,192 parks, 12,800 playgrounds, 124,031 bridges, 125,110 public buildings, 651,087 miles of highways and roads, and 103 golf courses. Perhaps the golf courses were included to appease Republicans. The young were hired. Artists and musicians were hired, perhaps to irritate the Republicans. The WPA operated as an independent agency with its own staff and budget, while selecting projects in consultation with state and local governments. For more details, see the Wikipedia articles on the Works Progress Administration and Harry Hopkins, while perhaps excusing some inadvertent plagiarism in my phrasing.

Extended unemployment insurance is all very well. But the dignity of work is essential for human morale. The WPA ended in 1943, when the demands of war production created a demand for the entire labor force and then some. Now we need a war against unemployment instead of a war against the Axis. We have so much work to do and so many people to do it.

Here is another idea for the next G20 meeting to consider: Ban foreclosures. Immeasurable damage is done to families thrown out of their homes, to the neighborhood, to the banks, and to the whole economy. The idea of foreclosures is insane. If mark to market can be revised for banks to revalue assets upward toward their "normal" level, why not homes for homeowners?

Since we are expected to pull the whole world out of the slump, why not legislate a new WPA and a No Foreclosure Act here and now and show the whole world how to do it?

May 2009

Subsequent events have shown that more developed and less developed countries have severe problems working together during a crisis because their financial policies, needs, and resources pull them apart. An ignorance of deficit finance makes matters much worse than they need be.

Recovery?

You can't be serious. Some economists are guessing that the recession-depression-bust, or whatever you call it, will hit bottom before the end of 2009 or early 2010. The GDP will start to grow again. The banks will be largely stabilized. The stock market will continue or resume its upward climb. International trade will start improving.

But 10 percent of the workforce, or about 15.4 million people, will still be unemployed, some large number will have run out of unemployment benefits, and the number of foreclosed homeowners will continue to rise. The recovery will not be an occasion for celebration. It will be tragic.

The problem lies in the management of the recovery by the Obama administration. Billions have been poured into banks, but they prefer liquidity, the well-known liquidity preference—they have money to lend but not enough qualified borrowers to lend it to. The administration's $787 billion budget, the American Recovery and Reinvestment Act, is a maze of red tape that doles out dollars to thousands of cities, states, federal government, and private organizations with no central command to decide who gets what and when. The result is a turf war, with delays, confusion, desperate citizens, and governors who won't accept funds to help their own constituents. If you are skeptical about this being a mess, see "The American Recovery and Reinvestment Act" on Wikipedia or the Web site of your choice, and review the list of the thousands of jurisdictions that are working against each other and have to be consulted and placated, and understand how complicated and protracted a job that will be.

Instead of creating a centralized WPA-like federal body with the authority to make a list of projects and hire the unemployed quickly, and yes with the cooperation of local authorities, the administration chose a decentralized, complicated, and protracted way to spend the stimulus money. My article in the May–June 2009 issue of *Challenge* (p. 281 in this volume) lists what the WPA accomplished. Between 1935 and 1943, it hired 8.5 million people who desperately needed jobs. The newly employed spent most of their money, which in turn got spent by others, so that the initial investment in jobs multiplied. Business improved with more paying customers to sell to. Banking improved with more solvent borrowers to lend to. The main problem with the WPA is that it wasn't big enough. It didn't complete the job of getting the economy out of the Depression. Deficit spending completely succeeded only with the onset of World War II, when private industry stretched the workforce to the limit and put the WPA out of business. Roosevelt wasn't bold enough. He was a pre-Keynesian living in a Keynesian world.

Obama's chief economic advisers, starting with Treasury Secretary Timothy Geithner, are blind to the advantages of centralized hiring because they are part of a clubby group of bankers who believe in banks first, people second. What sense did it make to appoint Timothy Geithner, who had a big hand in creating the boom to begin with by allowing insane leveraging of loans up to fifty times the capital of lenders (AIG, Fannie Mae, Freddie Mac, the shadow banking system that includes hedge funds, trust fund, and sovereign wealth funds)? He turned a blind eye to structured investment vehicles started by Citicorp and imitated by Bear Stearns, Lehman Brothers, and most of the nineteen largest banks, which were designed to rip off their clients. He also allowed, even fostered, large-scale subprime lending and excessive prime lending as home values were falling below the mortgages on them. Appointing Geithner was like hiring a bank robber to design and run the rescue plan because he knew where the money was.

We will continue to go through booms and busts until we alter the capitalist system in ways that will prevent them.

Everything is in jeopardy until we get rid of the bloat in the financial system. The bloat churns out profits for its managers, who are perceived to be geniuses in the boom and turn out to be dunces in the bust, with no positive effect on production, distribution, or services to the public. These geniuses-turned-dunces spin their wheels by overleveraging us into disaster. The U.S. economy had all the financing it needed in the 1950s and 1960s, when banks and insurance companies made up half the share of GDP that they did in 2008 at the height of the boom. In return for destroying the economy, the U.S. financial sector obtained about 16 percent of corporate profits between 1974 and 1985. In the 1990s it obtained 21 to 30 percent. In the current decade, it reached 41 percent. See David Brooks, *New York Times,* April 3, 2009. Now that we are in the dumps, the share has fallen to 28 percent.

The financial system needs to do only two things: transfer money from people and businesses with savings to people and businesses that need savings to invest and that have good credit ratings; and insure assets and lives. The old-fashioned banks and insurance companies could do the job very effectively. They didn't securitize loans into packages of unidentifiable paper, unidentifiable once combined into packages of thousands of loans, the value of which nobody knew but thought they knew, because rating agencies, who didn't know either, said that they knew. These so-called tranches of subprime, middling, and prime mortgages became opaque once they left the hands of their originators. The old-fashioned banks and insurance companies were responsible for making sure that borrowers were reasonable risks. If they weren't, the lenders took the consequences. But if a bank can get the loan out the door in return for a securitized debt obligation, the incentive to lend with care is out the door too. Even the nonsecuritized system got out of hand throughout our history with speculative manias for canals, railroads, gold rushes, stock and commodity markets, real estate, dot-coms—see the history of the United States. It need not happen. Speculative buccaneering can be recognized and prevented with effective financial rules made on the assumption that markets can go crazy unless they are reined in. Plain vanilla banks and insurance companies can do their necessary work without contracting financial fever and raising their blood pressure and everybody else's around them.

Then the issue of businesses too big to fail has to be faced. If they are too big to fail, they are *ipso facto* public enterprises in private hands. They are public utilities and need to be run as such with boards responsible to the public.

Behind all these problems is the increasing polarization of income and wealth, with 80 percent of families gaining little or nothing over the last several decades, while the top 1 percent, one-tenth of 1 percent, and one-hundredth of 1 percent gaining increasing wealth, which puts overwhelming economic and political power in the hands of a few thousand mostly like-minded individuals who have persuaded themselves that we live in the best of all possible worlds. At least half of the increased wealth went to CEOs, COOs, CFOs, and board members of the companies too big to fail: men, and a few women, who are responsible to no one, not even stockholders. They can and do run companies in the manner of medieval lords. The boards of directors and compensation committees appointed by the lords say the lords' worth is beyond measure. So everything is OK with the guardians. Steeply progressive taxes and the abolition of offshore tax havens would be nice ways to handle this problem, as well as a change in the philosophy regarding whom business lords are responsible to. The public, perhaps? A short-term, quick-profit modus is not fine. A long-term public interest modus is fine.

Let us return to the unemployed and the foreclosed. In a just and compassionate society, everyone who wants a job gets a job. The government is employer of last resort. A man or woman gets a job in the private sector if possible; in the public sector if necessary, not counting those who work in the public sector by choice—members of Congress, for example. In a just and compassionate society, no homeowner is foreclosed and cast into misery. Foreclosure is hardly distinguishable from debtor's prison, a punishment that does not fit the crime.

In a good society, as John Kenneth Galbraith called it, those who want to join a union can join a union, with no NLRB maze to walk through. That's about one-third of the workforce, according to polls, the percentage that belonged to unions before obstacles were put in the way. Strong unions then become a countervailing power, in Galbraith's words, to offset the power of businesses too large to fail, and lesser ones that follow in their wake. Unions and full employment help to redistribute income and wealth downward. Spending increases. The ability to save moves downward, for then every family benefits by investing savings, benefits from income that now largely accrues to the top 1 percent. In the 1940s, 1950s, and 1960s, unions created a new working-class middle class, decimated over the last quarter-century, much to the detriment of everyone.

All that is left, economically speaking, is to follow John Maynard Keynes's scientific observations: deficits are necessary to increase demand when the economy stumbles, and tax increases are necessary to remove excess demand when the economy floats upward.

This prescription adds up to markets that are effective at doing what markets do best; and governments that are effective at doing what governments do best. No perfection expected. Just trial and error with the actual economy and actual people in mind instead of the fantasies of economists and businessmen who think that we are still living in the economy and among the people of 1776, when Adam Smith wrote *The Wealth of Nations.*

I trust that most of us can enthusiastically support political democracy *combined with* economic democracy. Call it what you will.

Can Obama do it? Judging by his books, speeches, and actions, his heart and brains are in the right places. But he has to pick better economists.

Notes

1. The WPA was the largest New Deal agency. The name Works Progress Administration was changed to Works Projects Administration in 1939.
2. Timothy Geithner was president of the Federal Reserve Bank of New York, then under secretary of the Treasury for International Affairs during the terms of Treasury secretaries Robert Rubin and Lawrence Summers, whose protégé he is reputed to be.
3. The so-called shadow banking system is an unregulated and opaque section of the financial system that makes up its own rules.
4. Structured investment vehicles (SIVs) were part of the shadow banking system invented by Citigroup in 1988. They borrowed money from investors to buy short-term securities at low interest rates and used that money to buy long-term securities at higher interest rates, making a profit from the difference. SIVs usually ranged in size from $1 billion to $30 billion in assets. Their managers relied on mathematical models that did not take into account a sharp drop in real-estate values or a fall in long-term interest rates below short-term interest rates. In the recession, investors fled SIVs, leaving investment banks and other agencies no recourse other than shutting them down.
5. The NLRB (National Labor Relations Board) was established in 1934 to set up procedures for the formation of unions. With the advent of the Reagan presidency,

board members were often chosen because they opposed the formation of unions. The board was turned into an obstacle instead of a facilitator. The card check-off system, a simple procedure to get a "yes" or "no" answer, is a way to bypass the NLRB. Unions and their supporters are in favor of it.

6. In order not to unduly complicate the text, I did not mention the Public-Private Investment Program (PPIP), which would auction off the toxic assets of banks, assets substantially below their original market value. The Federal Deposit Insurance Corporation (FDIC) and the Federal Reserve guarantee private investors that they will not lose money and encourage them to buy the toxic assets on the assumption that they will rise in value. Perhaps. But the likelihood that these assets will rise to their previous value is dim, and the likelihood that the FDIC and the Fed will have to reimburse private investors for their losses is great. Then we will pay. The only sure thing is that the banks will have their toxic assets taken off their balance sheets and the private investors will get their money back. In *the New York Review of Books* of May 28, 2009, Benjamin Friedman wondered how your banker would react if you asked him or her to value your house at what you paid for it instead of what it is worth now. Timothy Geithner is a great advocate of the PPIP.

July 2009

Camp Runamuck

Two articles of interest appeared on the front page of the *New York Times* of July 31, 2009. One is about eighty or so out-of-work and out-of-means men and women who live under a bridge in Providence, Rhode Island. The other is about 4,793 traders and bankers from nine financial firms who received bonuses of more than $1 million each in 2008, of whom 311 made over $5 million and 47 made over $10 million. I am writing this note on August 1. By the time you read it in the September–October issue of *Challenge*, the situation might be different. The eighty or so people living under the bridge might be back at work. The 4,793 financiers might be restricted to bonuses in line with generally accepted standards of morality. In a recession of their own making, this means none.

The eighty indigents in Providence live under tarps. Interestingly enough, the 4,793 traders and bankers also live under a TARP (Troubled Asset Relief Program), from which their banks received $165 billion.

The homeless under the bridge live in a place they call Camp Runamuck. Their leader has a nice sense of irony, since he has made a play on the words "run amuck," a variation of "run amok." He has established an organization with written rules, shared tasks, and votes on issues. When the *Times* reporter Dan Barry visited, the down-and-outers were enjoying a communal dinner of "donated chicken, parboiled and grilled; donated corn on the cob; donated potatoes."

The *Times* did not report what the bankers and traders were doing that evening.

But we know that they live in their own Camp Runamuck, or Camp Runamok, as you prefer. New York State attorney general Andrew Cuomo compiled the following information. Twenty billion dollars in bonuses was distributed among the 4,793 traders and bankers in January, an average in excess of $4 million each. Nine-hundred-and-fifty executives at Goldman Sachs received more than $1 million each to run amok with. Four-hundred-and-twenty-eight at Morgan Stanley each had over a million to run amok with. Hundred of bankers and traders at weaker institutions like Citigroup and Bank of America ran amok with over $1 million each. The nine banks lost a total of $81 billion; altogether they distributed $32.6 billion in run-amok money when bonuses of less than $1 million are included. The *Times* article reports that this year bonuses will be higher because the banks *appear* to be making money.

A comparison of the two Camp Runamucks reminds me of Shaw's play *Major Barbara*. Major Barbara works at a Salvation Army center that provides food for poor people and prayers for their souls. Major Barbara is appalled to learn that her father, the Midas munitions-maker Andrew Undershaft, together with the owner of a huge brewery, supplies most of the money for the canteen. Undershaft sells to all who come, regardless of who they are or for what purpose they use the munitions. Why? Because Undershaft believes in power, his own power. As long as the world is the way it is, money is power. "The government of your country! I am the government of your country!" His motto is "Unashamed." After exchanging visits to the canteen and munitions plant, Major Barbara is convinced that the Salvation Army can accomplish nothing and joins her father to get the power to accomplish something. Shaw does not make clear what.

Certainly the 4,793 financial executives who each extracted over $1 million in bonuses during a near-depression and after receiving TARP money, are "unashamed." They are playing the hand that they were dealt. No middle-class morality for them.

Let us turn to Adam Smith and Charles Darwin for an explanation. In *The Theory of Moral Sentiments,* Smith observed that children are taught to see themselves in the place of others and thereby come to understand the feelings and concerns of others. In the case of the bankers, the "others" are other bankers, so their behavior is consistent with Smith's theory.

Darwin observed that *Homo sapiens* evolved as a social species for which cooperation was essential in order to survive. Insiders in a band or tribe cooperated. The rest of the world was inhabited by outsiders who might be enemies. But human brains are capable of changing the definition of insiders and outsiders, as demonstrated by history. We can conceive, without being unscientific, that every person in the world can come to regard every other person as an insider. So our job is to teach the bankers and traders that we are all insiders. Or to fence them off from the rest of us.

By the time you read these words, Congress may have declared that businesses "too big to fail" are public-private entities that must be managed in the public interest by boards responsible to the public.

Or it may have instituted steeply progressive income taxes to recoup assets taken by ordinary men who happened to be in the right place at the right time to take all that can be taken.

Or it may make it easier for employees to join unions, which at their height from the 1940s through the 1960s were a force for redistributing wealth, and in so doing creating a new working-class middle class, which earned money instead of borrowing it.

Congress may or may not have done any or all of these things before the end of the year. I intend to reread my words and compare them with the results.

Note

The nine banks discussed by Andrew Cuomo are Goldman Sachs, Citigroup, Merrill Lynch (now owned by Bank of America), Morgan Stanley, Bank of America, Bank of New York Mellon, Wells Fargo, State Street, and JPMorgan Chase. The following banks repaid their TARP money: Goldman Sachs, Morgan Stanley, Bank of New York Mellon, State Street, and JPMorgan Chase. Of the total 4,793 individuals who collected over $1 million, the total of 1,626 for JPMorgan Chase includes salaries.

September 2009

Dissatisfaction Guaranteed: An Account of Two Bubbles

A review of *Plunder and Blunder: The Rise and Fall of the Bubble Economy,* by Dean Baker. Sausalito, CA: PoliPoint Press, 2009.

You know the story of the Three Little Pigs. The first Little Pig built his house with straw. The second Little Pig built his house with sticks. The third Little Pig built his house with bricks. The Big Bad Wolf huffed and puffed and blew down the straw house and ate the first Little Pig. He huffed and puffed some more and blew down the stick house and ate the second Little Pig. He huffed and puffed again but couldn't blow down the brick house. So he climbed down the chimney and fell into a pot of boiling water, whereupon the third Little Pig ate him.

Why then did Little Pigs Alan Greenspan, Hank Paulson, Ben Bernanke, and Tim Geithner, and the heads of AIG, Fannie Mae, and Freddie Mac, build their houses out of straw? Why did the Little Pig CEOs of the biggest banks build their houses out of sticks? How did Nobel Prize winners Myron Scholes and Robert C. Merton convince all the Little Pigs who went to market that the Big Bad Wolf could never blow down the new and improved straw or stick houses, as proved by their new and improved mathematical model?

The tragedy of all the innocent Little Pigs who went to market is that the financial house could have been built of brick.

In non-allegorical language, the two overleveraged investment bubbles of the last fifteen years are put under a microscope by Dean Baker, co-director of the Center for Economic and Policy Research, in his book *Plunder and Blunder: The Rise and Fall of the Bubble Economy.*

The dot-com bubble of 1995–2001, i.e., house of straw, was created by Little Pigs who grossly overleveraged technology stocks on the assumption that new companies should madly scramble for market share before they even made a profit. The price-to-earnings ratio (PE) would make a real pig regurgitate. The straw house got blown down in the stock market crash of 2001.

The second bubble—house of straw—grew out of the first one when the sophisticated money started investing in real estate in 2002. After all, people always need houses. But the value of houses ballooned 20 percent above a 100-year trend-line, and a stable ratio between the cost of renting and the cost of buying was knocked to pieces by the ever-inflating cost of buying.

The clever straw idea of encouraging commercial banks to lend mortgage money and then sell the mortgages to investment bankers in return for bonds allowed the banks to use the bonds as capital to sell more mortgages. In technical language, they bought mortgage-backed securities. Since the banks were not responsible for the quality of the mortgages they had been sold, the banks took advantage of unqualified customers by issuing subprime mortgages. Once gotten out the door, they were bundled with thousands of other mortgages of all grades. No one could possibly know what the bundles were worth. But because the bundles were highly assessed by rating agencies that stood to gain by highly assessing them, trusting investors all over the world bought them, especially investment banks and sovereign wealth funds. After the subprime mortgages inevitably started defaulting, panic suddenly spread throughout the international market, which crashed in 2007, bringing the world banking system down with it, culminating in the bankruptcy of Lehman Brothers in September 2008. But you know all this. (Or if you don't, you can read Dean Baker's book.)

You also know about the credit default swaps issued by AIG as insurance against default by buyers of mortgage-backed securities and other collateralized debt obligations. But AIG had so little capital leveraged by so much debt that it too turned out to be a house of straw that had to be rescued by the federal government. The whole banking system had to be rescued by the federal government—socialism for banks—because it was a house of straw or, at best, sticks. In fact, the whole international banking system had to be socialized, like it or not.

What have we learned? The private financiers have learned nothing. They are already building a new house of straw and sticks. Their business, after all, is to get out of the straw or stick house before it is blown down and escape from the Wolf with the loot in their pockets. We don't know if the Fed and the Treasury, Congress and the White House have learned anything yet because they haven't done anything yet. Keynes and his followers taught us how to build a brick house that can't be blown down by the Big Bad Wolf. It remains to be seen how many straw or stick houses the Little Pigs will build before all the rest of us say enough is enough.

The worst of it is that 26 million Americans are unemployed, forced to work part time, or too discouraged to look for work. Forty million Americans are living in poverty in a big overlap with the unemployed and underemployed.

We could end this disaster by employing the unemployed and underemployed directly through deficit spending. They, in turn, would spend their paychecks because they would need to. Their spending would help the economy recover in a short time—relative to what is going on now—and make us all richer. I'm waiting to hear this rather straightforward idea discussed in the higher circles of government.

Where are you, Barack Obama, now that we need you?

November 2009

Obama's Failures

President Barack Obama has departed from reality with respect to the two decisive crises of his administration, unemployment at home and Afghanistan abroad. He now has the audacity of patience with unemployment and the fierce urgency of sometime later. He pleasantly assures us that the economy is on the mend. Unemployment will eventually be reduced. Possibly it will go down to 8 percent in the next few years.

The $787 billion allocated by Obama's American Recovery and Reinvestment Act of 2009, which I have puzzled over several times, depends, as far as I can discern, on the actions of hundreds if not thousands of jurisdictions with no centralized management and not much direct attention to consumer spending or jobs. Money has to filter through states, counties, towns, and government agencies. That is a creepingly slow way to get anything done. If this administration pushed to get some of that money to the jobless directly and quickly through a centralized agency, to repair infrastructure, even build new infrastructure, as Franklin Roosevelt did, that would no doubt make enemies. Someone with the audacity of hope might sound a call to the public to back him up and help him do, shall we say, the humane thing, and to hell with the enemies. Guess not.

The plain fact is that President Barack Obama gathered around himself members of the financial establishment, the very people who brought on the increase in unemployment in the first place, who don't have too clear a view of what unemployment entails for the unemployed.

During the boom that led to the bust, Lawrence Summers, Obama's director of the National Economic Council, said, "It seems to me that the overwhelming preponderance of what has taken place is positive."

In 2006, Timothy Geithner, now Obama's secretary of the Treasury, said, "In the financial system we have today, with less risk concentrated in banks, the probability of systemic financial crisis may be lower than in traditional bank-centered financial systems."

In 2005, Ben Bernanke, now Obama's Federal Reserve chairman, said, "I think it's important to point out that house prices are being supported in very large part by very strong fundamentals. . . . We have lots of jobs, employment, high incomes, very low mortgage rates, growing population, and shortages of land and housing in many areas."

These clever men spent all their waking hours rescuing the banks, only taking time to announce that employment would recover later, as if this were a law of nature instead of an act of policy.

Into these hands we commend ourselves. Into these hands Barack Obama has commended himself. Into these hands he has commended the unemployed, the foreclosed, the poor, and their unfortunate children.

In Afghanistan, we, via President Barack Obama, have commended ourselves into the hands of General Stanley McChrystal and the military establishment for which he stands, which is oblivious to the audacity of hopelessness and the fierce urgency of getting out now.

On August 30, 2009, General McChrystal sent a memo to Secretary of Defense Robert M. Gates, saying, "The weakness of state institutions, malign action of power brokers, widespread corruption and abuse of power by various officials, and ISAF's own errors, have given Afghans little reason to support their government. . . . Further, a perception that our resolve is uncertain makes Afghans reluctant to align with us against the insurgents." (The ISAF, or International Security Assistance Force, is the U.S.-led NATO coalition.)

Well said, General McChrystal. You will no doubt clean all that up before we start to get out in eighteen months. You will lecture the thief-president Hamid Karzai to mend his ways. You will convince the Afghans to overlook the occasional killing of wedding parties by our drones. You will turn this feudal land of quarreling chiefdoms into a peaceful domain. You will save face by soldiering on. You will please not make any comparisons with Vietnam. And do not, do not mention Lyndon Johnson.

We will deploy 100,000 soldiers in Afghanistan to make the land inhospitable to several hundred members of al Qaeda who are not there and then we will come home and they will come back if they want to.

Please convince me that our eloquent president has not joined the financial and military establishments of the United States of America and that unemployed people don't suffer as much as I think they do and that not too many people will be killed in Afghanistan.

December 1, 2009

(To whom it may concern: If you don't understand how to stabilize an unstable economy, read a virtual recipe on the subject, *The Keynes Solution: The Path to Global Economic Prosperity,* by Paul Davidson. If you want to ponder the futility of war, read *The Limits of Power: The End of American Exceptionalism,* by Andrew J. Bacevich. His son was killed in Iraq.)

Postscript: Economic conference at the White House, December 3, 2009.

President Barack Obama: "While I believe the government has a critical role in creating conditions for economic growth, ultimately true economic recovery is only going to come from the private sector."

Comment: A profound misconception of the roles of government and the private sector in a recession. The sudden decline in private spending in a recession must be compensated for by an increase in public spending large enough to restore the economy to full employment. If the private sector had sufficient financial reserves to bring about a "true economic recovery," we would not have had a recession in the first place. Only the federal government commands the financial resources to bring about a true economic recovery.

If President Obama does not understand the essential role of government in restoring prosperity, we will not have prosperity. We must be alarmed if our doctor is ignorant of a known remedy when we are sick. As our sickness drags on, we need our doctor to make an effort to learn about the known remedy. Our plan does not allow us to change doctors for four years.

Post postscript: I learned from Nicholas Kristof, *New York Times,* December 3, 2009, that a private effort, called the National Solidarity Program, is building schools, clinics, irrigation projects, and bridges in Afghan villages in agreement with the villagers. The Taliban most often leaves these projects alone because the local population supports them. "For the cost of deploying one soldier for one year, it is possible to build about 20 schools." But the inimitable Nicholas Kristof did not supply a cost-benefit analysis of the relative effect on the Afghans of twenty schools versus the deployment of one soldier.

January 2009

The Freefall That Isn't Free

A review of *Freefall: America, Free Markets, and the Sinking of the World Economy,* by Joseph E. Stiglitz. New York: W.W. Norton, 2010.

The recent sinking of the world economy, Joseph Stiglitz writes, resulted from an explosive mixture: deregulated financial markets; low interest rates that led to a mad runup of borrowing; a global real-estate bubble featuring stratospheric subprime financing; and a global economy pulled apart with the stresses of either dangerous fiscal and trade deficits or dangerous surpluses.

Banking doesn't have to rip the economy to pieces if the bankers stick to their business, which is to transfer depositors' money to creditors on purchases that depositors make; and assess and manage risk when the bankers make loans. Instead, the big bankers inflated their banks like balloons on collateralized debt obligations and by 2007 "earned" 41 percent of all corporate profits before they exploded.

We were then engulfed in market failures. The economy of goods and services was brought down by transactions of the financial sector to which most of us were not party. Like a factory that emits toxic smoke and blights an entire neighborhood, the banks emitted toxic securities and blighted the entire world economy. We have all paid the highest price on record for the recklessness of the small number of bankers at the top of the banking pyramid and the small number of regulators who were supposed to restrain them. The negative externalities, as Stiglitz points out, have cost the big banks nothing.

The opposite. In return for destroying the real economy of almost the entire world, they have siphoned up the profits like magnates, kings, and conquerors.

We immediately come up against the agency problem. Who are the head bankers working for? They are working for themselves to the detriment of others because there is no penalty for doing so; the moral code of Wall Street tells every man and woman to look out for themselves first. The separation of ownership and control has been taken to unimaginable extremes, with the stockholders in distant second place, leaving the managers with the incentive to aim at the highest short-term earnings—and the long-term health of the banks be damned. (The current distribution of earnings of the biggest banks is about 90 percent to employees and 10 percent to stockholders.)

Self-interested incentives led to the buying and selling of mortgage-backed securities, the quality of which the bankers knew nothing and the public less than nothing (information asymmetries), all inflated by the leveraging of initial assets by forty times or more, benignly approved by rating agencies and federal regulators. The interest of the public in this scheme is nowhere present, except when it comes to picking up the pieces when the banks collapse.

Perverse incentives lead to moral hazard, which means that the perpetrators can do immoral things to other people since they don't have to suffer the consequences of their actions. The government comes to the rescue because the newly awakened experts at the Fed and the Treasury assume that the banks are "too big to fail." The perpetrators pay themselves huge bonuses for record losses because we have no laws to stop them. They are exempt from risks; the "experts" have socialized the losses.

So we have a crash, in which the cumulative gap between actual output and potential output is in the trillions of dollars. The buildings are still there, the people are still there, the know-how is still there, nature is still there, but they are all strangely unusable.

As of 2008 we are in freefall. After the disintegration of Lehman Brothers on September 15, George W. Bush, through the mediation of his secretary of the Treasury Henry Paulson, comes to the rescue—of the banks. But not of the homeowners or the unemployed. TARP is conceived, the Troubled Asset Relief Program, a dissembling phrase for the bankrupt bank program. Paulson obtains $700 billion to throw at the banks, leaving the underlying economy unattended, akin, writes Stiglitz, "to giving a massive blood transfusion to a patient dying of internal bleeding" (p. 30). And Barack Obama continues along the same lines. Limitless support of the bad banks, too little support to revive the real economy (through the American Recovery and Reinvestment Act of 2009). Stiglitz invokes the Powell Doctrine: attack with overwhelming force. He announces the Krugman-Stiglitz Doctrine: when the economy founders, attack with overwhelming force. If you have too much ammunition, you can always hold back. (I assume that Paul Krugman was consulted about the naming.) In practice, the Obama Doctrine is: attack with underwhelming force, with the inevitable result of a longer and deeper recession.

The Bush and Obama administrations didn't follow the usual rules of capitalism. If a firm can't pay its debts, it goes into bankruptcy or receivership. The shareholders lose everything; the bondholders and creditors become the new shareholders. But our double standard applies: the executive stays, the public pays.

A well-designed stimulus, continues Stiglitz, does not muddle its objectives: 1. It must be fast. 2. It must be effective. 3. It must address long-term problems. 4. It must focus on investment that leaves the country in better shape. 5. It must be fair and help the general public. 6. It must deal with short-run exigencies created by the crisis: jobs, mortgages, health care. 7. It must be targeted to retrain workers where the job losses are permanent.

Now Stiglitz returns to the initial theme of *Freefall,* the mortgage scam, about which you already know too much. I will just recite some data supplied by the author. The underlying condition for excessive borrowing was the shortage of money in the hands of the general public. Median household income in 2005 was 3 percent lower than it was in 1999, while home prices rose 42 percent. Then comes the crash, and the banks have no incentive to restructure mortgages: they would be forced to write down their assets. Instead of using their preferred "mark to hope" they would have to use the conventional "mark to market." By the end of June 2009, one-third of all U.S. homes, 15.2 million, were underwater: the book value of the mortgages was greater than the value of the homes. By October 2009, only 651,000 mortgages had been modified out of 3.2 million eligible (20 percent).

Our friend Joseph Stiglitz proposes four ways to rescue homeowners *without* bailing out the banks. Emphasis his. (Although the big banks have already been bailed out, the homeowner rescue can still take place.) Pay the mortgage over a longer period. Lower the interest rate. Assist the mortgagee in making payments. Reduce the amount owed. All these possibilities would require new laws, such as a Chapter 11 for homeowners, which allowed for a reduction of the mortgage or a longer time to pay it off. Or a government assumption of mortgage debt at lower interest rates, which are virtually zero these days for government and bank borrowing.

Looking now at "The Great American Robbery," as Stiglitz calls it, we turn our attention to the collusion between the banks and the federal government. To quote: "Capitalism can't work if private rewards are unrelated to social returns" (p. 110). (Interjection: that has been the periodic problem of capitalism from its inception.) Further: "The failings of the Obama and Bush administrations will rank among the most costly mistakes of any modern democratic government at any time" (p. 110). The loans, guarantees, and bailouts approached 80 percent of a $14.2 trillion GDP in 2009, or $11.6 trillion.

The wrongs that were tolerated: 1. Wrong to accept unsocial incentives. 2. Wrong to accept "too big to fail." 3. Wrong to accept unmanaged securitization. 4. Wrong to allow commercial banks to imitate the high-risk returns of high finance (securitize mortgages). 5. Wrong to allow banks to prey on the poorest and most vulnerable. (I assume that you will allocate these wrongs fairly between the two administrations.)

Why didn't Obama direct the failing banks to file for Chapter 11 bankruptcy? Or enter into conservatorship, in which new entities take over ownership and management? *"Financial reorganizations giving a fresh start—are not the end of the world"* (p. 117; author's emphasis). If the banks had to follow the normal rules, incentives would have aligned better with the public interest and little public money or government intervention would have been needed. Risk was imposed on the public and removed from shareholders and bondholders under a "novel and unproven doctrine" (p. 118). "Too big to fail" is "too big to be resolved," that is, financially restructured. Under this assumption, "in the most munificent act in the history of corporate welfare, the government's safety net was extended to insolvent banks. Then it was extended even farther, to AIG, an insurance company" (p. 122).

TARP was originally designed to acquire toxic assets, that is, "cash for trash." The word "toxic," depreciated assets, was transmuted into "troubled," then under Geithner, "legacy," as if euphemisms turned sows' ears into silk purses, when in fact the banks and the Fed turned silk purses into sows' ears throughout the entire first decade of the twenty-first century. The banks were free to continue paying bonuses and dividends with no effective pressure to resume lending.

PPIP, or the Public-Private Investment Program, under Obama, took part of the TARP money to buy depreciated assets from banks ("cash for trash") and offered to sell them, leaving it to the public to make up any losses. "It was as if it [the Obama administration] had decided to use a private trash-hauling service, which would buy the garbage in bulk, sort through it, pick out anything of value, and dump the remaining junk on the taxpayer" (pp. 127–128). And "only certain members of the Wall Street club would be allowed to 'compete,' after having been carefully selected by the Treasury" (p. 128). The result was a huge transfer of wealth to certain banks, a win-win-lose proposition. Banks win, investors win, taxpayers lose to the extent that the program works for the banks.

The government could have given the TARP money—$700 billion—to well-managed banks or could even have chartered new ones. At a 12-to-1 lending ratio, $700 billion would have guaranteed $8.4 trillion in new credit, more than enough to meet the needs of the real economy. Instead, the bailout increased the size of the banks deemed "too big to fail" and "too big to be resolved." It did the opposite of what it should have done. "The banks that were the worst in risk management got the biggest gift from the government" (p. 135). The path taken was far worse than conservatorship or nationalization—"the privatization of gains and the socialization of losses" (p. 135).

If banks are too big to fail, they are too big to exist. They grind their wheels and contribute nothing. Assets don't trickle down; they are siphoned up. In 1995, the five largest banks combined had 8 percent of market share. Today they have 30 percent. Bank of America acquired Merrill Lynch. Wells Fargo acquired Wachovia. JPMorgan Chase acquired Bear Stearns. The

Obama administration's "oddest proposal" is to give the Fed more power to make regulation work. But the Fed already failed to use the power it had (p. 179).

Stiglitz refers to moving the deck chairs on the *Titanic*. Let me put it this way. Larry Summers, Tim Geithner, and Ben Bernanke are sitting together, and one of them is overheard to say, "What iceberg? We don't see an iceberg." After the crash, the captain asks them to organize the rescue operations.

Where do we go from here? The author has a whole chapter on reforming economics. I will not go into detail. Suffice it to say that the invisible hand is not only invisible, it does not exist. Sophisticated mathematical models using out-of-date statistics cannot predict the future if their designers assume that really bad things happen only once in a thousand years, which takes us back to 1010 CE. (In testimony before the House Financial Services Committee on January 22, 2010, Professor Stiglitz cited a model in which the designers postulated that the events of 2007–2008 happen less than once in the lifetime of the universe. But since the universe has not yet ended, this assumption seems implausible. The head of Goldman Sachs, Lloyd Blankfein, argued before the Financial Crisis Inquiry Commission on January 13 that "[w]e should resist a response . . . that is solely designed around protecting us from the 100-year storm." Jamie Dimon of JPMorgan Chase more conservatively found that a financial crisis "happens every five to seven years. We shouldn't be surprised." Not much we can do about it, really. So the estimated range is five years to the life of the universe.)

We should not let ourselves become befuddled by words that carry emotional baggage like "socialism," "privatization," or "nationalization." Public universities, for example, perform just as well as private universities. Efficient and inefficient firms can operate equally well or badly in the private or public sectors. The largest government steel mills in South Korea and Taiwan are more efficient than privately owned mills in the United States. The financial debacle in the *private sector* is a warning to take a long-run view of our needs, which is beyond the horizon of private firms. Not so easy for an electorate that is sketchy on facts. Only one person in four knows that it takes sixty senators to break a filibuster. Only one in three knows that no Republicans voted for the health-care bill (reported by Charles Blow, *New York Times,* January 30, 2010).

Since Joseph Stiglitz was chief economist at the World Bank between 1997 and 2000, and made himself very unpopular there, we expect him to think globally. He was unpopular because he pointed out that the United States and other rich countries had a double standard. I'm sure there were other reasons for his unpopularity as well. When a poor country had difficulty paying a loan, the World Bank and the International Monetary Fund forced it to pay up by cutting public expenditures, increasing taxes, raising interest rates, and balancing its budget, all of which throttled development and increased unemployment, but was good medicine by neoclassical standards. In the current crisis, what do you know, the United States and the other rich countries did the opposite and increased expenditures, lowered interest rates, gave tax rebates, and increased budget deficits. Meanwhile, China and India sidestepped the World Bank and IMF restrictions and experienced unprecedented growth.

The "global multiplier" is greater than the "national multiplier." But the global economy can no longer be managed by the United States alone, if ever it could. The United States cannot continue to act as "the consumer of last resort" or provide "the deficit of last resort" either in foreign trade—see the United States and China—or in stimulating the world economy. Stiglitz returns to the Keynes solution (to borrow the title of Paul Davidson's recent book): special drawing rights at the IMF, allocated among countries in proportion to their wealth, to be used as a center of currency exchange at a rate that does not rob one country to benefit another. Keynes advocated the use of a new international unit of exchange, the bancor, at the Bretton Woods meeting in 1944. Instead, given the enormous financial strength of the United States as World War II came to a close, the American delegation, led by Harry Dexter White, imposed the dollar on the IMF as the international medium of exchange. The strength of that arrangement is long past. Keynes also recommended that funds held by the bank in excess of a rich country's limit be donated to poor countries to aid their development. The postwar Marshall Plan is a perfect example of what Keynes had in mind. Marshall Plan aid helped Europe rebuild. At the same time, aid money created demand for U.S. exports; it created *positive externalities,* a free lunch. Stiglitz's proposals are much in the spirit of Keynes.

If I can summarize the message of this unsummarizable book, rugged individualism and market fundamentalism, little need for community, little need for trust, and government as the problem not the solution have taken us in the wrong direction. We need a morality and a vision of common interests for us and for the world, and the private and public institutions to act on this morality and this vision. It doesn't sound to me like the capitalism that we know and love.

Joe Stiglitz has written the most comprehensive book on the freefall and slow rise of the United States and world economies that we are likely to get, with extraordinary originality and sympathy. The best thing to do now is read it.

March 2010

Tea Party Politics

The first Tea Party that I encountered was the mad Tea Party attended by the March Hare, the Hatter, the Dormouse, and Alice. At the end, Alice left in a huff, since the Hare and the Hatter persisted in reproaching her for failing to solve unsolvable paradoxes.

The second Tea Party that I encountered took place on the night of December 16, 1773, when angry Bostonians disguised as Mohawks boarded three ships laden with tea and threw the tea into the harbor. The British Tea Act of 1773 allowed the East India Company to export tea to the colonies without paying a tax on it. Instead of rejoicing at the lower price of tea, the colonists were enraged at the prospect of American middlemen in the tea trade being driven out of business. They still had to pay the tax and therefore the price of their tea would be higher than the price of the East India Company tea.

Americans were angry because they didn't have to pay a tax.

I took part personally in the third Tea Party that I encountered at the Prince of Wales Hotel in Niagara-on-the-Lake in Ontario, Canada. Between 3 and 5 P.M., afternoon tea was served in the conservatory. An attentive hostess brewed Darjeeling, chamomile, mint, Earl Grey, or any other tea of your choice in a fine porcelain teapot, then poured it through a strainer into fine porcelain teacups. On a tiered stand resting on an elegant tea table, dainty tea sandwiches, cut square, triangular, or round, were served on very thin decrusted white bread, offering cucumber, ham with watercress, egg salad, cream cheese, smoked salmon, and scones served with clotted cream, jams, and jellies. On the top levels of the tiered stand, I found petits fours, miniature tarts, chocolates, and cookies. All this was served with the thoughtful provision of china plates, silver knives and forks, and crisp linen napkins. I have returned frequently to the Prince of Wales Hotel.

The next Tea Party that I encountered is taking place as we speak (or write).

It began with antitax protests early in 2009 in response to the millions and billions and trillions spent on the 2008 bank bailout and the 2009 stimulus package, then reached its stride with the proposal that billions more be spent to put the state between you and your doctor.

Men show up at Obama rallies with guns.

Crowds at Republican rallies shout "traitor," "liar," "fascist," "communist," "kill him." Signs show Obama with a Hitler mustache.

Representative Joe Wilson cries out "you lie" during Obama's speech before a joint session of Congress.

Texas governor Rick Perry tells a Tea Party rally that Texas might secede from the union.

House minority leader John Boehner warns that the country has twenty-four hours to avoid Armageddon if the health bill is passed.

"Kill the bill" is shouted from the House gallery with the approval of Republicans on the floor.

A crowd menaces House Democrats as they walk arm-in-arm toward the Capitol. Racial epithets are hurled at members of the Black Caucus. Representative Emanuel Cleaver is spat upon. Civil rights leader John Lewis is taunted "nigger." Representative Barney Frank is heckled "faggot."

Signs are waved at rallies: "Don't tread on me." "Disobedience to tyranny is obedience to God." "Obamacare equals death warrant for grandma."

From the House floor, Representative Randy Neugebauer shouts "baby killer" at Representative Bart Stupack.

Sarah Palin targets twenty Democrats with rifle crosshairs on her Web site. "Don't Retreat, Instead—RELOAD."

Ten members of Congress get death threats.

Tea Party leader Mike Vanderboegh writes on his blog: "To all modern Sons of Liberty: THIS is your time. Break their windows. Break them NOW."

Windows are smashed at Democratic Party offices.

Phone messages are sent to members of Congress: "Congressman Stupak, you baby-killing motherfucker. . . . I hope you bleed out your ass, get cancer, and die. You motherfucker."

To Representative Betsy Markey: "Better hope I don't run into you in a dark alley with a club, a knife, or a gun."

Governors around the country receive letters threatening to remove them forcibly from office if they don't step down in three days.

One-quarter of Republicans think that Obama might be the Antichrist.

The Republican leadership acknowledges that excessive language was used by a few Tea Party members. John McCain defends Palin's rhetoric as legitimate politics.

In 1965 Richard Hofstadter published a book of essays called *The Paranoid Style in American Politics.* The paranoid style is angry, suspicious, delusional, aggressive, grandiose, righteous, indignant, and apocalyptic. An individual might be paranoid according to a clinical definition, but a paranoid crowd is not clinically paranoid. A paranoid crowd feels persecuted as a group because its members perceive that their way of life is under attack by some powerful, alien force.

The American paranoid style started with the Salem witch trials and continued with attacks against blacks, Masons, Catholics, Mormons, radicals, liberals, antiwar protesters, and now against supporters of federal spending to revive the economy and to pay for a moderate health program. Spending trillions on dubious wars and going into debt trillions of dollars to finance them produced no paranoia. Most paranoid movements have an affinity for bad causes, as Hofstadter put it, but leftists have also engaged in paranoid episodes such as the Weatherman effort to overthrow the U.S. government. The Weathermen were scathingly denounced by liberals. We hear praise rather than denunciation of the Tea Party movement from leading conservatives.

The paranoid style is not confined to the United States. Hitler led a paranoid movement. Not all fear is paranoid. The fear felt by Hitler's neighbors was real. The fear felt by Jews was real. The fear felt by Stalin's victims was real.

The leaders of the Tea Party movement have nurtured lies. A paranoid movement has to coalesce around leaders. We have a black president to fear. He is a Muslim. His birth certificate was forged. He has a secret agenda. He is a socialist. He is the Antichrist.

The Republican leadership spread misinformation about the stimulus and the health-care bills. They denounced Obama for his failure to end unemployment, but they created unemployment. Republican leaders provided the table on which the Tea Party serves its tea. They propounded seemingly unsolvable paradoxes about taxes and spending that enraged the gullible.

Barack Obama is not without blame. He failed to head off anger over unemployment by doing something equal to the problem. His silence on health care during the summer of 2009 handed over the public forum to the Tea Party. He came roaring back in 2010 too late to undo the misconceptions.

Is the Tea Party protofascism? We don't know. If events gradually expose the lies, the Tea Party will die. It will take much longer to die than it would have if Obama had killed it in its infancy.

Samuel Johnson notoriously said, "Patriotism is the last refuge of a scoundrel." He was referring to England. In the United States it is the first refuge.

May 2010

The Futility of Force

The title of these ruminations derives from a book called *The Utility of Force: The Art of War in the Modern World,* by General Sir Rupert Smith, a retired high-ranking British commander. I do not deny that force has some utility. Consider intervention to stop ethnic cleansing or genocide. It's the way that the U.S. military has been using force in Afghanistan and Iraq that brings to mind the word "futility."

General Smith argues that most post-Korean wars are "wars amongst the people." The object of these wars is to "win the hearts and minds of the people," not to defeat an opposing army in the field of battle. The opposing force fights small skirmishes and blends in with the people.

When our side kills men, women, and children at wedding parties or funerals, kills children in schools, indiscriminately kills good people along with bad people by shooting missiles from remote-controlled drones, we are certainly fighting a war amongst the people, but we are not winning their hearts and minds. Instead, we are instilling hatred against us, which spills over borders throughout the entire Middle East and beyond. We are recruiting men and women who want to strike back at us—terrorists. We are recruiting entire nations that want us to get out.

What are the generals, admirals, presidents, and members of Congress thinking? What are we members of the public thinking?

If the tables were turned and the Afghanis and Iraqis invaded us and shot us up indiscriminately, we might get the point.

Why are our leaders acting stupidly?

Military solutions are bred into our bones. Vested interests push us toward military solutions. We think war is more effective than aid.

By bred into our bones I mean that we choose war because we presume that we are guided by a manifest destiny to bring our superior way of life to darker, less fortunate people. Our manifest destiny started with the occupation of Native American territory. We proceeded with the occupation of Mexican territory that happened to be in the way of American expansion. Then we went overseas to free an empire under the Spanish yoke in the Caribbean and Pacific. More recently, we have gone on to free other nations like Iraq and Afghanistan. Apparently the manifest destiny of other people is the opposite of ours.

Military solutions are bred into our bones. With respect to World War II, we had no choice. With respect to Korea, we had a choice. With respect to Vietnam, we had a choice. With respect to Afghanistan, we had a choice. With respect to Iraq, we had a choice.

To paraphrase Mr. Dooley, the Irish bartender-philosopher created by Peter Finley Dunne, we'll make ye free if we have ter break ivry bone in yer body t' do it. Mr. Dunne belonged to the Anti-Imperialist League. So did Mark Twain. But we don't use the word imperialism any more.

We used to have a small standing army except in wartime. But during the Cold War, we amassed a permanent military machine, modestly cut back after the fall of the Soviet Union in 1991, only to be amassed further in the "global war on terrorism" after 9/11.

Vested interests push us toward military solutions. Take the famous military-industrial complex. What is it? The military. The weapons manufacturers. The suppliers to the military and weapons manufacturers: that is, all the big businesses in the country. The big banks that finance them. The states that have military bases. The cities adjacent to military bases. The members of Congress from these states and districts that contain these cities, who are alarmed at the prospect of lost revenue if a base is closed. The lobbyists, obviously. The presidents, still thinking that big armies win, not thinking that "wars amongst the people" require "winning hearts and minds."

Add the vested interest in foreign bases, of which we have upward of 1,000. (See Chalmers Johnson, The Blowback Trilogy.) We still have bases in Germany that once protected the West from the Soviet Union. We still have a base in Okinawa that once hemmed in imperial Japan. We have nation-building bases in nations that don't want to be built. We have an archipelago of bases around the world, including floating bases on the seven seas, to protect us from everything.

If we closed 1,000 bases, that would entail a painful loss for suppliers, who would have to think of ways to convert to peacetime activities. As for the world, has anyone in authority ever wondered if it would be any worse off than it is now?

War is more effective than aid. We are spending around three trillion dollars on wars in Afghanistan and Iraq (see Joseph Stiglitz, *Freefall*), but we haven't thought about the alternative of spending three trillion dollars in development aid. What? Do you think we're crazy enough to spend that much money on development aid?

If we are not willing to create jobs for our own unemployed, rescue foreclosed homeowners, rescue small businesses, rescue our states, and rescue our educational system, how can we possibly think about *foreign* aid?

Our military spending is approximately equal to the military spending of the rest of the world together. The grand rationale was the Cold War, which permutated into the grand rationale of the "global war on terrorism," a war without limits, a war that crops up anywhere and everywhere, a war without end.

A war that undermines our own security and sinks us deeper into a morass of unsolved problems: our debt crisis, our energy crisis, our environmental crisis, our standard-of-living crisis, our vested interest crisis.

A vested interest is a stake in keeping things the way they are.

The "global war on terrorism" was manifest destiny dressed in new clothes by the Bush-Cheney administration. To our amazement, the Obama administration has put on the same now tattered clothes, having done nothing more than add a few colorful ribbons. No original thought, no change in direction, no sense of reality has been so much as hinted at, much to the consternation of the rest of the world, and most Americans too.

Here is a solid, indisputable, disconcerting fact. The "global war on terrorism" is illegal.

It doesn't matter whether you are a strict constructionist or a judicial activist. Both wings of the Supreme Court have chosen to overlook the unconditional constitutional mandate that grants Congress and only Congress the right to declare war. Congress itself has chosen to overlook its own unequivocal mandate, including members who go to bed with the Constitution under their pillows. Who is to say that the president, whoever he is, doesn't know best? The authors of the Constitution say so and would have to conclude that we are ruled by a government of outlaws.

On Sunday, May 8, I read an account of Sebastian Junger's *War,* reviewed by Dexter Filkins in the *New York Times Book Review.* Junger spent several months with an American infantry platoon in the six-mile-long Korengal Valley, "sort of the Afghanistan of Afghanistan: too remote to conquer, too poor to intimidate, too autonomous to buy off," quotes Filkins.

The job was to kill the Taliban and make friends with the Korengalis. But the Korengalis hated us as invaders.

Filkins concludes his article this way: "In April, the United States Army closed its bases in the Korengal Valley and sent the soldiers to other places. After five years of fighting and dying, American commanders decided the valley wasn't worth the fight. War indeed."

The war in Afghanistan has dragged on for nine-and-a-half years and violence in Iraq has continued for eight years. Our generals talk of asymmetrical warfare, which is shorthand for the kind of war we are waging now. They don't have the slightest idea what to do about it. If they did, we wouldn't be fighting. War indeed.

First comes the war. Then come the regrets.

July 2010

The Crisis of Capitalism

A comparison of the presidencies of Franklin Roosevelt and Barack Obama is instructive.

Roosevelt didn't find a way to end the economic crisis of the 1930s until everybody got a job as a worker or a soldier thanks to the voracious demand of world war. Yet Roosevelt remained popular throughout the twelve years and forty days of his presidency. He was elected four times and a Democratic majority in Congress was elected along with him.

First is the matter of his exuberant optimism. Personality is not policy, but Roosevelt's personality conveyed the feeling that he was on the side of the public. Everybody with a radio listened to his fireside chats, including me as a young boy caught in the uplift of his rhetoric. He gave frequent and frank press conferences. He raised the spirits of the country with his public appearances. He unleashed a whirlwind of work programs and bank regulations. He baited the "economic royalists," comparing them to the English royalists who oppressed the American colonies. The "royalists" called him a traitor to his class. Some meant his class at Harvard. That enmity persisted despite the fact that he saved their hides.

Roosevelt was indefatigable. In the first hundred days he declared a bank holiday and then reopened those that remained solvent. He supported the Glass-Steagall Act, which separated deposit banking from investment banking and created the Federal Deposit Insurance Corporation, easing depositors' worries about the safety of their accounts. He initiated the Civilian Conservation Corps, which sent young men into the countryside to work in the fields, forests, and national parks. He launched the Federal Emergency Relief Administration, which employed jobless men to perform unskilled work for town and state governments. He established the largest government-owned and run regional project in American history, the Tennessee Valley Authority, which built dams, controlled floods, and set up an electric grid that gave thousands of farm families the benefits of household electricity for the first time in their lives. Some fifty years ago I read the fervent account, *TVA: Democracy on the March,* written by its first director, David Lilienthal.

The National Recovery Administration, formed by Title I of the National Industrial Recovery Act, was the greatest of the great projects launched during the First New Deal, 1933 to 1935, and was a gigantic failure, declared unconstitutional by the Supreme Court. Contrary to the antitrust laws, businesses in each industry were invited to form cartels, raise prices, and reduce production, on the theory that these actions would cure the Depression. In my younger days, I saw the sign of the NRA, the Blue Eagle, in one storefront after another. Every businessman and woman wanted to pitch in and help. Labor was cajoled to go along by the inclusion of Section 7a, which legalized the right to organize unions, much to the consternation of the business "royalists." But Section 7a had no procedures or enforcement provisions, and an increasing number of strikes were broken up by official police, private police, and the National Guard. The private police were known as goons among the strikers, a recent coinage for the boss's thugs.

Title II of the NIRA established the Public Works Administration, which actually did get something done by building schools, hospitals, courthouses—in general public facilities still widely in use.

The Agriculture Adjustment Act ran parallel with the NIRA, authorizing farmers to cooperate in raising prices and reducing output by letting fields lie fallow and by slaughtering millions of pigs. The latter struck my young mind as atrocious, all the more so since millions of people were going hungry. An abstract theory can disorder the mind.

The unhelpful effect of these two programs was that the large businesses got together at the expense of the small ones and drove them into bankruptcy, while the large agribusinesses drove out the small farmers, tenants, and laborers.

The Second New Deal, 1935 to 1938, had a different character. The shift was strongly in favor of labor. The Works Progress Administration hired millions. The National Labor Relations Act replaced 7a and specified in detail the right of unions to organize, leading to the formation of the Congress of Industrial Organizations, which, together with the old American Federation of Labor, unionized one-third of the labor force by the 1950s. Much of the impetus for the pro-labor legislation came from Frances Perkins, secretary of Labor throughout Roosevelt's entire presidency and the first woman to be a member of the cabinet.

Taking account of all the successes and failures of the New Deal, Roosevelt did the best he knew how to end the Depression, and this fact lay behind the New Deal coalition of the unemployed, most of the working class and middle class, blacks, Jews, Catholics, many intellectuals, the liberal wing of business, and the Solid South.

The Solid South means white racists who voted Democratic. Roosevelt paid the price for the support of racists by turning his back on segregation, disenfranchisement, and lynchings. More to the point, blacks paid the price. At the instigation of the Solid South, the Social Security Act excluded domestic and farm workers, leaving out most blacks. The various work programs and the military remained segregated. Housing loans were discriminatory and government-supported mortgages required segregated housing. As an exception, when the threat of war became imminent, military contractors had to act as equal opportunity employers.

The fundamental flaw of New Deal economic policy was its failure to incorporate the idea that aggregate demand determines the level of economic activity and employment. Before Keynes, the idea was little known. The economists' dogma at the time equated the need of families to live frugally, hold cash, and stay as liquid as possible in an economic downturn with a presumed need for the government to do the same. Government borrowing created the danger of inflation, and debt was a burden to governments just as it was to families. Roosevelt violated the dogma in response to the sheer desperation of the unemployed. But when unemployment fell from a high of 25 percent in 1933 to 14.3 percent in 1937, he proceeded to balance the budget and revived the Depression in 1938 as unemployment rose to 19 percent. He resumed deficit spending in 1938 but not on a sufficient scale. In 1939 unemployment was still at 17.2 percent. The Keynes theory had not sunk in and did not until the 1940s, when there was no choice but to spend to win the war. By 1938, the Second New Deal came to an end. The American Liberty League of conservative Democrats, formed in 1934, launched an aggressive attack. Congress was no longer willing to support FDR's economic proposals.

Roosevelt was excoriated by conservatives for siding with labor against business, yet his persistent improvisations kept labor and the public sufficiently pacified to avoid looking for more radical solutions. Roosevelt aimed to humanize American capitalism, not destroy it, by implementing some of the most elementary features of a welfare state. The New Deal order persisted for some forty years. Even today, Social Security, the Federal Deposit Insurance Corporation, and what's left of the Securities and Exchange Commission, the National Labor Relations Board, and the labor movement remain.

His almost unlimited willingness to experiment is conveyed in John Kenneth Galbraith's book, *Name-Dropping*. One morning Harry Hopkins met Roosevelt to make the case for employment through the WPA. "Harry," Roosevelt said, "you are entirely right."

In the afternoon Harold Ickes came by to make the case for public works. Roosevelt said, "Harold, you are perfectly right."

Eleanor Roosevelt had been in the room for both meetings and remonstrated, "You say Harry is perfectly right, then Harold comes in and makes the opposite case, and you say *he* is perfectly right."

The president replied, "Eleanor, *you* are perfectly right."

In one respect, we cannot compare five years, 1933 through 1937, of Roosevelt's actions with one year and seven months (as I write) of Obama's actions. But in other respects we can. A majority of the public saw Roosevelt as a man on their side throughout the whole time. Obama has already lost the majority. Roosevelt sharply dissociated himself from Hoover's priorities. Obama embraced Bush's priority, to rescue the biggest banks through the Troubled Asset Relief Program, TARP, rather than make his priority the rescue of the unemployed. Obama could have nationalized the biggest banks or put them in receivership, made them smaller instead of larger, with new officers instead of the old ones, with the shareholders taking the financial hit instead of the public.

Obama made the very men who presided over the boom that turned into a bust his principal economic advisers: Robert Rubin, in charge of Obama's economic transition team; Timothy Geithner, secretary of the Treasury; Lawrence Summers, chairman of the president's National Economic Council; and Ben Bernanke, reappointed chairman of the Federal Reserve Board. All of them expected the good times to roll on. Roosevelt had some bank advisers, but they did not dominate his administration. His most intimate advisers, like Frances Perkins and Harry Hopkins, were former social work administrators and they were hell-bent on creating jobs.

Roosevelt kept the initiative on the economy for five years. Obama lost it in six months. By the summer of 2008 Obama faced public anger for coddling the biggest banks and failing to arrest the increase in unemployment. The stimulus did not stimulate. The $787 billion American Recovery and Reinvestment Act dribbled away through numerous constituencies and agencies. It was not big enough to do the job. It was not targeted to employment and its management was not centralized. Joseph Stiglitz recommended adopting the Powell Doctrine: strike with overwhelming force. The stimulus was insufficient, allowing the conservatives to say that deficit spending doesn't work. Obama's repeated feel-good assertion that jobs are being created fails to acknowledge that not enough jobs are being created. Unlike Roosevelt, he is either deceiving himself or not leveling with the public.

Obama has the advantage of living in a Keynesian world. We understand that a deficiency of private demand in a crisis must be made up by public demand. The resulting deficit will be paid for by taxes on the reemployed, economic growth, and God save the mark, a cutback in military spending and an increase in taxes on the affluent. In the pre-Keynesian world, before the widespread use of economic penicillin, Roosevelt could only keep the patient comfortable and in good cheer. But now we have penicillin. There is no excuse for failing to use it or for failing to use enough of it. The Obama doctors leaned over the patient and said, he seems to be getting better. Let's not give him the full dose. The patient is still sick.

Obama's start-and-stop style contributed to the resurgence of the conservatives. He disappeared from the public scene during the summer of 2009, allowing the Tea Party to take the initiative. His inflexibility led him to put health-care reform before reemployment. But the presidency requires improvisation. A president must deal with the problems before him. He cannot live only with a script. At the same time, the presidency is not a dress rehearsal. What is done is done. Obama has tried to live above the fray, leaving the details to Congress. And so he has lost the initiative along with the progressive movement that formed around him during the election campaign.

The members of that movement are startled by the fact that Obama did not champion a public option much less universal health care. They are taken aback by the financial regulatory act, which lays the groundwork for the next recession by failing to deal decisively with "too big to fail" banks, derivatives, the separation of consumer banking from investment banking— the Volcker Rule—and clear-cut consumer financial protection. The former members of that ephemeral progressive movement are dismayed by the hopelessness of Obama's continuing bloodletting in Afghanistan and Iraq. They were unable to see that he is a member of the business and military establishment because he did not talk like one. He still does not talk like one. But he acts like one. He is not a socialist.

At the same time, Obama did win the Nobel Prize for Peace by renouncing the Bush doctrine of preemptive war and reestablishing good relations with all foreign countries where good relations could be reestablished. He has worked for a reduction of atomic weapons. He did extend health care to some 30 million people even while helping the health insurance and pharmaceutical industries gain more customers. He did increase regulatory control over Wall Street even while helping the biggest banks expand. He did arrest the descent into depression even while opening the possibility of a decade of recession.

On a broader canvas, the Great Depression and the Great Recession are but two examples of a long history of economic crises, booms and busts, bank failures, unemployment, inflation, and other economic disasters. I count forty-eight such instances in the history of the United States. The suffering caused by these capitalist maladies is incalculable. They present a paradox: idle people ready to work and idle equipment ready for use.

The paradox extends to good times as well. Since 1999, productivity has risen in the United States, but median income has declined. Granted that the burst of the dot-com bubble in 2000–2001 was not a period of "good times," but the productivity arc from 1999 to the beginning of the subprime mortgage recession was ascending. GDP does not measure well-being. It includes the cost of cleaning up the oil spill in the Gulf as well as the cost of oil retrieved from wells that have not blown up. For a measure of well-being, we have to look at indices made for the specific purpose of measuring it. One such is the Index of Social Health in the United States from 1970 to 2005, presented in a book called *America's Social Health: Putting Social Issues Back on the Public Agenda* by Marque-Luisa Miringoff and Sandra Opdycke (which I published in 2008). This index is based on sixteen components such as infant mortality, drug abuse, unemployment, old-age poverty, and income inequality. For a list of all sixteen components, see the book or my article on page 260. The index shows a decline in social health of 19.7 percent from 1970 to 2005 and five years of consecutive decline during the most recent period. A modest use of imagination tells us that the decline in social health has been precipitous since the beginning of the 2008 recession.

Another measure, the Index of Economic Well-Being, includes consumption of all goods and services, leisure, life expectancy, accumulation of productive resources, income inequality, and unemployment. Comparing members of the Organization for Economic Cooperation and Development (OECD), the United States had the next to lowest level of well-being, followed by Spain. For a complete list of index components, read "The Index of Well-Being" in *Challenge*, July–August 2010, by Lars Osberg and Andrew Sharpe.

We, allegedly the richest country in the world, do not have an impressive record in rankings. Among selected wealthy countries, we rank last in infant mortality, next to last in child poverty, nineteenth in graduation rates from upper secondary schools, and last in homicide rates. For details, refer to the articles mentioned above. These are all measures of failure. Yet, according to everyone running for office, we are the greatest country in the world.

The phenomenon of inequality in the rich countries is worldwide, just worse in the United States. Remarkable for a presumed democracy, the richest 1 percent of Americans own wealth six times greater than the wealth of the bottom 80 percent. We have not only a culture of poverty, but also a culture of wealth. The poor perpetuate their poverty by being born into circumstances that they cannot control: poor health and poor habits of mothers; poor preschool and school education; lack of jobs; the prevalence of drugs; broken families; prison for black young men.

The culture of wealth means being born into circumstances that can be controlled. It means good health of the mother and child; good preschool and school education; good college education; and good job opportunities. For the very wealthy, the culture of wealth includes the best neighborhoods, the best prep schools, the best colleges, the best country clubs, the best resorts, the best opportunities for jobs at the largest corporations, and remarkable salaries and stock options. It means the chance to be a member of upper corporate and policymaking circles, small enough to form a network that binds everybody together and in which a convenient belief in well-earned privilege is common.

It means the possibility of becoming a top officer of a large corporation, which together with other large corporations finances think tanks that re-search alternative policies, as well as organizations that discuss and recom-mend prudent actions, contribute to political action organizations, maintain a corps of lobbyists in Washington and state capitals, and send funds to the Republican and Democratic parties.

Anecdotal evidence in the press and on the Internet suggests that a few men and some women have the power to make crucial decisions about almost everything that matters to them. We read about small groups who decided how to rescue the banks, how to stimulate the economy, how to write the health reform bill, how to write the financial regulatory bill, how to deal with Iraq and Afghanistan, and, in business, which deals to make and which not to make.

Every tract about the organization of American society routinely discusses the power of intimate groups that make critical decisions. In *Who's Running America?* the sociologist Richard Dye estimates that some 6,000 Americans belong to these small groups. The businessman David Rothkopf, a habitué of the World Economic Forum at Davos, Switzerland, compiled a similar list of some 6,000 world elite, the superclass, among whom, in any given field, twenty to fifty leaders who know or have access to each other, decide through e-mail, phone calls, and meetings on private jets, how, when, and why to shift capital, resources, and jobs from one place to another anywhere in the world. The details can be found in *Superclass: The Global Power Elite and the World They Are Making.*

The number 6,000 is an order of magnitude. Maybe 3,000 or 12,000 make the big decisions. That doesn't matter. The point is that political and economic power is highly concentrated. The composition of the top groups changes by the day. That doesn't matter either. Some old members drop out, some new members enter. Most of the newcomers are recruited from the upper 20 percent of the nation's families. They accommodate themselves in habits, manners, and beliefs. Nearly all are committed to preserving the system. Most are conservative. Very few are revolutionaries.

In *Who Rules America?* (the first edition long predates *Who's Running America?*), G. William Domhoff draws a picture of elite organization as three overlapping circles: the social upper class; the corporate community, mean-ing CEOs and directors of the largest corporations; and the policy-planning network, trustees and hired experts. The power elite is at the center and some members belong in all three circles. Most of the very wealthy do not participate. They are content to manage their wealth, or have it managed for them. I would add government as a fourth overlapping circle. Members of Domhoff's three circles enter government in high positions. Given the overlap, government is not an organization that must be influenced from the outside—except by the public. These are the circles of a plutocracy.

The capitalist world order is highly integrated. The subprime mortgage crisis that began in the United States spread around the world at electric speed. The world's wealthy are not innocent victims. They regularly dealt in highly leveraged derivatives of their own making as well as those that originated in the United States. The predictable result is a world recession with the accompanying mass misery. The fear of deficits means that the recession will be long and grueling and that unemployment will persist longer than necessary. The adoption of the euro by less developed countries such as Greece, Spain, Portugal, and Ireland, which incurred massive debts during the boom, means that these countries are stuck with euro zone economic policies that impose a drastic cutback of public services and prolonged unemployment. The alternative, receiving debt forgiveness from the creditor nations, which would allow them to be much more productive much sooner, and, through trade, benefit others as well as themselves, is ruled out.

Prior to the recession, most European social democracies used unemployment as a means of fighting inflation when an incomes policy would have done much better, allowing the jobless the dignity of working, with the extra benefit that all Europe would enjoy their contribution to a higher standard of living.

I cannot say anything more complimentary about the multinational economic institutions: the World Bank, the International Monetary Fund, and the World Trade Organization. Their leadership has shared a common philosophy called the Washington Consensus, which means the imposition of laissez faire throughout the world. The poor countries have paid a terrible price. When any of them has had difficulty paying an installment on a loan, the policy of the World Bank and the International Monetary Fund has been a demand for fiscal austerity, which means cutting back expenditure on health, on education, on housing, on business development, on everything, in order to squeeze out the money to pay back the Bank and the Fund. The result has been mass suffering in the poor nations, bankruptcies, and development going backward. Under this barrage of demands, all assets depreciate, at which time multinational corporations swoop in and acquire businesses and natural resources at depression-level prices. Instead of aiding development, the Bank and Fund have obstructed it. They do it behind closed doors. The poor countries have nothing to say about their policies. To make matters worse, the IMF and the World Bank have assisted dictatorships like those of Humberto Castelo Branco in Brazil and Augusto Pinochet in Chile, after declining to aid the democratic governments that preceded them. But in their own inimitable way they have helped development: the development of the world's largest banks and corporations.

The World Trade Organization, successor to the General Agreement on Tariffs and Trade, GATT, was formed to promote trade by removing obstacles like quotas and import duties and help maintain the balance of payments within reasonable limits. By treating all countries as equal beneficiaries of free trade, the WTO has tipped the scales in favor of the rich countries. Who could say that their intentions were not honorable? But it could be that poor countries need arrangements that facilitate development and that free trade is not one of them. It could be that they need to protect their infant industries as the United States did in the nineteenth century during its period of development into an industrial power.

China and other East Asian countries have dodged all the problems imposed by international organizations by not following their precepts.

NAFTA, the North American Free Trade Agreement, has similar problems. Free trade agreements between similarly developed countries like Canada and the United States help both sides because they trade as equals. The U.S. and Canada don't even need free trade agreements. When the agreement includes a less developed country like Mexico, which cannot trade as an equal, the advantage is all on the side of the biggest businesses, which are mostly in the United States. We too can buy up assets cheaply and drive small Mexican firms and farmers out of business. What are poverty-ridden Mexicans to do but cross the border into the United States as illegal aliens? If we were to give development aid to Mexico and help them raise their standard of living, the illegal aliens could stay home and Mexico would become a richer trading partner. I have not seen this eminently reasonable idea mentioned anywhere.

Then there is the matter of shipping jobs overseas to be performed by low-wage workers, a practice indulged in by all rich countries, at the expense of jobs at home. We should not impede the pursuit of comparative advantage, but only after everybody in the home country who wants a job has one and the workers in the low-wage countries work under decent conditions. Another idiosyncratic idea in these times.

Finally, although there is no finally, we come to the matter of trade between the United States and China. They keep their currency artificially low. We buy their low-priced goods at the expense of producing them here. This is a manipulated market, not a free market. If we manipulated back by imposing tariffs on Chinese goods, and encouraging them to raise the standard of living of the Chinese masses so they could buy the goods they produce, we could then trade what is mutually beneficial to trade and we would be able to start reducing our account deficit and their account surplus.

I suppose the point of the entire business of international economic relations is "mutually beneficial."

Contrary to what most Americans want to believe, we are a society of classes. In *Who Rules America?* Domhoff uses three indicators to determine whether a class has power. Who benefits? Who governs? Who wins? On all these measures, a very small minority of Americans determines the outcome of most economic and political issues to their own benefit, as I have suggested in discussing the culture of wealth. On his Web site (http://sociology.ucsc. edu/whorulesamerica/power/wealth.html), Domhoff presents the most recent statistics on wealth and income. No one can convincingly argue that we would get such skewed results in an egalitarian society or, to put it differently, a democratic society in which the interests of the majority prevail.

These are statistics from a new age of robber barons. In 2007, the richest 1 percent of households owned 34.6 percent of private wealth, the next 19 percent owned 50.5 percent, while the bottom 80 percent owned 15 percent. Which American politician has expressed concern about these figures?

Even more striking, the top 1 percent owns 49.7 percent of investment assets, the next 9 percent owns 38.1 percent, while the bottom 90 percent owns 12.2 percent. (These figures were calculated by Edward Wolff.)

The concentration of wealth has moved upward since the late 1970s, a period that coincides with the defeat of labor unions, which acted as a counterbalance to the upper class. For some forty years beginning in the mid-1930s, labor had some say in policymaking. Then American capitalism reverted to form. Almost all the say now comes from the business establishment and benefits the business establishment.

Incomes have followed the same trend. Since the early 1980s, tax cuts on upper incomes as well as strategies to avoid taxes altogether, such as multigenerational trusts, have increased the gap between the ultra-rich and everyone else. Between 1979 and 2004, incomes grew 27 percent, of which 33 percent went to the wealthiest 1 percent, while the incomes of the bottom 60 percent went down 5 percent.

An unpleasant truth is exposed in the fact that the top one-tenth of 1 percent commands more pre-tax income than 120 million people at the bottom. We are approaching the degree of class differences found under feudalism.

In our free-market economy, the *wages* of the top one-hundredth of 1 percent doubled between 2000 and 2007, rising to 6 percent. In 2003 the upper 1 percent commanded 57.5 percent of all the *capital gains* income compared with 40 percent in the early 1990s, while the bottom 80 percent received 12.6 percent, down by almost half since 1983. Income inequality is the highest since 1912. I am not making a comparison with the eighteenth-century British enclosure movement, although the thought is tempting.

When we come to making a comparison of white, black, and Latino income and wealth, the picture is bleak. Median household income for whites in 2006 was $50,000; for blacks, $30,000; for Latinos, $35,000. Median household net worth, including home value, was $143,600 for whites in 2007, $9,300 for blacks, and $9,100 for Latinos. Median household financial wealth, excluding homes, was $43,600 for whites in 2007; $500 for blacks; and $400 for Latinos.

We have a way to go. Young inner-city black men are sent to prison on drug charges instead of going to rehabilitation centers, and their civil liberties are curtailed as they remain under legal surveillance when they get out, which puts them in the vise of a caste instead of a class. More African Americans are in prison, jail, on probation, or on parole than the number of slaves in 1850, as stated in *The New Jim Crow: Mass Incarceration in the Age of Colorblindness* by Michelle Alexander. African Americans are arrested on drug charges at eleven times the rate of whites. Blacks are 12 percent of the general population but 44 percent of the prison population, the total of which happens to be the highest in the world. This is the way we do things here.

The free-market explanation of this growing polarization of wealth and income offers the claim that the winners are selling increasingly highly prized talents while the losers are selling talents that are decreasingly prized. Eighty to 90 to 99 to 99.9 percent of Americans are offering less of value than they did in the thirty years after the Second World War compared with the 20 or 10 or 1 or 0.1 percent of winners. Strange that productivity has been increasing all this time, presumably only at the top. At the same time, power has shifted increasingly to the top, the power to determine who benefits, who governs, and who wins. An essential part of power is to justify itself. Only the doubting question it and try to organize the doubters. The Tea Party might be on to something if they absorbed the facts instead of apparitions.

In the forties and fifties, the doubters joined unions. In the sixties they joined the civil rights movement. Since then they have joined the women's movement and the gay rights movement. At present we have no movement that represents the interests of the public as a whole. The size of unions was whittled away by the obsolescence of huge manufacturing plants, the outsourcing of work to low-wage countries, and the resurgence of corporate power. The heyday of unions is past. They now command 12 percent of the labor force and have a bad name.

A movement forms when a constituency is pushed beyond endurance and finds leaders who understand what the problems are, have a general idea of what the solutions are, and know how to form organizations. That constituency is the public. In a democracy, even if crippled, the powerless have an opening.

In 1985 I published *The Power of the Powerless* by a dissident little known outside of Czechoslovakia, Václav Havel, who became the first president after the overthrow of communism. He understood that most *Czechoslovaks* were against the regime, but acted as if they were for it until they got the courage to talk with neighbors about how bad life was. Once the talk spread through the whole country, the Party was doomed. The powerless became powerful when they understood that almost everybody was against the dictatorship and that they could act together to overthrow it. I am not making a comparison between a communist dictatorship and capitalist dictatorship. Our government is not a dictatorship and is subject to change much more readily than a communist regime. Our history is one attempt after another to put our founding theory into practice and not allow ourselves to be misled by rhetoric about the glories of the free market in which everybody gets his just desserts, and which is bound together forever with American democracy.

Creative destruction, a term coined by Joseph Schumpeter, characterizes the history of capitalism. The "discovery" of the Far East and the Americas created a world market with increasing demand for raw materials and products. The English government led the way in giving trade monopolies to joint ventures of wealthy merchants. The increase in demand was first met by specialization and the further division of labor, as Adam Smith observed, then by the use of steam power and machinery. A succession of inventions in production, transportation, and communications, and the rise of a class of owners and a class of industrial workers who moved from farms to towns, destroyed all old handicraft and factory industries and led to an unending stream of inventions of new and more efficient means of production. We are all familiar with this story. The slow pace of improvements in all previous history was replaced by the frenzied pace of improvements that continues to this day. Computers and cell phones seem to be replaced by new, advanced models every week. My one-year-old cell phone stopped working and the clerks in the cell phone store marveled at how I had survived with such an old model. As a publisher, I have experienced the greatest revolution since Gutenberg reinvented movable type and the printing press, having had to put every print book and journal that I have published online at the risk of going out of business if I didn't.

This is the process of creative destruction, so eloquently described by Schumpeter, who, by the way, sums up the original compelling description of this process by Karl Marx and Frederick Engels in *The Communist Manifesto,* which they saw with the utmost clarity in 1848. The creative side has brought us to the advanced state of technology that we experience today, with great expectations for medicine, clean power, and a decent standard of living for everybody in the world just around the corner.

The destructive side has wracked capitalism with bankruptcies, unemployment, booms and busts, towns and regions that have been ruined by the obsolescence or the departure of industries that once gave them vibrancy, the wiping out of entire occupations such as the typesetter in my own business, and the decline of entire countries, say the United States, that did not keep up with the most advanced developments. Behind Schumpeter's dispassionate account is widespread misery. The town where I was born and spent my first twenty years, Chester, Pennsylvania, ten miles south of Philadelphia on the Delaware River, never a cultural mecca, nevertheless was a thriving industrial center in the 1940s and 1950s. Then all the industries moved out, the affluent moved out, the skilled and the professionals moved out, and Chester became the poorest city in Pennsylvania and all the plants that were built there became useless. Now the place looks like the bombed-out former site of something. The remaining residents of Chester did nothing to bring on their misery. This is a typical story repeated hundreds if not thousands of times throughout the country. It just happens that in Chester, the remaining population is 70 percent black. Thirty percent live in poverty. Creative destruction, though celebrated by Schumpeter as the way upward and onward, not enjoyed by any previous civilization, is a system of anarchy in which business is responsible for creation but not responsible for destruction. Business and society enjoy the benefits of creation, if it is truly beneficial creation and not just another useless or harmful item to sell, but only society bears the cost of destruction, first striking the most vulnerable. Emerson wrote, "Things are in the saddle and ride mankind."

A program of reforms that serves the common interest is invariably denounced as too impractical, too untimely, too radical, too deviant from our universally accepted values. The time never comes to discuss what ought to be done except in a crisis. Then the issue is how to get out of the crisis and back to where we started from before the crisis. But we started from a previous crisis. The unpopular effort has to be made to consider what we have to do to avoid going from crisis to crisis. To put the issue positively, the effort has to be made to consider what we have to do to achieve a society regarded as serving the purpose stated in the preamble to the Constitution, to "promote the general welfare." The Constitution does not say anything about promoting the welfare of a privileged minority. The phrase means the common good.

What needs to be done?

A person's dignity depends on having a job. The world will not crumble if the government provides useful work as a supplement to employment by private business.

Employees are often at a disadvantage unless they have the unimpeded right to join a union.

Certainly the common good implies the right to good medical care, good housing, a good neighborhood, and a good education. None of these rights will materialize of their own accord. They must be assured by policy.

A good society cannot be dominated by the ultra-wealthy or suffer a class living in poverty. The remedy is to place upper and lower limits on wealth and income. The upper limit can be enforced through the tax code. The lower limit can be enforced through a minimum wage. A decent range between upper and lower should allow everyone sufficient income to accumulate savings. The benefit is not just to the individual family, but to society as a whole by spreading the ability to invest to everyone. Another way to eliminate the concentration of ownership at the top.

The world will not come to an end if the largest businesses are nationalized. The largest businesses have private power that is used for private ends, short-term profit that has concentrated wealth and power throughout the entire history of capitalism at the expense of the victimized majority. The single-minded if not ruthless pursuit of short-term profit has run the economy from boom to bust in cycles of creative destruction or, more accurately, destructive creation. The mania of immediate gratification at the cost of all else comes at the expense of a long-term view of what's good for everyone. Now even shareholders are subordinate to the power of the top corporate officers who help themselves to multimillion-dollar salaries and stock options, which make them the largest cohort to join the wealthiest one-tenth of 1 percent in modern history. They should simply be required to exchange their ownership shares for government bonds so that they work for the public.

The half-dozen largest banks have in effect become an extension of the Federal Reserve system, providing liquidity often where it is not needed and for no purpose other than self-enrichment. Why not just do away with the pretense that these banks are private and fold them into the Fed? Then the whole operation will be legitimately too big to fail.

The military-industrial complex now includes all large firms because they all do business with the military establishment. No one should make money by manufacturing the means of killing. We owe it to the munitions manufacturers to lift their guilt by nationalizing their firms and then downsizing them to peacetime proportions. We must patiently explain to the military-minded that we are not in a perpetual war. We used to have periods of peace. We should make an effort to regain that state of mind and perpetuate it indefinitely.

The long-term view, referred to above, means that we will be much better off if we collectively have several far-reaching objectives. Weaning ourselves off oil, gas, and coal, for example, which in turn saves the planet from global warming. Developing more livable cities and more rational and efficient transportation. Conquering cancer and heart disease. Supporting the arts so they can flourish and reach everyone. We unashamedly will have a private sector and a public sector. Each will do what it does best.

We will pay higher taxes, but we will get value in return: a civilized society. But taxes are taking away private property, I'm told. This is a myth. Private property is not a category of nature. It is a social convention. Private property is what we say it is. If we say that private property is what's left after taxes, then that's what private property is. If we all benefit from less private property and more public property, then we harm ourselves if we do otherwise. If economists have delusions on this subject, they will have to be kept off campuses until certified by a board of psychiatrists that they have recovered their senses.

A current controversy rages over our ability to afford Social Security and health care for an aging population, much less anything else. Why do the Cassandras assume a stationary state? At one time a majority of the population engaged in farming to support a minority in the cities. Now less than 2 percent of the population provides enough food for everybody. The number of workers in manufacturing, here and abroad, required to supply our needs is also declining. Full employment adds to wealth. A reduction of military spending and withdrawal from hopeless wars alone would add more than enough wealth to support the aging population. Progressive taxes; preventive medicine; healthier lifestyles; ending the waste of wealth in economic crises; even raising the retirement age for longer-living, healthier adults would give us more than we need for the elderly. Everybody else can use the surplus to shorten the workweek and take longer vacations.

We owe the rest of the world the use of our influence on the World Bank, IMF, and WTO to return to the original Keynesian idea of using them to keep the international balance of accounts within reasonable bounds, promote reasonable exchange rates, and help finance the development of poor countries with loans and grants on favorable terms, the opposite of what they have been doing for the last fifty years. The Washington Consensus of free trade must die and be replaced with a consensus on mutually beneficial trade if we are to have any hope of international cooperation between the developed countries and those that hope to develop.

By coincidence I have been reading *To Kill a Mockingbird* by Harper Lee on the fiftieth anniversary of its publication. Scout, or Jean Louise, the narrator, enters third grade. In Current Events the teacher writes the word DEMOCRACY on the blackboard (in caps). "Does anybody have a definition?" Scout raises her hand, and remembers an old campaign slogan: "Equal rights for all, special privileges for none." "Very good," says the teacher.

The teacher and students don't go into this, as some of the grownups did, it being the 1930s. The fact is that blacks had no political rights in the South, as Harper Lee makes exquisitely clear. Political democracy was difficult to impossible with special privileges for whites and none for blacks. We have not been accustomed to thinking about the privileges and power of great wealth and the management of great business empires until the rescue of the largest banks instead of the unemployed and the foreclosed caught our attention. Political democracy appears to be difficult to impossible, with unequal rights for all and special privileges for some, as Scout's wise teacher understood.

The mishandling of the banking crisis and the unemployment crisis shoves into our faces what we may not want to see: Political democracy is dependent on an economy that operates in the public interest. Capitalism is not a system of economic democracy. The market is not self-regulating. Capitalism is always in crisis.

A saying is current that the system is broken. It has always been broken. The sorcerer has conjured up forces that he cannot control (not the sorcerer's apprentice).

If the public takes control of this wildly out-of-control system, we will have entered a period of postcapitalism.

Will elected officials serve the public interest or their own? That depends on what we collectively agree is the public purpose. It depends on a new ethics of acceptable behavior. We all drive on the right side of the road in the United States and on the left side in Great Britain. No one has to enforce this rule because it has been accepted as the way to behave. Variations in the way officials behave in various countries, from very responsible to very irresponsible, allow us to believe that a culture of democracy is possible, if we follow the best examples. Civil society, the public, has to belong to the culture of democracy and make demands.

Some critics as well as supporters will call postcapitalism socialism. Socialism has undergone so many changes in meaning that a reader can get stuck on one meaning instead of another. I considered myself a dialectical socialist when I read Marx. I considered myself a Fabian socialist when I read Shaw. I considered myself a market socialist when I read Heilbroner. I considered myself a new socialist when I read Galbraith. I considered myself a spiritual socialist when I read Oscar Wilde, who wrote, "The trouble with socialism is that it takes up too many evenings." We shall have to give up at least some evenings. Democratic socialism, if you insist. But we don't have to have an "-ism." We can call our desired arrangement economic democracy. After all, that's what the free market was supposed to produce.

A good society, or a good enough society, must provide everyone the possibility of living a satisfying life. What are the chances of realizing it?

Kurt Vonnegut thought that the chances were zero. In *A Man Without a Country,* he recorded how, during the Depression and World War II, he dreamed of an America that had become humane and reasonable. "But I know now that there is not a chance in hell of America becoming humane and reasonable."

The time is not yet. It's too soon to tell.

September 2010

The Failure of Capitalism

A review of *Aftershock: The Next Economy and America's Future*, by Robert B. Reich. New York: Alfred A. Knopf, 2010.

I confess at the outset that *Aftershock* is both a satisfying and exasperating book. Robert Reich's introduction is called "The Pendulum." He identifies three periods of modern American capitalism in which the pendulum swung back and forth. The first is 1870 to 1929, when the concentration of income and wealth increased to fabled proportions. The second is 1947 to 1975, when a "basic bargain" was struck between capital and labor, which allowed prosperity—to a degree—to be shared. The third is 1980 to 2010, when the pendulum swung back to a concentration of income and wealth as great as the first. Now Reich expects us to begin a fourth stage in which the pendulum again swings toward shared prosperity.

I don't see any underlying law that can be based on three swings of a pendulum. What happens if the pendulum gets stuck? Toward the conclusion of *Aftershock,* Reich argues that the fourth swing "would require cooperation of all levels of society" (p. 141). "America's largest corporations and Wall Street banks will become concerned about the lackluster economy. . . . The CEOs will notice the public's increasing anger" (pp. 143–144).

Here is my exasperation. At no time in American history did the CEOs join a movement to reform capitalism in any fundamental way. During the New Deal and its aftermath, the CEOs were largely outside of the New Deal movement. The concessions to labor were extracted from them because labor unions had acquired the power to bargain forcefully and the public supported them. During the stagflation crisis of the 1970s, the "basic bargain," as Reich calls it, was snatched away.

Are we to expect the pendulum to swing back again at some fifth stage toward greater inequality? This is not an appealing prospect. In my previous *Challenge* article on the current and longstanding crisis of capitalism (p. 309 in this volume), I did not see any evidence that a permanent deal could be struck between the public and the CEOs, as Reich seems to acknowledge with his pendulum swings. Only the public has a permanent interest in abolishing unequal rights and special privileges. I wrote: "If the public takes control of this wildly out-of-control system, we will have entered a period of post-capitalism." This *is* an appealing prospect and one worth the effort. It is the only prospect about which I do *not* feel exasperated.

Let us put aside this troubling disagreement between Reich and me for a moment and turn to the first chapter of his book, a book that I think is excellent, for the most part.

Reich starts by pointing out that wages have not been sufficient to buy back what labor has been able to produce. Repeated crises emerge from this disparity, including the crisis we are in now. Professor Reich discovered or rediscovered the fact that Marriner Eccles made this very point during the Great Depression. Eccles was chairman of the Federal Reserve Board from 1934 to 1948. He had been a wealthy businessman before coming to the Federal Reserve and had the conventional views of wealthy businessmen. The economy would right itself on its own. Eccles despaired when it did not happen.

I quote Reich's quote from Eccles: "[M]en with great economic power had an undue influence in making the rules of the economic game, in shaping the actions of the government that enforced those rules, and in conditioning the attitude taken by people as a whole toward those rules" (p. 14).

Further from Eccles: "As mass production has been accompanied by mass consumption, mass consumption, in turn, implies a distribution of wealth . . . to provide men with the buying power equal to the amount of goods and services offered by the nation's economic machinery. Instead of achieving that kind of distribution, a giant suction pump had by 1929–1930 drawn into a few hands an increasing portion of currently produced wealth. . . . But by taking purchasing power out of the hands of mass consumers, the savers denied themselves the kind of effective demand for their products that would justify a reinvestment of their capital accumulations in new plants. In consequence, as in a poker game where the chips were concentrated in fewer and fewer hands, the other fellows could stay in the game only by borrowing. When the credit ran out, the game stopped" (pp. 17–18).

Eccles preached this doctrine to FDR along with the case for deficit spending to make up for the missing demand. He recorded his thoughts and actions in *Beckoning Frontiers,* published in 1951. Reich has found a narrator who was able to fathom the secret life of capitalism almost eighty years ago. Marriner Eccles, *requiescat in pace.*

By the late 1970s, the lessons of the Great Depression suppressed or forgotten, the disparity in income between the upper 1 percent and the bottom 99 percent began to rise. By 2007, the upper 1 percent took 24 percent of the income, approximately the same amount it took in 1928. The statistics are courtesy of the much-cited Thomas Pickety and Emmanuel Saez. (The division of financial wealth is also instructive: As of 2007, the upper 1 percent owned 49.7 percent of investment assets while the bottom 90 percent owned 12.2 percent.)

In a chapter called "How Americans Kept Buying Anyway: The Three Coping Mechanisms," Reich lists—

"Coping mechanism #1: Women move into paid work."

"Coping mechanism #2: Everyone works longer hours."

"Coping mechanism #3: We draw down savings and borrow to the hilt." (pp. 61–62, the author's italics.)

By 2007, the coping mechanisms were exhausted. We face a future without coping mechanisms. The "recovery" cannot be sustained. "[C]oncentrated income and wealth will threaten the integrity and cohesion of our society, and will undermine democracy" (p. 65).

"What's broken is the basic bargain linking pay to production. The solution is to remake the bargain" (p. 75).

The public is outraged at a "rigged game." Robert Reich proposes to unrig it. He proposes to remake the economy and the polity with an equalization program.

I quote his captions: A reverse income tax. A carbon tax. Higher marginal tax rates on the wealthy. A reemployment system rather than an unemployment system. School vouchers based on family income. College loans linked to subsequent earnings. Medicare for all. Public goods. Money out of politics (pp. 129–140).

Here is Reich's program with my comments:

Overall. We would be in a different and better world if we put his program into practice.

A reverse income tax. Good until we arrive at the time when the minimum wage provides a decent life.

A carbon tax. Good until we eliminate the spewing of carbon into the atmosphere altogether.

Higher marginal tax rates on the wealthy. Good and in line with my proposal in the previous issue of *Challenge* that a decent society requires minimum and maximum limits on incomes and wealth for the well-being of all, as well as the elimination of concentrated economic and political power of the wealthy.

A reemployment system rather than an unemployment system. Most unemployed people haven't gotten their old jobs back and often have to work for lower pay as the recession stretches out. Sophisticated economists talk about "structural changes" in the economy as the cause, but we need look no further than the lack of demand. Paul Krugman points out that the unemployed were quickly reemployed when demand radically increased during World War II (*New York Times,* September 27, 2010). That aside, Reich proposes wage insurance for up to two years, together with training for a new job. What's lacking here is the idea of government as employer of last resort. A plan to offer a job to everyone who wants a job cannot be made on the assumption that the private market will operate perfectly at all times and employ all workers all the time. There is much to be done in the public sector. Men and women employed in the public sector can make as useful a contribution as they can in the private sector.

School vouchers based on family income. An interim solution for the disparity of funds in rich and poor neighborhoods, but the object should be the financing of all schools at the level of the best schools.

College loans linked to subsequent earnings. An interim solution until we include college as part of the public educational system and support it with public expenditures.

Medicare for all. Another name for universal health care, the only civilized means of providing health care for everyone at the lowest cost.

Public goods. Agreed that we must have sufficient financing of all common goods such as public transportation, parks, museums, libraries, etc.

Money out of politics. Will be opposed by people with money in politics. All the more reason not to allow public offices to be bought and sold for huge amounts of money. Publicly financed elections with several months for campaigning is the diametrical opposite of campaigns that are conducted every day of every year with limitless amounts of money.

Robert Reich's list of reforms is a very good list, but it leaves out several crucial issues.

He assumes that raising incomes to a level sufficient to purchase everything that is produced will eliminate booms and busts. I believe this is his opinion, unless I missed something. But even with mass incomes sufficient to purchase everything that is produced, financial instability will nevertheless continue to plague us. As long as banks have the freedom to overinvest and invent new forms of derivatives at insane multiples of bank capital, and as long as a rising stock market attracts trusting investors to invest well beyond what is sustainable by the real economy, we will have booms and busts. Financial markets need to be sanely regulated and too-big-to-fail banks need to be broken up or absorbed by the Federal Reserve as part of the public banking system.

However, small businesses *should* be declared *too small to fail* after they have established, in ten years or so, that they are sound businesses. I have met a number of small business owners who have had to close their doors. They have put their money and their lives into their endeavors and are failing because of the poor economy, not because of any fault of their own. It is troubling to meet them and then see the "for rent" signs go up after they have moved out. The effect on their employees and the surrounding towns is equally troubling.

Even if total demand is sufficient to buy total supply, the excess or deficiency of supply in one sector or another is still a problem. My late and good friend Wassily Leontief addressed this problem, as well as the problem of matching total demand with total supply, with input-output analysis. This is little discussed now, but it needs to be brought back into the discussion. Input-output analysis has been neglected because a religious belief in the infallible free market seemed to make such analysis superfluous. Input-output analysis also suggests that some indicative planning of the market is necessary, a subversive thought not to be entertained by anyone of sound mind.

We also face the problem of intermittent commodity shortages, which can be addressed by stockpiling commodities in sufficient quantities to smooth out the supply cycle. In cases of recalcitrant suppliers, such as those in oil, the solution is to get off oil.

In my previous article, I discussed the need to control international trade and financial flows so that they operate to the mutual advantage of the countries involved. Of course this is easy to say and difficult to do, but we at least need to say it before we can do it.

I also discussed the concept of "negative externalities," which refers to the malign effects of a large business on a town or region. If the management of a large business decides to move out, the entire town or region pays the price and the large business pays nothing. The town and all its human and material assets are left to waste away. The principled acceptance of "creative destruction" as the price of progress is the Mephistophelian way to look at this. In a civilized society, any such business must be made responsible to meet the appropriate officials and nonofficials and work out a plan to preserve the jobs and the private and public assets of the town or region by finding something to replace the business that is leaving, and work out a timetable for a transition to take place.

Robert Reich's proposals cannot save the economy unless we do some planning. Not just contingent planning, but planning to realize what we want to achieve in education, health, the sciences, the arts, the environment, and in cities and regions. The idea is not subversive and will not lead to a police state. In the past we have had long-range objectives served by building canals, railroads, the interstate highway system, the space program, by supporting education and scientific research, and the largest one, developing the U.S. part of the New World, although that was not done with a fine respect for the American Indians or our neighbors to the south, who used also to be to our west.

We cannot be a good society until we are ready to renounce the military mentality that dominates American politics, which maintains that we must have the biggest mass murder machine in the world, while the facts show that, since the Korean War, the military machine has produced exactly the opposite of what we had hoped to accomplish while wasting trillions of dollars and hundred of thousands of lives. The American military machine specializes in producing the largest negative externalities in the world.

We also have to deal with the absurdity of calling a corporation a person, which Reich agrees is an absurdity. A corporation must have the right to limit the liability of stockholders so they do not lose the shirts off their backs if the corporation is sued or fails. It must have the right to make contracts. But to consider the corporation literally as a person instead of considering its personhood as a loose metaphor means that the officers of a large corporation, with many times the power and financial resources of an actual person, can make political contributions and influence our political life far in excess of a real person. But our Supreme Court thinks otherwise and sees an actual person, a very large one.

In a roundabout way, we return to the beginning of this article, which concerns "How It Could Get Done," to cite the title of Reich's final chapter. As I quoted, getting it done "would require cooperation at all levels of society." Why should we expect cooperation now when never in American history has the rich minority cooperated with the nonrich majority unless coerced? Reich refers to the New Deal. But for every Marriner Eccles, there were ninety-nine Andrew Mellons, secretary of the Treasury under Harding, Coolidge, and Hoover, who said, "liquidate labor, liquidate stocks, liquidate farmers, liquidate real estate . . . it will purge the rottenness out of the system."

Every banker I know is apoplectic over the modest financial reforms of the Obama administration, even though their banks are better off than they were before the recession began, while the rest of us are worse off. The prospect of their getting behind far-reaching reforms requires us to imagine a coalition of the willing and the unwilling.

Reich speculates about the backlash that will continue to grow until a newly formed Independence Party is elected in 2020, with Margaret Jones as president. The said Margaret Jones, as head of the Independence Party, proceeds to make the recession worse with a wildly destructive program against foreigners, politicians, and the rich, which pushes the economy into another great depression. My only question for Reich is: What makes you think that we need another party to make matters worse?

To get the lion to lie down with the lamb, Professor Reich will need divine intervention.

I argued in my previous *Challenge* article that fundamental reform in the interest of the public can only be made by leaders of organizations that represent the public. I also am counting on divine intervention.

Alexander Hamilton wrote: "The people, sir, are a great beast."

That's true.

An apocryphal exchange between F. Scott Fitzgerald and Ernest Hemingway runs:

Fitzgerald: "The rich are different from you and me."

Hemingway: "Yes, the rich have more money."

That's true.

The rich have definite explanations for their richness and everybody else's nonrichness. William S. Cohen, former secretary of Defense and current head of the Cohen Group, said in *Forbes/Life*, September 2010, concerning transportation to and from Washington, D.C.: "My favorite is a private plane in and out of Signature-Dulles. Then you escape the overly intrusive probes of TSA employees who treat errant paper clips as lethal box cutters and make you feel that your next step is Guantanamo."

That's true.

Immanuel Kant said that the crooked timber of humanity cannot be made straight. We can at least try to make it straighter.

Meanwhile, SNAFU. Situation normal all . . . You can look it up.

November 2010

Big Money

A review of *Winner-Take-All Politics: How Washington Made the Rich Richer—and Turned Its Back on the Middle Class,* by Jacob S. Hacker and Paul Pierson. New York: Simon & Schuster, 2010.

A few years ago, *Forbes* published a full-page poster in the Soviet style showing a man in a business suit waving a white, green, and black flag against a bright red background. Tall, white letters, standing out from the background, shout: "Capitalists of the world, UNITE!" I could not resist the temptation. I tore out the page, put it in a frame, and placed it on my desk.

Forbes's urging has not been in vain. The capitalists of the world have united. In particular, the capitalists of the United States have united. The recent history of the capitalist movement is the subject of *Winner-Take-All Politics*. The title is an exaggeration. The winners have not taken all. They have taken almost all.

Hacker and Pierson let the statistics speak first. Then they discuss the collusion that gave birth to the statistics. They appear to be right about everything. I will try to follow their lead through this review.

Here is what the statistics tell us. The winners in the United States have increased their share of winnings from the late 1970s to the present. Not modestly: exorbitantly, unashamedly, and *accelerando*. From 1979 to 2007 the top 1 percent of American households acquired 36 percent of the gain in income. From 2001 to 2006 they acquired 53 percent of the gain. During the same years, the top 0.1 percent—one in one thousand—acquired over 20 percent of the gain, compared with 13 percent for the bottom 60 percent.

The share of income of the top 1 percent was about 8 percent in 1974. In 2007 it was over 18 percent. With capital gains, the share rose to 23.5 percent. That was an average annual income of $1 million in 1974 compared with $7.1 million in 2007. The average annual income of the top 0.01 percent—one in ten thousand households—was less than $4 million in 1974. It rose to more than $35 million in 2007. (All numbers inflation-adjusted.)

To put it differently, the top 0.01 percent "earned" less than $1 of $100 earned in 1947, while in 2007 they "earned" $1 out of every $17, or more than 6 percent of the national income. At no time since 1913 has it been higher, and that is the year the statistics were first collected.

Well known to those who have the misfortune to follow these numbers, most of the gains went to the top executives of the largest corporations. Within this segment, the largest increases went to the bank barons.

Looking at the whole spectrum, the bottom of the labor force rose slightly, the middle rose slightly more, while the top shot away into space. From 1979 to 2006, the bottom fifth gained 11 percent, the second, third, and fourth fifths gained an average of about 24 percent, the upper fifth minus the top 1 percent gained 55 percent, while the top 1 percent gained 256 percent. Exclamation mark.

Words fail me. But I will say this. If you're planning to run for office, these are not the kinds of facts that you want to stress.

The pull-away of the winners was nonpartisan. The winners started winning bigger under Carter, and continued winning bigger under Reagan, George Herbert Walker Bush, Clinton, George W. Bush, and Obama. Never again can we say that the Republicans and Democrats always go in opposite directions.

Well, how did this happen? The winners became more organized while the losers became less organized. The winners—Big Money—got more clout in politics while the losers—labor unions—lost their clout. The labor unions dwindled to 7 percent of the private workforce. You can do a lot less with 7 percent than you can with 33 percent, which was about the fraction of the unionized workforce in the 1950s.

While organized labor was weakening, organized business was strengthening, pouring more and more money into think tanks, policy discussion groups, political action committees, lobbying firms, and directly to candidates, both Republican and Democratic, mostly Republican.

With more money, you can have more influence over the agenda. The agenda is what issues are discussed, what "facts" are adduced, what stories people are led to believe, which politicians they are led to believe will help them out. The only counterargument is suffering. Suffering led to the election of Obama. Continued suffering led to the rise of the Tea Party.

With respect to the "agenda," Mark Twain said: "A lie can travel half way around the world while the truth is putting on its shoes."

With more money, a new GOP emerged, pushed aside the old, and became the no-compromise party of lower taxes, deregulation, smaller government, demonized unions, supply-side economics, and a don't-blame-me credo that Big Money is just the innocent beneficiary of modern technology and globalization. Reagan gave it the big push. Gingrich pushed further. Except for G.H.W. Bush, who reneged on his "read my lips, no new taxes" promise, it's been onward and upward until today we have the party of No.

It used to be said that the communists believed "the worse the better."

Now the Republicans believe it. Defeat Obama if things are really bad. We will make sure that they are.

A few wise Democratic leaders understood the need to tack to the "center" and formed the Democratic Leadership Council in 1985. Bill Clinton became chief among them. The "center" should be read as meaning less support for the public, more support for business.

The political life of Senator Chuck Schumer illustrates the Democratic Party shift. Liberal on social issues, friendly to Wall Street because that's where the money is. And so Schumer became the biggest Democratic raiser of funds given from Wall Street pockets, able to hand out big contributions to fellow Democratic candidates. And he voted to repeal the Glass-Steagall Act so that commercial and investment banks could again merge and operate just as they did in the 1920s.

The California senators Dianne Feinstein and Barbara Boxer followed the same path. Liberal, but on good terms with Silicon Valley money, and opposed to any limitations on stock options for CEOs.

The Senate became the perfect arena for leaving Big Money alone. It's hard to change anything when you must get 60 votes to change anything, or stop a one-person filibuster, or overcome strict Republican adherence to the party line, or do anything when 70 percent of bills are filibustered.

With Democratic majorities in the House and Senate before the 2010 elections, the Republicans got help from Democrats in the center who became "Republicans for a Day," enough to hold up or defeat any attempt to restrain business. "No policy is a policy." A senator or congressperson doesn't have to be overtly against a bill. It can be sent back to committee for further study. Postponement, "drift," as Hacker and Pierson call it, is as good as a no. Even though more than 50 percent of workers favored unionization in recent polls, the Employer Free Choice Act, which would allow them to join a union merely by signing a card, was sent back to committee to be suffocated.

Politics is "organized combat," in the phrase of the authors. Organized combat used to be characterized as class conflict, the state as the executive committee of the ruling class. No need for inflammatory language any more. The conflict is between the winners and the losers. The state is the executive committee of the winners. No harsh words need to be spoken.

On with unemployment, foreclosures, and ghettoes. On with recession. On with historically high compensation for Wall Street. On with tanks, planes, and guns while balancing the budget. The esteemed former senator Alan Simpson, now co-chairman of a special commission on debt reduction, appointed by Barack Obama, said, "I can't wait for the bloodbath in April" when the time comes to raise the debt limit. "And boy, the bloodbath will be extraordinary" because his colleagues will demand a cut in spending for the losers. And what will the losers do?

Sir Walter Raleigh wrote:

> *Tell men of high condition,*
> *That manage the estate.*
> *Their purpose is ambition,*
> *Their practice only hate.*
> *And if they once reply,*
> *Then give them all the lie.*

January 2011

Violent Nation

Let me immediately acknowledge the moral superiority of the United States over all other countries in the world. I want to discuss only two small blemishes: the gun culture and the military culture.

We are acutely aware of the gun culture at the moment. The mass shooting in Tucson, Arizona, and the fight of Representative Gabrielle Giffords to survive a bullet that went in one side of her head and came out the other has left us in shock. We are aware of her daily effort to return to a normal life.

Everybody knows that the Tucson rampage followed others at Columbine, Virginia Tech, Fort Hood, and a several-page-long list. Everybody knows how we were shaken each time. Then the rampages recede with nothing done to prevent them from happening again. Every massacre is followed by the same refrain: Let's do something. Over 30,000 men, women, and children are shot dead every year and 66,000 wounded. Eighty lives a day are terminated by gunfire. Not that we are indifferent. Forty-six percent of us favor stricter gun control laws. Sixty-three percent want to ban assault weapons and high-capacity clips. Odd. We the people don't have the clout to get the government to do much of anything.

Every commentator has pointed out that we have more guns per capita than any other advanced country in the world. We also have more gun murders and suicides. At least we rank first in something. We have the best gun culture in the world, quantitatively speaking.

The reasons take us back to the beginnings of the European encroachment into a wilderness of the New World. Almost every move depended on guns. Getting the English, Spanish, and French to back off required guns. Driving the Indians westward to make way for farmers, ranchers, fur traders, and miners required guns. Hunting required guns. Protection of property from marauders required guns. Marauders required guns. The suppression of slaves required guns. Territorial disputes between pro-slavery and anti-slavery factions were fought with guns. The Wild West had no government other than the rough-and-ready justice enforced by lone families and ramshackle communities.

Then sheriffs and militias moved in, with guns. Law and order was established, with guns. Territories were established, with guns. New states entered the Union, enforcing the law with guns. Then Mexico was pushed south of the border, with guns.

The Big Thinkers of the time foresaw our manifest destiny as ruling a great continent from the Atlantic to the Pacific and acting as a beacon of liberty to the rest of the world. But not without guns.

The military culture is a twin of the gun culture, born out of the same wild continent. The army followed the settlers and moved west to establish lawful order. Fight Indians, suppress blacks, fight the Mexicans. Then fight the Civil War. Suppress Reconstruction. Then the navy comes in to help us move overseas to fight Spain and liberate Cuba, Puerto Rico, Guam, and the Philippines. Take over Hawaii. Oust dictators in Latin America. Uphold the legitimate interests of the United Fruit Company. Establish the nation of Panama, which graciously allowed us to build a canal. The army returns to break up strikes back home. Help the Ku Klux Klan enforce segregation and battle the civil rights movement.

We are a civilized country with guns. The National Rifle Association, first named the American Rifle Association, was founded in 1871 to perpetuate and defend this great tradition. Its prestige was so high that Ulysses S. Grant became its eighth president. Today guns are used for recreation and hunting. Guns are popular in movies, TV, and video games. But guns as recreation and culture is not the main purpose of the NRA. The main purpose of the NRA is to protect the Second Amendment right of citizens. Only citizens with guns can keep the government off their backs. That means free-for-all gun ownership. "Guns don't kill people, people do," they say. Strange as it may sound to the gun addicted, a murderer doesn't kill someone with a gun without a finger on a trigger.

The NRA is the strongest lobby in Washington because it gets most of the money in the gun fight. Politicians who oppose the gun lobby are an endangered species. Business leaders are not notably present in the movement to strengthen gun laws. Sometimes the fight over gun control is depicted as country against city. So don't blame us pro-gun people. Oh, bother the fact that equal numbers are killed by guns in urban areas as in rural areas.

After every massacre, critics list reasonable restraints. Background checks. Licenses. Limited sales per person. No open sales at gun fairs. No guns for criminals. No guns for the mentally unstable. No multi-firing magazines. No guns for drug users who need medical treatment. No guns for fanatics and terrorists. No guns at schools, churches, meetings. No violent political rhetoric. Nothing esoteric here. Why don't we do what's reasonable? The Brady campaign and other gun-control campaigns are far outmatched in decibels by the NRA. In this cacophony, gun control advocates can merely whisper and whimper.

Why then have Europe and Asia given up gun violence? They have just gone through too many wars. They have gotten tired of killing one another. They can't take it anymore.

Our military culture changed radically with the beginning of the Cold War. After each previous war, the army was demobilized. The generals did what they were expected to do: come when called and then stand down. Woodrow Wilson was elected on the slogan "He kept us out of war." Then we entered the war. When it was over we demobilized as usual until the war to end all wars did not end all wars. After one mad generation of rearmament in Europe and Asia, we and the Soviet Union became allies to defeat the fascists.

A pervasive fear then took hold. The battered Soviet Union would take over the world while the nuclear-armed United States would be the victim. The generals and admirals were not asked to stand down.

A titanic struggle between good and evil was about to take place. Democrats and Republicans together accepted the responsibility of fighting evil, everywhere.

Andrew J. Bacevich describes the nature and consequences of this crusade in his sixth book, *Washington Rules: America's Path to Permanent War.* Our political, military, and business leaders adopted a credo to lead, save, liberate, and transform the world. The credo puts the burden of world peace and order on us through the presence of our military power everywhere and our willingness to intervene against present or anticipated threats anywhere. These are the new Washington rules.

If you think about every president from Truman to Obama, you will not find a single one who has not embraced the credo. Truman renounced the wartime alliance with the Soviet Union and fought a proxy war in Korea. Eisenhower enunciated the Eisenhower Doctrine bolstering unstable but friendly governments in the Middle East and increased the number of regional alliances against the Soviet Union. Kennedy sanctioned the Bay of Pigs fiasco, came within a hair-trigger of atomic war during the Cuban missile crisis, and sent troops to Vietnam. Johnson presided over the escalating fiasco in Vietnam. Nixon spread the fiasco around Indochina. Ford embraced the credo even as we were finally forced out of Vietnam. Carter advanced the Carter Doctrine of increased presence in the Middle East. Reagan presided over a military buildup. Bush I launched the first Iraq war but left the Iraqi army intact. Clinton sent tens of thousands of bombing sorties over Iraq. Bush II enunciated the Bush Doctrine of preemptive war and shock-and-awed Iraq. Obama escalated the war in Afghanistan. The Washington rules smoothly morphed from Cold War to global war on terror, after a short but not sobering lull following our defeat in Indochina.

I don't mean to imply that nothing good was done by any president. Eisenhower warned against the military-industrial complex after he helped build it up. Reagan agreed with Gorbachev to reduce the number of nuclear weapons. Ford signed the SALT I Treaty reducing nuclear arsenals. Obama signed SALT II, reducing nuclear arsenals further.

Nor do I mean to imply that one strategy has persisted for the last sixty-six years. Colin Powell presided over the last (small) army-against-army conflict in the first Iraq war. Donald Rumsfeld disdained big armies and tried to fight a war of superior intelligence and smaller forces in the second Iraq war. David Petraeus adopted the counterinsurgency doctrine of winning hearts and minds in Iraq and Afghanistan. He counseled speed, because the public gets tired of long wars. All presidents, generals, and admirals agreed that they must keep as much military information as secret as possible. Let the public know nothing or next to nothing. The CIA keeps secrets. Now COIN, counterinsurgency, is the choice means and GCOIN, global counterinsurgency, is even better. Secrecy is the method of keeping bad news from the public and giving the generals, admirals, Pentagon, and president a free hand.

The strategy has changed but the credo remains the same.

The desired consequence of the credo, world peace and liberation through American military power, did not turn out as the American political, military, and business establishment expected. We cannot commit mass murder and expect the survivors to thank us. We have, among other super-cyber operations, a super-sophisticated intelligence and surveillance installation at Langley Air Force Base in Virginia, which monitors targets for the Predator drones that we fly over Afghanistan and Pakistan. But the human beings who do the monitoring cannot absorb all the information that comes flooding in. Their disease is called information overload. Mistakes are made. Mistakes are made in killing innocent men, women, and children in villages, in cars, at weddings and funerals, in killing allied soldiers on our side.

The Washington rules are rules of the insane. But the insane are unaware of their insanity. Madeleine Albright didn't change Washington policy, but she had a knack for expressing herself well. After the first Iraq war, she said, "If we have to use force, it is because we are America. We are the indispensable nation. We stand tall. We see further . . . into the future."

During the Balkans crisis, Colin Powell urged caution. Albright challenged: "What is the point of having this superb military that you're always talking about if we can't use it?"

In 1996, a television journalist asked Albright to comment on a report that sanctions imposed on Saddam Hussein had resulted in the deaths of half a million children. "It's a hard choice," she said, "but I think, we think, it's worth it."

These quotes are from Bacevich, who comments that Albright implies that "at least those children had died in a worthy cause. This was not cynicism or hypocrisy on Albright's part. It was conviction encased in an implacable sense of righteousness."

We now have the vampire twins, the gun culture and the military culture, feeding on blood.

The madness of crowds refers to leaderless groups that act irrationally and destructively. Prison rioters, street mobs that smash windows, violent spectators at soccer games, even crushes at department store sales, and currently investors who follow upward trends to create a boom followed by a bust, are all mad crowds. What about the madness of organized actions taken by leaders and followers? The rank and file act irrationally and destructively because they follow the irrationality and destructiveness of leaders. They are gripped by the madness of elites. The mad elites of America are sure of our righteousness and power and superiority and duty to rectify the world and carry out our world mission.

The madness of elites is not literal insanity, although that is not ruled out. It is madness from delusions, beliefs not based on facts, ignorance of reality, the inability to escape from a frame of reference that is held fast even when the opposite of what is intended is achieved. The truth is that we have a high murder rate because we have too many guns without enough safeguards. A further truth is that we have turned the Muslim world against us because we kill masses of Muslims. Those who are trapped in the gun culture and the military culture deal in polluted information. We don't have enough guns in the hands of good people. Al Qaeda threatens to kill everyone who cooperates with us. As most Americans would put it, believers stuck in the gun culture and the military culture can't think outside the box.

The following statement is sad but true. You cannot be president, a leading member of Congress, or a leader of the military-industrial-service complex in the United States without being a sociopath. Kurt Vonnegut used the word psychopath, but he meant sociopath. A psychopath is mentally ill, but a sociopath is socially ill, will kill tens of thousands because killing tens of thousands is for a good cause, will support dictators because they serve a grander design, will commit America to endless war because endless war is the way to achieve the good cause, as the light of the good cause grows dimmer and dimmer and moves further and further into the future.

You don't like the word sociopath? It's too harsh? We're talking about gentlemen and ladies, educated and cultivated people, men and women who are kind to their children, their mothers and fathers, their nieces and nephews, and they were elected by the people. But really, if both Democrats and Republicans are committed to open-ended war and guns for all, and the public desire to control the guns and end the wars is not represented, what are elections other than rituals and ceremonies? You have to be a sociopath to kill several hundred thousand people and get nothing in return. You have to be a sociopath to condone it and make billions from it.

Yes, some killing is necessary. Franklin Roosevelt used means that realized the ends, to defeat Hitler, Mussolini, and Hirohito. Horrible, unnecessary things were done, like the firebombing of Dresden, as Vonnegut described it. But those who use horrible means that cannot achieve valuable ends and don't give a damn about rethinking their premises, they are sociopaths.

My teacher Kenneth Boulding defined a paradox he called saliency. We know the victims in Tucson. They are not anonymous. We know the young Iranian woman named Neda, who was walking away from the street demonstrations in Tehran, of which she was not even a part, when she was shot through the heart. Her last words were, "It burns." All who listen to the news remember. But the hundreds, thousands, and tens of thousands killed and maimed in shootings and wars are anonymous. Their deaths and injuries are background noise unless we make a heroic effort to think otherwise. Even then we cannot imagine anonymous faces. Yet we know that no victims are background noise. The destructive cultures of guns and wars make them so.

What will it take to break out of these destructive cultures? Leaders of countermovements. Leaders who do not have a false consciousness but are conscious of falseness. Sane guides like Henry David Thoreau, Mark Twain, Eugene V. Debs, Bertrand Russell, Mohandas Gandhi, Dorothy Day, Nelson Mandela, J. William Fulbright, Martin Luther King, Mohamed ElBaradei, Howard Dean, Cindy Sheehan, and thousands more.

The English poet Stevie Smith wrote about the anonymous: *Nobody heard him, the dead man, But still he lay moaning: I was much further out than you thought and not waving but drowning.*

Will we be able to tell the difference some day?

March 2011

Postscript: The Egyptian Revolution, February 11, 2011

As of February 14, this much we know. The Mubarak dictatorship stood on three pillars: the secret police, the military, and the rich. All anti-regime organizations were outlawed. Defiance could lead to imprisonment, torture, or death.

The dictatorship siphoned off the wealth for itself and the privileged. The rest of Egypt lived in deprivation. Around 40 percent lived below or near the poverty line. College graduates endured ten times the unemployment average, which I learned on the Internet was "high."

Here are the bare facts about the revolution. The murder of twenty-eight-year-old Khaled Said by two policemen in June 2010 turned into rage. Asmaa Mahfouz showed his beaten body on Facebook. Young bloggers extended a protest network throughout the Middle East. The Tunisian revolution of January 14 gave Egyptians a glimpse of the future. The Google expert Wael Ghonim created a Facebook page with the searing slogan: "We Are All Khaled

Said." A young organizer, Ahmed Maher, called for a nonviolent demonstration in Tahrir Square, Cairo, on January 25. Hundreds of thousands of young people, professionals, union members, farmers, the middle class, especially women, the poor, and the unemployed turned out. Demonstrations spread to other cities. The army withheld fire. The demonstrations continued for eighteen days. On February 11, Mubarak fled. The military high command annulled the constitution, disbanded parliament, and called on Egyptians to prepare for free elections.

During the eighteen days of demonstrations, the Obama administration was of three minds. The U.S. ambassador to Egypt announced our support of Mubarak. The vice president, the secretary of state, and the secretary of defense counseled the Egyptians to slow down. Obama admonished his agents to change their tune, but was exceedingly restrained in supporting the demonstrators—until they won. Exceeding caution in supporting democracy followed thirty years of supporting a dictatorship with an annual stipend of $1.3 billion in military aid with no human rights conditions attached, as we were assured by Defense Secretary Robert Gates. As usual, the expenditure of some $39 billion in guns, tanks, and planes gained us precisely nothing, and gained the Egyptian public nothing but a dictatorship and misery.

Why were the crowds peaceful? They came for civilized demonstrations and, except for one day of attacks by Mubarak's hoodlums storming the square on horses and camels, they remained civilized.

The opposite of the madness of crowds is the sanity of crowds. In Tucson, onlookers acted spontaneously and humanely to subdue the gunman and help the wounded. In Cairo, the crowds showed up after hearing by word of mouth and the Internet that they should show up, but once having gotten to Tahrir Square, they organized themselves spontaneously and humanely. What makes a crowd sane is a constellation of known facts, intentions, trust, civility, and a common cause. A sane crowd can act spontaneously or follow customs and rules. Most of us act in the interest of others while driving a car, attending a meeting, or patiently standing in line at the airport. Or we can act in the interest of others without rules or customs simply out of a desire to help.

What will follow the Egyptian revolution? At the moment, we only know that February 11 was a day that belongs to us all.

March 2011

See page 355 for an account of the Arab Spring.

The Poorest Rich Country in the World: Address to the Graduating Class of 2011

Distinguished president, provost, and faculty; parents and graduating class of 2011:

You have taken the risk of inviting me as your commencement speaker knowing that my views on everything are negative. But no harm will come to your alma mater, Beneficent College, because tomorrow the college will close its doors permanently.

The endowment is broke, the state is broke, and Washington is broke. Gather all your grades, letters of recommendation, and yearbooks by the end of the day because nobody will be here tomorrow to give them to you. Get your own subscriptions to *Challenge*. The library will be closed.

The college cannot be harmed. You will be harmed. You will be harmed for inviting a radical speaker, and this fact will be in your records for the rest of your lives and thereafter. Your diminishing chances of employment will be diminished further by your rash decision.

Here are my negative thoughts for the class of 2011.

I looked at your course requirements. I am sure most of you have read *The Iron Heel, Brave New World, 1984, Fahrenheit 451,* or *Player Piano,* and recognize a dystopia when you see one. These books depict a world in which everything becomes worse in the future, and here we are in the future.

In these books, monopoly trusts rule the country. Nobody knows the truth anymore except the ruling class. We are perpetually at war. All knowledge of history and society is obliterated except among a few protestors. Work is done by machines and the unemployed are left to scramble for themselves.

Well, Jack London, Aldous Huxley, George Orwell, Ray Bradbury, and Kurt Vonnegut were waving red flags to warn us about a possible future. Here we are in the future. We used to be the richest rich country in the world. Now we are the poorest rich country in the world. We have become Dystopia USA.

Three of the authors were democratic socialists. Their opinions don't count.

You have been taught that we have all kinds of information. But have you been taught that most people don't know the meaning of the information? We have all kinds of information about the universe, but we don't know the meaning of the information except for those who make guesses. And they don't know the meaning either. We have all kinds of information about the USA, but we don't know the meaning of the information, except that teachers are the cause of our problems. A good guess. Or immigrants. Another good guess.

The ones who control the political marketing of ideas control the guessing. That's why the teachers are to blame. Never mind that they pay more taxes than GE, the largest corporation in the world until proven otherwise, which pays none. True, immigrants don't carry a great tax burden, for which they are to blame.

Students, you know that political marketing takes money and organization. You know that unions used to be the type of organization that did most of the political marketing for the public. Back in those days, we were less of a dystopia than we are now. The unions have been beaten. Their political marketing is sad.

Did you know that free speech, press, and assembly are harmless formalities exercised freely, and tolerated because they have no effect on policy? Contrary to the predictions made in all the literary dystopias, the leaders of our system don't need to establish a dictatorship. They already have one. Freedom of speech, press, and assembly create the illusion that we have no such thing as a dictatorship. I'm guessing that people prefer to hold on to their illusions.

So here's my advice, graduating class of 2011. Have fun, go to the beach, go dancing, listen to music, read books, make love, and when you know more, help to make the USA less a dystopia and more a country where everybody has enough to eat and drink, a nice place to live, a good education, a well-paying job, and equality for men, women, blacks, Latinos, gays, and American Indians. Where the army, navy, and air force are shrunk to a manageable size, and where teachers are not blamed for everything that is wrong. Or immigrants.

Just a reminder. Don't forget to collect your possessions after the diplomas are distributed.

May 2011

Ice-T and the Pathology of Poverty

A review of *Ice: A Memoir of Gangster Life and Redemption—from South Central to Hollywood,* by Ice-T and Douglas Country. New York: One World Ballantine Books, 2011. $25, 257 pages.

Ice is a furious account of black gang life in Los Angeles by a man who lived it and then escaped from it on the wings of gangsta rap. Ice-T is ice in his self-control but fire in his rage at ghetto misery.

Tracy Marrow, later Ice-T, spent his childhood in Summit, New Jersey. He decided that Tracy was a girl's name and went by Trey (although *Ice* is copyrighted by Tracy Marrow). His mother died when he was nine and his father died when he was thirteen. He was shipped off to live with an aunt in South Central L.A. His aunt didn't like him and he didn't like his aunt.

South Central was a trap, a ghetto trap. Poverty families, poverty schools, poverty drugs, poverty jobs (if any), poverty lawlessness, no way out. Except crime. Which was no way out. *Ice* is the story of the rare man who found a way out.

Trey had no idea how babies were made until his girlfriend got pregnant. He joined the army for the money to support her and his new daughter. Just before his four-year stint ended, his in-your-face sergeant said in his face: "Marrow, you fucking loser! You're only here because you *can't make it* in civilian life." He was wrong. Trey learned to be tough and he learned to steal. His commanding officer taught him. But the sergeant's remark was devastating.

He had gone to Crenshaw High in the 1970s—he was born in 1958. Crenshaw was dominated by a gang called the Crips and he learned to walk and talk like the Crips. The Crips in one neighborhood and the Bloods in another were home turf defense gangs. When he got back to South L.A. after his time in the military, the gangs had added robbery and violent gangbanging to their repertoire. Spraying enemies with AKs and Uzis was then commonplace and the sight of three or four dead bodies on a street corner was not unusual.

Trey went in for hustling (robbery), but not with guns. He didn't drink, do drugs, or smoke. "It wasn't a moral decision . . . my survival instincts kicked in real early." He and a "homey" sauntered into a jewelry store, pretended to be interested in a gift for a girlfriend, made acquaintance with the clerk, noting which case had the goods to snatch. After a few visits, the time for action came, but not before carefully plotting the exit route. Then he went back with a lookout. If the lookout signaled OK, Trey grabbed a small sledgehammer hooked to the back of his belt, smashed the case, grabbed the jewelry, and the two were far from the scene in five minutes. "In and out in five minutes." (That was before surveillance cameras came into play.) A haul could be worth $50,000 on the street, collected by gang retailers who shared the proceeds with the hustlers.

A similar method applied to department stores. All the back hallways and stairs were cased. Then grab and run. A side benefit of stealing Gucci and Louis Vuitton bags, Rolex watches, and a rack of mink furs was learning how to dress well. Trey also preferred Porsches.

At the same time, Ice-T (as he renamed himself) began rapping at clubs for free. When he won a contest, he realized there might be money in it. He started charging for gigs, while his popularity rose, particularly with young white audiences, which amazed him. He chose the name Ice-T out of respect for Iceberg Slim, whose books he read, admired, and quoted. Iceberg Slim had been a pimp in Chicago and his books warned young African-American readers what a hellish life pimping was, and admonished them to steer clear of it. (For example, *Pimp: The Story of My Life*.) Ice-T had observed pimping while in the army, and he did stay clear of it. Some of his best friends were pimps, nevertheless.

While leading a double life of rapping and hustling, there came a robbery when an off-duty security guard saw him running as an alarm went off. The guard started shooting and Ice-T started dodging as plate glass shattered and flew all over. He jumped through the window of the getaway car with his life intact but with the realization that he could get killed.

Meanwhile, Ice-T was getting noticed as a pioneer of gangsta rap, the lyrics of gang life and life in the 'hood. The language was gangsta language. Audiences started rapping in sync. A gig at The Radio, where Madonna performed, made him think, "Man, the coolest kids think I can play." He was living two lives each day. One night he closed his eyes at a stoplight, fell asleep, drove across the intersection, and was broadsided. But for his excellent physical shape, he would have died. During weeks in the hospital, he flashed back to his sergeant screaming he couldn't make it in the civilian world. "And here I was, nearly dead, and if I'd died in that Porsche, I'd have lived my whole life without accomplishing anything." After a few weeks out of the hospital, he said to himself, *"Let me stop running with these hustlers—risking prison every single day. Let me give this rap game a shot."*

Then came recordings, TV, movies, diverse companies of his own. In 1992 Warner Brothers released "Cop Killers."

> *I got my 12 gauge sawed off*
> *I got my headlights turned off*
> *I'm about to bust some shots off*
> *I'm about to dust some cops off . . .*

The whole country (it seemed) fell on Ice-T's head. Vice President Dan Quayle denounced him. Then Charlton Heston (leader of the NRA), Tipper Gore, and President George H.W. Bush himself denounced him. But Ice-T wasn't *advocating* killing cops. He was *reporting*. "It's a protest record. It's a song about a guy who lost his mind over brutal cops." It wasn't even new. Rappers had done this kind of reporting before. But only the cognoscenti knew. The uninformed had no context. You don't blame the actress playing Lady Macbeth for goading her onstage husband to kill Duncan. You know she's playing a part. Ice-T was playing a part: rapping a protest song. But putting out the news that he was reporting didn't help.

 Then came an invitation to New York from the producer Dick Wolf to do an episode on *Law & Order*—to play a cop. Wolf followed up with an invitation to be a regular on *Law & Order: Special Victims Unit*—to play a cop. That required a big move to New York. It also required a shift in his mindset. He didn't do "the method." He did his own method. "Whenever I show up on the set, it's like a little kid making believe I'm the police. . . . Ice-T pretending to be police."

When Ice-T reflects on a life of crime and redemption, legit business doesn't come off better than gang business. "One thing I've learned from straddling two worlds: Hollywood is *way* more gangster than the streets. Hollywood is way colder. Way more vicious. When I first started doing TV and movies, I never saw people get fired the way they do in show business. I never saw the coldness of the producers. They just don't care about anybody."

Further. "The higher up the mountain, the colder it gets. I've been around some of the most ruthless gangsters on the streets of South Central L.A., but I've never seen anything like Hollywood gangsterism. In the studios, they're dealing with billions of dollars. On the streets, you're dealing with hundreds of thousands of dollars. When cats are dealing with billions of dollars, anybody—I mean *anybody*—is expendable."

I've titled this review "Ice-T and the Pathology of Poverty." I should have added, "and the Pathology of Power." The powerful, *the really big gangs,* are dealing with *trillions* of dollars, have sent jobs overseas, have mindlessly engineered a recession, have engaged in hopeless wars, and perpetuate not just post-traumatic stress disorder but also concurrent traumatic stress disorder.

For a majority, the trauma is not *post.* The trauma comes from the *lack* of power. Trillions for offense, but not one cent for the ghetto and just a few cents for the middle class. The public can't do anything about it as long as it accepts fact-free economics and fact-free politics as gospel. Ice-T can't do it all by himself.

July 2011

China and the Future of the World

My first personal contact with the Chinese revolution came in 1948 when I was a student at Swarthmore College. I met George Chen, a young man of subtle brilliance who was in the U.S. to get a degree and was president of the Chinese Christian Students Association, which happened at that time to be a convenient cover for Chinese communist students. He was an avid supporter of the People's Liberation Army and kept a large map of China on the wall of his dorm room, charting the advance of the PLA with red pins and the retreat of the Kuomintang army with white pins. The procedure continued when he graduated in 1949 and moved to New York. That year his pins disappeared, replaced by the People's Republic of China. He then crossed the Pacific in a state of excitement with his bride Xiuxia. They had a girl and a boy, and George reverted to his Chinese name, Chen Hui.

During the Cultural Revolution from 1966 to 1976, in spite of his opinion that this was the most wonderful time to be alive in all of Chinese history, Chen Hui was sent to one village and his wife to another. They were intellectuals trained in the West and had to get all their bad thoughts washed out of their brains. I recall that the penitence lasted four years. Subsequently Chen Xiuxia became an executive of the China Society for People's Friendship Studies and Chen Hui became interpreter for Mao Zedong, Zhou Enlai, and Deng Xiaoping, managing editor of the *China Daily*, and for a time Chinese delegate to the World Bank.

I tell this story because it is typical of the ups and downs of Chinese leaders from 1949 to the present. Some were not as lucky as Hui and Xiuxia.

A very personal contact with the Chinese revolution came through my brother Lou Sharpe, who did business with the Chinese in the 1980s after Deng Xiaoping launched a market economy and urged Chinese businessmen to get rich. My brother sponsored an exhibit of machinery in Beijing to promote U.S.–China trade. The U.S. exhibitors prudently paid for "guards" when the exhibition hall was closed for the night. During the dark hours, Chinese technicians entered the hall and took apart every nut, bolt, and wire of the equipment in the hall, made drawings, then reassembled everything. How do we know? They made mistakes putting the machinery back together, a fact discovered in the morning.

In this way, the Chinese gained considerable technical knowledge from their U.S. counterparts.

Another incident is also typical. My brother negotiated for the rights to publish an in-flight magazine for the Chinese airline, CAAC. An agreement with Chinese officials was signed, but they were dissatisfied. They came back and demanded a better price. My brother pointed out that he would lose money if he agreed to sign a downwardly revised contract. The Chinese then withheld his passport, so he couldn't leave. Only the intervention of Chen Hui after two weeks of detention persuaded the negotiators, if that is what you call them, to give back his passport. Who knows, if it had not been for the intervention of Chen Hui, my brother might still be a prisoner in China.

Chinese officials are perhaps more sophisticated today, but I read that they are still fast and loose with intellectual property rights, copying every cubic inch of Hondas and Toyotas, replicating Yamaha engines, reproducing and mass marketing CDs and DVDs, copying and circulating tens of thousands of copies of Harry Potter books, even writing and selling their own Harry Potter books, or rewriting the endings of existing ones to the taste of newly discovered mass markets.

But let's get serious. The Chinese state and public are wrestling with monstrous problems: a population of 1.3 billion growing by more than 5 million every year; an annual influx of 10 million peasants into cities; the consequent fastest growth of cities in history; the fastest growth of industry in history; the reckless use of natural resources requiring imports from all over the world; the consequent pollution of air and water; the ruin of nature with megalomaniac dam projects; the poisoning of river water by tens of thousands of business establishments; the uncontrolled production of toxic products like milk powder that causes babies to wither away; and a culture of dishonesty that requires bribes at every level from top down to bottom up. The culture of dishonesty extends to the sale of fake papers at $100 or less for residential permits, work permits, university degrees, identity cards, PhDs in rocket science, and plates on official cars. (See *China Shakes the World* by James Kynge.) Then there is the added effect on the rest of the world of wrecking the international trade and monetary systems by keeping the renminbi artificially low in order to export cheaply and move jobs from elsewhere to China's sweatshops. On the other hand, about 250 million Chinese are now middle class and 115 are billionaires as of 2011, second only to the number in the United States.

So China is a laboratory for the rest of the poor and developing parts of the world. Is it even possible for the multitudes to achieve a decent life? At present, world population is about 6.5 billion. It will probably exceed 10 billion by 2055 and will probably stop growing before 2200 because of improved health and the dissemination of birth control information. (Unless something happens not foreseen by demographers.) When the number of people entering the world equals the number of people leaving it, we will have reached what is called the demographic transition. The question we need to ask is: What kind of life can the planet and the social system or systems support with a world population of 10 billion? The answer depends on the relation of inputs and outputs of matter, energy, and information, to use Kenneth Boulding's farseeing formulation of the problem in "The Economics of the Coming Spaceship Earth," published in 1966.

The biggest problem is the finite amount of matter or material resources available on Earth. Sometime in the future coal, oil, and other minerals will be used up. Coal and oil will be used up forever. The question about other resources, at present known or unknown, is how much can be recycled. It's hard to imagine that 100 percent of everything left can be recycled, and yet not impossible to imagine. At the same time we don't know how many people perfect recycling can support. Even the process of recycling requires the use of matter in the shape of equipment to do the recycling.

If we do it the Chinese way, we will not get there. The Chinese exploitation of nature is profligate. Much literally goes up in smoke. Cities sink into the ground because their support is eroded by mining and by the diversion of underground water. Production, no matter what the cost, which can be accomplished because the banks are awash with money, violates even the principles of neoclassical economics. Businesses that lose money start new product lines that lose money and then newer product lines that lose money on the assumption that the growing population and its demand for the good things of life will rescue them sometime in the future. With all the value added, the Chinese are engaged in value subtracted, not just of their own resources, but of resources around the globe. Imagine what would happen if every modernizing country tried to follow the Chinese example. We also practice value-subtracted economics, in economicese, negative externalities, such as the destruction of towns when large firms move away. So we ought not be the pot calling the kettle black. Part of the answer is, minimize inputs, do not maximize them. Minimize GDP and GWP—Gross World Production—do not maximize it. A startling thought for economists who are committed to the proposition that bigger is better.

The question of using energy is easier to deal with than the question of using matter. The energy resources buried in the earth will be used up. But we will not use up the energy from the sun, the tides, the wind, the atom, or the interior of the earth. In spite of all the crises with oil, coal, and wood, politicians are in no hurry to do anything intelligent. The Chinese are using up finite resources of energy at a crazy rate. They (and we) are a terrible example for the modernizing world as well as the modernized world. A conversion to near infinite energy resources needs to be made before large populations suffer for the conversions not having been made in time.

The answer to the question of information or knowledge is the most promising of all. The peculiar thing about knowledge is that it never gets used up. Some societies decay, and their social and cultural knowledge gets lost over several generations. But scientific knowledge accumulates and has accumulated faster since the industrial and agricultural revolutions. Here lies the solution to the use of matter, if there is a solution, and energy, which surely has a solution. To repeat, the Chinese are at a stage where most of their technical and scientific knowledge has been borrowed or stolen. They are in the same position now as the United States was in the nineteenth century, borrowing or stealing information from the British. If they continue to train scientists and engineers as they do currently, they will begin to add information instead of taking it.

Now we have come to the issue of information about organizing society. I and many others have valuable information about the way society should be organized, but society is not ready to use it. Is the Communist Party of China a good or bad form of social organization? Is the division between state-owned and privately owned enterprise good or bad? At different times the CPC has been good and bad. Under Mao, the Great Leap Forward from 1958 to 1961 was a disaster that ended in the starvation of an estimated 30 million peasants. It was nothing personal, just a matter of policy. Mao's attitude was, to hell with nature, man is in charge. The Cultural Revolution of 1966 to 1976 created an entire generation of uneducated ignoramuses. (As distinguished from our educated ignoramuses.) The current grease-my-palm corruption gets resources distributed in the most horribly inefficient way. Certainly the combination of a private market economy with a government-owned economy is a real great leap forward from exclusively relying on state-run enterprises and farm communes. But the Chinese have to have the social knowledge to run it and they don't.

The monopoly of power by one party, what to say about that, except that within the party vicious infighting has taken place between right and left factions from the founding of the party to the present moment. So it is really two parties with one name, distinct from the American model, which has two names but is really one party, as far as basic social philosophy is concerned. (except for the now-crashing Tea Party.) In both cases, the welfare of the public depends on their degree of enlightenment concerning their own interests and therefore their power to pursue those interests. In both China and the U.S., the situation is dire.

A word about Kenneth Boulding's phrase, spaceship earth. The earth is a spaceship in which the inputs and outputs must balance. Until recent centuries, the earth was viewed as a vast plain on which there was always someplace else to go if resources ran out. Then in the sixteenth century the earth began to be seen as a globe with great open spaces where people could move if life became oppressive. Now it is clear, at least to some, that the earth is not an open plain, but a spaceship where we cannot take out more than we put back. Most politicians in the world don't know this and neither does the benighted public.

As I said, China is a laboratory in which an experiment is taking place that will tell us much about the prospects for the future of the world. They already have had a great negative impact on the rest of the world's finances and resources. Some experts, writing the many books on China, predict that China will collapse. Others predict that China will dominate the world. Yet others predict that China will get along with the rest of the world. All this is just chatter. We have no way of knowing what twists and turns China will take in the future, much less what twists and turns the world will take.

Why do we Americans not insulate ourselves from the bad effects of the Chinese economy? Because our largest firms can buy merchandise from China for pennies and sell it here for dollars and make an enormous profit. In this way China makes a great contribution to the decline in workers' income and the transfer of wealth from the bottom to the top. The Chinese also hurt their own massive population by exporting their products instead of consuming them at home. The most difficult problem is when will we ever learn.

A Short Bibliography

Eamonn Fingleton, *In the Jaws of the Dragon*, 2008.
John Gittings, *The Changing Face of China*, 2006.
Martin Jacques, *When China Rules the World*, 2009.
Henry Kissinger, *On China*, 2011.
James Kynge, *China Shakes the World*, 2006.
Peter Navarro and Greg Autry, *Death by China*, 2011.

For Background

John King Fairbank, *China: A New History*, 1992.
Jonathan D. Spence, *The Search for Modern China*, 1999.

September 2011

The First Blossoms and Thorns of the Arab Spring

Nobody expected a new era to begin in North Africa and the Middle East in 2011. It's as if, when the sun rose one morning, everything looked different. Tunisians and Egyptians demonstrated in the tens of thousands and overthrew Ben Ali and Mubarak. Libyans launched a civil war and overthrew Gaddafi. Syrians massed in the streets against Bashar al-Assad and found themselves in a bloody stalemate. In neighboring countries sporadic protests sputtered on and off.

The issues were the same everywhere. The public was incensed by the blatant theft of national wealth by the dictators and the dictators' cronies. They were angered by the suppression of dissent. They were bitter about rising prices and falling standards of living and a high level of joblessness, among young people in particular. Some objected to the denial of rights for women. All these resentments and objections accumulated and built up over years and decades. Then in a flash, a split second in historical time, the murder of Neda Agha-Soltan in Iran and Hamza Ali Al-Khateeb in Syria, and the self-immolation of Mohamed Bouazizi in Tunisia and Khaled Saeed in Egypt turned years and decades of suppressed anger into uncontrollable rage. The martyrs would be taken aback by what they had wrought.

We don't know who will prevail after the first few weeks, months, and years. The armies are well organized and we don't know which side the generals will come down on. The Muslim Brotherhood promotes secular states in theory, but factions and offshoots promote Muslim states. The Shia and Sunnis are irreconcilable. Some political parties want to establish secular states and others want to establish Islamic states. The unions have a certain amount of power but we don't know how they will use it. The old guard and the wealthy are waiting in the wings. We don't know what the NATO powers will demand. We don't know what global corporations, the IMF, or the World Bank will demand. Turkey is a secular state and the strongest power in the region. Prime Minister Recep Tayyip Erdogan proposes a secular alliance with Egypt. Turkey with 79 million people and Egypt with 82 million are the two most populous states, and would exert massive power together. But Erdogan has expressed support for Muslim supremacy in the past. Prime Minister David Cameron of Great Britain and President Nicolas Sarkozy of France visited Libya and cheered on the rebels, but what comes next? The roles of Israel and the Palestinian Authority are exasperating. The United States supplies billions in arms and will want something in return. Have I forgotten anybody? Yes, the public. When the demonstrations are over and people go home, their power evaporates because they are not organized.

I have taken a look at the miserable path of earlier revolutions. They all had too many leaders and successors to figure out where they were headed no matter what the intentions were at the beginning. The complicated outcome of a revolution is measured in days, weeks, years, decades, and centuries. The colonial liberation movement in America split into the Federalists and the Democratic-Republicans. The Federalists, led by Alexander Hamilton, pushed for the development of business and banking. The Democratic-Republicans, led by Thomas Jefferson, pushed for the development of farming. Four score and five years later war broke out between the industrializing North and the agrarian slave-holding South. Two-hundred-and-thirty-five years later, the country founded on the conflicting ideals of Hamilton and Jefferson has declined into a state of hapless chaos. What comes next?

The French Revolution proceeded through the Estates General Assembly, the National Assembly, the National Constituent Assembly, the Legislative Assembly, the National Convention, then the Committee of Public Safety under Robespierre and the Jacobins, who guillotined their enemies, followed by the Thermidore Reaction and the guillotining of Robespierre and his fellow madmen. Then came the Directory. Then came Napoleon, who dissolved the Directory and after a tactful wait crowned himself emperor. Skipping ahead to the present, we find that France has slipped into a semi-comatose welfare state in which it can no longer afford the welfare to which it was committed.

The Russian and Chinese revolutions promised a future guided by the principle, from each according to his abilities, to each according to his needs . . .

And yet, in a convoluted way, considering all the advances and reverses, a few notable revolutions have given us more room to breathe. Non-absolutism looks better than absolutism, even when it requires some squinting. But the most important accomplishments of revolutions are the ideals. All men are created equal. Liberté, Egalité, Fraternité. The dictatorship of the proletariat. The people want to bring down the regime. The ideals survive to be dusted off and used again in the next revolution.

In one way or another, the Arab Spring will move the entire world.

November 2011

Index

Italic page references indicate charts and graphs.

A Man Without a Country (Vonnegut), 325
Absolutism, 356
Adam Smith in His Time and Ours (Muller), 167–171
Advising
  backward art of, 94–96
  Carter, 90–93
  Ford, 63–65
  graduates of 2011, 344–345
  interference versus guidance and, 74
  president and Congress, 90–93
Advisory Committee on National Growth Policy Processes, 51, 90–93
Affirmative action, 177, 179–180
Affluent Society, The (Galbraith), 237
Afghanistan wars, 228, 248, 295–296, 307–308, 339–340
AFL-CIO, 78–79, 157, 177–178
African Americans, 178–180, 267, 274, 319, 324
Aftershock (Reich), 326–332
Against the Storm (Myrdal), 21–23
Age of Extremes, The (Hobsbawm), 181–187
Aggregate supply and demand, 19, 74, 311
Agha-Soltan, Neda, 355
Agricultural Adjustment Act (1933), 144, 310
AIG, 291–292
Al Qaeda, 228–229, 246–247, 341
Al-Assad, Bashar, 355
Al-Khateeb, Hamza Ali, 355
Alaska purchase, 244
Albright, Madeleine, 340
Alexander, Michelle, 319
America Against the World (Kohut and Stokes), 246
America Needs a Raise (Sweeney), 177–178
American Dilemma, An (Myrdal), 21
American Federation of Labor, 310
American Liberty League, 311
American Recovery and Reinvestment Act (2009), 283, 294, 298, 312

"America's Ghetto Poor" (William Julius Wilson), 256
America's Social Health (Miringoff and Opdyke), 260–264, *261*, *262*, *263*, 314
Andelman, Bob, 173–174
Anderson, Marian, 267
Anderson, Orvil, 222
Anniversaries, taking stock in three, 118–119, 121
Anthropometric test to measure leader qualifications, 232
Antitrust Division of Justice Department, 145
Arab oil embargo (early 1970s), 24–27, 61
Arab Spring, 355–356
Arabs, blaming for oil embargo, 24, 26–27
Arnold, Thurman, 145
Asian Drama (Myrdal), 21
Assets for poor people, 255
AT&T, 149
Atlas, myth of, 32
Authority figures, accepting and identifying with, 29
Avery, Oswald, 109

Bacevich, Andrew J., 295, 339–340
Bailout of banking industry, 284–285, 288–290
Baker, Dean, 291–293
Balanced Growth and Economic Planning Act (1975), 51–55, 62
Bancor, proposed, 278
Bank of America, 288
Banking industry, 143, 278–279, 284–285, 288–290, 297–301, 324
Barry, Dan, 288
Bastard capitalism, 124
Bastard socialism, 124–125, 184
Bay of Pigs, 339
Beame, Abraham "Abe," 67
Beckoning Frontiers (Eccles), 327

Beliefs, 14, 75
Ben Ali, 355
Berezovsky, Boris, 194
Bernanke, Ben, 291, 294, 301, 312
Big business, 149. *See also* Corporations
Big-End, Little-End problem, 10
Big Government, 11, 140–141, 270–271
Big Money, 333–336
Bilmes, Linda, 246
Bin Laden, Osama, 228
Birth control programs, 28–30
Blair, Margaret M., 147–150
Blair, Tony, 217
Blankfein, Lloyd, 301
Blow, Charles, 301
Boehner, John, 304
Book reviews
  Adam Smith in His Time and Ours (Muller), 167–171
  Aftershock (Reich), 326–332
  Age of Extremes, The (Hobsbawm), 181–187
  America Needs a Raise (Sweeney), 177–178
  America's Social Health (Miringoff and Opdyke), 260–264, *261, 262, 263*
  Communist Manifesto, The (Marx and Engels), 202–206
  Conscience of a Liberal, The (Krugman), 257–259
  Crisis of Vision in Modern Economics, The (Heilbroner and Milberg), 158–162
  Disposable American, The (Uchitelle), 234–236
  End of Reform, The (Brinkley), 142–146
  Ending Poverty in America (Edwards, Crain, and Kalleberg), 254–256
  Freefall (Stiglitz), 297–302
  Good Society and Its Enemies, The (Galbraith), 163–166
  Guns, Germs, and Steel (Diamond), 195–201
  Human Development Report 1998, 211–213
  Ice (Ice-T and Country), 346–349
  John Kenneth Galbraith (Parker), 222–226
  Loyalty Effect, The (Reichheld), 172–173
  Mean Business (Dunlap), 173–174
  New Paradigm for Financial Markets, The (Soros), 268–269
  Plunder and Blunder (Baker), 291–293
  Report and Recommendations by the Commission on the Future of Worker-Management Relations (Dunlop), 151–157
  Resurrection (Remnick), 188–194
  Rethinking Corporate Governance for the Twenty-First Century (Blair), 147–150
  Social Health of the Nation, The (Miringoff and Miringoff), 217–218
  Teachings from the Worldly Philosophy (Heilbroner), 175–176
  To Renew America (Gingrich), 138–141
  Tyranny of the Bottom Line, The (Estes), 172
  We're Right, They're Wrong (Carville), 174–175
  When Work Disappears (William Julius Wilson), 178–180
  Who Rules America? (Domhoff), 239–242
  Winner-Take-All Politics (Hacker and Pierson), 333–336
Bottom-line measurement, 172
Bouazizi, Mohamed, 355
Boulding, Kenneth, 9–10, 137, 165, 255, 342, 350–352
Boxer, Barbara, 335
Brecht, Bertolt, 184
Bretton Woods Conference, 278, 302
Brinkley, Alan, 142–146
Bronowski, J., 114
Brooks, David, 284
Bubbles, economic, 268–269, 291–293
Budget
  balanced, 165
  cutting, 44
  deficits, 286
  economic planning and federal, 38
  household, 262, *262*
  military, 139–140
  military-favored, 251–252
"Bundling," 249
Burns, Arthur, 66–67
Bush Doctrine, 339
Bush, George H.W., 334, 339, 348
Bush, George W., 227–229, 246, 249, 251–253, 257, 298, 339
Business planning, 59, 136–137

CAAC (Chinese airline), 351
Cameron, David, 355
Canada, 317
Capital regulations, 49

Capitalism
  bastard, 124
  coinage of term, 122
  Communist Manifesto and, 205
  corporations and, 126
  as creative destruction, 150, 235–236,
    320–321
  crisis of, 309–325
  democracy and, 122–126
  as destructive destruction, 236
  failure of, 326–332
  government intervention and, 141
  Heilbroner and, 221
  Keynes and, 275–276, 279–280
  Landslide Age and, 186
  musings on, 122–126
  periods of modern, 326
  private rewards and social returns in,
    299
  savings of rich and, 279
  Smith and, 167, 170
  social contract and, need for, 170–171
  socialism and, 187
  Tanner's view of, 76
  unadulterated, 124, 126
  welfare state, 124, 126
  winners in, 333–336
Carey, Hugh, 69
Carter Doctrine, 339
Carter, Jimmy, 80–83, 85, 90–93, 128, 215,
  339
Carville, James, 174–175
Case for Big Government, The (Madrick),
  270–271
CEA, 37–38, 51–52, 56–57, 91, 224
Center for Statistical Policy and Analysis,
  91–92
Chalabi, Ahmed, 227
Challenge (magazine)
  advisory board, 3
  contributors, 137
  editor position, 119–120
  evaluation of, after thirty years,
    135–137
  house moving editorial (1975), 84–85
  incarnation of, 3
  influence of, 3
  interesting writing about economics
    and, 6
  points of view in, 3–4
  readership of, 3
  revival of (1973), 304
  thirtieth anniversary of, 135–137
  tradition of, 3
Character Index, proposed, 139

Chechnya, 193
Chekhov, Anton, 135
Chen Hui (formerly George Chen),
  350–351
Cheney Energy Task Force, 248
Chernomyrdin, Viktor, 188
Chesterton, G.K., 42
Children's Development Accounts, 255
China, 184–185, 278, 302, 317, 350–354
China Shakes the World (Kynge), 351
Chinese Christian Students Association,
  350
Chomsky, Noam, 113
Chubais, Anatoly, 188–189, 194
Churchill, Winston, 32, 184
CIA, 340
Citigroup, 286, 288
Civilian Conservation Corps, 309
Clarke, Richard, 228
Class, social, 122, 124–125, 255, 318
Cleaver, Emanuel, 304
Clemenceau, Georges, 275
Clinton, Bill, 140, 178, 217, 240, 339
Clinton, Hillary, 240
Coal, Great Britain's conversion to,
  129–131
Cohen, William S., 332
COIN (counterinsurgency), 340
Cold War, 191, 339
Collective bargaining, 154–155
Colonial liberation movement, 355
Comedy, source of, 77
Commission on Supplies and Shortages,
  proposed, 214–215
Commission on the Skills of the
  American Workplace (1990), 154
Commodity shortages, 43, 72, 330
Common good, concept of, 322
Communism, 184–185, 202–206, 334–335
Communist Manifesto, The (Marx and
  Engels), 202–206, 320–321
Communist Party, 182, 188
Company Man (Sampson), 148
Competitive market, 40
Competitive model of economics, 11
Confessions of a Union Buster (Levitt), 154
Conflicting interests in world, 9–10, 170
Confused egalitarianism, 125
Confused socialism, 125
Congress of Industrial Organizations, 310
Congressional Budget Office, 53–54, 57
Conscience of a Liberal, The (Krugman),
  257–259
Conservativism, 11, 160
Consumption, 279

Contingent workers, 155
Contract bargaining, 155
Controls, 20, 40–41, 44. *See also* Price-
wage controls
Corporate community, 239, 241
Corporate-conservative coalition,
241–242
Corporations. *See also specific name*
bottom-line measurement and, 172
capitalism and, 126
customer loyalty and, 172–173
democracy and, 126
disposable workers and, 234–236
gangs comparison to, 348
knowledge workers and, 235
layoffs and, 234–236
makeovers of, 173–174
ownership and control issues and,
147–150, 242
planning by, 59
power of, 148–150, 156, 239–240, 242,
334
stakeholders in, 15, 174
tax breaks for, 139
unions and, 177–178
Corporatism, 61
Cost-push inflation, 17–20
Council of Economic Advisers (CEA),
37–38, 51–52, 56–57, 91, 224
Council on Wage and Price Stability, 64
Country, Douglas, 346–348
Crain, Marion, 254–256
Creation theories, 109–114
Creative destruction, 150, 235–236, 280,
320–322, 330
Credit default swaps, 292
Crick, Francis, 109
Crisis of Vision in Modern Economics, The
(Heilbroner and Milberg), 158–162
Cronkite, Walter, 178
Crowly, Herbert, 242
Cuban Missile Crisis, 223
Cultural Revolution (1966–1976), 350,
353, 356
Culture of wealth, 314–315
Cuomo, Andrew, 288, 290
Currency devaluation, avoiding, 278
Customer loyalty, 172–173

Darwin, Charles, 109, 168, 289, 301
Davidson, Paul, 273, 277, 295, 302
De Gaulle, Charles, 149
Decentralization, 122–123
Decision making, decentralized, 122–123
Deficit spending, 276

Deficits, 286
Deforestation, 129–131
Demand, 19, 40, 43, 73–74, 311, 320, 330
Demand-pull inflation, 17–18
Democracy
Arab Spring and, 355–356
capitalism and, 122–126
corporations and, 126
economic, 324
musings on, 122–126
political, 324
social, 184
socialism and, 122–126, 324
Democratic Party, 335
Democratic socialism, 280, 324
Deng Xiaoping, 350
Descent of Man, The (Darwin), 168
Destructive destruction, 236
Dialectical socialism, 324
Diamond, Jared, 195–201
Diocletian, 76
Dionne, E.J., Jr., 162, 164
Disney corporation, 148
Disposable American, The (Uchitelle),
234–236
Disposable workers, 234–236
Dividends, 104
Division of Balanced Growth and
Economic Planning, 53
Djilas, Milovan, 184
DNA structure, 109
Dollinger, Genora Johnson, 144
Domhoff, G. William, 239–242, 315, 318
Dot-com bubble (1995–2001), 291
Drucker, Peter F., 50, 235
Dunlap, Albert, 173–174
Dunlop Commission, 151–157
Dunlop, John T., 151–157
Dunne, Peter Finley, 307
Dye, Richard, 315

Earth, cultivation of, 7–8
Eccles, Marriner, 143, 327, 331
Eckstein, Otto, 65
Eclecticism, 19
Economic planning
adjustments and, 50
Arab oil embargo and, 26–27
backing into, 26–27
bill, 51–55, 62
board, 33–39, 62
budget and, federal, 38
Carter and, letter to, 80–83
corporatism and, 61
critic of, reply to, 59–62

Economic planning *(continued)*
  in economy, 13
  fascism and, 62
  fear of, 48–50
  forecasting and, 81
  French, 35, 57
  imperative, 37–38
  implementation and, 82
  indicative, 37–38
  knowledge needed for, 49
  planning system of, 15
  politics and, 33–39
  power and, 13
  prices and, 15
  public opinion and, 14
  results of, 49
  Robbins's view of, 61
  socialism and, 15, 49, 61–62
  society and, 61
  successful, characteristics of, 38
  wages and, 15
Economic Planning Board, 62
Economic Planning Council, 62
"Economic Possibilities for Our
    Grandchildren" (Keynes), 280
Economic Transformation of America, The
    (Heilbroner and Singer), 149
Economics. *See also* Capitalism; Inflation;
    Socialism; Wealth
  analyses of, 7
  Big-End, Little-End problem, 10
  big government model of, 11
  breaking the rules and, 106–108
  as Bruegel painting, 9
  competitive model of, 11
  complexity of world and, 9
  as deductive discipline, 160
  demand and, 19, 40, 43, 73–74, 311, 320,
    330
  as dismal science, 47
  fiction versus nonfiction, 158
  floundering of, 11
  Ford's summit and, 43–45
  G20 Summit and, 281–282
  Galbraithian world of, 12–13
  Heilbroner and, 221
  Higher, 10
  housewife in modern, 13
  income distribution and, 81, 158,
    177–178, 213, 264, 285, 318, 333
  incomes policy and, 102–105, 115–117,
    127–128
  institutional, 11, 21–23
  interesting writing about, 5–8
  of Iraq war, 246–248, 252

Economics *(continued)*
  Knight's view of, 4
  Landslide Age (1973–), 186
  Little Red Riding Hood scenario and,
    106–108
  Lower, 10
  mainstream, 21–23
  market, 22
  multinational institutions and,
    316–317, 323
  Obama's failures and, 294–296
  planning bill, 51–55
  policy, 4
  politics and, 11
  predictions about, impossibility of,
    28–32
  reflexivity and, 268–269
  reforms, 14–15, 212–213, 321–323,
    328–329, 331
  Reich and, 328–329
  social health and, 260–264, *261, 262,
    263*
  stabilization policy and, 17
  supply and, 19, 40, 73, 330
  Tanner on studying, 76
  tax-based incomes policy, 115–117
  textbook world of, 12–13
  theories, 99, 158–162
  Three Little Pigs scenario and, 291
Economics and the Public Purpose
    (Galbraith), 12–16, 237
"Economics of the Coming Spaceship
    Earth, The" (Boulding), 352–354
Economists. *See also specific name*
  analytical, 21–22
  career of, 4
  conservatism of, 11
  "crisis of vision" and, 160
  disaccord among, 6, 9–11
  disappearance of, 4, 22
  economic law and, 78–79
  institutional, 21–22
  as planners, 21
  prescience of, 23
Economy. *See also* Inflation; Market;
    Recession; Recovery; *specific crisis*
  Arab oil embargo and (early 1970s),
    24–27, 61
  bubbles in, 268–269, 291–293
  capital regulations and, 49
  cycles in, 313, 322
  economic planning in, 13
  financial crisis (2008), 265–266,
    278–279
  free market, 46, 48, 297–302, 318–319

Economy (continued)
  freefall of, 297–302
  full employment and, 70–74, 279
  Great Compression and, 257
  growth of, 63–64
  guidance versus interference and, 74
  health of American, 217–218
  interest rates and, 139, 277–278, 299
  market, 348
  monopolies and, 169
  New York City's financial crisis (1975),
    66–69
  in 1950s and 1960s, 284
  parts of, 13
  prices and, 15, 115–117
  Russian, 189–194
  stagflation and, 128
  stimulus for, 298–299
  stimulus packages and, 283, 294, 298
  unemployment and, 18, 65, 164,
    281–282
  wage-price controls and, 17–20, 40–42,
    44–45
  wages and, 15, 104, 115–117, 263, 264
  Wall Street bankers and traders and,
    288–290
Edwards, John, 254–256
Egalitarianism, confused, 125
Egypt, 355
Egyptian revolution, 342–343
Eichner, Alfred S., 103, 160
Einstein, Albert, 77
Eisenhower Doctrine, 339
Eisenhower, Dwight, 241, 339
Eisner, Michael, 148
Electoral coalition, 258–259
Electoral participation, 241–242, 249–250
Elite, 240–241, 265–266, 315, 341
Employer Free Choice Act, 335
Employment Act (1946), 70, 78
Employment, full, 70–74, 279
End of Boom and Crash, The (Heilbroner),
  130
End of Reform, The (Brinkley), 142–146
Ending Poverty in America (Edwards,
  Crain, Kalleberg), 254–256
Energy use, 26–27, 352–353
Engels, Friedrich, 124, 202–206, 320–321
Enlightenment, public, 123–124
Erdogan, Recep Tayyip, 355
Estes, Ralph, 172
"Euthanasia of the rentier," 279
Euthanasia of stockholders, 15
Evolution, 109–114
Exchange rates, 79

Externalities, 170, 302, 330
ExxonMobil, 247

Fabian Essays (Shaw), 5
Fabian socialism, 324
Fascism, 62
Federal Deposit Insurance Corporation
  (FDIC), 287, 309
Federal Election Commission, 249
Federal Emergency Management Agency
  (FEMA), 229–230
Federal Emergency Relief Administration,
  309
Federal Energy Administration, 62
Federal Reserve Board, 37, 51, 58
Federal Reserve System, 66, 277, 322
Feinstein, Dianne, 335
FEMA, 229–230
Filkins, Dexter, 308
Financial crisis (2008), 265–266, 278–279
Financial Crisis Inquiry Commission,
  301
Financial Product Safety Commission,
  proposed, 256
Financial sector, 143, 277–279, 284–285,
  288–290, 297–301, 324, 335
Fiscal policy, 19, 45, 70–73
Fitzgerald, F. Scott, 332
527 tax code, 250
Folklore of Capitalism, The (Arnold), 145
Ford, Gerald, 40, 45, 63–65, 66–69, 214
Ford's summit (1974), 43–45
Forecasting, 81
Foreclosures, banning housing, 282
Foreign policy revolution (2008),
  273–274
Frank, Barney, 304
Free market, 46, 48, 170, 183, 297–302,
  318–319
Free speech, press, and assembly, 345
Freefall (Stiglitz), 297–302, 307
French Revolution, 356
Freud, Sigmund, 29, 77
Friedman, Milton, 137, 158, 179
Full employment, 70–74, 279
Full Employment and Balanced Growth
  Act (1978), 58, 62, 78, 136, 215, 225
Future of Capitalism, The (Thurow), 160

G20 Summit (2009), 281–282
Gaddafi, Muammar, 355
Gaidar, Egor, 188–189, 193–194
Galbraith, John Kenneth
  analysis of theories of, 12–16
  biography of, 222–226

Galbraith, John Kenneth *(continued)*
  as contributor to *Challenge*, 137
  countervailing power and, 212
  courage of, 237
  five socialisms of, 14–16, 237–238
  good society and, 163–166, 237, 285–286
  Initiative Committee for National
      Economic Planning and, 215
  interview of, 120
  labor and, well-paid, 273
  message of, 13
  New Deal and, 311
  power between corporations and
      unions and, 156
  price control and, 40–41
  pride of, 97–101
  puppet play about, 97–101
  reflection on, 237–238
  socialism and, 14–16, 100–101, 141–146,
      237–238, 324
  technostructure and, 16
Galbraithian revolution, possibility of,
    12, 15–16
Gang violence, 346–349
Gans, Herbert, 138
Gates, Robert M., 295, 343
GATT, 317
GCOIN (global counterinsurgency), 340
Geithner, Timothy "Tim," 284, 286–287,
    291, 294, 300–301, 312
General Agreement on Tariffs (GATT),
    317
General Theory (Keynes), 12, 275, 279
Genes, 109–114
Geoghegan, Thomas, 156
George, Henry, 5
George, Lloyd, 275
Ghonim, Wael, 342–343
Gingrich, Newt, 138–141, 334
Glass-Steagall Act, 309, 335
Global multiplier, 302
Goffman, Erving, 257
"Golden Age" (1947–1973), 185–186
Goldfinger, Nat, 65, 120
Goldman Sachs, 288
Good society, 163–166, 237, 280,
    285–286, 322, 325
Good Society and Its Enemies, The
    (Galbraith), 163–166, 237
Gorbachev, Mikhail, 186, 191–193
Gore, Tipper, 348
Government. *See also* Budget; Democracy
  capitalism and intervention of, 141
  impartiality of, 169–170
  prosperity and, 296

Government *(continued)*
  Smith's view of, 169–170
  social programs and, 174–175
Graduation rates, U.S., *263*, 264
Great Britain's conversion to coal,
    129–131
Great Compression, 257
Great Depression, 142–143, 309, 313, 327
Great Divergence, 258–259
Great Leap Forward, 353
Great Recession, 313
"Great risk shift," 255
Greenspan, Alan, 43, 139, 291
Gromyko, Andrei, 191–192
Guild socialism, 15
Gulbenkian, Nabur, 24
Gun culture, 337–338, 340
Guns and gun control, 140, 338
Guns, Germs, and Steel (Diamond),
    195–201

Hacker, Jacob S., 255, 333–336
Haldane, J.B.S., 9
Hamilton, Alexander, 331, 356
Hard money, 242
Havel, Václav, 320
Haydn, Joseph, 45
Hayek, Friedrich A. von, 46–47
Hazlitt, Henry, 59–62
Health care, 323
Health insurance, universal, 258–259
Heartbreak House (Shaw), 161
Heilbroner, Robert "Bob," 22, 28–32, 130,
    137, 149, 158–162, 175–176, 221, 324
Heller, Walter, 137, 224
Hemingway, Ernest, 332
Henderson, Leon, 143
Hercules, 32
Heston, Charleton, 348
Higher Economics, 10
History of the English-Speaking Peoples, A
    (Churchill), 32
Hitler, Adolf, 305
Hobbes, Thomas, 270
Hobsbawm, Eric, 181–187, 202, 204
Hofstadter, Richard, 304–305
Homo sapiens, evolution and behavior of,
    109–114, 168, 195–197, 201, 289
Hopkins, Harry, 282, 311–312
Hu Jintao, 281
Huizinga, Johan, 32
Human Development Report 1998, 211–213
Human nature, 76
Humphrey-Hawkins Full Employment
    Act (1978), 58, 62, 78, 136, 215, 225

Humphrey, Hubert, 51, 62, 136, 225
Hurricane Katrina (2005), 229–231
Hussein, Saddam, 228, 246–247, 340

Ice (Ice-T and Country), 346–349
Ice-T, 346–349
Ickes, Harold, 311
Ideas, 75, 345
IMF, 301–302, 316, 323
Imo (ape), 113
Imperative economic planning, 37–38
Incentives, financial, 71, 297–298
Income distribution, 81, 158, 177–178,
    213, 264, 285, 318, 333
Incomes policy, 102–105, 115–117,
    127–128, 277
Index of Economic Well-Being, 314
Index of Social Health, 217, 262
Index of Social Health and Gross
    Domestic Product, *261, 263*
Index of Social Health of the United
    States, 260, 314
"Index of Well-Being" (Osberg and
    Sharpe), 314
India, 302
Indicative economic planning, 37–38
Individual Development Accounts, 255
Industrial Revolution, 130–131, 170
Industrialization, 29
Inequality, 314
Infant mortality, U.S., 260, *263*, 264
Inflation
    commodity shortages and, 43
    continuing, 18
    controls and, 41
    cost-push, 17–20
    curing, 18–20, 116–117, 127–128
    cycle of recession and, 20
    dangers of, 277
    demand and, excess, 43
    demand-pull, 17–18
    exporting, avoiding, 73
    fear of, 164
    Ford and, 63–65
    Ford's summit on, 43–45
    full employment without, 70–74
    as futile game, 20
    importing, avoiding, 73
    incomes policy and, 116–117, 127–128
    inevitability of, 127–128
    Keynes and, 277
    kinds of, 43
    moderate rate of, 164–165
    recovery and, 63–64
    World War II and, 41

Information, ubiquity and meaning of,
    344–345
Initiative Committee for National
    Economic Planning, 51, 54, 57, 59,
    136, 215
Innovation, 320
Inquiry into the Human Prospect, An
    (Heilbroner), 28–32
Institutional economics, 11, 21–23
Intellectual property rights in China, 351
Interest rates, 139, 277–278, 299
Interindustry supply and demand, 73
International Monetary Fund (IMF),
    301–302, 316, 323
International trade, 330
Interviewing experiences, 120–121
Investment, export-led, 278
Invisible hand, 301
Iraq wars, 227–229, 246–248, 251–252,
    307, 339–340
"Is the End of the World at Hand?"
    (Solow), 5–6
Israel, 356

Jackson, Andrew, 243
James A. Baker Institute of Public Policy
    report (2001), 248
Javits, Jacob K., 51, 62, 136, 225
Jefferson, Thomas, 243, 356
Job training programs, 71
Jobs, 178–180
John Kenneth Galbraith (Parker), 222–226
John Maynard Keynes (Davidson), 273, 277
Johnson, Chalmers, 251, 307
Johnson, Lyndon B., 225, 339
Johnson, Samuel, 171, 305
Joint Economic Committee, 53–54, 57,
    78, 92
Jones, Margaret, 331
Junger, Sebastian, 308

Kalecki, Michal, 44
Kalleberg, Arne L., 254–256
Kant, Immanuel, 332
Karzai, Hamid, 295
Kennedy, John F., 39, 223–224, 339
Keynes, John Maynard, 10–12, 16, 99, 143,
    223, 275–280, 286, 302
Keynes Solution, The (Davidson), 295
Keynesianism, 34, 70, 223, 276–280
Knight, Frank H., 4
Knowledge, 351
Knowledge workers, 235
Kohut, Andrew, 246
Korengal Valley, 308

Korean War, 306–307
Kotz, David, 188, 190
Kristof, Nicholas, 296
Krugman, Paul, 257–259
Krugman-Stiglitz Doctrine, 298
Kurds, 227
Kynge, James, 351

Labor
collective bargaining and, 154–155
contingent workers, 155
contract bargaining and, 155
disposable workers and, 234–236
division of, 5, 7, 123
Dunlop's view of, 151–157
Galbraith's case for well-paid, 273
identities of, conflicting, 204
inner-city African Americans and,
178–180
job training programs and, 71
knowledge workers and, 235
unions, 104, 117, 144, 151–157, 177–178,
242, 322, 335
unskilled workers and, 71
wage disparities with management and,
177–178
Labor-liberal coalition, 241–242
Labor-Management Group, 102
Labour Party (Great Britain), 275
Lamb, William, 77
Landslide Age (1973–), 186
Language, emergence of, 113–114
Last Chronicle of Barset, The (Trollope),
86–89
Law, economic, 78–79. *See also specific law*
Leadership, 232–233, 342
Lee, Harper, 323–324
Lekachman, Robert "Bob," 136
Lenin, Vladimir, 182, 205
Lenin's Tomb (Remnick), 188
Leonhardt, David, 246
Leontief, Wassily, 51, 80, 137, 214–216
Lerner, Abba P., 20
Levitt, Martin Jay, 154
Lewis, John, 304
Lewis, John L., 144
Liberal Party (Great Britain), 275
Libya, 355
Lilienthal, David, 309
Limits of Power, The (Bacevich), 295
Lincoln, Abraham, 182, 247
Lindblom, Charles E., 123, 126
Little Red Riding Hood scenario, 106–108
Long Gilded Age, 257–258
Look for the Union Label (Tyler), 155

Lower Economics, 10
Loyalty Effect, The (Reichheld), 172–173
Lucas, Robert E., Jr., 149, 159
Luce, Henry, 223
Luxemburg, Rosa, 182

MAC, 69
Mackay case, 156
Madness of crowds, 341
Madrick, Jeff, 270
Mainstream economics, 21–23
Major Barbara (Shaw), 289
Management, 122–123, 130, 177–178
Manifest destiny, U.S., 306
Mansfield, Michael "Mike," 90
Mao Zedong, 350, 353
Market. *See also* Economy
competitive, 40
economics, 22
economy, 348
failures, 297
free, 46, 48, 170, 183, 297–302, 318–319
self-regulation, 268
socialism, 324
system in economy, 13
Markey, Betsy, 304
Marrow, Tracy "Trey" (later Ice-T),
346–349
Marshall Plan, 278, 302
Marshall, Ray, 152
Martin, William McChesney, 39
Marx, Karl, 5, 75, 77, 79, 97–98, 124, 126,
202–206, 235, 247, 272, 320–321,
324
Maslin, Janet, 209
Maurice, François, 110
McCain-Feingold Bipartisan Campaign
Reform Act (2002), 249
McCain, John, 302
McChrystal, Stanley, 295
McGovern, George, 63
McKinley, William, 244
Mean Business (Dunlap), 173–174
Meany, George, 78–79
Medvedev, Dmitri Anatolievich, 281
Megacorp and Oligopoly (Eichner), 103
Melman, Seymour, 140
Memoirs (Gorbachev), 191
Mercantilism, 169
Merkel, Angela, 281
Merton, Robert C., 291
Mexico, 317
Middle class, 255
Mideast violence, 342–343, 355–356
Milberg, William, 158–162

Military
  budget, 139–140
  culture, 337–342
  solutions, 306–308
  spending, 252
Military-industrial complex, 241, 322,
  339
Mill, John Stuart, 213
Millennialism, 126
Mills, C. Wright, 241
Miringoff, Marc, 217–218, 260
Miringoff, Marque-Luisa, 217–218,
  260–264, 314
Mondale, Walter, 136
Monetarism, 158–159, 277
Monetary policy, 19, 70–73
Money, 44, 242, 250
Monod, Jacques, 110
Monopolies, 169
Morgan Stanley, 288
Mortgage scandal, 284, 299, 316, 324
Mubarak, Hosni, 342–343, 355
Muller, Jerry Z., 166–171
Multilateral agreements, 73
Multiplier effect, 252, 302
Muslim Brotherhood, 355
Mutual Assistance Corporation (MAC), 69
My Russia (Zyuganov), 188
Myrdal, Gunnar, 21–23, 46–47, 137
Myths, Heilbroner's view of, 32

NAFTA, 317
Name-Dropping (Galbraith), 311
National Commission on
  Intergovernmental Relations, 92–93
National Commission on Supplies and
  Shortages, 45
National Growth and Development
  Commission, 92–93
National Industrial Recovery Act (NIRA)
  (1933), 143–144, 310
National Labor Relations Act (1935), 144,
  310
National Labor Relations Board (NLRB),
  154, 286–287
National multiplier, 302
National Recovery Administration, 143,
  309
National Rifle Association (NRA), 338
National Solidarity Program, 296
Natural resources, using, 29–31, 350–351
Nef, John U., 129–130
Negative externalities, 170, 330
Nemesis (Chalmers Johnson), 251
Neoconservatism, 249

New Classical Economics, 159
New Deal
  first (1933–1935), 142, 145–146, 148–149,
    183, 215, 223, 309–311
  flaw of, 311
  Galbraith's view on, 311
  new, 257–259
  revilement of, 141–142
  second (1935–1938), 310–311
New Industrial State, The (Galbraith), 14
New Jim Crow, The (Alexander), 319
New Keynesian Economics, 158–161
New Orleans, 229–231, 246
New Paradigm for Financial Markets, The
  (Soros), 268–269
New Rich, New Poor, New Russia
  (Silverman and Yanowitch), 190
New socialist imperative, 14–15
New United Motors Manufacturing Inc.
  (NUMMI), 153
New York City's financial crisis (1975),
  66–69
Newcomen, Thomas, 130
Newton's model of self-regulation,
  169–170
NIRA (1933), 143–144, 310
Nixon, Richard M., 19, 24, 44, 339
NLRB, 154, 286–287
Non-absolutism, 356
North American Free Trade Agreement
  (NAFTA), 317
NRA, 338
NUMMI, 153

Obama, Barack, 267, 272–274, 281, 286,
  293–296, 298, 300, 305, 311–313, 339,
  343
Obama Doctrine, 298
OECD, 281, 314
Office of Balanced Growth and Economic
  Planning, 51–55, 57–58, 62
Office of Management and Budget, 51, 91
Office of Price Administration (OPA), 41
Oil and Energy Working Group of State
  Department, 248
Oil and oil prices, 26, 248, 277
Oil industry, 25–27, 61
Oil Producing and Exporting Countries
  (OPEC), 25
Okun, Arthur, 65, 115–116
Okun form of TIP, 115–116
OPA, 41
Opdyke, Sandra, 260–264, 314
OPEC, 25
Order, social, 122–124, 126

Organizational for Economic Cooperation and Development (OECD), 281, 314
Osberg, Lars, 314
Ownership
  corporate, 147–150, 242
  public, 124

Pahl, R.E, 61–62
Palestinian Authority, 356
Palin, Sarah, 304
Paranoid style, 304–305
Paranoid Style in American Politics, The (Hofstadter), 304
Parker, Richard, 222–226
PATCO (Professional Air Traffic Controllers Organization), 156
Paulson, Henry "Hank," 291, 298
Perestroika, 191–193
Perkins, Frances, 145, 312
Perry, Rick, 304
Petraeus, David, 340
Philosophy, 175–176
Pickety, Thomas, 327
Pierson, Paul, 333–336
Pigou, Arthur, 170
Pimp (Ice-T), 345
Pinmaking, 5, 7
Planning. *See* Business planning; Economic planning; Energy planning
Plunder and Blunder (Baker), 291–293
Policy-planning network, 240–241
Political Element in the Development of Economic Theory, The (Myrdal), 21
Political marketing of ideas, 345
Politicians. *See specific name*
Politics. *See also specific politician*
  Democratic Party, 335
  economic law and, 78–79
  economic planning and, 33–39
  economics and, 11
  incivility in, 303–304
  leadership and, 232–233
  as organized combat, 335
  paranoid style in, 304–305
  Republican Party, 141, 304–305
  Solid South and, 310
  superpower status of America, 243–244
  Tanner's view of, 76
  Tea Party and, 303–305, 313, 319, 334
Politics and Markets (Lindblom), 123
Polk, James K., 243
Population growth, 28–30, 351–352
Positive externalities, 302
Post-Korean wars, 306–307
Postcapitalism, 280, 326

Poverty
  assets for poor people and, 255
  character and, 139
  child, 260, *263*, 264
  cycle of, 254–255, 314
  definition of, 254–255
  Edwards's book on, 254–256
  "great risk shift" and, 25
  in New Orleans, 229
  pathology of, 346–349
  in Social Indicator performance (2005), *263*
  in urban areas, 179–180
  U.S. rate of, 217, 260, *263*, 264
  welfare and, 138–139
Powell, Colin, 340
Powell Doctrine, 298, 312
Power
  analysis of American, 239–242
  in China, 351
  of corporations, 148–150, 156, 239–240, 242, 334
  countervailing, 212, 257–258
  economic planning and, 13
  elite, 240–241, 315
  military, 339–340
  pathology of, 348–349
  powerless and, 320
  private, 149–150
  public, 149–150
  superpower status of America and, 243–244
  of unions, 156
Power of the Powerless, The (Havel), 320
PPIP, 287, 300
Predator State, The (Galbraith), 273
Presidential election (2008), 249–250, 272–274
Price stability, 71–72, 116, 128
Price-wage controls, 17–20, 40–42, 44–45, 71–72, 76
Prices, 15, 115–117
Primates, evolution and behavior of, 112–113
Problems of Economics (journal), 118
Property taxes, 270–271
Proudhon, Joseph, 270
Psychopathic personalities, 232, 252, 341
Public enlightenment, 123–124
Public opinion, 14
Public ownership, 124
Public-Private Investment Program (PPIP), 287, 300
Public Works Administration (PWA), 142, 310

Publishing, 119–121. *See also* Book reviews; *specific title*
PWA, 142, 310

Quayle, Dan, 348
Quotes, stray, 77

Racism, 267, 310
Raleigh, Sir Walter, 336
Rap music, 347–348
Rational expectations, 159
Reagan, Ronald, 268, 334, 339
Real estate bubble, (2002), 291–292
Reality versus illusion, 207–210
Recession, economic
  in curing inflation, 18
  cycle of inflation and, 20
  1937, 143, 145
  perpetuation of, 63–65
  private spending in, 296
  public spending in, 296
Recovery, economic
  inflation and, 63–64
  1975, 63–65
  2009–2010, 283–286
Recycling issue, 350
Redistribution wars, predicted, 29
Reflexivity, 268–269
Reforms
  economic, 14–15, 212–213, 321–323, 328–329, 331
  social, 30
Regulation, 49, 165. *See also specific law*
Reich, Robert B., 326–332
Reichheld, Frederick F., 172–173
Remnick, David, 188–194
Report and Recommendations by the Commission on the Future of Worker-Management Relations (Dunlop), 151–157
Republican Party, 141, 304–305
Resource allocation, 40
Resurrection (Remnick), 188–194
Rethinking Corporate Governance for the Twenty-First Century (Blair), 147–150
Revolution from Above (Kotz and Weir), 188, 190
Revolutionist's Handbook, The (Tanner), 75–77
Rice, Condoleezza, 228
Robbins, Lionel, 61–62
Rohatyn, Felix, 69
Roosevelt, Eleanor, 311
Roosevelt, Franklin D., 142–143, 149, 178, 183, 284, 294, 309–312, 341

Roosevelt, Theodore, 149
Rothkopf, David, 265–266, 315
Rove, Karl, 249
Rubin, Robert, 165, 312
Rumsfeld, Donald, 340
Rusk, Dean, 224
Russell, Bertrand, 16, 342
Russia, 188–194
Russian Revolution, 356

Saez, Emmanuel, 327
Said, Khaled, 342–343
Saliency, 342
SALT I Treaty, 339
SALT II Treaty, 339
Sampson, Anthony, 148
Samuelson, Paul, 65
Sarkozy, Nicolas, 281, 355
Say's Law, 276
Scholes, Myron, 291
Schroeder, Gerhard, 217
Schumer, Charles "Chuck," 335
Schumpeter, Joseph, 150, 235, 280, 320–321
Scientific knowledge, 353
Scott, Hugh, 90
Scott Paper corporation, 173
Scott, Sir Walter, 171
Second Amendment, 140, 338
Self-interest, 167, 170, 298
Self-regulation, 169–170
Seward, William H., 244
Shadow banking system, 286
Sharpe, Andrew, 314
Sharpe, Lou, 350–351
Shaw, George Bernard, 5, 7–8, 12, 42, 161, 232, 289, 324
Sheahan, John, 57
Sheehan, Cindy, 227
Sherraden, Michael, 255
Shiites, 227
Silverman, Bertram, 190
Simpson, Alan, 335
Singer, Aaron, 149
SIVs, 286
Slaughterhouse Five (Vonnegut), 232
Slightly tarnished socialism, 125
Smith, Adam, 5, 7, 74–75, 77, 97–98, 166–171, 280, 286, 289, 320
Smith, Rupert, 247, 306–308
Smith, Stevie, 342
Social class, 122, 124–125, 255, 318
Social contract, 170–171
Social democracy, 184
Social democrats, 184–185

Social Health of the Nation (Miringoff and Miringoff), 217–218
Social Indicator performance (2005), *263*
Social insurance, 255
Social order, 122–124, 126
Social problems, 21, 260–264, *261, 262,* 351. *See also specific type*
Social programs, 138–139, 174–175. *See also specific type*
Social reform, 30
Social Security, 142, 257, 323
Social Security Act (1933), 142, 145, 310
Socialism
  bastard, 124–125, 184
  bureaucratic symbiosis and, 15
  capitalism and, 187
  changes in, 324
  coinage of term, 122
  confused, 125
  democracy and, 122–126, 324
  democratic, 280, 324
  dialectical, 324
  economic planning and, 15, 49, 61–62
  euthanasia of stockholders, 15
  Fabian, 324
  five types of (Galbraith's), 14–16, 237–238
  future of, 206
  Galbraith and, 14–16, 100–101, 141–146, 237–238, 324
  guild, 15
  Heilbroner and, 221
  market, 324
  millennialism and, 126
  musings on, 122–126
  new socialist imperative, 14–15
  Obama and, 274
  postcapitalism, 324
  slightly tarnished, 125
  spiritual, 324
  after World War I, 181
Society
  economic planning and, 61
  Goffman's view of, 257
  good, 163–166, 237, 280, 285–286, 322, 325
  organizing, 351
  social health of, 260–264, *261, 262, 263*
  technological, 122–123, 126
Sociopathic personalities, 341
Soft money, 250
Solid South, 310
Solow, Robert M., 5–6
Soros, George, 268–269
Soros, Robert, 269

Soviet system, 125
Soviet Union, 188, 206, 248, 339
Speer, Albert, 222
Spetter, Henry, 135–136
Spiritual socialism, 324
Stabilization policy, 17
Stagflation, 128
Stakeholders, 15, 174
Stalin, Joseph, 182, 205, 305
Stanley Works company, 234
Steam engine, 130
Stein, Herbert, 31, 92, 120, 137
Stigler, George, 11
Stiglitz, Joseph E., 246, 297–302, 307
Stimulus, economic, 298–299
Stimulus packages, 283, 294, 298
Stockholders, 15, 174
Stokes, Bruce, 246
"Strategy Energy Policy" (2001 report), 248
Structured investment vehicles (SIVs), 286
Stupack, Bart, 304
Subprime lending, 284, 299, 316, 324
Summers, Lawrence "Larry," 294, 301, 312
Sunnis, 227
Super-bubble, 268–269
Superclass (Rothkopf), 265–266, 315
Superpower status, U.S., 243–244
Supply, 19, 40, 73, 330
Sweden, 221
Sweeney, John J., 151–152, 157, 177–178
Symbiosis, bureaucratic, 15
Syria, 355

Taliban, 296
Tanner, Jack, 75–77
TARP, 279, 288–289, 298, 300, 312
Tarshis, Lorie, 162
Tax-based incomes policy (TIP), 115–117, 277
Taxes, 49, 139, 270–271, 303, 323, 334
Tea Party, 303–305, 313, 319, 334
Teachings from the Worldly Philosophy (Heilbroner), 175–176
Technical knowledge, 351
Technological society, 122–123, 126
Technostructure, 16
Teleonomy, 111
Tennessee Valley Authority (TVA), 35, 309
Terrorism, war on, 247, 308
Thatcher, Margaret, 268

Theory of Moral Sentiments, The (Smith), 167, 280, 289
Theory of Price Control, A (Galbraith), 41
Thermidore Reaction, 356
They Only Look Dead (Dionne), 162, 164
Three Little Pigs scenario, 291
Thurow, Lester, 160
Tight money, 44
Timon of Athens (Shakespeare), 5–6
TIP, 115–117, 277
To Kill a Mockingbird (Lee), 323–324
To Renew America (Gingrich), 138–141
Tobin, James, 43–44
"Too big to fail" concept, 285, 289, 299–300, 313
"Too small to fail" concept, 329
Trade, international, 330
Tragedy, source of, 77
Tranches of subprime, 284
Trollope, Anthony, 86–89
Troubled Asset Relief Program (TARP), 279, 288–289, 298, 300, 312
Truman Show, The (film), 207–210
Tunisia, 355
Turkey, 355
TVA, 35, 309
Twain, Mark, 334
Tyler, Gus, 155
Tyranny of the Bottom Line, The (Estes), 172

Uchitelle, Louis, 234–236
Ultraconservatives, 242
Unadulterated capitalism, 124, 126
UNDP, 211–213
Unemployment, 18, 65, 164, 281–282, 292, 324
Union-management cooperation, 153–154
Unions, 104, 117, 144, 151–157, 177–178, 242, 322, 335
Unions and Economic Competitiveness (Marshall), 152
United Nations Development Programme (UNDP), 211–213
United States. *See also* Politics; *specific economic issues and government departments*
  China and, 348, 352
  as dystopia, 344–345
  export-led investment and, 278
  financial crisis (2008) and, 265–266, 278–279
  graduation rates in, *263*, 264

United States *(continued)*
  gun culture in, 337–338, 340
  guns and gun control in, 140, 338
  history of, 140
  infant mortality in, 260, *263*, 264
  manifest destiny and, 306
  military culture in, 337–342
  poverty rates in, 217, 260, *263*, 264
  "save the world" credo and, 339–340
  as superpower, 243–244
  violence in, 337–342
Universe's expansion, 9
Unskilled workers, 71
U.S. Supreme Court, 156, 308–309
Utility of Force, The (Smith), 306–308

Vanderboegh, Mike, 304
Vietnam War, 307, 339
Violence
  gang, 346–348
  in Mideast, 342–343
  in United States, 337–342
Volcker, Paul, 128, 277
Volcker Rule, 313
Vonnegut, Kurt, 232–233, 252–253, 325, 341–342
Voting, 241–242, 249–250

Wage-price controls, 17–20, 40–42, 44–45, 71–72, 76, 117
Wage stability, 116
Wages, 15, 104, 115–117, *263*, 264
Wagner Act, 142, 153
Wagner, Robert, 144
Wall Street bankers and traders, 288–290, 335
Wallace, Henry, 144
Wallich, Henry, 115–116
Wallich-Weintraub form of TIP, 115–116
Waning of the Middle Ages, The (Huizinga), 32
War Against the Poor, The (Gans), 138
War (Junger), 308
Warren, Elizabeth, 256
Wars. *See also specific name*
  of redistribution, predicted, 29
  supply and demand and, 40
Washington Rules (Bacevich), 339
Watson, James B., 109
Wealth, 169, 239–242, 258, 264, 285, 314–315, 318
Wealth of Nations, The (Smith), 5, 168–171, 286
Weapons of mass destruction (WMD), 246–247

Weathermen (left-wing extremist group), 305
Weidenbaum, Murray, 137
Weintraub, Sidney, 115–116
Weir, Fred, 188, 190
Welfare, 138–139
Welfare state capitalism, 124, 126
We're Right, You're Wrong (Carville), 174–175
When Work Disappears (William Julius Wilson), 178–180
Which Side Are You On? (Geoghegan), 156
White, Harry Dexter, 278, 302
Who Rules America? (Domhoff), 239–242, 315, 318
Why Economics Is Not Yet a Science (Eichner), 160
Wilde, Oscar, 38–39, 324
Wilson, Joe, 304
Wilson, William Julius, 178–180, 256
Wilson, Woodrow, 149, 339
Winkler, J.T., 61
Winner-Take-All Politics (Hacker and Pierson), 333–336
WMD, 246–247
Wolf, Dick, 348
Wolff, Edward, 318
Woodcock, Leonard, 51, 120, 215, 225
Wordsworth, William, 4

Works Progress Administration (WPA), 142, 282–283, 286
World
  complexity of, 9
  conflicting interests in, 9–10, 170
  expansion of universe and, 9
  Heilbroner's predictions for, 28–32
  history
    Diamond's book, 195–201
    Hobsbawm's book, 181–187
  population growth of, 28–30, 349–350
  report on development of (1998), 211–213
World Bank, 301–302, 316, 323
World Trade Organization (WTO), 316–317, 323
World War I, 181–182
World War II, 41, 44, 183–184, 341
WPA, 142, 282–283, 286
Wright, Jeremiah, 267
WTO, 316–317, 323

Yakhontoff, Victor, 118
Yanowitch, Murray, 190
Yeltsin, Boris, 188, 190, 193–194

Zhou Enlai, 350
Zyuganov, Gennady, 188

Photo by Liz Sharpe

About the Author

Mike Sharpe is the founder of M.E. Sharpe, Inc., which publishes academic books and journals in the social sciences, international studies, business, and management information systems. His previous books include *John Kenneth Galbraith and the Lower Economics, Thou Shalt Not Kill Unless Otherwise Instructed: Poems and Stories,* and *Requiem for New Orleans,* a collection of poems.

For Product Safety Concerns and Information please contact our EU
representative GPSR@taylorandfrancis.com
Taylor & Francis Verlag GmbH, Kaufingerstraße 24, 80331 München, Germany

www.ingramcontent.com/pod-product-compliance
Ingram Content Group UK Ltd.
Pitfield, Milton Keynes, MK11 3LW, UK
UKHW050951280425
457818UK00033B/857